Gender in the Middle Ages

Volume 19

WOMEN, DANCE AND PARISH RELIGION
IN ENGLAND, 1300–1640

Gender in the Middle Ages

ISSN 1742-870X

Series Editors
Jacqueline Murray
Diane Watt

Editorial Board
Clare Lees
Katherine J. Lewis

This series investigates the representation and construction of masculinity and femininity in the Middle Ages from a variety of disciplinary and interdisciplinary perspectives. It aims in particular to explore the diversity of medieval genders, and such interrelated contexts and issues as sexuality, social class, race and ethnicity, and orthodoxy and heterodoxy.

Proposals or queries should be sent in the first instance to the editors or to the publisher, at the addresses given below; all submissions will receive prompt and informed consideration.

Professor Jacqueline Murray, Department of History, University of Guelph, Guelph, Ontario, N1G 2W1, Canada

Professor Diane Watt, School of Literature and Languages, University of Surrey, Guildford, Surrey GU2 7XH, UK

Boydell & Brewer Limited, PO Box 9, Woodbridge, Suffolk IP12 3DF, UK

Previously published volumes in the series are listed at the end of this book.

WOMEN, DANCE AND PARISH RELIGION IN ENGLAND, 1300–1640

NEGOTIATING THE STEPS OF FAITH

Lynneth Miller Renberg

THE BOYDELL PRESS

© Lynneth Miller Renberg 2022

All Rights Reserved. Except as permitted under current legislation
no part of this work may be photocopied, stored in a retrieval system,
published, performed in public, adapted, broadcast,
transmitted, recorded or reproduced in any form or by any means,
without the prior permission of the copyright owner

The right of Lynneth Miller Renberg to be identified as
the author of this work has been asserted in accordance with
sections 77 and 78 of the Copyright, Designs and Patents Act 1988

First published 2022
The Boydell Press, Woodbridge

ISBN 978-1-78327-747-6

The Boydell Press is an imprint of Boydell & Brewer Ltd
PO Box 9, Woodbridge, Suffolk IP12 3DF, UK
and of Boydell & Brewer Inc.
668 Mt Hope Avenue, Rochester, NY 14620–2731, USA
website: www.boydellandbrewer.co.uk

A CIP catalogue record for this book is available
from the British Library

The publisher has no responsibility for the continued existence or accuracy of
URLs for external or third-party internet websites referred to in this book, and
does not guarantee that any content on such websites is, or will remain, accurate
or appropriate

This publication is printed on acid-free paper

For Dr. John T. Maple, who encouraged me to become a historian and helped me attain that dream, and for my parents, Bill and Linda Miller, who supported and encouraged me every step of the way.

CONTENTS

Acknowledgments	ix
List of Abbreviations	xi
Introduction	1
1 Reforming and Redefining True Religion	19
2 Dance and Protecting Sacred Space	51
3 Dance and Disrupting Sacred Time	77
4 "Satan Danced in the Person of the Damsel"	105
5 "In Her Dance She Had No Regard Unto God"	131
6 Performing Dance, Sin, and Gender	157
Conclusions	187
Appendix	195
Timeline	207
Bibliography	211
Index	249

ACKNOWLEDGMENTS

This book has been many years in the making; its completion is largely due to the support it has received from multiple institutions, funds, and individuals along the way. Grants and fellowships from organizations including the North American Conference on British Studies, the Centre for Medieval Studies through the Medieval Academy of America, Phi Alpha Theta, the Mid-Atlantic Conference on British Studies, and Baylor University made the initial archival research for this project possible. My thanks especially to the archivists at the Bodleian, the British Library, Cambridge University Library, Trinity College Dublin, the Lambeth Palace Archives, and York Minster for their support and help. Conference funding grants from the Sixteenth Century Society and Conference, the American Historical Association, the North American Conference on British Studies, Baylor University, and Anderson University allowed me to present portions of the project and receive invaluable feedback as I developed my arguments and analysis. I am particularly grateful to the editors of collections with the Records of Early English Drama, including John Geck, Sylvia Thomas, C. E. McGee, Alexandra Johnston, Audrey Douglas, Diana Wyatt, David N. Klausner, and Sally-Beth MacLean, for allowing me to use their unpublished editorial work and transcriptions in my research. Special thanks go to Alexandra Johnston and Sally-Beth MacLean for their help in identifying the most relevant REED collections and standardizing citations to their materials. In the final stages of writing and editing, the librarians at Anderson University, particularly Darlene McKay and Fred Guyette, have been invaluable in making resources accessible even through the challenges of the ongoing pandemic. The Faculty Development Committee at Anderson University also provided financial support that helped with the final research for the project. Finally, publication of this book was made possible, in part, by financial support from the Founders' Prize of the Sixteenth Century Society and Conference; I am exceedingly thankful for the Sixteenth Century Society's support and aid in bringing this work to completion.

I also owe a large debt to those who have provided feedback and support throughout the research, writing, and revision process. Feedback and support from Beth Allison Barr, David Whitford, Joseph Stubenrauch, Katherine French, Kathryn Edwards, and Jesse Spohnholz helped me conceptualize, sharpen, and hone the book's arguments and analysis, as well as navigate the proposal and publication process. I am thankful for their time, investment,

Acknowledgments

wisdom, and generosity. Caroline Palmer has made the publication process both painless and helpful; I am so appreciative of her work and guidance. Lastly, I owe much gratitude (and many hours of editing) to my writing groups: to Ryan Butler, Paul Gutacker, and Elise Leal, who provided support and encouragement in the initial research and writing process and beyond; to Taylor Sims, Hayley Bowman, Danielle Alesi, Bradley Phillis, and Jennifer Binczewski, whose feedback and accountability helped move the book through revisions, rewrites, and the publication process; and to Elizabeth Marvel and Lindsay Privette, who offered comments on the manuscript in its entirety. The community of scholars within which I have had the privilege to work has made my own scholarship far stronger than I could have hoped; any errors or weaknesses that remain in this book are entirely my own.

Finally, I am indebted to those who have provided personal support over the time in which this book was written. In addition to those already mentioned as members of my writing groups, many of whom have become close friends through the years, I also need to thank Jenny Hudnall, Heather Conley, Kristi Butler, Paige Gutacker, Skylar Ray, Anna Wells, Tim Orr, Roger Flynn, Allan Wilford, Katherine Wyma, Kris Barnett, Chuck and Jessie Fuller, and Jessica Keene for their friendship, encouragement, and support. I am grateful to Rob and Amy Renberg, Brian and Hannah Hodgson, Ryan and Emily Weener, and Holly Renberg for their care and support, and particularly for their enthusiasm at each step of the way through the publication process. Ben and Leanna McKenzie, Ryan and Peggy Allbritten, and Peter Miller have listened patiently to many hours of talk about research and revisions; thank you to all of you for being constant sources of humor and support. My parents, Bill and Linda Miller, have helped support me in more ways than I can name as I have worked on this project; thank you for listening, for encouraging, and for making some of the archival trips for this book far more fun than they would have been without you. And finally, to my husband, Adam Renberg: thank you for believing in this book from the first time you read it (and for reading it many times after that to help with revisions and prose and edits). I am so grateful that you support me and my work not just through words and affirmation, but also through multiple conversations about how to work out a tricky part of the argument and through doing far more than your share of the dishes, chores, and laundry. This book, and my scholarship, are far stronger for having you as my partner.

ABBREVIATIONS

BL	British Library
Bodl.	Bodleian Library
Camb.	Cambridge
CUL	Cambridge University Library
EEBO	Early English Books Online
EETS	Early English Text Society
ES	Extra Series
HCL	Hereford Cathedral Library
HRO	Hereford Record Office
PL	Patrologia Cursus Completus, Series Latina
OS	Original Series
REED	*Records of Early English Drama*
SRO	Somerset Record Office
STAC	Star Chamber
TNA	The National Archives
WSA	Wiltshire Swindon Archives

INTRODUCTION

In the early thirteenth century, Stephen Langton, Archbishop of Canterbury (1206–1228), used the text of a dance song, "Bele Alis," to begin a sermon in which he exhorted his audience to "dance to God" with "a sonorous voice, that is, holy preaching, pleasing both to God and to men; the entwining of arms, that is, a twofold charity, namely, the love of God and neighbor; and the stamping of feet, that is, works harmonizing with our preaching, in imitation of our Lord Jesus Christ, who undertook first to do good works, and then to teach."[1] The preacher utilized the dancing Alis in this sermon to represent the Virgin Mary and invoked Christ's Davidic lineage to remind "the hearer of David's dancing before the Lord."[2] In this medieval English sermon, dancers represented saints, and dancing exemplified true Christian living. In an era in which preaching was used to convey doctrine and proper behavior to the laity, such a message from the pulpit seems a powerful endorsement of the holiness of dance.

Indeed, medieval Christians did "dance to the Lord," both allegorically and literally. Saints such as Elisabeth of Spalbeek were known for their dancing of the passion, while tales such as that of the Virgin's *jongleur* indicate divine approval of dancing.[3] In many churches throughout medieval Europe, Easter celebrations included a dance to the risen lamb. According to one

---

[1] It is worth noting that the author of the sermon is sometimes identified as "Pseudo-Langton," as the sermon authorship cannot be fully confirmed. Robert A. Taylor et al., "The Bele Alis Sermon: Homiletic Song and Dance," *Florilegium* 24 (2007): 186–187. Taylor's article contains a full transcription of the sermon in Latin, followed by a translation of the text. The word used for dance is "tripudio," a Latin word not found in the Vulgate and used to refer specifically to ritual dance.

[2] Ibid., 178–179.

[3] Karen Silen, "Elisabeth of Spalbeek: Dancing the Passion," in *Women's Work: Making Dance in Europe before 1800*, ed. Lynn Matluck Brooks (Madison: University of Wisconsin Press, 2007), 207–227; Jessica Van Oort, "The Minstrel Dances in Good Company: Del Tumbeor Nostre Dame," *Dance Chronicle* 34, no. 2 (May 2011): 239–275; Jan M. Ziolkowski, *The Juggler of Notre Dame and the Medievalizing of Modernity* (Cambridge: Open Book, 2018); Kathryn Emily Dickason, *Ringleaders of Redemption: How Medieval Dance Became Sacred* (Oxford; New York: Oxford University Press, 2021).

fourteenth-century description, the Easter service began as the priests processed into the sanctuary, singing a song of praise to the risen lamb. Then the priests moved into the center of the cathedral and began an intricate dance on the cathedral's maze-patterned flooring, dancing through the maze while tossing a ball from priest to priest, singing a round in which the melody bounced from singer to singer in tandem with the ball.[4] And while ordinary laity could not participate in this dance of worship, they did dance, and often, as a part of their religious practice: at parish ales, at maidens' lights, at saints' feasts, and in processionals throughout their town. At these events, medieval parishioners danced not primarily in pairs, but in groups, performing Langton's call to community arm in arm with their neighbors. Dance was a regular part of medieval worship, and the idea of dancing to God in a literal sense was not foreign – the sermon from the Archbishop of Canterbury quoted above was not just an allegorical call to dance the Christian life.[5]

Even as the theological ground shifted under the feet of ordinary English parishioners in the English Reformations, dance remained an important part of Christian celebration at the local level. For despite the many theological changes of the sixteenth century, in the early years of the European Reformations, at least, Christians continued dancing – although theologians and pastors increasingly debated whether their parishioners danced after God or the devil. Parish dances, danced processionals, and similar festivities continued almost until the English Civil War, despite increasing controversy over ceremonialism, liturgy, parish practice, and texts like the Book of Sports, with its sanction of dances on Sunday. And outside of these church-sponsored events, laity continued to dance, at weddings, on holidays, and on Sundays. In the face of ministerial challenges to dance practices, the dancers of the parish often doubled down on their traditions, with dances like Morris dances surging in popularity concurrently with redoubled sermon rhetoric against dance.[6]

---

[4] Wright's description reads as follows: "Each year, from at least 1396 until 1538, the canons and chaplains of the cathedral of Auxerre [in France] gathered in the early afternoon of Easter Sunday around the maze situated in the nave of their church. Joining hands to form a ring-dance, or chorea, they chanted antiphonally the sequence Praises to the Easter Victim (Victimae paschali laudes) as they danced on the labyrinth." Craig M. Wright, *The Maze and the Warrior: Symbols in Architecture, Theology, and Music* (Cambridge, MA: Harvard University Press, 2001), 138–140; Harris also discusses the Easter ball dance in his work. Max Harris, *Sacred Folly: A New History of the Feast of Fools* (Ithaca, NY: Cornell University Press, 2011), 54–62.

[5] Kathryn Dickason's sweeping new study of the sacralization of medieval dance contains numerous examples of dancing the faith and of dance as a form of faith. Dickason, *Ringleaders of Redemption*.

[6] John Forrest provides an expansive and important study of the boom in Morris dancing's popularity in the sixteenth century. See John Forrest, *The History of*

Introduction

By the end of the Reformations, though, dancers were described as dancing not with angels in heaven but with demons in hell, and holiness was marked by stillness rather than dancing. Visitation records from the sixteenth and seventeenth centuries repeatedly checked whether anyone had danced in the churchyard or on a holy day, seeking to be sure no parishioner was misbehaving or polluting sacred space through their dancing.[7] Authorities repeatedly admonished and reprimanded parishioners for dancing. If parishioners neglected to sufficiently repent of their dances, ecclesiastical authorities pulled the dancers in front of their neighbors and forced them to confess to their sins. Preachers referred to dancing laity as given over to the devil, as sinners rather than saints.

What led to the stillness of the saints? To the transformation of dancers from saints dancing after Christ into sinners dancing after the devil? And why does it matter? These questions lie at the heart of this book, which explores changing understandings of dance as it relates to religion, gender, sin, and community. An overview of dance practice in the English parish shows that for medieval and early modern people, dance played an integral role in creating, maintaining, and uniting (or fracturing) community. But to simply consider how and when ordinary people danced misses the collision of rhetorical conceptions of dance with the gendering of dancing bodies. As theological understandings of sacrilege, sin, and proper worship changed, the meanings of dance and gender shifted as well. Through following variations in theological and rhetorical understandings of dance, this book explores the shifts in theological footing that dramatically altered the intricate steps of the performance of holiness and gender within the lives of ordinary men and women.

Ecclesiastical concern with dancing gendered bodies did not originate with the late Middle Ages, and the recognition of the creation and calcification of gender binaries through religious discourse is also not new. But concern with female bodies specifically was not a constant within religious discourses about dance, nor was concern about gender central to ecclesiastical constructions of dance until the late Middle Ages. Judith Bennett, in her call for studies of patriarchy as a historical constant, notes that "because [scholars] take women's oppression as a given, they neither analyze the dynamics of male

---

   Morris Dancing, 1438–1750, Studies in Early English Drama (Toronto: University of Toronto Press, 2016).

7 For two examples of this common practice, see *Records of Early English Drama* [henceforth *REED*]: *Salisbury*, ed. Audrey Douglas, Sarum 1549–50, Bishop of Salisbury's Detecta Book, Episcopal Visitation Articles, 9 July, fol. 7; *REED Salisbury*, ed. Douglas, Sarum 1552–1553, Bishop of Salisbury's Detecta Book, Episcopal Visitation Articles, 4 March, fols. 96v–97. Forthcoming with *REED: Wiltshire*, ed. Roslyn Hays and C. E. McGee, REED Online.

Women, Dance and Parish Religion in England, 1300–1640

power nor critique it, and their works can sometimes thereby almost disguise it."[8] In the assumption of a consistent religious perspective towards dance as a gendered and embodied activity, current scholarship has similarly obscured the dynamics of male power at play in the church's approach to dance, both in theology and in practice. Discussions of dance or gender rarely took center stage in the sermons and texts written for ordinary men and women, but a closer look at these texts shows that their authors repeatedly engage dance and gender as they teach about how to live as a member of the church. Simply noting that medieval and early modern authors often sexualized dance or treated dance through a misogynistic framework leaves the mechanisms by which misogyny was spread, reified, and applied in the daily lives of ordinary men and women invisible. To understand the complexity in the outworking of religion and gender in medieval and early modern parishes, dance's role as a rhetorical mechanism of misogyny then applied in parish discipline and governance needs examination.

In many ways, the church's approach to dance, with its tension and paradox, parallels the church's approach to women and their bodies. This ambivalence in the church's approach to dance wove throughout the works of patristic authors like Augustine and Chrysostom. According to these early church fathers, only the best of saints or the worst of sinners danced – but there were both dancing saints and dancing sinners. Dance was treated as an *adiaphora*: a matter on which the biblical text was unclear and on which multiple perspectives could be held within the framework of orthodoxy.[9] This ambivalence and accompanying multipotentiality for dance continued through much of the medieval period. Similarly, and in an important parallel for an embodied practice such as dance, the church's approach to bodies and materiality as a whole has always been marked by paradox, perhaps never more than in the late Middle Ages, as noted by Caroline Walker Bynum. Her discussion of the inherent paradox contained in medieval approaches to matter, viewed as both "radical threat and radical opportunity," highlights the "intense awareness of the power of the material" in medieval religion.[10] This paradox becomes even

---

[8] Judith M. Bennett, *History Matters: Patriarchy and the Challenge of Feminism* (Philadelphia: University of Pennsylvania Press, 2006), 28.

[9] For a discussion of the difference between *adiaphora* and heresy, see Louise Nyholm Kallestrup and Raisa Maria Toivo (eds.), *Contesting Orthodoxy in Medieval and Early Modern Europe: Heresy, Magic and Witchcraft*, Palgrave Historical Studies in Witchcraft and Magic (Cham: Springer International, 2017), 9.

[10] Caroline Walker Bynum, *Christian Materiality: An Essay on Religion in Late Medieval Europe* (New York; Cambridge, MA: Zone Books, 2011), 20. See also Caroline Walker Bynum, *Fragmentation and Redemption: Essays on Gender and the Human Body in Medieval Religion* (New York; Cambridge, MA: Zone Books, 1991); Caroline Walker Bynum, *Holy Feast and Holy Fast* (Oakland: University of California Press, 1987).

Introduction

clearer when the bodies under consideration are female. Dyan Elliott's *Fallen Bodies: Pollution, Sexuality, and Demonology in the Middle Ages* notes that "within the altered conditions of the high and late Middle Ages" the clergy reinterpreted "inherited sexual and religious traditions." Part of this involved an increased focus on the female body, "perceived both as self-contaminating … and as a source of contagion to others."[11] And, as Elliott details and scholars such as Mary Douglas and Jane Tibbetts Schulenburg have argued, "a state of defilement was fundamentally linked with the sacred, since both conditions were contagious, dangerous, and circumscribed by numerous prohibitions."[12] Elliott points out that the portrayal of the female body as polluting and dangerous is a "constant pulse" throughout the history of Christianity.[13] Although patristic and early medieval theologians noted their potential for holiness, women, like dance, consistently caused unease.

Previous scholars have noted this religious nervousness about both women and dance, to the point of stereotype: the modern colloquial description of dance as a "vertical expression of a horizontal activity" captures this religious apprehension about dance as a potential form of sexual expression. However, more recent scholarship on medieval dance and religion seeks to challenge this perception of dance as at odds with western Christian tradition. Both Kathryn Dickason and Laura Hellsten propose new models of understanding medieval dance as a mode of redemptive performance in medieval Christianity.[14] Both Dickason and Hellsten start with patristic perspectives, recounting the familiar tune of concern about dance but then pulling out hidden dissonance and counterpoints through considering the often-overlooked potential for dance as theological construction, as holiness, as sacred performance. Their scholarship represents a much-needed consideration of dance as theology in the early and high Middle Ages, complicating the traditional narrative found in broader surveys of dance and religion like E. Louis Backman's or Barbara Ehrenreich's works.[15] Yet, while these recent studies complicate understandings of dance and the church, gender does not act as a central focus

---

[11] Dyan Elliott, *Fallen Bodies: Pollution, Sexuality, and Demonology in the Middle Ages* (Philadelphia: University of Pennsylvania Press, 1999), 1, 3.

[12] Ibid., 3. See also Jane Tibbetts Schulenburg, *Forgetful of Their Sex: Female Sanctity and Society, ca. 500–1100* (Chicago: University of Chicago Press, 2001); Michael Frassetto, *Medieval Purity and Piety: Essays on Medieval Clerical Celibacy and Religious Reform* (London: Taylor & Francis, 1998).

[13] Elliott, *Fallen Bodies*, 3.

[14] Dickason, *Ringleaders of Redemption*; Laura Hellsten, *Through the Bone and Marrow: Re-Examining Theological Encounters with Dance in Medieval Europe* (Turnhout: Brepols, 2021).

[15] Barbara Ehrenreich, *Dancing in the Streets: A History of Collective Joy* (New York: Macmillan, 2007); E. Louis Backman, *Religious Dances in the Christian Church and in Popular Medicine* (London: Allen & Unwin, 1952).

of their arguments. This is a significant omission: the dancing body is always a gendered body, and gender certainly mattered to the theologians and sermon authors addressing dance.

Considering dancing bodies primarily as gendered bodies reveals that the potential holiness allowed to both dance and women shifted between 1300 and 1600. In the thirteenth century, where this book begins, a common concern with the protection of the sacred drove ecclesiastical unease about bodies – particularly dancing bodies and female bodies. This concern with protecting the holy appeared in the Crusades, in campaigns against heretics throughout late medieval Europe, and in the thorough programs of reform set in motion at Fourth Lateran Council in 1215. At this council, the church redefined what it meant to practice "true religion" – a phrase I use throughout this book to indicate what church authorities considered proper doctrine and practice, Christian belief both rhetorical and embodied in the actions of the members of the parish. In the process of clarifying doctrine and practice, Fourth Lateran (and the texts that distilled and adapted its canons for application within the parish) changed the way that the church talked about sacred space, about dance, and about women. And it was this council that led to the creation of a new set of church laws meant to protect the church from the world: to separate holy things from profane ones. New canon laws separated priests from congregations, nuns from the world, women from priests, and women from the altar. These theological changes transformed religious and social practice while subtly redefining the church's approach to gendered bodies and the proper performance of holiness. Medieval sermon authors tied both dance and women, together and individually, to sacrilege and sinful behavior. Over the course of the fourteenth and fifteenth centuries, two distinct discussions about dance and about women, both concerned with profane behavior, slowly intertwined into a single diatribe about sacrilegious dancing female bodies.

This late medieval shift in approach to dance continued into the sixteenth-century Reformations, as theological changes restructured communities and created new standards for appropriate social behavior and morality. Scholarship on the changes to the medieval parish with the coming of the Reformations certainly shows the disruption to community, tradition, and society thus brought about.[16] Yet, as Carlos Eire demonstrates, particularly in Reformed tradition, the key focus was on idolatry and on true worship. According to Eire, within the Reformed tradition, reform of social order and behavior grew out of a concern with sacrilege.[17] The same underlying

---

[16] Eamon Duffy's works provide perhaps the best noted consideration of this. Eamon Duffy, *The Stripping of the Altars: Traditional Religion in England, 1400–1580*, 2nd edn (New Haven, CT; London: Yale University Press, 2005).

[17] Carlos M. N. Eire, *War against the Idols: The Reformation of Worship from Erasmus to Calvin* (Cambridge: Cambridge University Press, 1989); Cressy's work on Tudor–Stuart England is also particularly important for this project. See David

Introduction

concern with practicing "true religion" (albeit true religion with different theological priorities) drove the Reformations, particularly within the parish. And because this underlying concern remained the same, the connection between dance and sacrilege did not dissolve, nor did the connection between women and sacrilege disappear with the advent of the Reformations. Instead, discussions of dance, sacrilege, and women became increasingly intertwined. The transgressions of dance and of sacrilege were centered on female bodies and identified as female sins. The theological preoccupations of the reformers differed from their medieval predecessors, but their approach to dance simply carried medieval frameworks to their logical endpoint of stillness as holiness.

Dance, while seemingly a peripheral issue to the study of religion or gender, touches on the deepest concerns of both late medieval and early modern religion. As Dyan Elliott put it, "the superficially marginal is often imaginatively (and hence ideologically) central" – and dance serves exactly this role within both late medieval and early modern texts.[18] While both late medieval and early modern reforms sought the creation of a purer Christian faith, these reforms did not simply do so throughout focusing on big theological tenets, like soteriology or justification. The priests and pastors of ordinary men and women in both periods sought to provide an understanding of the doctrines of the faith, true. But this doctrinal education for laity always had a practical end in mind: how then should we live? In expounding on that question, clerics created models of behavior and performance that focused on actions and relationships, on the performance of virtue within community in daily and practical actions. Thus, the application of these theological reforms eventually affected all aspects of lay life, and it is in these more practical and theologically peripheral issues that continuities in thought between the two eras become most apparent. By exploring the particular issue of dance, broader medieval problems and concerns about sacred space, true worship, and women come into sharper focus. The continuity of the patriarchy as well as the continuity of theological thought becomes clearer; the mechanisms through which misogyny shifted shape and survived distinct theological breaks become more apparent.

The first significant contribution of this book, in uncovering and analyzing the mechanisms by which misogyny became more embedded into church teaching and practice, relates closely to its second major contribution: an understanding of the parish that transcends traditional chronological divides between medieval and early modern. The parish has been the focus of much recent scholarly study, with rich results for the understanding of the lived

---

Cressy, *Birth, Marriage, and Death: Ritual, Religion, and the Life-Cycle in Tudor and Stuart England* (New York; Oxford: Oxford University Press, 1997); David Cressy, *Travesties and Transgressions in Tudor and Stuart England: Tales of Discord and Dissension* (Oxford: Oxford University Press, 2000).

18 Elliott, *Fallen Bodies*, 11.

religion of ordinary men and women. Studies have considered material piety, liturgical drama, social dynamics, law, art, and literature.[19] Typically, however, scholars have treated the Reformations as a distinctive break in parish practice and dynamics. This book complicates this picture. By centering dance, a subject usually treated tangentially as a small part of broader parish life, my work shows that while the Reformations changed the details of parish debates, the foundational concerns of parish teachings and practice remained centered on sacrilege and gender, despite shifting definitions for both. Remarkable continuities endured into modernity.

Stepping back to again consider the ambivalence with which patristic and early medieval authors viewed dance, however, makes clear that continuity in theological concern between 1300 and 1600 does not tell the full story, for the church's approach to gendered bodies did undergo a very real shift during this period. Through repeated statements about *adiaphora* like dance, statements often embedded within sermons or texts focused on other things, gender became a defining factor in considerations of sacrilege and parish practice, with important ramifications for the potentiality of female bodies. And as dance and sacrilege both became discussed in more gendered terms, bodies themselves became less fluidly gendered. Gender slowly shifted from a spectrum of potentialities to a more binary rubric, with accompanying standards for performing holiness and sin. The lived experience of dance and of gender within the parish remained remarkably consistent, but the rhetorical status of both dance and women shifted dramatically, bringing by the seventeenth century dramatic change in lived experience. These mechanisms of misogyny – the rhetorical and practical ways in which toxic approaches to women and to gender shifted form and function – need to be

---

[19] The following represent some of the most significant and relevant works on the English parish: Katherine L. French, *The People of the Parish: Community Life in a Late Medieval English Diocese* (Philadelphia: University of Pennsylvania Press, 2001); Katherine L. French, *The Good Women of the Parish: Gender and Religion after the Black Death* (Philadelphia: University of Pennsylvania Press, 2008); Bronach Christina Kane, *Popular Memory and Gender in Medieval England: Men, Women and Testimony in the Church Courts, c.1200–1500* (Woodbridge: Boydell Press, 2019); Bronach Kane and Fiona Williamson (eds.), *Women, Agency and the Law, 1300–1700* (London: Routledge, 2016); Ian Forrest, *Trustworthy Men: How Inequality and Faith Made the Medieval Church* (Princeton: Princeton University Press, 2020); Alec Ryrie, *Being Protestant in Reformation Britain* (Oxford: Oxford University Press, 2015); Sally Harper, P. S. Barnwell, and Magnus Williamson (eds.), *Late Medieval Liturgies Enacted: The Experience of Worship in Cathedral and Parish Church* (Aldershot: Routledge, 2019); Beat A. Kümin, *The Shaping of a Community: The Rise and Reformation of the English Parish, c. 1400–1560* (Aldershot: Scholar, 1996); Robert Whiting, *The Reformation of the English Parish Church* (Cambridge: Cambridge University Press, 2014); Muriel McClendon, *The Quiet Reformation: Magistrates and the Emergence of Protestantism in Tudor Norwich* (Stanford: Stanford University Press, 1999).

Introduction

explored and unpacked, in all their subtlety and in their manifestations in small asides in larger texts and contexts. This book's most important contribution comes in its unpacking of these rhetorical mechanisms. The gradual ideological and theological shifts in approach to dance did not remain abstract but brought about tangible consequences for real people. Anchoring the sins of sacrilege and of dance to the female body had important implications for women, as rhetoric about gender and sin developed to address dance specifically expanded to address all women at all times. As dance transformed from an ambivalent action whose acceptability was determined by place and time to an essentialized, embodied transgression, perceptions of women's bodies shifted accordingly, with the potential to perform holiness well enough to overcome one's gendered form gradually erased. The gendering of dance and sacrilege contributed to an early modern and Anglo-Protestant culture in which women and their bodies were consistently blamed for the transgressions of men, whatever those transgressions might be.

Thus, to return to my initial question: what led to the stillness of the saints and to this shift in approach to dance? I argue that attempts at eliminating sacrilegious behavior and reforming the church led to growing concern about both dancing and female bodies. Dance moved from something that could be either problematic or acceptable, celebratory and communal or sinful, to sacrilegious (collectively) and then sacrilegious and sexualized (individually). This shift took place because of changes in the ways in which medieval clerics and communities thought about sacrilege and transgression in relation to gender. These medieval discourses about dancing and female bodies increasingly intertwined and collided throughout the late medieval period, until eventually, by the start of the sixteenth century, both sacrilege and dance were defined as transgressions gendered female. And defining sin as gendered female had very real ramifications for both men and women, as new definitions of what it meant to perform one's gender collided with discourses about holiness and transgression. With the narrowing of potentiality for what it meant to be a holy man or woman, the ways in which one could properly perform one's gender narrowed as well, leading to closer scrutiny and monitoring of the bodies of the faithful. The medieval and early modern parish saw little change in women's daily experience or in the practice of dance but tremendous change in the rhetorical status of both dance and women, laying the foundation for religious practice centered on an idea of women as transgressive.

Three key assumptions underpin this study and shape its structure. The first assumption is tied to text and audience. The goal of this book is to understand not theological arguments about dance or sacrilege, but instead what lay audiences were taught about sin and holiness and how those teachings shaped their daily lives. Thus, the focus is on the preaching and practice of ordinary parishes, not on court dances or elite theological texts. Accordingly,

Women, Dance and Parish Religion in England, 1300–1640

the theological texts considered in this monograph are ones that would have been accessible to most men and women: sermons. These sermons are almost all in the vernacular, and almost all meant to be delivered orally rather than read. Lengthy theological treatises, musicology or medieval theories of music, courtly dance practices or dance manuals remain topics for another study. Underpinning this project is the assumption that what was taught from the pulpit mattered and had sensory power. Whether audiences acted upon the teachings or not, the internalized ideologies about gender and transgression shaped gender roles and norms in both the late medieval and early modern periods. The subtle development of a misogynistic framing for dance mattered for how ordinary men and women understood dance, religion, and gender. The question of audience reception and application of teaching is an important one, and one considered through the addition of records of dance performances in English parishes when available. More of these records survive for the latter periods of this project, and thus, dance performance itself plays a greater role in the early modern chapters of the monograph.[20]

My second key assumption regards the nature of performance as a practice both rhetorical and embodied. This assumption first appears in my treatment of the performativity of gender, an idea introduced by Judith Butler and now so well known as to need little introduction.[21] I treat gender as inextricably connected both to rhetoric and to embodiment, two ways of constituting, signifying, and stabilizing gendered scripts. Similar treatments of gender appear in other studies of discourse and ephemeral performance, like Sandy Bardsley's or Laura Gowing's studies of speech and gender or Theresa Coletti's study of theatrical performances and gender.[22] This study's combination

---

[20] One more note about sources must be made before moving on. Several of the chapters in this work – notably, Chapter 2 and Chapter 4 – draw on medieval sermon cycles for much of their evidence. The text quoted in each chapter is, unless noted otherwise, drawn from edited print editions of these cycles. Extensive archival work backs the research in this project, and nearly every extent manuscript witness to each sermon cycle has been examined in person, as is reflected in the bibliography. However, the portions of each cycle relevant to my argument show no major revisions from manuscript to manuscript; the differences are slight spelling changes rather than changes to words, sentences, or the structure of the narrative. Thus, for simplicity's sake, I have chosen to cite to the more accessible edited versions of the sermon cycles and have not cited individual manuscripts in the footnotes unless I am citing something specific to an individual or unpublished manuscript.

[21] Judith Butler, "Performative Acts and Gender Constitution: An Essay in Phenomenology and Feminist Theory," *Theatre Journal* 40, no. 4 (December 1988): 519–531.

[22] Sandy Bardsley, *Venomous Tongues: Speech and Gender in Late Medieval England* (Philadelphia: University of Pennsylvania Press, 2006); Laura Gowing, *Domestic Dangers: Women, Words, and Sex in Early Modern London* (Oxford; New York:

Introduction

of peripheral discourse and ephemeral practice in the form of dance helps provide new insight into the performance of gender in the years between 1300 and 1600, accessing difficult to reconstruct performances and ideologies about gender through this lens.

A related assumption regards the conceptualization and meaning of "dance" within my sources and within this project. Dance, as a performed practice located within specific social temporalities, is always difficult to recover. The type of dance that I am interested in – choreographies, spontaneous or planned, of ordinary bodies within parishes rather than courts – proves even more difficult to define and conceptualize. Recently, dance scholars have done excellent work theorizing and problematizing the idea of premodern dance, utilizing innovative conceptual frameworks to more fully illuminate the boundaries of performance. Seeta Chaganti's field-changing work, *Strange Footing*, conceptualizes medieval dance in reciprocal and dynamic relationship with poetic form, proposing "a methodology that elucidates the collaboration of dance and text to produce an experience of poetic form."[23] Kathryn Dickason, meanwhile, frames dance as a form of kinetic devotion, a performance of penance and grace that was "equally about redemption and domination."[24] Other scholars apply concepts like virtuality or kinesis to create conceptualizations of dance.[25] Yet, none of these frameworks quite fit with how I see dance appearing in my sources. The authors, audiences, and dancers in this study saw dance as a broad phenomenon that could encompass many forms of motion for many occasions; its embodied performance was part of their ordinary lives. In texts and sermons about dance, clerical authors thus treated dance broadly and vaguely, as an ordinary communal action with many possible permutations, none of which these authors considered it important to define or delineate.

In line with this, I treat "dance" in this book first and foremost as a discursive rhetorical construct, broadly defined and construed by medieval and early modern clerics more concerned with preventing transgressive action than with careful conceptualization or delineation of forms of movement. These authors applied this broad rhetorical construct to embodied motion

---

Oxford University Press, 1996); Theresa Coletti, *Mary Magdalene and the Drama of Saints: Theater, Gender, and Religion in Late Medieval England* (Philadelphia: University of Pennsylvania Press, 2004).

[23] Seeta Chaganti, *Strange Footing: Poetic Form and Dance in the Late Middle Ages* (Chicago: University of Chicago Press, 2019), 3–4.

[24] Dickason, *Ringleaders of Redemption*, 3–5.

[25] See, for example, Susanne Langer, "The Dynamic Image: Some Philosophical Reflections on Dance," *Salmagundi*, no. 33/34 (1976): 76–82; Rebecca Straple-Sovers, "Kinesic Analysis: A Theoretical Approach to Reading Bodily Movement in Literature," in *The Cursed Carolers in Context*, ed. Lynneth Miller Renberg and Bradley Phillis (New York: Routledge, 2021), 21–38.

and action, assuming that their audiences would connect "dance" to their own regional practices of communal motion. Because of the breadth of the rhetorical conceptualization of dance in my sources, I apply dance in a similarly expansive way when considering embodied practice and action. In my study, I treat dance as an example of what Geraldine Heng has described in her work on medieval race-making as a technology of power: dance is a rhetorical framework deployed through parish teaching and management to create, enforce, and naturalize power relationships based on selectively essentialized bodies and traits.[26]

My third key methodological assumption concerns the importance of challenging traditional epochal, regional, or genre divisions. Thus, Judith Bennett's *longue durée* methodology for gender history guides the chronological parameters for this study.[27] As Bennett argues, continuities and changes in patriarchal structures do not appear without a wide chronological lens. Thus, this book takes a broad chronological scope, exposing hitherto overlooked constructions and consequences through that lens. The divide between medieval and early modern studies has been helpfully challenged, reconceptualized, and discussed by literary scholars like James Simpson and Nancy Bradley Warren, scholars of religion including Eamon Duffy and Ronald Rittgers, as well as scholars working on gender like Christine Peters, to name only a few.[28] However, studies of the parish – the center of lived religious experience for most medieval and early modern individuals – have remained more bifurcated across the assumed chronological divide between medieval and early modern, as have studies of dance. Considering parish approaches to dance, in sermons and in practice, helps us understand the lived religion that continued across the medieval/early modern divide and shows that while theology and parish governance changed dramatically, in many ways, lived religious experience did not.

Similarly, this book takes a broad geographic scope in its study of English parishes. There were, indubitably, significant differences in parish practice throughout England, with certain parishes more inclined to festive celebrations

---

[26] Geraldine Heng, *The Invention of Race in the European Middle Ages* (Cambridge: Cambridge University Press, 2018), 28.

[27] Bennett, *History Matters.*

[28] Brian Cummings and James Simpson, *Cultural Reformations: Medieval and Renaissance in Literary History* (Oxford: Oxford University Press, 2016); Nancy Bradley Warren, *Chaucer and Religious Controversies in the Medieval and Early Modern Eras* (Notre Dame, IN: University of Notre Dame Press, 2019); Duffy, *Stripping of the Altars*; Ronald K. Rittgers, *The Reformation of Suffering: Pastoral Theology and Lay Piety in Late Medieval and Early Modern Germany* (Oxford: Oxford University Press, 2012); Christine Peters, *Patterns of Piety: Women, Gender, and Religion in Later Mediaeval and Reformation England* (Cambridge: Cambridge University Press, 2002).

Introduction

including dance than others. And styles of dance, types of parish traditions, and individual community dynamics clearly appear in any in-depth analysis of parish and diocesan records. Works by Eamon Duffy, Katherine French, David Cressy, Audrey Douglas, Emily Winerock, and others highlight the importance of regional difference in understanding parish culture, religion, and the actual performance of dance and other like activities.[29] But while these regional differences do matter, particularly in studies that are more concerned with social history and dance practice, there are also transregional commonalities – approaches and rhetoric about dance and women that appear over and over in both sermons and parish records, regardless of the context of the county or parish. Alessandro Arcangeli notes that "when authors came to discuss [dance], their starting point was often an acknowledgement that, to a certain degree, dance itself is morally neutral. Thus, it can become a sin only under particular conditions, according to a repertoire copied from the series of circumstances that, in the rhetorical tradition, the orator has to remember to mention in his speech: time, place, person, manner, intention."[30] But Emily Winerock nuances this claim, stating that "since dance, as a physical practice, was *always* done in some kind of social and cultural context, it was only 'indifferent' in theory. In practice, it was always either good or bad, orderly or disorderly, permissible or forbidden."[31] I take Winerock's assertion a step farther. Looking at not only parish records, but also at sermons, from a distance – doing a sort of "deep reading," as it were – shows that regardless of the specific contexts in which dance occurred, rhetorically at least, many late medieval texts and most early modern ones did not actually treat dance as morally neutral. The rhetorical conception of dance developed in sermons, regardless of their geographic or regional context, followed a remarkably consistent trajectory in connecting dance first to sacrilege and then to sexualized female bodies. These commonalities have something significant to say about broader trends in approaches to both religion and gender.

It is for the sake of these commonalities and what they can show us about the contours of lay belief and lived religious experience that this book prioritizes breadth of scope over close contextual analysis, for both texts and parish records. I consider primarily sermons in this study, but on occasion pull

[29] Eamon Duffy, *The Voices of Morebath: Reformation and Rebellion in an English Village* (New Haven, CT: Yale University Press, 2001); French, *The People of the Parish*; Cressy, *Birth, Marriage, and Death*; Audrey Douglas, "'Owre Thanssynge Day': Parish Dance and Procession in Salisbury," *Folk Music Journal* 6, no. 5 (1994): 600–616; Emily F. Winerock, "Reformation and Revelry: The Practices and Politics of Dancing in Early Modern England, c. 1550–1640" (Ph.D. diss., University of Toronto, 2012).

[30] Alessandro Arcangeli, "Dance under Trial: The Moral Debate, 1200–1600," *Dance Research* 12 no. 2 (1994): 130.

[31] Winerock, "Reformation and Revelry," 4.

in other religious didactic literature, such as instruction or conduct books, pamphlets, glosses, or commentaries. Despite differences in genre, I consider these works as related and comparable texts: vernacular literature aimed at teaching religious belief and morality to a largely lay audience. Similarly, I utilize the work of the Records of Early English Drama (henceforth REED) project to look at dance in parish records. The REED works do provide insight only into the episodes in which dance is mentioned, not the broader parish conflicts in which these episodes are set. Yet I argue that this approach has great merit for understanding the broad changes in approach to dance, religion, and gender that I seek to unpack. When, despite different parish personalities and settings, common patterns in approach to dance appear, we can see more clearly the contours of the broader trend in treating dance as sacrilegious and gendered. Individual parish tensions and circumstances certainly played a role in determining the appropriateness of dance and dancers, but broad parameters remained. By emphasizing the malleability of dance's appropriateness based on specific literary, regional, chronological, or religious contexts, we have thus far missed the significant shift in fundamental cultural and ideological approaches to dance that took place between 1300 and 1600. By overlooking this shift, we have also ignored important yet gradual changes for the people of the parish.

The narrative of this book unfolds along both chronological and thematic lines. I begin with a broad first chapter, "Reforming and Redefining True Religion." In this first chapter, I provide chronological grounding for the case studies that follow, looking comparatively at teaching, living, and protecting the faith in the late medieval and early modern eras. In this chapter, I highlight continuities in reform from Fourth Lateran through the English Reformations, focusing on discussions of sacrilege and false religion and on the structure and function of the parish. Despite significant theological differences between the two periods, the primary concerns about true worship and creating a truly Christian Europe remained the same. Looking at these reforms through the lens of dance highlights these continuities, as well as an important interplay in the construction of scripts of piety and transgression. As transgressions became gendered, discussions that began as theological deliberations setting moral parameters ended up as proscriptive discourses regulating earthly bodies.

The next two chapters explore the gendering of sacrilege: how the association of dance with sacrilege helped create an emphasis on sacrilegious female bodies. The second chapter, "Dance and Protecting Sacred Space," looks at late medieval attempts at dealing with sacrilege, particularly sacrilegious dance and sacrilegious bodies. It does so through a case study following one of the most popular medieval sermon tales, the tale of the cursed dancing carolers, over several centuries. Taught widely to English lay audiences in multiple iterations, this tale highlights both a growing concern with sacrilege in the

Introduction

wake of Fourth Lateran and the start of the attaching of the sin of sacrilege to female bodies. Chapter 3, "Dance and Disrupting Sacred Time," provides an early modern counterpoint. By examining discussions of dance in early modern sermons, it shows that sacrilege in the form of Sabbath breaking remains a key concern of early modern sermons. The underlying concerns remain the same as in the medieval texts, but the sacred space being disrupted is now temporal rather than spatial. And the individuals doing the disruption are now, according to the sermons, almost always women. The continuation of this specific medieval discourse binding sacrilegious dance to female sin feeds into the creation of new narratives about dance and female sin, such as witchcraft dances. As the discourse became more entrenched, the consequences for women became more tangible. Both these chapters connect narrow concerns about dance with larger anxieties about sacred space, time, and bodies, and conversely with fear of the profane.

Dance as sacrilege, the focus of Chapters 2 and 3, is a major and foundational concern for late medieval and early modern religious figures, connected to broad changes in theology and practice. But as shown in Chapters 4 and 5, concern with sex is layered onto that foundation of sacrilege. This secondary concern with sexuality is never as broadly significant in its theological framing. It does not intersect with the major theological discussions of either the late medieval or the early modern eras, which means that Chapters 4 and 5 are the most narrowly focused chapters in this work, looking more closely at texts that show rhetorical change rather than at wider theological currents. These two chapters serve as focused case studies of vernacular presentations of the dance of Salome, the young dancing girl from the gospel narratives. These two chapters explore the ways in which dance became not just a transgression gendered female but a sexualized sin tied to the female body, following a chronological trajectory over the two chapters. In Chapter 4, "Satan Danced in the Person of the Damsel," the medieval foundations for this change appear through the ways in which Salome's narrative is adapted to focus on the sins of the women in the text. In Chapter 5, "In Her Dance She Had No Regard Unto God," this focus on the female body becomes a rubric for the gendered performance of sin and holiness, a rubric applied to all women, whether in the past or in the present. The flattening out of gendered potentiality that is so crucial in later discussions of dance is clearest in these chapters, as tracing a single narrative over several hundred years clearly shows the shifts in approach to gendered bodies and gendered transgression. The anchoring of sacrilege to dancing female bodies in the thirteenth and fourteenth centuries helped drive the feminization and sexualization of all dancing bodies in the sixteenth and seventeenth centuries.

The massive and practical ramifications of layering sex onto sacrilege in rhetorical conceptions of dance become apparent in Chapter 6, "Dance, Transgression, and the Performance of Gender." This final chapter focuses solely on the sixteenth and seventeenth centuries, balancing discourse and practice in pulling together both the continuities and changes explored in earlier chapters. Daniel Price's 1580 sermon provides one example of the gendered discourses this chapter explores and shows well the confluence of the main themes of this project:

> The devil had no other engine in Paradise but the woman, she was the wheele to turne about all the world. Ahabs Iezebell is his instrument to slay the Prophets, Herodias daughter to strike of Iohn Baptist his head ... whether it be that women by their nature are more flexible, or by law lesse lyable to punishment (though very many of them haue beene holte worthy Saints and Martyrs of God), yet many haue beene most faithfull servants to their infernall Master, they be the loadstones and loadstars in all evill, the Iesuit not more serviceable to the Pope then Idolatrous women to the devill.[32]

Much of the language in this sermon intentionally reminded an audience of dance, with its references to "turning about" and flexibility. At the heart of the list of the engines of the devil sits the dancing daughter from the gospel narratives, Salome, recast not simply as the idolatrous servant of the devil but also as a parallel to the Jesuits serving the pope, a strong claim to make in 1580. This sermon demonstrates how Salome's narrative had become used to typify the dangers that women posed to true religion: dance was simply one of many ways in which the devil utilized women as his tools. The narratives about the dangers of women dancing have expanded to become more general narratives about the dangers of women, with ramifications for constructions of masculinity in rhetoric and in parish discipline. And in the court cases and parish records this chapter explores, it is not hard to see the negative consequences for both men and women that come from referring to women as the servants of the devil and the engines of his evil.

As the ideologies and beliefs traced out in this monograph seeped into tradition and became an unquestioned part of what it meant to practice true Christianity, the ramifications for the ordering of communities and the treatment of individuals became very tangible. With the narrowing of potentiality for what it meant to be a holy man or woman, the ways in which one could properly perform one's gender narrowed as well, leading to closer scrutiny and monitoring of the bodies of the faithful. Case studies from Somerset and Berkshire show the ramifications of this discourse on dance, as in two separate instances of parish discipline, ecclesiastical courts treat fornication and dancing as comparable sins, with dancing ultimately regarded as the more problematic action. By the seventeenth century, the lived experience

---

[32] Daniel Price, *Spirituall Odours to the Memory of Prince Henry* (At Oxford: Printed by Ioseph Barnes and are to be sold by Iohn Barnes dwelling neere Holborne Conduit [, London], 1613), 21. Price was recognized as a gifted preacher, "especially against the papists."

Introduction

of religion had shifted to reflect the reframed theological understandings of sacrilege and gender. How do church teachings on theologically marginal issues – on *adiaphora* – affect the church's treatment of individuals? Using dance to explore this question reveals the hardening of approaches to gender created through discourses about these marginal issues and the cost of rigidly maintained binaries, whether of gender, religion, or historical periodization.

CHAPTER 1

REFORMING AND REDEFINING TRUE RELIGION

How does one create a church in which ordinary men and women can give an answer for what they believe and live according to that belief? The answers to these questions shifted between Fourth Lateran Council in 1215 and the Reformations of the sixteenth century, but the questions themselves drove both reform movements. Pope Innocent III, his medieval cardinals, and sixteenth-century reformers would likely all be offended by this categorization of their reforms as more similar than not. Yet, despite differences on the role of scripture, justification, sacraments, ecclesiology, and numerous other issues, these reforms had similar aspirations. Furthermore, the ways in which these medieval and early modern reformers sought to teach the faith, ensure that laity lived the faith, and protect the faith often took similar forms.

Held in 1215, Fourth Lateran aimed at clerical and lay education along with greater regulation within the medieval church. Convened by Pope Innocent III, Fourth Lateran sought mainly "to reinvigorate the health of the local churches" and to "prepare the laity to be able to identify heretics ... the council and [its decrees] generated a 'revolution' in pastoral care."[1] Canons 10 and 21, dealing with preaching and confession respectively, set new standards for clerical behavior and authority and necessitated the creation of new materials for clerical education.[2] Other topics addressed in the remaining seventy canons included heresy, clerical behavior, church governance, and social order. And while one of Innocent III's goals in calling the Council was to reform the church, a second goal, tied to Canon 3 and its discussion of heresy, was articulated in Canon 71 with its call for another crusade. The Albigensian Crusade, the Holy Land Crusades, and the *Reconquista* show the late medieval continuation of Fourth Lateran's focus on heretics and infidels, while the late medieval boom in lay piety and vernacular texts highlighted the ways in which Fourth Lateran's focus on the health of the laity shaped faith and practice up until the Reformations of the early modern period.[3]

---

[1] Kevin Madigan, *Medieval Christianity* (New Haven, CT: Yale University Press, 2015), 310.

[2] Mary E. O'Carroll, *A Thirteenth-Century Preacher's Handbook: Studies in MS Laud Misc. 511* (Toronto: Pontifical Institute of Mediaeval Studies, 1997), 8–9.

[3] For an in-depth look at Innocent III's focus in opening Fourth Lateran, see his

Women, Dance and Parish Religion in England, 1300–1640

While Fourth Lateran's better-known efforts at creating Christian hegemony came in its campaigns against European heresies, Jews, and the Muslim occupants of the Holy Land, its positions on clerical (and hence lay) education sought to promote a similar hegemony, albeit through subtler means and smaller institutions.[4] Medieval clerics worried not just about heresy on a large scale in distant lands but also about heresy on smaller scales closer to home. The Council's emphasis on pastoral care, perhaps the most famous of its emphases, reflected this concern with caring for the souls of ordinary men and women: with teaching, protecting, and encouraging the living of the faith. While recent scholarship has challenged the dominant scholarly view of Fourth Lateran's influence, other scholars such as Andrew Reeves show the Council's impact on vernacular pastoral literature and, I argue, through that literature on the lives of those in the parish.[5]

Fourth Lateran, with its emphasis on moral practice and prevention of heresy, had direct implications for activities such as dance, implications not yet explored in scholarship on the late Middle Ages. Much like campaigns against heresy, campaigns against dance were not entirely new. While earlier councils such as the 589 Fourth Council of Toledo prohibited dance during divine services, these councils did not exclude dance from sacred ground entirely. They focused more on decorum during services than on dance as a form of sacrilege.[6] Patristic and early medieval councils placed dance outside

---

    sermon in Pope Innocent III, *Between God and Man* (Washington, DC: Catholic University of America Press, 2004).

4 For discussions of the influence of Fourth Lateran on medieval conceptions of heresy, see, among others, R. I. Moore, *The War on Heresy* (Cambridge, MA: Harvard University Press, 2012), 264–266, 268–271; Malcolm Lambert, *Medieval Heresy: Popular Movements from the Gregorian Reform to the Reformation*, 3rd edn. (Oxford: Blackwell, 2002), 112, 200–201.

5 Jeffrey Wayno's article provides helpful challenges to the prevalence of Fourth Lateran's canons, posing questions of local adaptation and textual transmission to challenge the dominance of the Council's impact. However, Andrew Reeves's work on Fourth Lateran in specifically English contexts provides a helpful counterpoint to Wayno's analysis. While Wayno's arguments are certainly significant, Reeves's consideration of the English transmission of Fourth Lateran shows that the Council's canons certainly filtered into English pastoral literature and then into the parish. For various perspectives on Fourth Lateran's impact on vernacular literature and laity, see Jeffrey M. Wayno, "Rethinking the Fourth Lateran Council of 1215," *Speculum* 93, no. 3 (June 29, 2018): 611–637; Andrew Reeves, "'The Nourishment of God's Word': *Inter Caetera* (Canon 10) in England," in *Literary Echoes of the Fourth Lateran Council in England and France, 1215–1405*, ed. Maureen B. M. Boulton (Toronto: Pontifical Institute/Brepols, 2019), 46–73.

6 Alessandro Arcangeli, "Dance and Punishment," *Dance Research* 10, no. 2 (1992): 130. Church councils that issued prohibitions against dance, in some form or another, included the Council of Auxerre, the Council of Toledo, and the Council of Chalons-sur-Saone. See Harald Kleinschmidt, *Perception and Action in Medieval*

Reforming and Redefining True Religion

the mass but not necessarily outside the boundaries of true faith.[7] Prior to Fourth Lateran, dance as a part of mass, as a means of ritual celebration in churchyards or cemeteries, or as an act of worship could be interpreted as a mirroring of heavenly dances performed by angels, and evidence indicates that dance formed an important part of high medieval Christian practice. But during the eleventh through thirteenth centuries and particularly after Fourth Lateran, many clerical perceptions of dance in theological discourses slowly inverted from a heavenly dance performed by angels into a dance of demons. Late medieval clerics began to see dance not as a possible connection to a sacred heavenly sphere but as an act that disturbed a divinely created order, and thus as an act that could not be allowed in churches.[8]

The thirteenth-century councils thus took a more holistic approach to dance than these earlier councils, with a clearer approach to dance starting to appear. While Fourth Lateran focused on teaching clergy and laity alike foundations of belief and behavior, the Council of Avignon spelled out specifically how those two things connected to dance. The Council of Avignon in 1209 prohibited dance during sacred services and on sacred ground: "It is our edict that in churches on saints' eves there shall be no dance-mimes, no obscene movements and no round-dances; nor shall love-songs be sung there, nor dance-songs."[9] The Avignon prohibitions moved dance further from the sacred and closer to the edges of proper Christian behavior. Yet, despite these prohibitions, multiple sources show that the practice of dancing in churchyards remained widespread.[10] As the medieval church sought broad reforms

---

Europe (Rochester, NY: Boydell Press, 2005), 45. Other medieval condemnations of dance appear in Bishop Caesarius of Arles, "Sermo CCLXVI," cap. 4, in PL vol. 39, col. 2239; and Childebert, King of the Franks, Constitutio, in PL vol. 72, col. 1122.

[7] Alessandro Arcangeli, *Dance and Law* (Ghent: The Institute for Historical Dance Practice, 2000), 52; for specific examples in an early medieval English context, see Arthur West Haddan and William Stubbs, *Councils and Ecclesiastical Documents Relating to Great Britain and Ireland* (Oxford: Clarendon Press, 1869), vol. 3, pp. 133, 369, 315. Numerous other regulations and prohibitions appear in local councils from throughout Europe.

[8] According to Arcangeli, late medieval clerics defined dance as a lingering pagan rite, and "the battle against dancing as a part of the war against paganism." Arcangeli, "Dance under Trial," 127.

[9] As quoted in John Stevens, *Words and Music in the Middle Ages: Song, Narrative, Dance, and Drama, 1050–1350* (Cambridge: Cambridge University Press, 1986), 162.

[10] See Elina Gertsman, *The Dance of Death in the Middle Ages: Image, Text, Performance* (Turnhout: Brepols, 2010), 54; Marilyn Daniels, *The Dance in Christianity* (New York: The Paulist Press, 1981), 46; Nancy Caciola, *Afterlives: The Return of the Dead in the Middle Ages* (Ithaca, NY: Cornell University Press, 2017), esp. 3–4, 141–142, 249, 252; Jean-Claude Schmitt, *Ghosts in the Middle Ages: The Living and the Dead in Medieval Society*, trans. Teresa Fagan (Chicago: University of Chicago Press, 1998), 84, 117–119, 139–140, 182, 214–217.

in how its members worshipped and learned, dance became an issue that was used to highlight improper belief and practice. Between Fourth Lateran and the early modern Reformations, the always-extant tensions between Christianity and dance crystallized into concerns that impacted the practice and beliefs of all believers, men and women alike.

While medieval clerics do show a growing concern with dance in the thirteenth and fourteenth centuries, dance proved to be a greater preoccupation for the early modern reformers of the sixteenth and seventeenth centuries, perhaps because medieval authors took dance so much for granted. For late medieval authors and parishes, the biggest concern with dance came with its use in worship (or in disrupting worship, as we will see in the next chapter); their concern was first with actions that disrupted sacred space or time, and then with the bodies performing those actions and jeopardizing holy matter. By contrast, early modern reformers fixated on dance as embodied and gendered, particularly as medieval changes in the conceptualization of dance meant that early modern authors now thought of dance as first a moving sexualized body, then as an action. The gendering of dance flipped the order of concern and changed the discussion from one of sacrilege to one about sex – an action paramount on the list of priorities for early modern reformers.

With a renewed emphasis on scriptural texts and a rejection of papal authority, these early modern reformers wrote and preached a new form of faith and practice, leading to the reworking of doctrine, of churches, and of communities. Reformers redefined standards for clerical behavior and authority, created new materials for the teaching of clergy and laity, and produced new scripts for morality. Much like the reforms of the thirteenth- and fourteenth-century church, these reformations of the sixteenth and seventeenth centuries were not without violent suppression of opposition. Under the authority of scripture and true belief, reformers drove out or executed those who were deemed sacrilegious or profane. Within both the medieval and the early modern parish, then, attempts at parish discipline and regulation revolved around this priority of protecting the faith (and the faithful) from profane bodies or false beliefs.

What exactly qualified as false belief or as true religion during the English Reformations was a loaded question, and the answer changed dramatically decade by decade, for England's Reformations infamously swung between one extreme or another, with official state policy (and the theology and praxis that accompanied it) shifting under each monarch and under each archbishop, bishop, and theologian.[11] Henry VIII's pivot from defender of the papacy to self-proclaimed head of the English church, driven by his desire for a male

---

[11] Peter Marshall, *Heretics and Believers: A History of the English Reformation* (New Haven, CT: Yale University Press, 2018), xii.

heir and the pope's refusal to grant a divorce or annulment, may have been the initial impetus behind the 1534 Act of Supremacy, and much of the effort of the Henrician Reformations accordingly went into securing respect for and loyalty to the new head of the church. However, throughout the Henrician Reformations, Henry's own willingness to allow multiple Protestant reformers to make their case for their own vision of a reformed English church meant that the Henrician Reformations were not simply state reforms. They were complex, erratic, and idiosyncratic attempts to bring together various forms of religious idealism into a single uniform religious policy, one united primarily by its emphasis on the monarch as the church's head but also marked by a spectrum of Protestant positions.

After Henry's death in 1547, the English Reformations became more clearly defined in goals and theological emphases under his son and heir, Edward VI, with a shift from emphasis on the church's leadership towards an emphasis on theology and liturgy as spread through new prayerbooks, confessions, and articles of faith. The Edwardian Reforms, from 1547 to 1553, and the Marian Reforms that followed between 1553 and 1558, both pursued more internally consistent theological ends, although the Protestant goals of the Edwardian Reforms, pushed by such figures as Thomas Cranmer, John Hooper, and Miles Coverdale, directly contrasted with Mary I's restoration of Catholic teaching and practice under such clerics as Stephen Gardiner and Edmund Bonner. The Elizabethan settlement of 1559, with its new Act of Supremacy and Act of Uniformity, sought to bring some stability after these relatively rapid and dramatic changes in policy, pursuing some of the middle ground of the Henrician Reforms but in a far more coherent and consistent manner. Yet, the process of division and confessionalization under the broad umbrella of official state policy continued through Elizabeth I's reign and into the reigns of the first two Stuart monarchs, leading into the debates between Laudians, Puritans, and other factions that would ultimately spark the English Civil Wars in the 1640s. Despite this diversity in theological vision and goals, however, each of these stages of the Reformations sought to create uniformity within the English church, using prayer books, sermon collections, regulations of parish life, and more punitive means to try to make each reformer's vision a reality.[12]

As Peter Marshall notes, it is too simplistic to describe the English Reformations only as an "'Act of State,' simply imposed upon the nation by its successive governments."[13] While, yes, the state did play an outsized role in setting the broad framework for each stage of the Reformations, wide variations existed in tension with others within official policy, each promoted by

[12] Ibid. Marshall's book gives a roughly chronological and far more detailed overview of the various stages of the English Reformations for those interested in some of the specific details of each stage.

[13] Ibid.

Women, Dance and Parish Religion in England, 1300–1640

reformers with their own individual views of what it meant to bring about the practice of true belief. The development of distinctive forms of faith, often tied to specific theological nuances, reformers, or local customs, took place alongside the broad state-supervised push for uniformity within the English church. Thus, the experience of the Reformations could look quite different for individuals from different parishes, and these political shifts from monarch to monarch, bishop to bishop often shaped political changes more than lay religion, at least in the short term.[14]

Set against this ever-shifting political backdrop, in England, the transition from medieval reforms into early modern ones was particularly gradual. As early as 1216, bishops worked to transmit key Lateran canons into their dioceses. These efforts continued throughout the thirteenth century, particularly with the work of Richard Poore, Bishop of Salisbury, Robert Grosseteste, Bishop of Lincoln, and John Peckham, Archbishop of Canterbury. Poore's efforts resulted in a set of synodal statutes transmitting portions of Fourth Lateran between 1217 and 1219, while Peckham was among the earliest advocates for vernacular education of clergy and laity. His Lambeth council, convened in 1281, resulted in a syllabus of what every parish priest must teach his parishioners.[15] Grosseteste's work resulted in, among other things, the 1281 Synod of Oxford and the 1280 *South-English Legendary*.[16] These early efforts by theologically minded reforming bishops helped spur a boom in vernacular literature and lay piety in fourteenth-century England, with texts like John Mirk's *Festial*, Robert Mannyng of Brunne's *Handlyng Synne*, the *Northern Homily Cycle*, and *Speculum Sacerdotale* proliferating alongside parish guilds, saints' cults, and other religious practices.[17] In the fifteenth century, the threat of Lollardy, in and of itself another reform-focused movement, led to the Arundel prohibitions that attempted to slow the creation of new vernacular texts. However, lay religious involvement only increased, with the expansion of mystery plays, Corpus Christi observations, and other forms of performed

---

[14] See, for example, McClendon, *The Quiet Reformation*.

[15] Andrew Reeves, "Teaching the Creed and Articles of Faith in England: 1215–1281," in *A Companion to Pastoral Care in the Late Middle Ages*, ed. Ronald Stansbury (Leiden: Brill, 2010), 41.

[16] O'Carroll, *A Thirteenth-Century Preacher's Handbook*, 10–11; Klaus Bitterling (ed.), *Of Shrifte and Penance: The ME Prose Translation of Le Manuel des péchés* (Heidelberg: C. Winter, 1998), 10; Andrew Reeves, *Religious Education in Thirteenth-Century England: The Creed and Articles of Faith* (Leiden: Brill, 2015).

[17] See, among others, Jennifer Garrison, "Mediated Piety: Eucharistic Theology and Lay Devotion in Robert Mannyng's 'Handlyng Synne,'" *Speculum* 85 (2010): 894–922; Beth Allison Barr, "'Sche Hungryd Ryth Sor Aftyr Goddys Word': Female Piety and the Legacy of the Pastoral Programme in the Late Medieval English Sermons of Bodleian Library MS Greaves 54," *Journal of Religious History* 39, no. 1 (2015): 31–50; French, *The People of the Parish*; Coletti, *Mary Magdalene and the Drama of Saints*.

Reforming and Redefining True Religion

parish culture.[18] The long English Reformations, formally starting with Henry VIII's 1534 Act of Supremacy and unfolding over the next hundred years through numerous acts, statutes, and texts, heightened division over forms of religious practice but continued the same emphasis on correct doctrine, lay education, and active piety that had begun centuries before. The slow transformation of dance from ambivalent to profane through shifts in understanding of holiness and gender occurred, step by step, against these continual pushes for reform and piety.

There is already a robust and expansive scholarship on medieval religious reforms and the early modern Reformations.[19] Thus, the point of this chapter is not to provide an in-depth study of these reform movements. Instead, this chapter uses dance as a lens for a broad overview of reform, laying the groundwork for the case studies in the chapters that follow. This dance-focused overview reveals several key continuities. The first is a concern with the propagation of rightly understood and practiced faith to laity. However, clear differences in approach to scripture appear within this broad continuity. These exegetical differences shape approaches to transgression, true religion, and bodies. The second continuity is a concern with false worship, found at the heart of both reform movements.[20] One cannot protect true faith without first defining false faith, and in the process of defining sacrilege, a "persecuting society," as Moore so famously put it, is formed.[21]

---

[18] Judy Ann Ford, *John Mirk's Festial: Orthodoxy, Lollard and the Common People in Fourteenth-Century England* (Cambridge: D. S. Brewer, 2006); Shannon McSheffrey, *Gender and Heresy: Women and Men in Lollard Communities, 1420–1530* (Philadelphia: University of Pennsylvania Press, 1995); Miri Rubin, *Corpus Christi: The Eucharist in Late Medieval Culture* (Cambridge: Cambridge University Press, 1991); Lawrence M. Clopper, *Drama, Play, and Game: English Festive Culture in the Medieval and Early Modern Period* (Chicago: University of Chicago Press, 2001).

[19] A limited selection of works in these expansive fields includes works such as Madigan, *Medieval Christianity*; Anne T. Thayer, *Penitence, Preaching and the Coming of the Reformation* (London: Taylor & Francis, 2017); Steven E. Ozment, *The Age of Reform (1250–1550): An Intellectual and Religious History of Late Medieval and Reformation Europe* (New Haven, CT: Yale University Press, 1980); William H. Campbell, *The Landscape of Pastoral Care in 13th-Century England* (Cambridge: Cambridge University Press, 2018); Duffy, *Stripping of the Altars*; Peter Marshall, *Reformation England, 1480–1642* (Oxford: Oxford University Press, 2003); Christopher Haigh, *English Reformations: Religion, Politics, and Society under the Tudors* (Oxford: Oxford University Press, 1993); Carlos M. N. Eire, *Reformations: The Early Modern World, 1450–1650* (New Haven, CT: Yale University Press, 2016); Julie Chappell and Kaley A. Kramer (eds.), *Women during the English Reformations: Renegotiating Gender and Religious Identity* (New York: Palgrave MacMillan, 2014).

[20] Eire, *War against the Idols*, 3.

[21] Robert Ian Moore, *The Formation of a Persecuting Society: Authority and Deviance in Western Europe, 950–1250*, 2nd edn. (Oxford: Blackwell, 2007).

Women, Dance and Parish Religion in England, 1300–1640

Third, and most significantly: as boundaries between true and sacrilegious beliefs, bodies, and behaviors hardened into punishable binaries, they did so not only because of disagreement on key theological issues but also because of *adiaphora* – peripheral issues that tap into bigger concerns and questions but have no clear black-and-white answer in scripture. The lack of a single clearly defined position means that it is in these peripheral issues, such as dance, that boundaries excluding the "other" and regulating troublesome bodies were often drawn. From the debates over these grey areas, discourses with binary approaches to holiness and transgression emerged, leading to a persecuting society in which "true religion" and "true practice" were starkly and harshly defined.

TEACHING THE FAITH

The first step in creating a "purer" version of Christianity was to teach the faith: to enable ordinary men and women to give an account of their beliefs and of the basic tenets of Christianity. To some degree, these basic tenets of the Christian faith varied from place to place and between periods. For a medieval English context, the 1281 Synod of Oxford gave a fairly clear idea as to what teaching the faith consisted of:

> Every priest having charge of a flock, do, four times in each year (that is, once each quarter) on one or more solemn feast days, either himself or by someone else, instruct the people in the vulgar language, simply and without any fantastical admixture of subtle distinctions, in the Articles of the Creed, the Ten Commandments, the Evangelical Precepts, the Seven Works of Mercy, the Seven Deadly Sins with their Offshoots, the Seven Principal Virtues, and the Seven Sacraments.[22]

These priorities highlight well the tension in vernacular texts aimed at the laity: the need to communicate theological concepts like the nature of the sacraments and the creeds alongside practical guidelines to lived faith like the seven deadly sins and the seven principle virtues. While, as Wayno notes, the degree to which synods and statutes passed on Fourth Lateran's canons varied widely, English pastoral literature is remarkably consistent in noting what should be taught to the laity, and the rapid proliferation of pastoral texts indicates that bishops took at least Fourth Lateran's admonition to teaching seriously.[23] In an early modern context, the central tenets of teaching the faith

---

[22] As translated in Joseph A. Mosher, *The Exemplum in the Early Religious and Didactic Literature of England* (New York: AMS Press, 1966), 115.

[23] Wayno discusses a series of regional adaptations of the Council's canons, including Richard Poore's collection of statutes from Salisbury, compiled between 1217–1219. See Wayno, "Rethinking the Fourth Lateran Council of 1215," 625–627.

Reforming and Redefining True Religion

varied a little more. As Euan Cameron observes, "by 1600 protestant theology was a complex body of academic teachings, far more widely distributed than ever was medieval scholasticism, and sustained with much more doctrinaire determination."[24] But teaching the faith remained the primary priority of the reformers. Amy Nelson Burnett notes that "the Protestant reformers believed that their chief responsibility was to communicate a message," the message of true faith, through sermons, catechism, and church discipline.[25] For laity, learning the faith included both intellectual propositions and guidelines for lived experience. Clerics sought to teach the laity a practical theology that would then shape their interactions with things like dance. But while synodal decrees were clear on how to teach and explain the sacraments, these decrees and those implementing them were far less clear regarding how to teach on dance or gossip, leaving much more leeway for those teaching the faith to create their own theologies of dance for the laity.

How would the faith have been taught? In both the medieval and early modern periods, laity learned their faith primarily through preaching. In recent years, scholars have highlighted the importance of preaching – and of sermons – in late medieval religion and piety.[26] As noted by Alan Fletcher, Susan Wabuda, Anne Thayer, Beverly Mayne Kienzle, G. R. Owst, and others, sermons played an essential role in establishing Christian communities and communicating the church's teachings, forming an integral part of medieval religion.[27] Medieval clerics carefully filtered and reframed creeds and other theological texts for lay audiences, primarily through vernacular sermons. As sermons became an increasingly central part of late medieval religion, sermon cycles – collections of texts that met the requirements of creedal education – proliferated. Sermon cycles were compiled for three distinct groups: friars, regular clergy, and secular clergy. With a few exceptions, texts for the friars and regular clergy were in Latin, and texts for secular clergy were in the vernacular.[28]

---

[24] Euan Cameron, *The European Reformation* (Oxford: Oxford University Press, 2012), 417.

[25] Amy Nelson Burnett, *Teaching the Reformation: Ministers and Their Message in Basel, 1529–1629* (Oxford: Oxford University Press, 2006), 4–5, 262.

[26] Alan J. Fletcher, *Late Medieval Popular Preaching in Britain and Ireland: Texts, Studies, and Interpretations* (Turnhout: Brepols, 2009), 275.

[27] See Beverly Mayne Kienzle, *The Sermon* (Turnhout: Brepols, 2000); Larissa Taylor (ed.), *Preachers and People in the Reformations and Early Modern Period* (Leiden: Brill, 2001); Thayer, *Penitence, Preaching and the Coming of the Reformation*; G. R. Owst, *Preaching in Medieval England: An Introduction to Sermon Manuscripts of the Period c. 1350–1450* (Cambridge: Cambridge University Press, 2010); Susan Wabuda, *Preaching during the English Reformation* (Cambridge: Cambridge University Press, 2008).

[28] Fletcher provides an extensive discussion of these categories in his book. He also notes that there is one important exception to this rule. Texts composed by Augustine canons (canons regular) blurred the lines between regular and secular.

Women, Dance and Parish Religion in England, 1300–1640

These vernacular sermons were the ones intended for lay audiences, and thus, I argue, most indicative of the religion and doctrine communicated to the majority of the population.[29] These compilations were typically quite structured, providing sermon collections that systematically addressed the entire church year through *temporale* sermons tied to Sundays and church holidays and *sanctorale* sermons tied to saints' lives.[30] A parish priest equipped with such a cycle would have at his fingertips all the material he needed to ensure the safety of the souls of his congregation.[31] Considering the state of the book at the priest's fingertips provides a solid indication that many of these texts were indeed intended for use in a parish, as many of the cycles show signs of heavy use. Many vernacular sermon cycles also contain multiple scribal hands and texts, little decorative illumination, small margins, and other cost-saving measures that indicate an awareness of expense and a relatively low budget.[32] It is for the purpose of teaching a lay audience on a parish level that the majority of the surviving English sermon cycles were composed, and thus, what these sermons say about dance can help us understand how ordinary men and women understood dance and its relationship to their faith and lives.[33]

Prior to Fourth Lateran, preaching most likely came from the monks associated with cathedral monasteries; however, even then, parish priests and secular clergy fulfilled much of the parish demand for preaching.[34] Mendicant friars, the Dominicans and Franciscans, played a significant

---

    Mirk's *Festial* is one such text, and a good example of the difficulty of classifying sermon cycles. Fletcher, *Late Medieval Popular Preaching in Britain and Ireland*, 14–22; see also Owst, *Preaching in Medieval England*.

[29] Owst, *Preaching in Medieval England*, 223.

[30] Fletcher, *Late Medieval Popular Preaching in Britain and Ireland*, 165. However, although these sermon cycles were structured, it was not necessarily according to the *ars predicandi*. They were often influenced in their form more by the demands of rendering theological concepts, often originally in Latin, into clear English with relative ease. Once these sermon cycles began to draw primarily upon other English sermons for their source material, the discrepancy between the ideal sermon as envisioned by grammarians of sermon form and these secular sermon cycles became even more pronounced.

[31] Ibid., 23. Fletcher notes that smaller, more piecemeal cycles were often intended for personal use rather than for preaching. He states that "when a preaching compilation is found to be thoroughly eclectic in its sermons and other contents, it will also prove to be a personal product, while the manuscript that contains the longer and systematic sermon cycle, by contrast, will prove to be institutionally sanctioned or a product of professional scribes who had a practical eye to the clerical book market."

[32] Fletcher mentions Bodl. MS Hatton 96 and CUL MS Gg.6.16, both manuscripts considered in this monograph, as his two examples of sermon cycles intended for parish-level use. Ibid., 25.

[33] Ibid., 161.

[34] Reeves, "'The Nourishment of God's Word.'"

Reforming and Redefining True Religion

role in supplementing the preaching of secular clergy in the thirteenth and fourteenth centuries.[35] Medieval sermons could thus come from one's parish priest (a figure well known and involved in the daily life of the laity), from a regular cleric (most likely an Augustinian canon) from a nearby cathedral school or monastery, or from an itinerant mendicant friar (a Franciscan or Dominican). Sermons from the parish priest would likely be delivered within the parish church as a part of regular services and would be fairly short: John Mirk's sermons in *Festial*, for example, were likely between ten to fifteen minutes in duration.[36] Sermons from a mendicant might be delivered in other public spaces like the churchyard or the marketplace. Some of these sermons, along with sermons aimed at a university audience, might be substantially longer. Thomas Wimbledon's widely circulated *"redde racionem villicacionis tue,"* for example, would have taken over an hour to deliver.[37]

Whether brief or lengthy, in the church or in the public square, the delivery of the sermon itself was a performance, with careful thought given not only to content but also to delivery, to style, and to other performative elements.[38] Sermons were, in other words, a public performance in a public space, an occasion for entertainment as well as edification: an activity not too dissimilar from parish dance. This continued into the early modern era. Parish priests delivered sermons at least once a week, if not more frequently, while university faculty and clergy known for their speaking abilities delivered sermons in public spaces, for example outside St. Paul's Cathedral in London. Such Paul's Cross sermons might last hours, would be delivered to an audience of perhaps thousands, and would even involve refreshments.[39] Parishioners, if unsat-

---

[35] D. L. D'Avray, *The Preaching of the Friars: Sermons Diffused from Paris before 1300* (New York: ACLS History E-Book Project, 2005); Anne Thayer, "The Medieval Sermon: Text, Performance, Insight," in *Understanding Medieval Primary Sources: Using Historical Sources to Discover Medieval Europe*, ed. Joel T. Rosenthal (New York: Routledge, 2012), 43–58.

[36] Beth Allison Barr, "Medieval Sermons and Audience Appeal after the Black Death," *History Compass* 16, no. 9 (2018).

[37] Nancy H. Owen, "Thomas Wimbledon's Sermon: 'Redde Racionem Villicacionis Tue,'" *Mediaeval Studies* 28 (1966): 176–197; Sabine Volk-Birke, *Chaucer and Medieval Preaching: Rhetoric for Listeners in Sermons and Poetry* (Tübingen: Gunter Narr Verlag, 1991), 160–174; Siegfried Wenzel, *Preaching in the Age of Chaucer: Selected Sermons in Translation* (Washington, DC: Catholic University of America Press, 2008), 254–269.

[38] Carolyn Muessig (ed.), *Preacher, Sermon, and Audience in the Middle Ages* (Leiden: Brill, 2002); Charlotte Steenbrugge, *Drama and Sermon in Late Medieval England: Performance, Authority, Devotion* (Kalamazoo, MI: Medieval Institute Publications, 2017).

[39] The Virtual Paul's Cross Project provides a helpful introduction to metropolitan preaching and its experience and gives a sense of the significance of early modern sermons in public life. See https://vpcp.chass.ncsu.edu/ and John N. Wall, "Virtual

Women, Dance and Parish Religion in England, 1300–1640

isfied with their own parish preacher, would go to nearby parishes to hear preachers whose sermons they preferred, in a practice known as "sermon-gadding."[40] Sermons, like dance, were a part of the fabric of daily life for the laity of medieval and early modern England, and the voice of the preacher threaded through the community from the pulpit and from the square. Thus, in helping laity understand and live out their faith, the voice of the preacher would perhaps be the strongest theological influence on laity and parishes. The preacher's theology of dance, whether intentionally created or inadvertently constructed through repeated sermon mentions, set the expectations and rhythms for lay lived experience.

Contrary to early modern criticisms that accused medieval authors of neglecting scripture, medieval sermons were full of scriptural allusions and texts. Even *sanctorale* sermons, framed around saints' lives and thus a target of much Protestant ire, drew on multiple scripture passages. References to the gospels abound, as do references to Pauline texts. Threaded throughout these sermons, mentions of dance appear – rarely in extensive discussions or as a topic of full sermons, but consistently, in exposition of scripture passages and more frequently in sermon tales, throughout the liturgical year.[41] The use of dance in vernacular sermons highlights well the way that medieval reformers thought their faith should be taught. One such example appeared in a lengthy late fourteenth-century vernacular sermon by Thomas Wimbledon, "*redde*

Paul's Cross: The Experience of Public Preaching after the Reformation," in *Paul's Cross and the Culture of Persuasion in England, 1520–1640*, ed. Torrance Kirby and P. G. Stanwood (Leiden: Brill, 2014), 61–92; Arnold Hunt, *The Art of Hearing: English Preachers and Their Audiences, 1590–1640* (Cambridge: Cambridge University Press, 2010).

40 Hunt, *The Art of Hearing*, 14–15, 187–228.

41 The *Repertorium of Middle English Prose Sermons* indicates that, out of all catalogued vernacular sermons in England, four scripture verses that mention dance are referenced, in four distinct prose sermons, with a fifth direct reference to a dance scripture appearing in the verse *Northern Homily Cycle*. Vernacular English sermons directly reference Matthew 11:16–17, Ecclesiastes 3:4, Job 21:11–12, and Lamentations 5:15. These sermons also directly reference Matthew 14 and Mark 6, where the dance of Salome is presented; her dance will be discussed in a later chapter and thus does not appear here. Given that at least nineteen scriptures reference dance directly and that so many medieval sermons exist, it should be apparent that instances in which dance was discussed in vernacular sermons are comparatively rare. Eric Stanley's article breaks down every possible Latin word that could be translated to mean dance and contains far more than nineteen references. Nineteen is the number of references to dance that survived in the King James Version (1611), and, I argue, the minimum number of dance references contained in scripture. Eric Stanley, "Dance, Dancers and Dancing in Anglo-Saxon England," *Dance Research: The Journal of the Society for Dance Research* 9, no. 2 (1991): 18–31; Veronica O'Mara and Suzanne Paul (eds.), *A Repertorium of Middle English Prose Sermons* (Turnhout: Brepols, 2007).

Reforming and Redefining True Religion

racionem villicacionis tue," on Luke 16:2. A reference to Lamentations came at the very end of this rather lengthy sermon, in the conclusion on the rewards due "to wyse seruantis and goode, and ... false seruauntis and wickede."[42] The author moved from a list of sins – including envy, wrath, slowness to good deeds, lechery, gluttony, and covetousness – to a description of the reward for these sins:

> But fier, brymston, and the spirit of tempestis, that is the fend of Helle schulleth be a party of here peyne, as it is write in the Sautere. Whan these dampned men beth in this woo they schulleth synge this rewful song that is writen in the Book of Mornynge:
>
>> The ioye of our herte is ago:
>> Oure wele is turned into woo.
>> The couroune of oure heued is falle vs fro.
>> Alas, for synne that we doo.
>
> But ioye, and ioye, and ioye to hem that beth saued! Ioye in God! Ioye in hemself![43]

The Lamentations reference is contained in the quatrain regarding the disappearance of joy and transformation of "wele to woo" – dancing to mourning, as rendered in the scriptural text. While the sermon's translation of "wele" does not directly correlate to the idea of dancing, the movement from a state of joy to one of woe conveys the emotional transition of Lamentations precisely. The focus in the teaching of the faith in this widely circulated verse is more on action than belief: more on the cessation of sin than on the biblical text itself. Medieval authors prioritized practical applications over theological or exegetical depth in messages aimed at laity, and scriptures about specific actions like dance were paraphrased to create sermons constructed around larger moral lessons.

---

42 The popularity of this sermon is substantiated by the seventeen manuscripts and twenty-two early modern printed texts (dating from 1540 to 1732) that survive. Wimbledon's sermon, while not part of one of the major sermon cycles, did reach a large audience in both the late medieval and early modern periods. See Owen, "Thomas Wimbledon's Sermon," 196. For extensive analysis of the Wimbledon sermon's style and structure, see Volk-Birke, *Chaucer and Medieval Preaching*, 160–174. Christopher Fletcher summarizes the current state of scholarship on Wimbledon in a footnote before his discussion of the theme of youth in the sermon. Christopher Fletcher, *Richard II: Manhood, Youth, and Politics, 1377–99* (Oxford: Oxford University Press, 2008).

43 Owen, "Thomas Wimbledon's Sermon," 197. Owen's edition of this sermon comes from the earliest known manuscript of the sermon – Camb., MS Corpus Christi College, 357. Another edited edition is based on MS Hatton 57, which Owen dismisses as a "careless or hurried copy" (176).

Women, Dance and Parish Religion in England, 1300–1640

So, if medieval sermons did not rely primarily on close scriptural exegesis to teach theological knowledge to laity, what aids did they use? *Exempla*, anecdotes intended to convey clear moral and theological messages, were the key means by which medieval clergy taught their parishioners the faith.[44] The *exemplum*, like the sermon, was not a prevalent medieval tool until the thirteenth century, when it became the primary tool utilized by the mendicant orders.[45] In the aftermath of Fourth Lateran, *exempla* became a central part of church teaching and preaching, utilized to communicate moral standards and basic theology to the laity, either through sermons for the illiterate or through beautifully decorated compendiums of tales intended for a wealthy lay audience.[46] Preachers often used these *exempla* to illustrate and communicate major theological points. For example, in John Mirk's *Festial*, the homily on Corpus Christi utilized a tale about Saint Ode, bishop of Canterbury, to reaffirm the doctrine of transubstantiation by discussing the doubt of priests and a miracle performed by the bishop in which he was able to show the priests the changed elements and to bring about belief.[47] Throughout *Festial* and other medieval sermons, *exempla* that more tangibly explicate a doctrine in narrative form often follow portions explaining the basics of the faith.

Beth Allison Barr has used Margery Kempe's *Book* to show that sermons and the *exempla* contained within affected the piety of lay audiences, and it is in Margery's *Book* that one example of lay absorption of dance *exempla* appears.[48] Margery described the appearance of the Blessed Virgin Mary in a dream and the dance of the Virgin and her maidens in heaven, indicating familiarity with *exempla* like the one on the maiden Musa, who, like Margery, gained entrance to the heavenly dance through earthly abstention.[49] While

---

[44] Jacques Berlioz and Marie Anne Polo de Beaulieu, "Exempla: A Discussion and a Case Study," in *Medieval Women and the Sources of Medieval History*, ed. Joel T. Rosenthal (Athens, GA: University of Georgia Press, 1990), 38.

[45] Arcangeli, "Dance and Punishment," 30; Berlioz and Beaulieu, "Exempla: A Discussion and a Case Study"; Fritz Kemmler, *"Exempla" in Context: A Historical and Critical Study of Robert Mannyng of Brunne's "Handlyng Synne,"* (Tübingen: Gunter Narr Verlag, 1984); David Jones (ed.), *Friars' Tales: Thirteenth-Century Exempla from the British Isles* (Manchester: Manchester University Press, 2011).

[46] Sullens references the beautiful illuminations of these texts as evidence of lay and clerical circulation. See Robert Mannyng, *Handlyng Synne*, ed. Idelle Sullens (Binghamton, NY: Medieval & Renaissance Texts & Studies, 1983), xvii.

[47] John Mirk, *Mirk's Festial: A Collection of Homilies*, ed. Theodor Erbe, EETS ES 96 (London: K. Paul, Trench, Trübner & Co., 1905), 170–171.

[48] Barr, "'Sche Hungryd Ryth Sor Aftyr Goddys Word.'"

[49] Exemplum #1424 in Frederic C. Tubach, *Index Exemplorum: A Handbook of Medieval Religious Tales* (Helsinki: Suomalainen Tiedeakatemia, 1981), 114. Versions of this *exemplum* appear in twenty-one different manuscripts, indicating its prevalence. Margery Kempe, *The Book of Margery Kempe: An Abridged Translation*, trans. Liz Herbert McAvoy (Cambridge: D. S. Brewer, 2003), 68–69.

Reforming and Redefining True Religion

Margery's *Book* is full of scriptural language and multiple allusions to the text, oftentimes the moral lessons she drew from the many sermons she heard come from *exempla* or from direct connections to the life of Christ rather than from careful exegesis of scriptural texts. Thus, the relative scarcity of references to scriptures about dance in medieval sermons does not necessarily mean that medieval audiences were not imbibing ideas about dance from the sermons that they heard, for dance *exempla* abound in medieval sermons.

Sermons likewise played an important role in educating laity and cultivating piety in early modern England. Eric Carlsen and Susan Wabuda, among others, have explored the importance of sermons during this period, with Carlsen asserting that sermons were the key means of communicating doctrine and bringing sinners to repentance in England prior to the Laudian reforms of the late 1620s–1630s.[50] In a continuity from late medieval practice, for the laity, the Reformations were more heard than read, and thus, sermons retained their central place in lay piety, shaping theological understandings and setting standards of moral behavior. Anne Thayer's work shows the extent to which sermons shaped lay theology and action, outlining regional differences that she convincingly traces back to penitential preaching.[51] However, despite continuities in importance and place in parish life, these sermons differed from their medieval forerunners in several ways, one of the most notable being the disappearance of *exempla*. These *exempla*, described in one early modern sermon as "*ridiculous legend-preaching* to make the people laugh," were replaced with "the vleauened bread of *sinceritie* and truth" – a compendium of scripture references and close exegetical readings, drawing occasionally on reformers or church fathers.[52]

As vernacular translation and presentation of scripture became more of a priority, discussions of dance scriptures in sermons became more widespread.

   The passage connects dancing and appropriateness with virginity: "Ah, Lord, there are virgins now dancing happily in heaven. Shall I not do so? … Because you are a virgin in your soul, I shall take you by the one hand in heaven and my mother by the other hand, and so shall you dance in heaven with other holy maidens and virgins, for I may call you dearly bought and my own beloved darling." Tubach's *Index Exemplorum* lists out nineteen distinct dance exempla, found in over seventy cycles and texts, each of which survives in multiple manuscript copies.

50 For recent scholarship on sermons in the early modern period in England, see, among others, Eric Josef Carlson, "The Boring of the Ear: Shaping the Pastoral Vision of Preaching in England, 1540–1640," in *Preachers and People in the Reformations and Early Modern Period*, ed. Larissa Taylor (Leiden: Brill, 2001), 249–294; Wabuda, *Preaching during the English Reformation*; Taylor (ed.), *Preachers and People in the Reformations and Early Modern Period*.

51 Thayer, *Penitence, Preaching and the Coming of the Reformation*.

52 From "The First Frvits of the Resvrrection," in John Prideaux, *Eight Sermons* (Imprinted at London: by Felix Kyngston, for Iohn Budge, and are to be sold at his shop in Pauls Church-yard, at the signe of the greene Dragon, 1621), 30–31.

Women, Dance and Parish Religion in England, 1300–1640

Prose sermons from the medieval period referenced only five scriptures that mention dance, including the Salome narrative, while David's dance does not appear at all.[53] Vernacular presentations of psalms mentioning dance, which appear in vernacular psalters but not in medieval sermons, do not use the word dance but instead use the more ambiguous "choir" or "croude."[54] In contrast, the early modern sermons quote the psalmist as having exhorted his audience to "praise the Lord with dance." They also frequently discuss verses that reference dance from Matthew, Ecclesiastes, Job, and elsewhere, along with David's dance (mentioned forty-four times in the around three hundred early modern sermons surveyed). Ironically, as dance slowly disappeared from parish life, it became more and more prevalent in sermons. The voice of the preacher gradually drowned out the pipes of the parish dances.

A close study of how early modern sermons use these scripture references to dance highlights some of the key exegetical differences in texts aimed at laity between 1300 and 1600.[55] Several early modern authors scold those who

---

[53] A less common way that dance featured in medieval sermons was through the presentation of biblical figures who danced. A study of the *Repertorium* indicates that although the most common scriptural dancers (David, Salome, Miriam, Jephthah's daughter, and Judith) are referenced a total of 197 times in thirty-nine different manuscripts, very few of these references actually mention their dances. David receives 169 mentions, Judith 10, Herodias/Salome 9, Miriam 5, and Jephthah's daughter 4. Four of the nine references to Salome explicitly mention her dance, which also appears in three verse sermon cycles. For specific manuscript information, see O'Mara and Paul, *A Repertorium of Middle English Prose Sermons*. In fact, none of the other scriptural exemplars who danced in worship or in celebration dance in Middle English sermons, with only Salome making an appearance. The golden calf narrative from Exodus 32 is likewise rare in medieval sermons; only seven sermons in four manuscripts reference the chapter, with the only sermon that references the verse in which dance occurs discussing "wantonness" instead of dancing. See BL Add. MS 40671, fol. 40v.

[54] These psalters complement the arguments made in this monograph, although they do not fit within this project and remain a subject for future study. See Annie Sutherland, *English Psalms in the Middle Ages, 1300–1450* (Oxford; New York: Oxford University Press, 2015); Robert Ray Black, Raymond St.-Jacques, and J. J. Smith (eds.), *The Middle English Glossed Prose Psalter: Edited from Cambridge, Magdalene College, MS Pepys 2498* (Heidelberg: Universitätsverlag Winter, 2012); Richard Rolle, *Two Revisions of Rolle's English Psalter Commentary and the Related Canticles*, ed. Anne Hudson (New York; Oxford: Oxford University Press, 2012).

[55] See Basil Hall, "Biblical Scholarship: Editions and Commentaries," in *The Cambridge History of the Bible, Vol. 3: The West from the Reformation to the Present Day*, ed. S. L. Greenslade (Cambridge: Cambridge University Press, 1963), 76–80, 83, 87–88; Victor Harris, "Allegory to Analogy in the Interpretation of Scriptures," *Philological Quarterly* 45, no. 1 (January 1, 1966): 10; David C. Steinmetz, "Calvin and the Patristic Exegesis of Paul," in *The Bible in the Sixteenth Century*, ed. David C. Steinmetz (London: Duke University Press, 1990), 118.

Reforming and Redefining True Religion

use scripture to support the dances of their day, connecting scriptural support for dance to sacrilegious interpretations of scripture. One sermon argued that:

> We are to come to the Word, not to learne to maintaine our owne errours and heresies, or to maineteine our sins. As because of the drunkennesse of *Noe*, or by the filthinesse of *Lot* with his daughters to take occasion to maintaine drunkennesse and whore domes, this is an horrible abuse of the Word: In *Amos* wee see them reproued that would play with *Dauids* instruments, hauing no skill or Art, that is no heart to vse them wel; whereas *Dauid* had skill by them to stir vp his affections: So do they that mainetaine their filthy dances by *Dauids* dancing.[56]

This sermon explicitly tied together a number of scripture passages and represents one use of scripture in early modern sermons: proving a point through multiple citations rather than through a narrative or exemplar. Another sermon on dance, referencing Ecclesiastes 3:4, expanded upon the reasons why supporting dance from scripture is profane and displayed a different exegetical approach:

> There be some which mainteine daunsing, and these be there words: wee can proue by the Scripture yt daunsing is allowed, *there is a time* (saith Solomon) *to daunce*. I noted before, and they which obserue well the course of things here spoken, shal find it true, that he disputeth not what is done lawfullie, but what is done. But I will not holde them in his straight, I will graunt in this one particular of dansing, that he speaketh of a thing lawfull: yet shall ye see that they doe fouly abuse gods word in the sence they alledge it. There are more kindes of daunsing than one. If they will haue this Scripture serue their turne, they must shewe that such daunsing as it is vsed now a daies: wanton dansing, by which men and women nourish and feede their fleshly lustes, is here mainteyned. By such dauncing sinne is much increased, God is not glorified by it. Are they not then ashamed to make Gods word alow it, and so to be contrarie to it selfe? For Gods word doth condemne chambering and wantonnesse. *Rom. 13*. If any replie, and say we can doo it with a chast mind, onely for recreation, and in sober maner, when at a marriage such mirth is to be vsed. I answere, that such are not to be so disalowed as the rest. But yetwith all wee must take this, that euery one is to haue regard not onely of his owne chastitie, but also for the preseruation of the chastitie of all other. If thou doo that which is a baite to stirre vp, and kindle euill lustes in other, thou doest breake the rule of loue, thou doest hurt they neighbour, therefore take heed how thou daunce.[57]

---

56 Thomas Cartwright, *A Commentary Vpon the Epistle of Saint Paule Written to the Colossians* (London: Printed by Nicholas Okes, and are to be sold by George Norton, dwelling neere Temple-barre, 1612), 201–202.

57 "The Fifth Sermon," in George Gifford, *Eight Sermons* (At London: Printed by Iohn Windet for Toby Cooke, at the Tygers head in Paules Church-yard, 1589),

Women, Dance and Parish Religion in England, 1300–1640

This sermon takes one of the scriptures most often used in presentations of dance as potentially godly and ties it to several key themes: sexual transgression, sacrilegious use of God's word, and leading others into sin. In both approaches, the narratives and extratextual components that characterized medieval sermons are missing.

Both medieval and early modern reformers focused on teaching the faith to the laity, leading to comparable bodies of vernacular texts. And despite dramatic theological and exegetical differences, when it comes to *adiaphora* such as dance, these sermons show clear continuities. Dance was not a central issue for either medieval or early modern reformers but rather a peripheral issue related to Christian living, to true faith, and to transgression. *Adiaphora* like dance were used to push audiences towards right living more than towards right belief. Through persistent mentions of dance in medieval and early modern sermons, particularly through persistent mentions of dance in association with women and sin, preachers and sermon authors created rhetorical and theological structures that could then function as mechanisms for the perpetuation of misogyny. Similarly to the weaponization of religious dissent in the campaigns and crusades of the late Middle Ages, we see a weaponization of gender in the parish in the name of a campaign for true belief and proper practice.

LIVING THE FAITH

The goal of both medieval and early modern reformers was to bring about not only knowledge of faith but also rightly lived faith in practice. For most people between 1300 and 1600, and indeed for centuries after, their parish provided the context for that rightly lived faith. As Katherine French has noted, the parish served as the center for late medieval communities.[58] People were baptized and married in their parish churches, then buried in their church-yards. Much of the life that took place around and among those events played out within the parish community as well: negotiation of community tension, business deals, wills, property transfers and sales, and much more. But the significance of the parish as a center for communal life, not just personal transactions, should not be understated. Lay involvement in parishes through the guilds (organized by life stage, by gender, by devotion to a particular saint, or a variety of other factors) or other sub-parochial groups meant that within each parish, the laity were not passive recipients of sermons or theology but active participants in their religion, often through interest groups with their own

---

79v–80v; for another example of a similar sermon, see Edward Elton, *An Exposition of the Epistle of St Paule to the Colossians* (London: Printed by Edward Griffin for Ralph Mab and are to be sold at his shop, at the signe of the Grey-hound, in Pauls-Church-yard, 1615), 1064, 1076.

[58] French, *The People of the Parish*, 2.

Reforming and Redefining True Religion

administrative structures and activities. The parish itself was a community, created not simply by geographic borders or ecclesiastical mandate but also through lay interaction, relationships, organization, and traditions.[59]

Parishes comprised the lowest level of the medieval ecclesiastical hierarchy: within any given diocese, as explained by French, "parishes with their chapels were grouped into rural deaneries, which in turn were grouped into archdeaconries ... each deanery had its own court that addressed a variety of spiritual, moral, and administrative issues such as adultery and failure to attend church, but it also oversaw the appointment of diocesan administrators and the probate of wills."[60] The bishop (or his vicars-general and suffragan bishops – episcopal administrators with less political clout than the bishop) technically oversaw the diocese and its archdeaconries, deaneries, and parishes, but within each diocese, areas known as peculiars sat within the diocese yet outside the oversight of the bishop. The parishes within these peculiars were sometimes attached to cathedrals, sometimes not, but in each case under the oversight of the courts of the peculiar rather than the courts of the deaconry. Within the parish itself, authority resided with an assortment of individuals, different in number by parish: priests, vicars, curates, clerks, sextons, churchwardens, and "trustworthy men," to name a few. These individuals were chosen differently in each parish but in all instances oversaw church finances and upkeep, the behavior of the parishioners, and the various needs and functions of the parish. They also negotiated with the bishop and his representatives for the interests of the parish. As both Katherine French and Ian Forrest have shown, parishes were not straightforward sites of ecclesiastical control but instead sites of negotiation in which individuals and communities defined, protected, and advocated for individual and communal interests and needs.[61]

The changes wrought by the Reformations did not immediately overturn the vision of rightly lived faith in practice that shaped late medieval discussions and supervision of dance but simply increased the level of scrutiny from outsiders. However, the English Reformations eventually brought significant changes to the lived experience of laity within the parish.[62] Changes to the

---

[59] See French's chapter "Defining the Parish" for more detail. French, *The People of the Parish.*

[60] Ibid., 6.

[61] Forrest, *Trustworthy Men*; French, *The People of the Parish.*

[62] See, for example, Duffy, *Stripping of the Altars*; Duffy, *The Voices of Morebath*; Beat Kumin, "Late Medieval Churchwardens' Accounts and Parish Government: Looking beyond London and Bristol," *The English Historical Review* 119, no. 480 (February 1, 2004): 87–100; Kümin, *The Shaping of a Community*; Alexandra Walsham, *The Reformation of the Landscape: Religion, Identity, and Memory in Early Modern Britain and Ireland* (Oxford; New York: Oxford University Press, 2012); Gary G. Gibbs, *Five Parishes in Late Medieval and Tudor London* (New York: Routledge: 2021).

Women, Dance and Parish Religion in England, 1300–1640

ecclesiastical hierarchy paired with changes to liturgical practice to create a new parish, one that was as much a political entity as a religious one. Churchwardens assumed more responsibility for secular affairs, while the various guilds were gradually dissolved. With the frequently shifting definitions of "true faith," visitation took on an increasingly important role, to ensure conformity with the latest prayer book, the latest set of regulations, and the latest scripture translation. Simultaneously, government officials, for example overseers of the poor and of the highways, proliferated, ultimately reducing the influence and scope of the parish's authority.[63] Yet, despite the changes, the parish remained the heart of communal life for most ordinary men and women between the thirteenth and sixteenth centuries.

Within these parish contexts, rightly lived faith was inextricably connected to the sermons that conveyed the moral standards it required. Thus, sermons focused not only on the key doctrinal points as laid out by Fourth Lateran or by various reformers but also on how to live one's life: how to worship, how to conduct business, how to engage one's community, how to function within relationships, and smaller actions like when to dance or not to dance, when to eat or drink or not, when to laugh or not laugh. Discussions of dance in medieval and early modern sermons show this use of preaching to define, negotiate, and communicate moral standards, either through *exempla* or through lengthy exposition of scripture. This negotiation took place alongside lived faith in the form of parish dancing, for dance played a role almost as large as that of sermons in the English parish between 1300 and 1600 – a role which, like that of sermons, remained relatively consistent. As scholars like Katherine French have shown, dance was a part of church fundraisers, taking place in the form of maidens' lights, fundraisers organized by the maidens of the parish to raise funds for lights (candles) in the parish church. Some of these maidens' lights were dances, but other maidens' lights raised funds through different means. In some parishes, wives' dances likewise helped supplement church funds and stores.[64] Church processionals on Whitsunday and other liturgical celebrations often involved groups of dancers.[65] In less liturgically sanctioned dance performances, dancers would gather to socialize in dancing to popular ballads or would perform dances like the Morris

---

[63] J. S. Craig, "Co-Operation and Initiatives: Elizabethan Churchwardens and the Parish Accounts of Mildenhall," *Social History* 18, no. 3 (1993): 357–380; Keith Wrightson, "The Politics of the Parish in Early Modern England," in A. Fox, P. Griffiths, and S. Hindle (eds.), *The Experience of Authority in Early Modern England* (London: Palgrave, 1996): 10–46.

[64] Katherine L. French, "Maidens' Lights and Wives' Stores: Women's Parish Guilds in Late Medieval England," *The Sixteenth Century Journal* 29, no. 2 (July 1, 1998): 399–425.

[65] Douglas, "'Owre Thanssynge Day.'"

Reforming and Redefining True Religion

dance.[66] These social dances – still primarily performed in groups rather than pairs – would mostly take place on holidays and feast days (to the consternation of clerics, sometimes during services), either in public spaces that permitted large gatherings or (more controversially) in private homes. Emily Winerock's doctoral dissertation provides a picture of just how widespread dance was in the English parish. Her study of the REED records for the counties of Lancashire, Cheshire, Shropshire, Herefordshire, Worcestershire, Gloucestershire, and Somerset from 1550 to 1642 shows that:

> dance is the central focus in 49% (160) of these records, one component among several in 46% (150), and a tangential detail in 5% (15) of the records examined. Of these records, 76% (248) are court prosecutions mentioning dance – with 62% (202) from ecclesiastical courts and 14% (46) from secular courts – 10% (34) are visitation articles; 8% (27) are payments for dance performances, lessons, and special attire; and 7% (23) are poetic, dramatic, and other types of literary records.[67]

Dance – like sermons – threaded throughout the daily lives of English parishioners.

Part of determining how to rightly live one's faith in the English parish between 1300 and 1600 involved negotiating the contingency surrounding activities like dance or wrestling or bowling or drama – pastimes that were not explicitly condemned in scripture or by church authorities but that could also problematically distract parishioners from the mass or from the purpose of feast days through providing alternative activities during these times. Dance's sinfulness, like that of so many other communal parish activities, was contingent on the circumstances under which it was performed, with frequency, location, and participants all informing its moral standing.[68] Case studies that highlight this contingency in practice appear in later chapters; for now, we will remain focused on rhetorical models of living the true faith through dancing (or not dancing) presented to parishioners in sermon literature.

---

[66] Judith Bennett, "Ventriloquisms: When Maidens Speak in English Songs, c. 1300–1550," in *Medieval Woman's Song: Cross-Cultural Approaches*, ed. Anne Klinck and Anne Marie Rasmussen (Philadelphia: University of Pennsylvania Press, 2002); Forrest, *The History of Morris Dancing, 1438–1750*; Robert Mullally, *The Carole: A Study of a Medieval Dance* (Farnham: Ashgate, 2011); Ronald Hutton, *The Rise and Fall of Merry England: The Ritual Year, 1400–1700* (Oxford: Oxford University Press, 2001).

[67] Winerock, "Reformation and Revelry," 15. Winerock's introduction provides a helpful overview of the legal context of dance in the early modern period, and the first chapter of her dissertation provides an overview of early modern dance styles and practices.

[68] Arcangeli, "Dance and Punishment," 128, 130.

We see the emphasis on teaching the true faith discussed in the previous section in the use of sermons to help parishioners navigate the complex matrix delineating acceptable leisure activities from dangerous or sinful ones. Sermon *exempla* in particular played a key role in helping laity navigate these complicated contingencies about standards for Christian living. In one early example of this, the *Liber Exemplorum*, an English collection of *exempla* compiled between 1275 and 1279 that survives in only a single manuscript, presents an *exemplum* that discusses "a priest in the area around Worcester in England" who was disrupted by carolers. "He had heard the song with its refrain all night long while the dancers circled the church ... On the following day he stood at mass in his priestly robes and, instead of the greeting the people with "*Dominus vobiscum*" and so on, he sang out in a loud voice the English refrain "*Swete lamman dhin are.*"[69] The author of the *Liber Exemplorum* advises readers to "take care in what they do. For they enjoy their dances and their foolish songs in this life, but without doubt they can see from this example that their games are nothing to them but a preparation for everlasting death."[70] In teaching what it meant to live the Christian life, *exempla* like this one clearly communicated that what mattered was not just what one was taught, but also what one did (and where and when one did it). One's actions, like dance, could identify an individual as either a Christian or not. Control over one's body and bringing one's body in line with proper behavior marked one as holy rather than transgressive; failure to do so had dire consequences for the individual and for the practice of true faith, making proper regulation of bodies a priority. Parish dancing built community and provided opportunities for the individual performance of piety. Sermon tales about dance, preached in parish churches and public communal spaces, highlighted that you were what you did and closely aligned moral virtue with the physical body.

Later chapters turn to some of the ways in which parishes applied this rhetorical conception of dance in parish management and discipline. But for the moment, we need to consider one further intersection between sermon literature and life in the parish. As sermon literature and discussions of dance developed from the thirteenth through sixteenth centuries, sermons shifted the focus to embodiment and action rather than intention. This increased focus on embodiment, the duality of approach to the material in the medieval world, and the physical nature of dance gave fourteenth- and fifteenth-century clerics another angle to use in their attack on dance.[71] Clerics thus sought to protect the physical bodies of those under their care, to teach the laity the importance of controlling their own flesh, and then to help regulate the

---

[69] Jones, *Friars' Tales*, 139. Translated, "Swete lamman dhin are" means "my sweetest friend, your lover desires your favors."

[70] Ibid., 138.

[71] Arcangeli, "Dance under Trial," 149.

Reforming and Redefining True Religion

ways in which the laity under their care lived. Again, this priority appears in the moral lessons spelled out in *exempla* on dance in medieval sermons. In the years following Fourth Lateran, controlling the bodies of women through stopping or preventing dancing became an increasingly prevalent theme in *exempla*. Multiple *exempla* discuss fearful visions that cure young girls of dancing, or girls who stop dancing because of torment by hellfire.[72] The gendering of transgression taking place in *exempla* shows the ways in which *adiaphora* like dance eventually shaped much larger discourses like approaches to the proper performances of religion and of gender. Like the characters in these *exempla*, as we shall see in later chapters, individuals in the parish who transgressed standards for normal and godly behavior were punished, as this shift to focus on embodied action affected negotiations about dance's appropriateness in the early modern parish.

In the Middle Ages, *exempla* helped laity navigate living their faith; in the sixteenth century, however, expositions of scripture provided the key means of moral direction on how to live one's faith. And again, in closely looking at dance and other issues of lived experience, complex negotiations of new scripts of piety and morality appear. Scholars such as Susan Karant-Nunn have studied how the early modern Reformations reworked expectations for piety and the performance of righteousness, while Beth Plummer and others have explored the reworking of social expectations these Reformations brought about.[73] But it is important to note that, in redefining positive exemplars and moral standards, early modern sermon authors also redefined transgression, again largely through discussions of *adiaphora* like dance.

Early modern sermons connect not simply dancers but also supporters of dancers to violations of God's word and direction and to failures to live the Christian life as taught through scripture. As one sermon puts it, in supporting dancing, "some persons, goe not onelie against the plaine euidence of the word, but against their owne consciences."[74] Another sermon states:

> They that haue grace may learne, that the lyfe of a Christian man, is neyther playe, nor pastime, neither daunsing nor daliance, neither fleshly, nor licentious liberty: but a laborious and dangerous warfare, a charie and circumspect keeping of a Godlie and innocent life. Let carnall Gospellers

---

[72] #1424, 1427, 1428, and 1429 in Tubach, *Index Exemplorum*, 113–114.

[73] See as examples Susan C. Karant-Nunn, *The Reformation of Ritual: An Interpretation of Early Modern Germany* (London; New York: Routledge, 1997); Susan C. Karant-Nunn, *The Reformation of Feeling: Shaping the Religious Emotions in Early Modern Germany* (Oxford: Oxford University Press, 2010); Marjorie Elizabeth Plummer, *From Priest's Whore to Pastor's Wife: Clerical Marriage and the Process of Reform in the Early German Reformation* (Farnham: Ashgate, 2012).

[74] Edward Elton, *An Exposition of the Epistle of St Paule to the Colossians Deliuered in Sundry Sermons* (London: Printed by Edward Griffin for Ralph Mab and are to be sold at his shop, at the signe of the Gre-hound, in Pauls-Church-yard, 1615), 768.

Women, Dance and Parish Religion in England, 1300–1640

perswade themselues they haue God by the toe, or in their boseme neuer so much: if they be not in a ward of this warfare to fight against the Deuill, the victorie of Christ shall not auaile them.[75]

True Christians, according to this sermon, do not dance; only "carnall Gospellers," those serving the devil instead of the Lord, still dance.[76] Another sermon connecting false believers and dance condemns:

> the assemblies of our time, such as are gathered together in the dedications of Churches and in very many feastes of the Christians, where a men shall see nothing but riot and superfluitie, and an vnbrideled libertie of drinking, daunceing, playing and reuelling: they sanctifie their assemblies, not vnto God, but vnto *Bacchus* and *Venus*, and shall one day bee punished of God, whose name they so shamefully and impudently abuse.[77]

In the sixteenth century, most of these sermons present dance as a boundary used to separate the "sacrilegious" or profane "Christians" from the true followers of God. The wicked of the world, false followers of Christ, danced "after the fashion that is spoken of in Moyses," despising God while claiming to follow him.[78]

---

75   Thomas Bentham, *A Notable and Comfortable Exposition* (At London: Printed by Robert Walde-graue, dwelling in Foster-Lane, ouer against Goldsmiths Hall, 1583), 2r–3v.

76   Another sermon contrasts the actions of those serving the devil with those serving God, in a call to repentance: "As you haue giuen ouer your members from sinne to sinne, to serue the Deuill, your tongues to sweare, to lie, to flatter, to scold, to iest, to scoffe, to baudie talke, to vaine iangling, to boasting, &c. Your hands to picking, groping, idlenesse, fighting, and c. Your feete to skipping, going to euill, to dancing, &c. Your eares to heare fables, lyes, vanities, and euill things, &c. So now, giue ouer your members to godlinesse." See John Bradford, *A Double Summons* (London: Printed by George Purslowe, 1617), fols. F.5r–F.6v.

77   Rudolf Gwalther, *The Homilies or Familiar Sermons of M. Rodolph Gualther* (Imprinted in London: [By Thomas Dawson] for William Ponsonnby, 1582), 53r; for more examples of uses of dance as a way to separate "sheep" from "goats," as it were, see "His Desires Limitation," in Stephen Jerome, *Moses His Sight of Canaan* (London: Printed [by T. Snodham] for Roger Iackson, and are to be solde at his shop, neare to the conduit in Fleetstreete, 1614), 123–124; "The Soules Solace Against Sorrow," in William Harrison, *Deaths Aduantage Little Regarded* (At London: Imprinted by Felix Kyngston, 1602), 12; "Third Sermon," in John Dod 1549 and Robert Cleaver, *Three Godlie and Fruitful Sermons* (London: Printed [by N. Okes and F. Kingston] for William Welby, and are to be sold at his shop in Pauls Church-yard, at the signe of the white Swan, 1610), 117; "The Conclvsion of the Rehearsal Sermon," in John Hoskins, *Sermons Preached at Pauls Crosse and Else-Where* (London: Printed by William Stansby for Nathaniel Butter, and are to be sold at his shop at Saint Austens gate, 1615), 33.

78   "The ccxxvj sermon," in Jean Calvin, *Sermons of Master Iohn Calvin, Vpon the*

Reforming and Redefining True Religion

Discussions in these early modern sermons and in the debates over the controversial *Book of Sports* reveal the extent to which Carlos Eire's point about sacrilege applies to any study of early modern religion. Many of the sermons about dance tie it back not simply to morality or to living out one's faith, but to idolatry, to sacrilege, and to the devil. In short, dance became a yardstick by which true and false Christians were measured – a doctrine found nowhere in the scriptures these sermons explicate. These discussions also highlight the ways in which the practice of the Reformations was worked out. For ordinary men and women, the doctrines of the Reformations were not necessarily set out in debates about sanctification or justification. They were set out in discussions about dicing or dancing, in rules about who could do what when, and in regulations placed on earthly bodies. The details about theologically tertiary issues like dance mattered in discussions of how to live one's faith, and parish discipline reflected this priority. The devil truly was in the details.

PROTECTING THE FAITH

Debating and defining the boundaries of true religion almost inevitably results in a group of actions or individuals pushed outside those boundaries. Thus, once the boundaries are set, they must then be defended and protected from those they exclude. In the wake of the reforms this chapter has explored, guarding the faith from various threats became a priority. As R. I. Moore's classic *The Formation of a Persecuting Society* pointed out, a concern with protecting the faith from heresy drove the entire structure and program of Fourth Lateran. Thus, the growing effort to suppress heresy in the twelfth and thirteenth centuries was not due to an increase in heretics or heretical teaching, but simply because heresy was emphasized as a much more significant problem than in the past. To quote from Moore, "deliberate and socially sanctioned violence began to be directed, *through established governmental, judicial, and social institutions*, against groups of people defined by general characteristics such as race, religion or way of life."[79] The movements following Fourth Lateran highlighted the ways in which this reprioritization played out, through the Albigensian Crusade, the Crusades for the Holy Land, the Inquisition, the expulsion of the Jews from England, and eventually the witchcraft trials of the late medieval and early modern world. The reforms of Fourth Lateran made protecting the faith from a variety of threats a greater priority, with violent repercussions for marginalized groups.

But, as made clear through the multiple canons directed at educating the laity and enforcing confession, the faith needed protection from accidental

---

Booke of Iob (London: Imprinted by Henry Bynneman, 1574), 618.

[79] Moore, *The Formation of a Persecuting Society*, 4.

heresy performed by unwitting laity as well. While parish teaching played an important role in this, parish discipline also helped. In its most basic form, parish priests worked with individual parishioners to help them confess their sins, do penance, and make restitution for their actions. Church court officials also brought correction cases against wayward parishioners, in the archidiaconal courts of archdeacons or in the consistory courts of the archbishop for the most serious cases.[80] Parishioners cited to appear before the court faced excommunication for failure to appear; courts assigned penalties including public penance in the parish court, fines, or simple repentance, with the goal being the restitution of right order in the parish community.[81] This process varied by diocese but continued in much the same form between 1300 and 1600, creating consistency in what it looked like to use parish discipline to protect the faith from transgression throughout the period considered in this book.

This process of church discipline helped deal with actions like dancing during church services, gossip, or other problematic behavior. But in our consideration of protecting the faith, we also need to note how gendered bodies played a role in this aspect of late medieval and early modern reform movements. The *adiaphora* negotiated to protect the faith did not simply involve actions, but also bodies, particularly female bodies. Prior to Fourth Lateran, prohibitions intended to separate women and sacred objects appeared in Gratian's twelfth-century *Decretum*; these were echoed in thirteenth-century texts by Fishacre (d. 1248), Bonaventure (c. 1217–1274), Duns Scotus (d. 1308), Richard of Middleton (c. 1249–1308), and Thomas of Chobham (d. c. 1236).[82] It was in these prohibitions and the reforms of the eleventh and twelfth centuries that a fundamental shift in how the church dealt with women and their bodies took place. Liturgies for the purification of women's bodies after parturition first developed in the late eleventh century, while efforts to present the Virgin Mary as spared from the usual contaminants of a female body redoubled.[83] Contemporaneously, numerous prohibitions against

---

[80] Ralph A. Houlbrooke, *Church Courts and the People during the English Reformation, 1520–1570* (Oxford; New York: Oxford University Press, 1979), 8, 33, 53.

[81] Houlbrooke, *Church Courts and the People during the English Reformation, 1520–1570*; Kane's recent study of men, women, and testimony in church courts gives striking insight into the dynamics of church courts and their function. Kane, *Popular Memory and Gender in Medieval England*.

[82] A. J. Minnis, "'De Impedimento Sexus': Women's Bodies and Medieval Impediments to Female Ordination," in *Medieval Theology and the Natural Body*, ed. Peter Biller and Alastair J. Minnis (York: York Medieval Press, 1997), 122–123. Chobham, as noted by Minnis, did not simply prohibit women from touching sacred items or giving mass, but attempted to keep a physical distance between women and priests during mass, "because their presence would inflame priests and other clerics with lustful desires."

[83] Elliott, *Fallen Bodies*, 5.

Reforming and Redefining True Religion

women in sacred space proliferated, and sermon tales about the dangers of women in close proximity to priests or to the Host burgeoned.[84] Even movements such as *periculoso*, a thirteenth-century reform meant to protect sacred female bodies from the profane influences of the world, indicated a different approach to female bodies.[85] Part of purifying and regulating sacred space and Christian practice involved removing lay women and protecting women religious. Thus, women were increasingly excluded from theological learning, and women well versed in theology were associated with heretical movements such as Lollardy.[86] Women found their forms of piety limited, as indicated by concern about how the bodies of female pilgrims might taint pilgrimage sites.[87] As the next chapter will explore, sacrilege became an action often treated as a female sin, and in the fourteenth-century implementation of the Lateran reforms of the thirteenth century, women, like dance, were pushed out of sacred space.

It is important to note that nowhere in Fourth Lateran was there a clear spelling out of a comprehensive doctrinal shift in approach to women, Jews, lepers, heretics, or any of the other groups Moore and subsequent scholars discuss. It is also important to note that some of Fourth Lateran's canons dealing with these groups may not have filtered into most contexts. Wayno's consideration of Fourth Lateran's transmission into Bishop Richard Poor's 1217–1219 Salisbury statutes shows that, indeed, some of the Fourth Lateran canons on Jewish–Christian relations, heresy, simony, and other issues did not appear in every context.[88] Yet the general spirit behind Fourth Lateran – of reforming clergy and laity, teaching proper belief and behavior – certainly appeared in the Salisbury statutes and then in the vernacular literature developed to address each author's specific priorities. Through this vernacular literature, through regulations of peripheral issues and small actions expressed in moralizing texts and sermons, more comprehensive positions on topics like heresy, sacrilege, and gender gradually developed. Through a series of decisions about small "inconsequential" things like dance, clerics and authors created broad positions and much starker boundaries between sacred and profane, male and female, holy and transgressive bodies. Authorial asides

---

[84] Elliott provides a lengthy study of this in Chapters 4 and 5 of Elliott, *Fallen Bodies*.

[85] Elizabeth M. Makowski, *Canon Law and Cloistered Women: Periculoso and Its Commentators, 1298–1545* (Washington, DC: Catholic University of America Press, 1999).

[86] Alcuin Blamires, "The Limits of Bible Study for Medieval Women," in *Women, the Book, and the Godly*, ed. Lesley Smith and Jane H. M. Taylor (Cambridge: D. S. Brewer, 1995); Alcuin Blamires and C. W. Marx, "Woman Not to Preach: A Disputation in MS Harley 31," *The Journal of Medieval Latin* 3 (1993): 34–63.

[87] Susan Signe Morrison, *Women Pilgrims in Late Medieval England: Private Piety as Public Performance* (London; New York: Routledge, 2000).

[88] Wayno, "Rethinking the Fourth Lateran Council of 1215," 627.

Women, Dance and Parish Religion in England, 1300–1640

referring to dance as problematic, as a woman's pastime, or as dangerous to piety in vernacular sermons on broader topics functioned as the mechanism by which late medieval misogyny solidified and spread.

These stark late medieval boundaries around "true faith" only became clearer and harsher with further reform in the early modern period. Indeed, as Eire contended, "by pointing to a distinction between 'true' and 'false' worship and charging their followers to abstain from religious pollution, the Reformers – most notably Calvin – intensified the social divisions caused by theological disagreements."[89] Like in the thirteenth century, when Fourth Lateran redefined true worship and pushed for a purification of Christian practice and teaching, sixteenth-century preachers sought to abolish the "pagan" practices of their medieval predecessors. As these reformers redefined sacrilege and true worship, they rejuvenated the discourse about dance and sacrilege. A 1583 translation of a sermon by Calvin provided a description of medieval Christianity that deems the reforms of the medieval church a failure, showing no distinction between the behavior of "pagans" and the late medieval church that Fourth Lateran sought to reform:

> Wheras men saw that the heathen made great feasts, and kept a great number of solemne holy dayes in honour of their Idols: O (quoth they) wee must no more doe soe, for that were a seruing of the diuell: but let euery parishe make a Church-holyday, to play, to daunce, and to feede in till they burst againe, and all in the honour of God. Besides this, let euery one haue their patron, and let them worshippe him. And so in steade of the solemne feastes that were among the heathen, let others be brought in among vs. O sirs (say they) these thinges are not doone any more in honour of the Idols; but in honour of Saint Martine. And then let them daunce and playe the drunkerdes, for all is well enough so it be done in the honour of God.[90]

This sermon clearly connects the rituals and liturgies of the medieval church to false, sacrilegious worship, placing dance at the center of the profane behavior and setting up Catholicism as the new target for condemnations of sacrilege. A sermon by Thomas Adams, printed in 1615, makes the same point, describing how "that inchanting cup of *fornications* preuailes ouer" the "besotted soules" of the Catholics:

> Come you into their Temples, and behold their Pageants, and histrionicall gestures, bowings, mowings, windings, and turnings; together with their seruice in an vnknowne *language*, and (like a deafe man, that sees men dancing, when hee heares no musicke) you would iudge them *madde*.

---

[89] Eire, *War against the Idols*, 313.

[90] "LXXXJ Sermon," in Jean Calvin, *Sermons ... Vpon the Fifth Booke of Moses Called Deuteronomie* (London: Printed by Henry Middleton for George Bishop, 1583), 495.

Reforming and Redefining True Religion

Behold the masse-Priest with his baked god, towzing tossing, and dandling it, to and fro, vpward and downward, forward and backward, till at last, the iest turning into earnest, he choppes it into his mouth at one bitte; whiles all stand gaping with admiration.[91]

In a way, with these descriptions of "masking and mumming Masse Priests, in all glorious shew to the eye, with piping and singing, with bely cheare, with their Robinhoods, and morrice dances, and all their relegion like a stage play, ful of carnal delights, and bewitching vanities," discussions of dance and sacrilege have come full circle.[92] Again, dance is an action at the center of discussions about reforming the church and its clergy by removing pagan influences and enforcing proper respect for the sacred.

As one further example shows, early modern authors did not use dance only to separate Catholics from Protestants. They also used it as a mark of true religion, as a means of separating "carnal" believers from ones who truly followed the gospel. Strikingly, sermon authors placed many of the individuals otherwise ostracized in early modern society – Jews, Turks, and Catholics – above dancers in this moral hierarchy:

So in the heads Oeconomicall, wee shall see little spirituall … Let experience speake: looke into their houses, into their regiment, into their carriage and disportment; and yee shall see their exercises such as vvere vsed in the Siege of Thebes, couetous carding and dicing, or wanton and promiscuous dauncing: you shall finde moe shewes of Religion in the vse of the Word, in the house of a Iew, more seeming prayers in the house of a Turke, Papist, or Pagan (who pray oftner to Saints and Idols then they) then in their houses, which are rather dens of Diuels, and cages of vncleane Birds, then Churches.[93]

Stillness truly was a mark of the saints and dancing an action that demonstrated a threat to faith. This discourse played out in sixteenth- and seventeenth-century parishes and dioceses as well. To give only one example, a 1640 petition against Bishop Wren from the Diocese of Ely complained that the bishop, through his visitation articles, required the churchwardens and other officers to work for:

---

[91] Thomas Adams, *Mystical Bedlam* (London: Printed by George Purslowe for Clement Knight, and are to be sold at his shoppe in Paules Church-yard at the signe of the Holy Lambe, 1615), 70.

[92] "IIII Sermon," in William Burton, *Ten Sermons Vpon the First, Second, Third and Fourth Verses of the Sixt of Matthew* (Imprinted at London: By Richard Field for Thomas Man, 1602), 168.

[93] "His Desires Limitation," in Jerome, *Moses His Sight of Canaan with Simeon His Dying-Song*, 123–124.

The advancem{en}t of Romish Superstit{i}on, & to the hindrance of the power & progresse of Religion, to the encouraging and pressing the reading of the booke of sport{es} & recreac{i}ons strengthened by the Bishopp{es} owne example in bowling & in the afternoone, & chatechiseing if it be (as the Article phraseth it) sermonwise. Add to this the strict pressing of the last of our now dread Sou{er}aigne touching wakes & such like ffeast{es} (as they are called w{i}th us) & in that addition stiled the whereby the com{m}on prophanat{i}on of the Lord{es} daie w{i}th beastlie drunck-ennes, lacivious Dauncing{es}, quarrelling{es} & fighting{es} & manie of all religious hart{es} amongest vs) hath been exceedinglie encouraged, whereas we cannot conseiue y{a}t ever there with such insolencies as these, w{hi}ch more suit w{i}th dedicac{i}on of Temples to Bacchus and Venus than to the service of Al Consciences, to the impoverishing y{ou}r petic{i}oner{es} & the enriching of Ecclesiasticall Officer{es}.[94]

The Bishop's support of dance in the churchyard and his Sabbath bowling provide proof for a list of serious charges – of Romish superstition, of hindering the advance of religion, of profaning the Lord's day, and of impoverishing the church.

In a parallel to the results of the thirteenth-century reforms, these early modern reforms and accompanying discourse about dance and sacrilege crystallized into a new set of boundaries for dancing bodies, boundaries entrenched as gendered ones. Eire noted in his work that the Reformed emphasis on iconoclasm led to "an increased masculinization of piety ... the richly symbolic feminine aspects represented by the Virgin Mary as 'Mother of God,' and by other female saints, were suddenly replaced by those of a transcendent, but overtly masculine God."[95] What has not been as thoroughly noted is that the emphasis of the Reformations on protecting true religion also led to a masculinization of piety through continuing the medieval emphasis on sacrilege as a gendered transgression. Those who opposed the actions and changes put in place by the reformers were often referred to as women, as in this sermon: "There be many Micols in this land which haue mocked King Dauid for dauncing before the Arke. There are many whiche terme vs heady and foolish men, because we come and throng, and prease thus to a sermon: but as Christ said, *Father forgiue them, they knowe not what they doe.*"[96] Continuing with this gendered imagery, sermons frequently portrayed

---

[94] *REED Cambridgeshire*, ed. John Geck with Anne Brannen, REED Online (forthcoming 2022). Diocese of Ely, 1640, Petition against Bishop Wren, BL MS Egerton 1048, fols. 24v–24.

[95] Eire, *War against the Idols*, 315.

[96] "Food for New Borne Babes," in Henry Smith, *The Sermons of Maister Henrie Smith* (At London: Printed by Richard Field [, T. Orwin, and R. Robinson] for Thomas Man, dwelling in Pater Noster row, at the signe of the Talbot, 1593), 1026.

Reforming and Redefining True Religion

sacrilegious individuals using language gendered female, or simply as women, as in this sermon:

> Yea, shee is a religious Strumpet too, this day have I paid my vowes; she goes to Church, but more to intangle simple ones in her eye-lids, then to heare a Sermon: Oh, shee rides in her Coach like a Queene of beautie. Thus the wanton is taken, with these and many the like; with ditties, and daunces, with rose-beds, and garlands, and crownes of roses. Thus also doeth our tempter deale with vs, by temptations on the left hand.[97]

This sermon, with its portrayal of women as "strumpets" who entangle men in their eyelids, shows how discourses about dance and transgression often blurred with discourses about gender. The boundaries set in debates about issues with no clear scriptural support or prohibition started to seem to apply not to actions but to individuals, individuals often placed into categories based on their gendered bodies.

CONCLUSION

So, despite dramatic theological differences and a massive chronological span, considering the years between 1200 and 1600 *in toto* is an exercise that highlights more commonalities than differences. Between the reforms of Fourth Lateran and the end of the early modern Reformations, those responsible for the care of ordinary men and women shared a common approach and concerns. As a result, reformers created a body of texts aimed at clearly communicating key doctrine, along with vital moral codes for Christian conduct. In these didactic texts, how to live and protect true faith was not mandated in sweeping theological arguments but negotiated in detailed discussion of individual issues like dance, worked out and enforced through parish practice, courts, and discipline.

As is apparent from the fraught diatribes about dance from Fourth Lateran onwards, there is more significance to explore here than lies simply in the action of dancing itself. The stakes were not simply whether one danced or not, but rather whether one was pious or sacrilegious, a true believer or a heretic. It is in the *adiaphora* and presentations of daily actions that theologies of lived faith were worked out for the laity; it is these discussions that must be considered in order to understand how definitions of holiness and transgression shifted between the medieval and reformed churches. It is in these discussions of the details of Christian living that broader paradigms

---

97 "The Cause of Ionahs Anger," in Robert Vase, *Ionah's Contestation about His Gourd* (London: Printed by I[ohn] L[egat] for Robert Bird, and are to be sold at his shoppe, at the signe of the Bible in Cheape-side, 1625), 23.

Women, Dance and Parish Religion in England, 1300–1640

for gender and its performance were gradually constructed, as the next two chapters will show through considering two key concerns of religious figures from both the medieval and early modern periods: defining and protecting the boundaries of sacred space and time.

CHAPTER 2

DANCE AND PROTECTING SACRED SPACE

What did it look like to take rhetorical ideas about true faith and put them into practice in the parish? To demarcate the sacred from the profane, and then protect holy things from the world? Ecclesiastical figures exerted tremendous energy in this marking out of boundaries between sacred and profane in the centuries following Fourth Lateran. Much of this involved identifying true doctrine, teaching right belief, and enforcing proper practice, as discussed in the previous chapter. But, as shown in the tale of the cursed dancing carolers and other medieval sermon tales, authors and parish priests also focused on literal boundaries between the sacred and the profane, enforced in an earthly context through the regulation of matter and bodies. Caroline Walker Bynum's work has shown that late medieval audiences were increasingly concerned with materiality. Although, as Bynum puts it, "the later Middle Ages has been characterized in recent scholarship as moving toward inner piety and visuality ... matter was a more insistent and problematic locus of the sacred in the twelfth to sixteenth centuries than in the early medieval period."[1] The problematic nature of matter meant that discussions of sacred matter, whether that be relics, spaces, or bodies, were nuanced and fraught. Sacred matter had to be carefully defined, separated from dangerous matter, and protected.

As medieval materials and spaces became more clearly demarcated into sacred and profane, safe and dangerous, so did medieval time. The creation of sacred time was inextricably intertwined with the goal of sacralization of the world and thus with the reforms of Fourth Lateran. As Jacques Le Goff put it, to medieval authors, "Christianity has the means to structure and sacralize the time of human life in such a way as will lead humanity to salvation."[2] Thus, the tools of reform, including medieval sermons, were rooted in time. Jacobus de Voragine's saints in the *Legenda Aurea* were anchored in the time of the liturgy. *Exempla* in sermon collections like *Handlyng Synne* were explicitly anchored in time and location. When marking out the parameters

---

[1] Bynum, *Christian Materiality*, 19.

[2] Jacques Le Goff and Lydia G. Cochrane (trans.), *In Search of Sacred Time: Jacobus de Voragine and the Golden Legend* (Princeton: Princeton University Press, 2014), xiii.

Women, Dance and Parish Religion in England, 1300–1640

of Christianity in the reforms of the late Middle Ages, time and place mattered just as much as body and materials. For Jacobus de Voragine and the other reformers of the thirteenth century, time could be properly sanctified only through a synchronous sanctification of space.[3] Sacred time was as important as sacred matter to late medieval believers, and medieval authors sought to demarcate and protect both.

This chapter uses the tale of the cursed dancing carolers in English vernacular texts to trace out the boundaries of sacred time and space along with what these boundaries meant for the believers who lived out their lives within them. Based on the narratives about a purported event in eleventh-century Saxony, the popular tale of the cursed dancing carolers tells the story of the consequences when sacred space is not protected from dance and dancing bodies. A group of men and women congregate in a churchyard on Christmas Eve, and, in a holiday mood, begin to sing and dance a carol. The priest, hoping to begin his mass, comes out and admonishes them, asking them to be quiet. Frustrated when they take no notice of his warning, the exasperated priest asks God to make the dancers continue in their dance, hand in hand, for a year. Perhaps to everyone's surprise, the priest's prayer for vengeance is granted, and the dancers continue their carol, in rain, sleet, and snow. Even attempts to drag the dancers apart cannot stop the dancing. The fate of the dancers at the end of this year is either death or a continuation of their dancing, as the dancers who survive hop about for the remainder of their lives, permanently marked by their sin.

If popularity is any indication of significance, it is clear that this odd medieval tale contained significant meaning for its audiences, for it was one of the most popular medieval sermon tales.[4] But what was that meaning? Seeta Chaganti's exploration of the medieval carole points to the multivalent meanings possible in the form's concentric circles, poetic form, and the virtuality of the encounter between the two.[5] Yet, much of the meaning Chaganti explores comes from the performance of premodern dance and its intersection with poetic lyric, neither of which feature prominently in the tale of the cursed dancing carolers. The English versions of the tale neither reproduce the entirety of the dance song nor provide much of a description of the dance. A recent edited collection, *The Cursed Carolers in Context*, focuses specifically on the tale of the cursed carolers and shows how the meaning of the tale – its significance and its moral – shifted with each transmission into a different literary, geographic, and political context. The tale could be about proper

3   Ibid., 177.

4   Arcangeli, "Dance and Punishment," 35.

5   Chaganti, *Strange Footing*, 189–276. Chaganti mentions the tale of the cursed dancing carolers, but as the text of the dance song performed by the carolers does not appear in the tale, it falls largely outside the scope of her analysis of poetic form and caroles.

Dance and Protecting Sacred Space

crusading, about pastoral care, or about the virtues of female community, depending on who was hearing it.[6] The danced curse remains consistent in each iteration of the tale – but little else did.

Vernacular English versions of this tale presented a consistent message to their primarily lay audiences, one that was not about sex but about sacrilege. Given broader late medieval concerns about the sexual nature of dance, one would expect the variations of this tale to explicitly condemn men and women dancing together: to identify sexual sin as the reason for their punishment. But the tale does not appear to criticize the dancers for dancing in a mixed group or for their physical contact due to the form of the dance. Not only was this *exemplum* not really about sexual sin, it was also not really about dance, at least for its English audiences. In each vernacular English version of this popular medieval *exemplum*, dance was not the key sin addressed by the author; indeed, dance was not treated exclusively as a sin, and its sinfulness was displayed as contingent upon the circumstances of its performance. The tale used the attention-grabbing plot to communicate the need to protect the boundaries of sacred space and to connect into much larger medieval discussions about protecting the sacred from the profane. From its appearance in the thirteenth-century Anglo-Norman *Manuel des péchés* to its iteration in Peter Idley's fifteenth-century *Instructions to His Son*, the tale functioned as a text intended to purify sacred time and space by removing the profane.[7]

---

6   Lynneth Miller Renberg and Bradley Phillis (eds.), *The Cursed Carolers in Context* (New York: Routledge, 2021).

7   The four vernacular versions of the tale presented in England in the *Manuel*, *Handlyng Synne*, *Of Shrifte and Penance*, and Idley's *Instructions to His Son* draw upon the Othbert and Theodoricus texts, the two original sources for the tale from purported eyewitnesses to the Kölbigk event. The *Manuel*'s version appears to draw on the Othbert narrative, which is argued to be the oldest of the three source texts. In contrast, Mannyng's version was based on the Theodoricus text, considered to be about a decade more recent than the Othbert narrative. See Robert Evan Mullin, "The Exempla in *Handlyng Synne*" (masters' thesis, Emporia Kansas State College, 1974), 93; Mannyng seems to have accessed the Theodoricus text through passages from the eleventh-century monk Goscelin's "Life of St. Edith of Wilton." Goscelin presents Theodericus's version of the events, and uses the story to "point out the power and grace of St. Edith of Wilton in obtaining the cure of one of the dancers, Theodericus." Kemmler and Mannyng, *"Exempla" in Context*, 133. The Wilton Chronicle presents a surviving version of St. Edith's life in which the tale appears. As this version of the events is arguably intended for a different audience from the *Manuel* or *Handlyng Synne*, it will not be analyzed in depth in this text. For the text and analysis, see Mary Dockray-Miller (ed.), *Saints Edith and Æthelthryth: Princesses, Miracle Workers, and Their Late Medieval Audience: The Wilton Chronicle and the Wilton Life of St Æthelthryth* (Turnhout: Brepols, 2009), 278–292. The two fifteenth-century adaptations draw directly upon the *Manuel* and *Handlyng Synne* rather than on the original source texts, and thus reflect both the Othbert and Theodoricus versions of the tale, albeit versions filtered through these

Initially, the focus of the tale was clearly on protecting sacred space through removing problematic actions, such as dance. However, as the tale was changed and refined over the late Middle Ages, as the *adiaphora* of dance was worked out, that focus shifted. In discussions aimed at laity, dance became defined as sacrilege, and then, through a parallel discussion of women and sacrilege, became associated primarily with sacrilegious female bodies. In multiple *exempla*, and in the tale of the cursed dancing carolers in particular, defending the sacred from the profane started to subtly lead to defining as transgressive not just actions committed by bodies, but certain bodies themselves. As became clearer through each iteration of the tale, purifying the sacred began with removing dance and other disruptive behaviors and ended with removing female bodies.[8]

SACRED SPACES, HOURS, AND MATTER

Dance featured prominently in the efforts of medieval authors and parishes to consecrate their hours and their churchyards. In some thirteenth- and fourteenth-century contexts, dance's involvement with the creation of liturgical space and time helped to consecrate the hours. Kathryn Dickason's discussion of dancing the hours shows well the potential for holy liturgical dance, especially in French and Italian contexts, during this period.[9] As Dickason writes, "in the Christian defense of psalmody and dance, the liturgy accomplished the rediscovery of sacred time."[10] But for most of the people in an ordinary English parish, dancing the liturgy within the church was not an option; clerics and authors viewed unconsecrated lay bodies as threats more than part of worship. The liturgical dances explored by Dickason and others

---

two penitential manuals. Manuscript history information given in Bitterling, *Of Shrifte and Penance*, 15–29.

8   These iterations appear not just in the creation of new texts, but also in revisions to the manuscripts of each text. Yet for *Handlyng Synne* these revisions had little effect on the tale of the cursed carolers. Although the number of known manuscripts has doubled since the creation of Furnivall's EETS edition (cited throughout this chapter), Furnivall's edition remains a reliable text for this specific tale. I have consulted seven of the nine extant manuscript copies of *Handlyng Synne* (CUL MS Ii.4.9, BL MS Harley 1701, BL Add. MS 22283, Bodl. MS Ashmole 61, Bodl. MS 415, and Folger Shakespeare Library MS V.b.236). I have also consulted the only extant copy of *Of Shrifte and Penance* (Camb., St. John's College MS 197), and a copy of Idley's *Instructions to His Son* (Camb., Magdalene College MS Pepys 2030, BL MS Arundel 20). This manuscript work has shown no variants beyond spelling variations, and thus, for the ease of the reader, citations will be to published edited versions of each text.

9   See Ch. 3, "Dance of the Hours: The Liturgy," in Dickason, *Ringleaders of Redemption*, 77–102.

10 Ibid., 82.

Dance and Protecting Sacred Space

were usually open only to the appropriate performers: to clergy and carefully chosen individuals who could be trusted to dance in a way that enhanced worship rather than distracted from it.[11] In a document from Sens in France, the description of the liturgical dance makes clear that only male clerics could acceptably perform the liturgical dance:

> Male ecclesiastics, those beneficed and wearing the habit of the metro-politan church of Sens, as well as the archbishop, if he be present, after the midday meal on Easter, gathered in the courtyard of the cloister, and there dancing a round-dance – not jumping as in other peculiar dances – they sang hymns of the resurrection of Christ and other Latin texts in praise of God. But because a large number of people of both sexes ran to join in the said round-dance, where perhaps much evil might be perpetrated ... in order to remove a danger to souls, that custom should be wholly abolished.[12]

The addition of laity into the dance provided cause for the suppression of this danced liturgy, especially since the laity involved included women. Furthermore, Craig Wright notes that in the eyes of medieval clergy, "dancing within the church often degenerated into boisterous, even indecent behavior. Lay persons who led the dance in church (*ducere choream*) were usually stigmatized along with practitioners of other dubious professions – actors, mimes, prostitutes, and gamblers."[13] Yet, increasingly in this period, dance was part of parish life and the correct practice of faith. Dance functioned as a means of raising support for the church, of creating church community, and of celebrating the saints. Maidens' lights, hocktide festivities, Whitsun proces-sionals, dance within mystery plays and cycles, and danced parish rituals were part of the festive liturgical time lived out by late medieval parishes.[14] Many of these customs, particularly lights and processionals, were communally performed dances that helped bind the parish together, raise money for the parish church, and create a visual display of the body of Christ. Even for those excluded from formal liturgical dances during mass, dance served as a means of communal piety within the sacred time of feast days.

To be fair to those seeking to manage medieval parishes, lay behavior within the church, churchyard, and during service often gave clerics reason

---

[11] See also Hellsten, *Through the Bone and Marrow*.

[12] Poitiers, Bibliothèque municipale, MS 336, fol. 90–90v, as translated and presented in Wright, *The Maze and the Warrior*, 146.

[13] Ibid., 138.

[14] For some of the best discussions of these festivities in an English parish context, see French, "Maidens' Lights and Wives' Stores"; French, *The Good Women of the Parish*; French, *The People of the Parish*; Duffy, *Stripping of the Altars*; Duffy, *The Voices of Morebath*; for examples in continental contexts, see Harris, *Sacred Folly*; Max Harris, *Christ on a Donkey: Palm Sunday, Triumphal Entries, and Blasphemous Pageants* (York: Arc Humanities Press, 2019).

for concern. Synodal decrees from the thirteenth and fourteenth centuries repeatedly admonished clerics to keep games, dancing, and wrestling out of the churchyard, for these activities drew people out of the mass and into secular pastimes. Synodal statutes from the late thirteenth century in Winchester, for example, urge that "on the celebrations of feast days or at other times, let not wrestling matches take place, dances be conducted, or other showy games be held," so that the mass could be properly observed.[15] Even if games and dancing were out of the question, the mass might still not be the focus, for laity then often gossiped or flirted instead. Daniel Jütte's article about sleeping in church displays what many laity saw as the alternative to games and misbehavior: boredom and slumber.[16] For many thirteenth- and fourteenth-century parishioners, dancing was simply more fun and more interesting than paying attention to the mass – and thus, clerics saw it as a threat to their hoped-for reforms and pastoral care.

We see this clerical preoccupation with the dangers of lay dance as a threat to liturgical space and time in some of the sermons and *exempla* mentioned in the previous chapter. From a broad overview of dance *exempla*, the exact focus of clerical concerns about dance becomes clearer. Taking a broad overview of primarily continental medieval texts and *exempla*, Alessandro Arcangeli notes that the placement of dance *exempla* like the tale of the cursed dancing carolers within a late medieval religious text revealed what sins late medieval clerics associated with dance. Occasionally, dance appeared as its own entry, under the term *chorea*. This indicated a view of dance as more threatening than other performed arts, such as music or drama, which did not merit their own entries as categories of sin.[17] Dance was also occasionally placed within discussions of game-playing and referred to as "the game of dances."[18] However, these were not the usual classifications of dance within these continental sources. When the text was organized into sections dealing with the seven deadly sins, dance was commonly discussed under sections dealing with lust. *Exempla* used dance's physicality and supposed sexual nature to

---

[15] See, for example, Diocese of Winchester, 1262–5, Register of Bishop John de Pontissara. HRO, 21M65/A1/1, fol. 56. *REED Hampshire*, ed. Peter Greenfield and Jane Cowling (REED Online: 2020), https://ereed.library.utoronto.ca/collections/hamps/.

[16] Daniel Jütte, "Sleeping in Church: Preaching, Boredom, and the Struggle for Attention in Medieval and Early Modern Europe," *The American Historical Review* 125, no. 4 (October 21, 2020): 1146–1174.

[17] Arcangeli, "Dance under Trial," 129.

[18] Ibid., 138. A possible reason for this classification is the late emergence of a word referring specifically to dance in the German and English vernacular languages; it was not until around 1200 that the English language developed a word that referred specifically and solely to dance. See Stanley, "Dance, Dancers and Dancing in Anglo-Saxon England." Prior to this date, words such as "karole" were used, words that referenced specific dance styles or song-dances.

Dance and Protecting Sacred Space

connect it to the sin of lust. More interestingly, dance was also often classified under the sin of gluttony. As Alessandro Arcangeli explained, this was due to Gregory the Great's classification of dance as "inane rejoicing" and thus akin to "excessive eating and drinking."[19] When a source classified sins using the Ten Commandments as a guide, dance typically appeared under discussions of the commandments regarding adultery, coveting a neighbor's wife, or respecting the Sabbath.[20] Despite this broad range of sins connected with dance in continental medieval texts, vernacular English texts often took a different and more focused approach. In the vernacular English texts considered in this chapter, dance *exempla* appear not in discussions of lechery or adultery or lust, but only in sections on the third commandment (keeping the Sabbath holy) and on sacrilege. Dance's placement in these thirteenth- and fourteenth-century texts reveals what profane actions medieval English authors most associated with dance: not sexual sin or lust but the violation of sacred space, either spatially or temporally. Discussions of dance were part of the attempt to mark out the boundaries of sacred space, and tales like the cursed dancing carolers narrative were so popular because they were memorable and relevant, meant to teach how to honor the sacred spaces and times that laity encountered every time they walked past their parish church.

The medieval churchyard sat at the center of these concerns with sacred space and time, both literally and ideologically. It was in defense of both sacred space and sacred time that clerics deployed many late medieval *exempla*. In a late medieval context, dance was frequently used as a tangible anchor for discussions of these spiritual dangers. Dance in sacred spaces was dangerous to Christian worship, for the place of performance made the action of dancing far more disruptive. Likewise, the disruption caused by dance in sacred spaces upset societal boundaries between the sacred and the secular and endangered the priest's authority through drowning out his voice and teachings, both symbolically and literally. And preventing dance in sacred spaces, both spatial and temporal, was a constant struggle in the medieval world. In most medieval communities, the church and its churchyard were the only community spaces accessible to all. Additionally, for the majority of the population, Sunday, or holy feast days, were the only days they could dance or hold community celebrations. This explains the repeated appearance of dance within discussions of keeping the Sabbath holy.[21] Authors used the particular sacrilege of dancing during the mass

---

[19] Arcangeli, "Dance under Trial," 129.

[20] Ibid., 130.

[21] Ibid. For detailed studies of the liturgical year and its feasts in several specific communities, see Charles Phythian-Adams, "Ceremony and the Citizen: The Communal Year at Coventry 1450–1550," in *Crisis and Order in English Towns, 1500–1700*, ed. Peter Clark and Paul Slack (New York: Routledge, 2013), 57–85; Mervyn James, "Ritual, Drama, and Social Body in the Late Medieval English

Women, Dance and Parish Religion in England, 1300–1640

to mark out boundaries for sacred spaces in a memorable way, boundaries meant to apply to all sorts of disruptive lay behavior. This use of dance as a representative problematic behavior helps show how parishes and clerics navigated the growing importance of holy matter and liturgical time and lay threats to these sacred spaces, spatial and temporal.

Before turning to the tale of the cursed dancing carolers and its role in turning dance into sacrilege, we need to consider one final concern that clerics had when contemplating holy things and medieval churches. Medieval churches were the site of the miracle of the Eucharist and the locus of sacred matter. The liturgies and masses within which the Eucharist was performed were the locus of sacred time. Thus, to medieval reformers and authors, "a church is a place in which a sacred time is constantly alive and always prevails."[22] The presence of holy matter within the church provided another focus for clerical concern. Historians have repeatedly acknowledged that matter and bodies were of vital importance to medieval religion. And as Bynum noted, the significance of matter only increased in the later medieval era. In one example, authors of sermons, tales, and theological texts increasingly focused on the incarnation. Le Goff argued that thirteenth-century texts like the *Legenda Aurea* "display a tendency common in its century to give increasing importance to Christmas over Easter. That tendency is clearly linked to the evolution of Christian spirituality, which, after having made of Christianity essentially the religion of a resuscitated God, began to accord more and more importance to the celebration of his incarnation."[23] Accordingly, as Miri Rubin's authoritative study records, Corpus Christi celebrations reached their height in the late medieval era, along with Christocentric piety focused on the Eucharist itself.[24] Matter itself became increasingly important in parish piety as well, as shown in Katherine French's studies of parish life. Individuals showed their devotion to parish saints and to their faith through material gifts – through consecrating ordinary materials to the saints, making matter sacred in the process.[25] The significance of sacred spaces and matter in the late Middle Ages was not only ideological. The theological shifts in approach to holy matter and the deep paradoxes these debates housed shaped the lives and practices of laity. As theologians sought to negotiate how a fallen earthly world could be made both spiritually and materially sacred, laity contributed to these discussions by practicing their faith as they understood it should be

---

Town," *Past & Present* 98, no. 1 (1983): 3–29; Hutton, *The Rise and Fall of Merry England*; Ronald Hutton, "Seasonal Festivity in Late Medieval England: Some Further Reflections," *The English Historical Review* 120, no. 485 (February 1, 2005): 66–79.

[22] Le Goff and Cochrane, *In Search of Sacred Time*, 180.

[23] Ibid., 20.

[24] Rubin, *Corpus Christi*.

[25] French, *The Good Women of the Parish*.

Dance and Protecting Sacred Space

practiced. An emphasis on holy matter drove an emphasis on material and embodied piety.

The significance of this late medieval emphasis on holy matter appears not only in theological definitions of the holy but also in definitions of the profane. As late medieval religion focused more on holy matter, holy spaces, and holy bodies, there arose a corresponding focus on transgressive and profane matter, spaces, and bodies. Shining a light onto the profound potential of the sacred cast things, spaces, and bodies labeled profane into starker relief. And this is exactly what happened in the *exempla* and sermon tales that proliferated to teach the true faith in the thirteenth and fourteenth centuries, for the laity could not understand the full glory of the sacred without understanding the full horror of the profane. The emphasis on holy and sacred matter and spaces brought a parallel emphasis on the abuse and destruction of these things and an increased focus on protecting them.

This dual focus on sacred and profane matter appears in a wide variety of medieval *exempla*. Some of the most common are the *dauerwondern* (Eucharistic miracle tales) discussed by Bynum and Rubin.[26] An example from fourteenth-century England appears in Robert Mannyng of Brunne's *Handlyng Synne*, in his section on the sacraments. A man doubts the reality of transubstantiation and to counter this doubt, the elements of the Host transform into the flesh of the child Christ himself, with awe-inspiring results:

> Whan þe preste shulde parte þe sacrament,
> An aungel dowun from heuene was sent,
> And sacryfyed þe chylde ryȝt þare;
> As þe prest hyt brak, þe aungel hyt share;
> Þe blode yn-to þe chaleys ran
> Of þat chylde, boþe God and man ...
> Þan gan he cry, with loudë steuene,
> "Mercy! Goddys sone of heuene!
> Þe brede þat y sagh on þe auter lye,
> Hyt ys þy body; y se hyt with ye.
> Of þe brede, þurgh sacrament,
> To flesshe and blode hyt ys alle went;
> Þys y beleue, and euer y shal;
> For verryly we se hyt alle.[27]

---

[26] Bynum, *Christian Materiality*, 168–176; indeed, Rubin's masterful study of the rise of Eucharist-centric culture in the late Middle Ages highlights this emphasis on the material elements of medieval Christianity, with their connection to the divine. See Rubin, *Corpus Christi*.

[27] Robert Mannyng, *Robert of Brunne's "Handlyng Synne," A.D. 1303, with Those Parts of the Anglo-French Treaties on Which It Was Founded, William of Wadington's "Manuel Des Pechiez,"* ed. Frederick James Furnivall, EETS OS 119 & 123 (London: EETS, 1901), 313–314.

Women, Dance and Parish Religion in England, 1300–1640

Mannyng's *exemplum* about this miraculous display of transubstantiation, meant to teach true belief in the Eucharist, is tame in comparison to other *dauerwondern* about deliberate misuse of the Host, but still communicates the essential message: sacred matter is not to be profaned, either by action or by doubt. Read as a whole, Mannyng's discussion of the sacrament of the Host well displays how a focus on the holy led to a corresponding focus on the profane. Mannyng discussed the marvel of the sacrament of the Eucharist at length, dwelling on its power and its efficacy for believers. But he also spent an equal amount of time highlighting all the ways in which the sacrament can be endangered by human sin – through fallible priests, through taking the sacrament in sin, through abuse by nonbelievers, and on and on. He was careful to note that none of these transgressions can actually remove the power of the Eucharist, but nonetheless emphasized the severe gravity of profaning the sacred through action, thought, or carelessness.

Exempla on medieval dance parallel these *dauerwondern* in their focus on protecting sacred things from sacrilegious actions. And indeed, many (if not most) medieval dance *exempla* focused on protecting the sacred from sacrilege perpetuated through dancing. One tale told of a dancer who, in an echo of the golden calf narrative from Exodus often used to illustrate idolatry, dances around a ram and curses a priest, bringing down destruction upon the entire region. Several tales spoke of devils dancing in mockery of the mass, profaning the sacrament of the altar through the action of dancing. Dancers who were dancing in a place of pilgrimage were struck down by lightning; a dancer who disturbed a sermon is shamed by her priest, who ripped her wig and adornments from her head. A dancer who went to dances and games instead of to church was tortured by perpetual fire until confession lifts the burning.[28] In these tales, it is clear that the Eucharist was not the only sacred thing that needed protecting from misbehaving parishioners. These dance *exempla* sought to protect the masses, priests, and churchyards that thirteenth- and fourteenth-century authors saw as important and vulnerable.

Through these thirteenth- and fourteenth-century texts, we see the changing priorities of the medieval parish: a reclamation of the churchyard as a space for sacred activities and consecrated bodies alongside the sacralization of time. Each of these changing priorities carried consequences. With the increased emphasis on the Eucharist came an emphasis on its abuse and the ways in which the holy could be profaned. And with the increased use of dance and processional in material piety and parish life came a parallel push against dance in improper places and times. A clearer picture of what holy dance looked like led to a clearer definition as to what profane dance looked

---

[28] Tales 1417, 1412, 1423, 1425, 1427 as listed in Stith Thompson, *Motif-Index of Folk-Literature: A Classification of Narrative Elements in Folktales, Ballads, Myths, Fables, Mediaeval Romances, Exempla, Fabliaux, Jest-Books, and Local Legends* (Bloomington: Indiana University Press, 1955), 113–114.

Dance and Protecting Sacred Space

like. It is precisely because of the vibrant parish life explored by French, Duffy, and others that dance became more contentious.[29] It is precisely because of the frequency of dance in church-adjacent spaces or even in the church itself that tales such as the tale of the cursed dancing carolers came about.

Significantly, the surge of female piety noted by French and others corresponds with these dance tales' increasing focus on women, despite what Dyan Elliott has described as "an ostensible relaxation of pollution concerns" tied to the female body in the high and late Middle Ages. In short, Elliott argues that concerns about the physical body shifted to concerns about intentionality and action, in line with the move towards a more interior religion noted in much of the scholarship on late medieval religion. Thus, as Elliott discusses, debates about the sacrilegious act of sexual intercourse within a church shifted from a focus on the act itself to the intentions of each party.[30] The tale of the cursed dancing carolers, in its multiple iterations across the thirteenth through fifteenth centuries, also reflects this shift, with all the versions considered in this chapter emphasizing sacrilegious actions and the intentions behind them.

Yet, looking at the gendering of danced sacrilege shows that bodies still mattered to those teaching the laity and managing medieval parishes. Bynum's aforementioned argument regarding matter in the late Middle Ages dovetails with Elliott's contentions and with the subtle shifts in the tale of the cursed dancing carolers. As Bynum points out, part of the reason that the later Middle Ages have been discussed as a period that emphasized visions and inner piety over matter and material is because of the growing mysticism of lay piety at that time, the flourishing of a "visionary and visual culture ... in which revelations to women played a crucial role."[31] This reason for the receptiveness of women to visions was, however, still intimately bound with the material. Women were more often receptive to mystic visions and inscriptions because of their softer, more impressionable physical forms. Even a turn towards interiority maintained an emphasis of sorts on the female body. Elliott succinctly stated this relationship by noting that "the female soul was believed to be relentlessly permeated by her body."[32] Thus, neither Bynum nor Elliott minimizes the role that matter and bodies continued to play in late medieval religion, in both positive and negative senses. In the fourteenth and fifteenth centuries, even with the turn towards interior piety and affective meditation, medieval religion remained very much interested in the material, particularly when it came to women. As Le Goff notes in his study of Jacobus de Voragine's *Legenda Aurea*, "it is worth remarking that the essential element in female sanctity continued to be the female body, even among the thinkers of the new

---

[29] For example, Duffy, *Stripping of the Altars*; French, *The People of the Parish*.
[30] Elliott, *Fallen Bodies*, 6, 61–80.
[31] Bynum, *Christian Materiality*, 19.
[32] Elliott, *Fallen Bodies*, 48. See also pp. 42–43.

Women, Dance and Parish Religion in England, 1300–1640

mendicant orders and even when sanctity was clearly a consequence of the virtues and pious lives of the women" rather than of their martyrdom.[33]

When the defining factor in sanctity remained the female body, it follows that the defining factor in transgression would be the female body as well. As the tendency to associate holy women and spiritual authority with visionary experiences and interiority increased, so the association of sinful women with the body and embodied experiences increased accordingly. Women remained, more than their male counterparts, inseparably both body and imagination, spirit and physical form.[34] The fraught relationship between gender and matter, and indeed with matter in general, meant that by the end of the fourteenth century, increasingly transgression was a gendered and embodied action, whether that transgression be dance, sex, or sacrilege. Before unpacking the shift in focus from action to bodies, however, we need to first consider dance as sacrilege, starting with dance in the vernacular texts that present the tale of the cursed dancing carolers for an English lay audience.

SACRED AND PROFANE ACTIONS: SACRILEGE AND DANCE

While profane actions can be defined only in opposition to holy actions, in a sense, the majority of the actions discussed in texts such as *Handlyng Synne* or *Of Shrifte and Penance* are profane. In teaching the basics of the faith – the Ten Commandments and the seven deadly sins in particular – the emphasis was on what it looked like to break these precepts or to commit these sins. Thus, many of the *exempla* in these texts, including all the medieval dance *exempla* in these vernacular English texts, revolve around transgressions and how to repent rather than around holiness or sacred behavior.

The manuscripts that present the tale of the cursed dancing carolers highlight the extent to which discussions of dance in a medieval English context revolved around sacrilege rather than around lust or sexuality. In one example, in *Of Shrifte and Penance*'s discussion of the third commandment, following a thirty-five-line discussion about the sins and dangers of working on the Sabbath, the twenty-line section on other disorders that violate the third commandment begins as follows: "Knowe ʒe also for sothe þat wyckedly þey trespasseth þat lede caroles ar daunces on þe holyday and hey þat seth hem. Fvl muche evel cometh of seche iapes, and þerfore forbede hem at þe chyrche."[35] And in the lengthiest discussion of dance offered in these sermon cycles, the tale of the cursed dancing carolers, each manuscript places the *exemplum* within a section focused on sacrilege, providing clear definitions of sacrilege before using the tale to illustrate them. Mannyng, for example,

---

[33] Le Goff and Cochrane, *In Search of Sacred Time*, 28.

[34] Elliott, *Fallen Bodies*, 36.

[35] Bitterling, *Of Shrifte and Penance*, 50.

Dance and Protecting Sacred Space

defined sacrilege as "mysdedë to holynes," which could include not only dancing but also anything ranging from stealing from the church, striking clergy, defiling the churchyard, burying those who are not clergy (or baptized) in a church, withholding church property, women's tempting of clergy, having sexual intercourse in holy places, playing in churchyards, to using the church for unholy purposes.[36] *Of Shrifte and Penance* likewise placed the tale in its section on sacrilege, beginning by discussing forms of sacrilege the audience might not recognize, like trespassing on the churchyard, improper burial, women in the sight of the priest during the mass, exacerbating sin by sinning in sacred space, or using the goods of the church for secular purposes. The text sought to help its audience understand that although "he þat kepeth nat clene a circheȝerde, he may dowte þat he hath trespassed. Þe chyrcheȝerd is over hows, whare alle we schul reste and abyde þe iugement of God. Þerfore we schulde kepe hyt þe more clennore."[37] Idley's version of the tale of the cursed dancing carolers is one of only two *exempla* in his section on sacrilege, representing a significant abridgement of Mannyng's text, with its seven *exempla*. Thus, from the outset, the reason for the discussion of dance is clear: dance needed to be discussed in order to protect the sacred.

In one of the only pieces of scholarship written specifically about the sacrilege sections of any of these four works, Mark Miller, in an analysis of Mannyng's version of the tale in *Handlyng Synne*, notes that the placement of this tale in the sacrilege section makes sense within a late medieval context. "Caroling is a clear case of sacrilege; it is a sin against the church itself by way of a perversion or parody of the celebration inside the church, the mass whereby the Christian community is rightfully constituted and affirmed."[38] In early versions of the tale of the cursed dancing carolers in particular, the use of dance in the violation of sacred space and of the priest's authority was the sole criticism that the tale brought against dance. The placement of the priest's curse first made this point, and a later aside to the reader, noting that "Just as the priest had prayed to God/ They danced the entire year./ It would have been better if they had ceased/ When they were admonished," reasserted the

---

[36] Mannyng, *Handlyng Synne*, 271; Mullin, "The Exempla in *Handlyng Synne*," 56. Chapter 3 in Elliott's work provides a thorough analysis of one of these offenses, that of having sex in sacred space. This discussion reached its zenith around the same time that the discussions of dance in sacred space began to intensify. Elliott, *Fallen Bodies*.

[37] Bitterling, *Of Shrifte and Penance*, 99.

[38] Mark Miller, "Displaced Souls, Idle Talk, Spectacular Scenes: *Handlyng Synne* and the Perspective of Agency," *Speculum* 71, no. 3 (July 1996): 610; see also Kate Greenspan, "Lessons for the Priest, Lessons for the People: Robert Mannyng of Brunne's Audiences for *Handlyng Synne*," *Essays in Medieval Studies* 21 (2004): 109–121.

Women, Dance and Parish Religion in England, 1300–1640

connection between dance in sacred space and divine punishment.[39] These textual cues indicated the central moral of the tale: violation of sacred space and interruption of worship is a sin. The author of the *exemplum* did not leave it to his reader to interpret these clues, though. The thirteenth-century *Manuel* stated its moral, explicitly and succinctly, at the end of the tale: "Through which [this tale] is perceived/ And understood that it is neither lighthearted nor wise/ To sing and dance near the church/ Or in a cemetery to talk aloud/ In order to disturb the priest/ When he sings in the church."[40] Mannyng's fourteenth-century version in *Handlyng Synne* made the connection between sacrilege and disruption through activities like dance even more clear:

> Karolles, wrastlynges, or somour games,
> Who-so euer haunteþ any swyche shames
> Yn cherche, oþer yn cherchëȝerd,
> Of sacrylage he may be a-ferd.
> Or entyrludës, or syngynge,
> Or tabure bete, or oþer pypynge,
> Alle swychë þyng forbodyn es,
> Whyle þe prest stondeþ at messe.[41]

The moral of the tale of the cursed dancing carolers was not subtle or ambiguous in its approach to dance: dance in sacred space, either spatial or temporal, was sacrilege. This again aligns with the synodal decrees that remain from the thirteenth and fourteenth centuries: prohibitions of churchyard dancing centered on the violation of the churchyard with secular things, not on sexual sin, as in Bishop William of Raleigh's thirteenth-century synodal statutes:

> Likewise since great reverence is due to the relics of saints, we have served the body of one who, being holy of holies and glorious among his saints, made others saints. Honour must be bestowed. And so we, wishing to preserve due honour for that one to whom honour and glory is due, under penalty of excommunication, forbid that in cemeteries or churchyards, games or wrestling matches be carried out and that women presume to conduct dances there wantonly with the singing of lay songs, since from these things, because reverence for the lord and honour for the saints are held in contempt, brawls and disputes and human mores are wont to arise.[42]

---

[39] "Sicum le prestre out Deu prie/ L'an entire unt karole./ Meus lur vaudreit auer cesse/ Quant il furent amoneste." Mannyng, *Handlyng Synne*, 286. All translations from the *Manuel* are my own.

[40] "Par tant sumes aparceu/ Qe ceo ne est mie gas ne iu,/ Just l'eglise karoler,/ Ou en cymiter pleder,/ Pur le prestre disturber/ Quant il chante al muster." Ibid., 290.

[41] Ibid., 283.

[42] Diocese of Winchester, 1247–9, Synodal Statutes of Bishop William of Raleigh,

Dance and Protecting Sacred Space

A similar decree appears in Bishop Richard de Wyche's thirteenth-century statutes for the Diocese of Chichester: "we prohibit round dances or base and shameful pastimes which might incite (people) to immorality from being held in churchyards."[43] In each vernacular variation of the dancing carolers tale and in the thirteenth-century synodal decrees that sought to guide parish behavior, the real issue with dance was with its use as an instrument of sacrilege, not with the act itself.

Within these ecclesiastical texts, the main concern with dance is its violation of the "true Christianity" that Fourth Lateran hoped to instill and the ways in which this unholy action endangered holy spaces. But in the thirteenth century, the concern is primarily with the action of dancing itself, not with the bodies committing the action. Particularly in thirteenth-century documents, both didactic texts and synodal statutes, the authors focus on what the people (both men and women) did in sacred spaces and at sacred times rather than on their gendered bodies. Similarly, other discussions of sacrilege focus on a long list of problematic actions. In its discussion of the third commandment, *Of Shrifte and Penance* places dance in a list of other sacrilegious actions like wrestlings, tavern-going, romances, fables, songs, and public hangings.[44] Mannyng's *Handlyng Synne* likewise exhorts its listeners to avoid a list of actions on the Sabbath, at their peril:

> Ȝyf þou make karol or play,
> Þou halewyst nat þyn holyday.
> Ȝyf þou come ouergladly þar tyl,
> And ȝyuest þarto mochyl þy wyl,
> Yn þat hast þou mochyl plyȝt,
> For synne wyl come þurgh swychë syȝt.
> Ȝyf þou euer settyst swerde eyþer ryng
> For to gadyr a wrastlyng,
> Þe holyday þou holdest noght,
> Whan swyche bobaunce for þe ys wroȝt.[45]

The list continues to discuss drawing women into town with flower garlands and crowns, lechery, pride, and, prior to covering tavern attendance, drinking, gluttony, chess, and games, turns to "jangling" (gossip, chatter, and disruptive speech and fidgeting) in the mass:

    Salisbury Cathedral Archives, FG/1/1, fol. 401, col. 1. As transcribed in *REED Hampshire*, ed. Greenfield and Cowling, https://ereed.library.utoronto.ca/collections/hamps/.

43 Bodl. University College MS 148, p. 189 col. 1, as translated and transcribed in *Records of Early English Drama: Sussex*, ed. Cameron Louis (Toronto: University of Toronto Press, 2000), 224.

44 Bitterling, *Of Shrifte and Penance*, 50–51.

45 Mannyng, *Handlyng Synne*, 36.

> 3yf þou euer ianglyst at messe
> Yn þe cherche with more or lesse,
> And lettyst men of here preyers,
> For hem perel soþely þou berys;
> Þe holyday þou holdest nat ry3t,
> And lettyst to wurschyp god almy3t.[46]

All these lists of problematic behavior address a broad "you," an anonymous, genderless listener. While men or women receive occasional mentions in tandem with particular behaviors (for example, women with flower garlands and crowns), the authors focus largely on what unruly parishioners might do, not on the bodies they would commit these actions in.

We start to see a change in emphasis – from action to bodies – in discussions of jangling occurring around the dance narrative, beginning with the moral of the tale. This theme of "jangling" in church appears in all the versions of the text, starting with the *Manuel*: "Pursue peace as a truth, because/ That which you have babbled/ The devil will repeat/ When he shows his roll of names/ Unless that be amended/ And purged through confession."[47] Mannyng's version of the tale likewise moves directly from dancing to jangling in church, making the same connections between caroling, jangling, sacrilege, and the devil's roll. And to further hammer home this connection, the next *exemplum* in the *Manuel* and *Handlyng Synne* continues on the same theme of jangling in church. In Mannyng's presentation of the tale, a man laughs when the priest reads out the gospel for the day. When asked by the priest why he had such an inappropriate response, he stated that "twey wymmen iangled þere besyde" and a devil had been taking down their words; his laughter was sparked by the devil's difficulty in pulling out more parchment to record the words of the still-gossiping women.[48]

Clearly, dancing and gossiping are both key concerns in these discussions of sacrilege. And these concerns are framed as related – the *exempla* focused on each transgression flow into each other, and the moral of the tale of the cursed dancing carolers references the seemingly related sin of jangling. Jangling has been the focus of several excellent works on late medieval transgression. Bardsley's *Venomous Tongues* notes that although dangerous and excessive speech had a long historical association with women, "this association grew both more intense and more tangible in its consequences" in the late Middle Ages.[49] Ina Habermann, Laura Gowing, and Karma Lochrie make

---

[46] Ibid.

[47] "Duter poes pur verite,/ Qe quant qe auez la iangle,/ Del deable vus ert reherece/ Quant sun roule ert muster,/ Si ci ne seit amende/ E par confessium ouste." Ibid., 290.

[48] Ibid., 291.

[49] Bardsley, *Venomous Tongues*, 1.

Dance and Protecting Sacred Space

similar arguments in their work, pointing to the ways in which the sins of the tongue like slander, defamation, and gossip became sins of female tongues.[50] Through repeated association in texts, sermons, and court cases, transgressions like "jangling" became transgressions associated almost exclusively with women – in short, transgressions gendered female.

Similarly to the gendering of slander and other "verbal" transgressions, the related transgressions of sacrilege and dance became gendered transgressions over the course of the late Middle Ages. The versions of the tale found in the *Manuel* and in its revision in *Of Shrifte and Penance* do not emphasize the sin of one particular gender. It specified that "Three women were in the group/ And four men, dancing."[51] Additionally, these men and women were "tied together to honor God" as they danced, just as they had been when they began the carole.[52] The punishments described in the text are for sacrilege and for ignoring the priest's authority. They do not vary according to the gender of the dancer, with no additional emphasis on the women over the men. This changes in other versions of the tale. While the thirteenth-century *Manuel* places its emphasis on sacrilege more generally, in *Handlyng Synne*'s fourteenth-century iteration of the *exemplum*, female sacrilege is deemed more problematic and transgressive than male sacrilege.[53] In Mannyng's *Handlyng Synne* and in Idley's fifteenth-century *Instructions to His Son*, sacrilege within the text is presented as gendered. These later versions of the tale appear to be presenting all the sins of the narrative in a way that implicates dance as the action that causes the other forms of sacrilege, and women as the figures who facilitate the dancing. By doing so, women initiate the multiple acts of sacrilege within the tale. In an attempt to define proper actions, the authors of these texts turned to examples of sin and transgression; the individuals featured in these examples, increasingly women, started to be associated with the transgression more directly. Concern about dancing shifted to concern about dancers, and with the shift from an action to a body, gender became a more important factor in the discussion.

SACRED AND PROFANE BODIES: GENDERING SACRILEGE

By following these iterations of this *exemplum*, it becomes clear that the tale of the cursed dancing carolers, emerging concomitantly with the redefinitions of true Christian worship and uses of sacred space, highlights concern

---

[50] Ina Habermann, *Staging Slander and Gender in Early Modern England* (Aldershot; Burlington, VT: Ashgate, 2003); Gowing, *Domestic Dangers*; Karma Lochrie, *Covert Operations: The Medieval Uses of Secrecy* (Philadelphia: University of Pennsylvania Press, 2012).

[51] "Treis femmes en la semble,/ E quatre homes, unt karole." Mannyng, *Handlyng Synne*, 286.

[52] "Tiele nut pur Deu honurer." Ibid., 285.

[53] Kemmler and Mannyng, *"Exempla" in Context*, 133.

about dance in sacred space as sacrilegious. This concern with delineating and protecting sacred space from dance forms the core of each version of the tale. However, later versions of the tale of the cursed dancing carolers display a growing concern with female dancers, emphasizing the greater danger posed by the combination of women and dance in sacred space. The stress gradually shifts to focus on not simply sacrilegious dancers, but sacrilegious female dancers. It shifts away from problematic actions to problematic bodies, from sacrilegious dancers to sacrilegious dancing women.

One of the first gendered representations of sacrilege that the reader encounters in Mannyng's version of the tale of the cursed dancing carolers appears in how the figures of the dancing carolers are gendered. Mannyng's version contains twelve carolers, five of whom are named. Three of the five named carolers are women. The only named male caroler in the beginning of the tale is the one identified as the "lodesman" (leader), Gerlew. One other male caroler, "seynt Teodryght," is identified at the very end, in the discussion of his miraculous cure at the tomb of St. Edith. The other three named carolers are identified as "maydens" and the "prestes doghtyr" and appear throughout the tale.[54] Mannyng specifically states that those who called the priest's daughter Ave out to join the caroling were the two women, Wybessyne and Merswynde.[55] So, it would appear that in Mannyng's version of the tale, the focus is on the female dancers. When read in the context of the other sermon tales in Mannyng's section on sacrilege, the implication that the main offenders in sacrilegious sins were women becomes much clearer.[56]

Examples of gendering the sin of sacrilege appear throughout Mannyng's discussion of sacrilege: the two tales preceding the dancing carolers narrative and the tale immediately following it (the tale about "jangling" discussed earlier) focus on women committing sacrilege. In these tales, the women in question often committed sacrilege merely through their presence, voice, or intrinsic sexuality, whereas in the three sacrilege tales in *Handlyng Synne* that feature only men, misuse of the church for financial gain or improper burial and blatant idolatry occur. Mannyng seems to imply that for women, sacrilege often occurred in thoughtlessly committed ordinary actions, while for men, sacrilege required a more serious breach of divine law. This fits with a growing trend in medieval texts, as Ruth Mazo Karras highlights: "exempla tend to show men as wicked in their particular roles as merchants, monks, or kings, not because of their masculinity. Women, in contrast, appear wicked simply because they are female."[57] In the transgressive world of the dancing carolers, Mannyng emphasized the presence of female dancers, making the

---

[54] Mannyng, *Handlyng Synne*, 283.

[55] Ibid., 284.

[56] Ibid., 284, 289.

[57] Ruth Mazo Karras, "Gendered Sin and Misogyny in John of Bromyard's 'Summa Predicantium,'" *Traditio* 47 (1992): 237.

Dance and Protecting Sacred Space

issue appear to be one not merely of dance in sacred space, but also of women in sacred space.

Idley's text clearly reflects the shifts in the gendering of sacrilege to which *Handlyng Synne* points. The dancers, with one named man and three named women in the group of twelve, caroled in the churchyard during "ȝule nyȝt".[58] Idley added a line to his version of their carole song, deepening the sexual transgression of the tale by adding the specification that the dancers were there for the women: "why stand we? Take we theis meydyns!"[59] Then his tale continues along the same lines as Mannyng's – the priest's angry curse, the attempt to pull the priest's daughter Ave from the dance, the removal of Ave's arm, the repeated attempts at its burial, the collapse of the dancers at the end of the year, the death of Ave, and the continued hopping of the other dancers evermore.

An examination of the framework of the tale in Idley's text reveals that here, even more so than in Mannyng's earlier work, the entire focus of the section on sacrilege is on women. The presentation of the dancers in the tale focused, from the beginning, on the sexualized maidens' bodies, layering a focus on bodies over the tale's focus on sacrilege. Furthermore, Idley went on to add at the end of the tale a few additional stanzas not found in Mannyng's text:

> And specially theis women, as I dare sey,
> Haue besy talking of huswyffrye;
> Gangle as a gosse and Iangyll as a Iey,
> And how their husbandes be full off Ielosye.
> Sumset their myndes galantes to asspye,
> Beholdyng the schort garments round all abouȝt
> And how the stuffing off the codpiece berys ouȝt.
> Sum cum to chyrche to shew feyr bedys;
> Sum cum also the boroll ffor to shew;
> Sum tell the councell off their husbandes dedes;
> Sum how their husbandes is a crokyd shrew;
> Sum seme holy, iff ther be but a ffewe;
> Thus with dyuers thynges occpacion thei ffynde –
> As for God and oure lady ar lytyll in mynde.[60]

In two of these last three stanzas of his discussion of sacrilege, Idley moved from the sacrilegious carolers to the many forms of sacrilege committed by women while attending church – again returning to the idea of "jangling." We see again here the connection between sin and women, sacrilege and female bodies. While Mannyng ended his section with a general exhortation

---

[58] Peter Idley, *Instructions to His Son*, ed. Charlotte D'Evelyn (Boston; London: D. C. Heath and Co.; Oxford University Press, 1935), 207.

[59] Ibid.

[60] Ibid., 210.

against sacrilege, Idley focused in on the specific forms of sacrilege committed by women. Although he then added in a final stanza that "to speke only off women I ware to blame" and acknowledged that "men also be culpable in the same," this brief seven-line closing statement does not negate the emphasis on female sacrilege and the sins caused by the presence of female bodies in sacred space prevalent in the preceding stanzas.[61] Although Idley made no significant adaptations to Mannyng's retelling of the tale, the framing of his sacrilege section, with its selection of *exempla* focused on women's bodies and his added closing stanza, drew greater attention to the role of women in sacrilege and to the connections between female bodies and sacrilege, whether the specific act be dancing or gossiping. Thus, in the latest medieval adaptation of the tale of the cursed dancing carolers in England, the connections between female bodies and sacrilege were traced out most strongly, with Idley specifically and pointedly singling out women as the key perpetrators of sacrilege, whether through their presence, their actions, their words, or their dances.

Concern with the sexuality of women's bodies was not new to the fifteenth century. But it is important to note that this trepidation about female sexuality was increasingly tied to a fear of sacrilege starting in the thirteenth century. Through tracing discussions of dance, I argue that it becomes clear that sacrilege, not lust, was the sin at the core of much thirteenth- and fourteenth-century medieval concern with women. Even the framing of the very first *exemplum* in *Handlyng Synne* highlights this. In Mannyng's discussion of the first commandment – thou shalt have no other god before me – the sinner in the *exemplum* is a monk who forsakes God and forsakes his vows because of his lust for a woman. Discussions of sacrilege increasingly centered on female bodies; fornication and dance and other such sins were merely the actions that facilitated the core sin of sacrilege, almost always driven by the presence of women. This is not to say that concern with lust and sexual sin did not play a role in these admonitions and discussions, for it clearly did. But, when read alongside other discussions about sacrilegious actions like dance, it becomes clear that sacrilege played a substantial role even in discussions about female sexuality. And if medieval moralists worried most about sacrilege, not sexuality, that reframes the implications for women. Sexuality could, hypothetically, be carefully contained behind convent walls or monitored. If women's bodies were inherently sacrilegious, women could not ever attain the same access to holy matter, spaces, and perhaps even to a holy God as their male counterparts.

This very separation of female bodies from the sacred is what appears in numerous late medieval texts, *exempla*, and trends. Authors and clerics systematically removed not only dance but also women from sacred spaces. The larger collections within which the tale of the cursed carolers appeared

---

[61] Ibid.

Dance and Protecting Sacred Space

reflect this trend. Mannyng's presentation of the tale of the monk who abandoned his vows for a woman, the tale with which he opened *Handlyng Synne*, gave his audience one example of why women need to be removed from the sight of clerics and monks. He also noted in his section on sacrilege that:

> Ʒyt do wymmen gretter folye
> Þat vse to stoned among þe clergye,
> Oþer at matyns, or at messe,
> But Ʒyf hyt were yn cas of stresse;
> For þerof may come temptacyun,
> And dysturblyng of deuocyun;
> For foule þoght cumþ of feble ye-syƷt,
> And fordoþë grace with riƷt;
> And with a tale hyt may be shewed,
> Þat ys gode boþe for lered and lewed.[62]

Mannyng then moved into the tale of the temptation of St. John Chrysostom's deacon. Notably, this *exemplum* is the only other tale Idley chooses to present in his section on sacrilege. In this *exemplum*, the devil causes a pious deacon to sin by appearing to the deacon in the form of a woman, and causing "such desyrous lust by the fendes temptacion,/ that he fforgat the Lorde off hys saluacion."[63] The body of a "woman" was the catalyst for the deacon's sacrilege and failure to properly perform his duties. Idley used this tale to remind his reader that "syƷt off a woman bredes a shrew" and to caution his audience that women should be kept out of sight and out of sacred space. In the presentation of this tale alongside the heavily gendered version of the tale of the cursed dancing carolers, Idley's emphasis on female sacrilege is quite clear.

The gendering of sacrilege does not appear only in these texts, however, but in other *exempla*, canon laws, and parts of parish life as well. The push for clerical celibacy in the wake of the Gregorian reforms, intensified in the reforms after Fourth Lateran, revolved around concern that married priests would be contaminated by their wives and unable to perform the mass efficaciously.[64] And as this discourse about the pollution of women's bodies and intentions continued, the boundary between women and the sacred, particularly the physical space of the church, became firmer. Simeon of Durham's version of the life of St. Cuthbert gave one example of this in a discussion of how St. Cuthbert had prohibited women from entering churches in which he had served or been present, during his life and even after his death:

> As she [Sungeova] was one night returning home from an entertainment, was continually complaining to her husband that there was no clean piece

---

62 Mannyng, *Handlyng Synne*, 277.
63 Idley, *Instructions to His Son*, 206.
64 Elliott, *Fallen Bodies*, 83.

Women, Dance and Parish Religion in England, 1300–1640

of the road to be found, in consequence of the deep puddles with which it was everywhere studded. So at last they determined that they would go through the churchyard of this church (that is, of Durham) and that they would afterwards make an atonement for this sin by almsgiving. As they were going on together, she was seized with some kind of indefinite horror, and cried out that she was gradually losing her senses. Her husband chided her, and urged her to come on, and not be afraid; but as soon as she set foot outside the hedge which surrounds the cemetery of the church, she immediately fell down; and being carried home, she that very night ended her life.[65]

Both the firmer boundary around the churchyard – the prioritization of sacred space discussed at length in this chapter – and the greater sin of women in sacred space become apparent in this short tale. Both Sungeova and her husband were aware that intruding upon sacred space was a sin, yet only Sungeova died for the offense. And significantly, the sacrilegious offense was Sungeova's idea. The sacrilege of the tale was yet again initiated by a woman, and the sacrilege of the woman could not be atoned for, as could the sacrilege of her husband. Sungeova's female body was depicted as unredeemable after this sacrilegious offense. In another tale in the same text, Simeon described how a woman, driven by the desire to see the beauty of the church, "walked through the cemetery of the church. But she did not go unpunished; for presently she was deprived of her reason – she bit out her own tongue; and in her madness she ended her own life by cutting her throat with her own hand."[66] Sacrilege is again connected to the female body, and, like jangling, to female speech. At least discursively, sacrilege had become a gendered transgression.

The ramifications of this discourse did not take long to become apparent, as sacred space became increasingly and inherently masculine in the thirteenth and fourteenth centuries. St. Cuthbert's supposed creation of an entirely separate outdoor worship space for women was not the medieval norm but rather an extreme implementation of these theological frameworks. But separation of women from the altar, from priests, and even from male congregants was common, as seating arrangements carefully kept women seated separately from men. This was certainly not a new practice, as noted by Katherine French and others, but a practice that nonetheless gained more attention in texts like Mannyng's, praised as a means of protecting sacred space, the decorum of the service, and clerical chastity.[67] The practice of

---

65 Simeon of Durham, "A History of the Church of Durham," trans. J. Stevenson in *The Church Historians of England* (1858). Taken from Emilie Amt, *Women's Lives in Medieval Europe: A Sourcebook* (New York: Taylor and Francis, 2013), 191.

66 Ibid., 192.

67 Katherine L. French, "The Seat Under Our Lady: Gender and Seating in Late Medieval English Parish Churches," in *Women's Space: Patronage, Place, and Gender in the Medieval Church*, ed. Virginia Chieffo Raguin and Sarah Stanbury (Albany: State University of New York Press, 2005), 142–143. See also Margaret

72

Dance and Protecting Sacred Space

separate seating arrangements within the church represents a tangible and daily demonstration of the impact of the discourse traced out in this chapter on even the most pious of women.[68] The details of the ideology so carefully worked out in theological discourses may not have been fully translated to laity, but its underlying concern with the control of women's bodies, vividly portrayed in *exempla*, certainly did. Concerns about the minutia of church seating, like concerns about dance in sacred space or female presence within consecrated areas, ultimately connected to broader concerns about women's morality and motion.[69] As the discourse about protecting the sacred moved from generals to particulars through the negotiation of actions like dance and then from negotiating actions to defining bodies, the end point of the discussion was, to a more precise degree than previously, the monitoring and controlling of women's bodies.

In a counter to this interpretation of late medieval reforms' impact on women as one of increased clerical control, Katherine French notes how women used "their" space within the church to show status, to negotiate rank, and to cultivate a female-centric community of piety, one unintentionally created by regulations intended to create a more male-centric space. As she points out, "giving women a space within the nave was recognition that they were a part of the parish community, but a part that needed definition and perhaps confinement."[70] Still, the fact remains that this part of the parish community, and the generally female-centric parish culture with its hocktides, processionals, and material piety, flourished not because of clerical encouragement but in spite of frequent male efforts at suppression. The intention of the discourse centered around the sacred and around women was to remove women from the center of church life and worship, not to include them. Similarly, while Beth Allison Barr alleviates the picture of medieval misogyny in her work on pastoral care by noting gender-inclusive pronouns and specific instructions for caring for the souls of women as a pastoral tool developed to meet the admonitions of Fourth Lateran, the separation between women and sacred space or individuals remained.[71] Even in attempts to care for women, the dangers women's bodies posed to sacred things – whether priests, altars, relics, or time – remained paramount in the minds of medieval authors. The

---

Aston, "Segregation in Church," in *Women in the Church*, ed. W. J. Sheils and Diana Wood (Oxford: Blackwell, 1990), 237–281.

[68] For more thorough discussion, see Jane Tibbetts Schulenburg's and Crine Schleif's chapters in Virginia Chieffo Raguin and Sarah Stanbury (eds.), *Women's Space: Patronage, Place, and Gender in the Medieval Church* (Albany: State University of New York Press, 2006); see especially pp. 185–206.

[69] French, "The Seat Under Our Lady," 143.

[70] Ibid., 155.

[71] Beth Allison Barr, *The Pastoral Care of Women in Late Medieval England* (Woodbridge: Boydell Press, 2008).

Women, Dance and Parish Religion in England, 1300–1640

growth of lay piety and mysticism in the late Middle Ages may have afforded greater agency to women, but as long as women remained in earthly bodies, they remained bounded by the profane, with unequal access to sacred space or time.

CONCLUSION

The tale of the cursed dancing carolers, in its many versions, shows how debating out *adiaphora* like dance led to subtle but important changes. Its initial point, and the foundation for concern with dance, was the clerical fear that dance was sacrilegious. This apprehension connects to what seems to be one of the most important priorities of late medieval authors in a religious environment increasingly defined by a bifurcation between holy and profane matter. And, from the ways that women feature in the later versions of the tale and from the numerous other late medieval movements connecting women with danger to sacred space and worship, it is clear that sacrilege as an action slowly became a gendered transgression between the thirteenth-century *Manuel* and Idley's fifteenth-century revision. But how?

A second key point from Mark Miller's analysis of *Handlyng Synne* helps explain how Mannyng's concerns about actions in the church shifted to Idley's concerns about women's bodies and their disruption of the sacred. Miller analyzes the ways in which the tale is not simply a straightforward admonition to avoid playing in churchyards and argues that the sin (or sins) considered in the tale is not one-dimensional. To Miller, "what begins as the depiction of the carolers' sinful condition seems from the moment of the priest's cursing to be equally a depiction of his failures."[72] Ultimately, Miller argues that Mannyng uses the tale to illustrate both "the problem of human sinfulness" and "the constraints attendant on a discourse that seeks to engage that problem."[73] To Miller, and in his reading, to Mannyng, the real problem is not a simple act of sacrilege or the sinfulness of dance and women, but the sinfulness of humanity and the all-encompassing spectrum of sins, sins not easily separated into individual, punishable acts. I contend that it is precisely because of this intersectionality of transgression that clerical discussions of actions considered *adiaphora* like dance or gossiping during mass break down, shifting the focus of these discussions to bodies. Parsing action from action proved to be unwieldy, to lead to rubrics of moral behavior almost too difficult to follow. As authors and audiences attempted to keep these rubrics straight, repeating and revising them in each subsequent text, the lines separating actions from bodies blurred. Separating profane actions from

---

[72] Miller, "Displaced Souls, Idle Talk, Spectacular Scenes: *Handlyng Synne* and the Perspective of Agency," 611.

[73] Ibid., 616.

Dance and Protecting Sacred Space

sacred spaces began to instead mean separating profane bodies from sacred spaces. To say that concerns about dance or concerns about women were not about sex is an oversimplification. But, as the emphasis of medieval sermons on dance makes clear, the initial concern with dance was not sex but sacrilege – particularly sacrilege that could lead to sex. In defining dance as sacrilege and then in parsing out exactly what sacrilege meant, a vital shift took place, making the discussion about dance more about bodies than about actions, more about female bodies than male ones.

These theological ideas impacted lay medieval understandings of gender and parish management. As Ruth Mazo Karras explains, "the stories that medieval people heard could not help but affect their mental constructions of their world ... when preachers or compilers of preaching aids used women in their *exempla*, they may have been speaking or writing about something other than women, but they did choose women as vehicles to make their point, and this choice helped shape their audience's views about gender."[74] And increasingly, preachers discussed dance only in relation to women. The *exempla* of Jacques de Vitry, roughly contemporaneous with *Handlyng Synne*, mention dance only as performed by women. In one *exemplum*, dancing women are compared to the instrument used to catch quail, in a reference to how dancing women ensnare others in sin.[75] Another *exemplum* asserts that dancing women belong to the devil: "When a man does not want to lose his cow, he ties a bell to its neck. To this cow may be compared the woman who leads in the dance. When the devil hears the sound he is reassured, and says: 'I have not yet lost my cow.'"[76] The moral of medieval *exempla* was more and more frequently that both dance and women were inescapably profane. And as dance and women were repeatedly connected to disrespect for the sacred and to sacrilege, the mental constructions that medieval individuals built around both dance and women increasingly focused on transgression and on punishment of women in their communities. For what respect was owed to those who did not respect God? What care was owed to the devil's cows?

---

[74] Karras, "Gendered Sin and Misogyny in John of Bromyard's 'Summa Predicantium,'" 257.

[75] *Exemplum* CCLXXIII in Jacques de Vitry, *The Exempla Or Illustrative Stories from the Sermones Vulgares of Jacques de Vitry* (London: Folklore Society, 1890), 114, 253.

[76] *Exemplum* CCCXIV in ibid., 131, 269.

CHAPTER 3

DANCE AND DISRUPTING SACRED TIME

"What shall we say of the assemblies of our time, such as are gathered together in the Churches ... where a man shall see nothing but riot and superfluity, and an unbridled liberty of drinking, dancing, playing, and reveling: they sanctify their assemblies not unto God, but unto Bacchus and Venus."[1] So reads one sixteenth-century sermon lamenting the abuse of the church and churchyard in early modern England. Sermons repeated this lament over and over throughout the sixteenth and seventeenth centuries. The physical space of the church itself was a hotly debated one within the context of the English Reformations, as battles over liturgy, vestments, and ritual raged in both country and city parishes. And debates over the keeping of the Sabbath showed that disputes over the use of sacred space were not confined to physical space but included time as well. Like in the thirteenth and fourteenth centuries, arguments over the proper use of these two spaces – physical and temporal – often overlapped. This was particularly apparent in arguments about dancing, as many of the events at which dancing occurred as a regular part of parish life happened in the parish churchyard on Sundays or religious holidays, since these remained the only days kept entirely free from labor in the sixteenth and seventeenth centuries.[2] The controversies over King James I's 1618 *Book of Sports*, which declared dancing on the Sabbath to be a "lawful recreation," well display this struggle to define these boundaries of sacred space and time and the accompanying fight for authority over sacred space that played out through many of the sacramentalist and ritualist controversies of the English Reformations.[3] In short, the battle for the churchyard did not end with the carolers of the medieval period but continued into a conflict with the Morris dancers and parish procession dancers of the sixteenth and seventeenth centuries.

Many scholars have looked at Sabbatarianism as a sixteenth-century development. Ronald Hutton, Christopher Marsh, David Katz, Kenneth Parker,

---

[1] Gwalther, *The Homilies or Familiar Sermons of M. Rodolph Gualther Tigurine Vpon the Prophet Ioel. Translated from Latine into Englishe, by Iohn Ludham Vicar of Withersfielde*, 53r.

[2] Winerock, "Reformation and Revelry," 33.

[3] Ibid., 36.

and James T. Dennison, among others, have considered the growing debate over the Sabbath between the various factions of the English Reformations, a debate that often centered on reserving Sunday for worship and good works.[4] Within this discussion, scholars generally treat dance as a peripheral issue tied to changing parish festivities and rituals rather than as something integrally bound to the larger theological concerns of Sabbatarianism. But using dance as a framework for viewing both medieval and early modern concerns about sacrilege shows that Sabbatarianism is actually quite medieval and that dance remains more central to the issue of sacrilege than current scholarship has noted. Rather than a distinct new development, early modern discussions of dance and the Sabbath build on the same concerns as their medieval forerunners. In both medieval and early modern texts, concern about challenges to church authority and disruption of services frame the ways in which these religious authorities approached dance and holy time.

There were continuities between the medieval and early modern perspectives on sacrilege, the significance of which become apparent when analyzed through the framework of dance. But their primary significance does not lie in the ways in which these continuities extended the negative trajectory of the church's approach to dance, particularly dance in sacred space and time. Their primary significance lies in the gendering of sacrilege as a female sin, tied to female bodies in early modern discussions of dance and the Sabbath. The gendering of sacrilege traced out in the previous chapter becomes even starker as sacrilege is tied more firmly to the female body, in discourse if not in practice. Through this discourse, authors created space for discussions about other forms of sacrilege like witchcraft (another transgression tied in this period to dance and to women). As the discourses about dance, women, and sin became more entrenched and more tied to bodies than to actions, the consequences for women became more tangible. This chapter will trace out both the discourses and realities regarding dance, women, and Sabbath-breaking during the early modern era, starting with the continuities between medieval and early modern conceptions of sacrilege. The connection of dance, sacrilege, and women helped build the connections between sacrilege, witchcraft, and women, providing another means for asserting male control and separating women from the sacred, both discursively and in practice.

---

[4] Parker's work is particularly relevant, tracing as it does the connections between medieval views of the Sabbath and early modern approaches. See Hutton, *The Rise and Fall of Merry England*; Christopher Marsh, *Popular Religion in Sixteenth-Century England: Holding Their Peace* (London: Macmillan, 1998); David S. Katz, *Sabbath and Sectarianism in Seventeenth-Century England* (Leiden: Brill, 1988); Kenneth L. Parker, *The English Sabbath: A Study of Doctrine and Discipline from the Reformation to the Civil War* (Cambridge: Cambridge University Press, 2002); James T. Dennison, *The Market Day of the Soul: The Puritan Doctrine of the Sabbath in England, 1532–1700* (Kentwood, MI: Reformation Heritage Books, 2001).

Dance and Disrupting Sacred Time

SABBATARIANISM, MEDIEVAL AND EARLY MODERN

Sabbatarianism – a specific theological position about keeping the Sabbath holy – became a key flashpoint in the debates of the English Reformations. At least as articulated by early authors like Thomas Rogers, who wrote a revised version of his *Catholic Doctrine of the Church of England* in 1607, the debate about the Sabbath flared up during the reign of Elizabeth I, as a pernicious new doctrine advanced by Presbyterian dissenters claimed that "the Lord's-day, even as the old sabbath was of the Jews, must necessarily be kept, and solemnized of all and every Christian, under the pain of eternal condemnation both of body and soul."[5] As noted by Kenneth Parker, however, Rogers's account is misleading in how it presents the works of early Sabbatarian advocates like Nicholas Bownde and in its identification of Sabbath doctrine as a new innovation of the 1580s and 1590s. In fact, conformist or mainstream figures such as Henrich Bullinger, Thomas Becon, and Archbishop Matthew Parker all advocated for the concept of a morally binding Sabbath – a holy day on which one could do no work and must observe a day of rest. The 1563 second *Book of Homilies*, the governmentally authorized collection of sermons for circulation in parishes without an educated cleric, likewise laid out the Sabbath as key to proper parish practice, spreading the Sabbath as a theological priority into even the smallest of English parishes.[6] In sixteenth-century debates about theology, the idea of a broad and binding command to observe the Sabbath served as a point of unity, despite debates over what exactly that meant for practices like holy days, the relationship of Sunday to the Sabbath, and the extent to which Old Testament restrictions applied.[7] Ultimately, the Sabbatarian debates about what exactly it meant to keep the Sabbath holy centered on the idea of sacred space and time, just like medieval debates about churchyards and activities during mass.

While there may have been some consensus over the need to keep the fourth commandment, the vehement debates of the English Reformations about how exactly to do so illustrate that demarcating and protecting the boundaries of sacred time and space remained a priority for early modern reformers. Many of these debates remained centered on the same themes, spaces, and topics as their medieval counterparts. As Alexandra Walsham pointed out, the sacred spaces and places of the medieval world did not suddenly become less sacred with the intrusion of the Reformations of the sixteenth century.[8] Although spaces like churchyards and matter like the Eucharist gradually transformed in

---

5 Thomas Rogers, *The Catholic Doctrine of the Church of England: An Exposition of the Thirty-Nine Articles* (Cambridge: Cambridge University Press, 1854), 17–20.

6 Kenneth L. Parker, "Thomas Rogers and the English Sabbath: The Case for a Reappraisal," *Church History* 53 (1984): 334–336.

7 Ibid., 336–341.

8 Walsham, *The Reformation of the Landscape*, 11.

Women, Dance and Parish Religion in England, 1300–1640

their exact supernatural significance, the Reformations brought about gradual desacralization rather than dramatic changes. In many ways, the sacred and enchanted spaces at the center of medieval debates, both geographic and temporal, remained there up until the 1630s.[9] In the English context, the changes were even more gradual than in the continental context. While reformers like Luther and Calvin regarded the consecration of churchyards as an *adiaphora*, in England the physical space of the churchyard remained officially sacred for a full century after the Reformations began.[10] As in the late medieval period, dance came up frequently in these early modern discussions about sacrilege and holy space. In these discussions, it becomes clear that sacred time was more of a concern than sacred material or spaces; late medieval anxieties about first space and then time flipped, and early modern reformers prioritized time over space. But beyond this shift, ecclesiastical fears remained much the same: protecting the sacred from the disruption of dance and debating out the parameters needed to ensure this protection. In short, the concern remained sacrilege, more frequently framed in early modern sermons as idolatry. Sixteenth-century versions of *Certain Sermons and Homilies* lay out an early definition of idolatry in *An Homily Against Peril of Idolatry*, which starts with noting the reverence due to God and his house: "the church or house of God is a place appointed by the Holy Scriptures, where the lively word of God ought to be read, taught, and heard, the Lord's holy name called upon by public prayer ... therefore all that be godly indeed ought both with diligence at times appointed, to repair together to the said church, and there with all reverence to use and behave themselves before the Lord."[11] While the sermon goes on to discuss images and idols, it begins its discussion of idolatry and sacrilege (defined as stealing from the Lord the reverence he is due) with the church and the service.

Sermons about dance and sacrilege in the form of Sabbath-breaking still focused on the ways in which dance during sacred time challenged the authority of the church to control godly living and practice. One 1571 sermon by William Kethe presents a story about disorder in a parish, in which the minister's authority was doubly challenged:

> The Minister seyng the great disorders in hys Parish, the next Sabboth day after they had obtained licence, wrote to the Iustice of yt same, and

---

[9] Ibid., 9.

[10] Emily F. Winerock, "Churchyard Capers: The Controversial Use of Church Space for Dancing in Early Modern England," in *The Sacralization of Space and Behavior in the Early Modern World: Studies and Sources*, ed. Jennifer Mara De Silva (Farnham: Ashgate, 2015), 238–239.

[11] Homily the Fourteenth, in Ronald B. Bond (ed.), *Certain Sermons or Homilies (1547): And, A Homily against Disobedience and Wilful Rebellion (1570): A Critical Edition* (Toronto: University of Toronto Press, 1987).

Dance and Disrupting Sacred Time

wrote nothyng but that he will yet stand to. The Iustice called those that had abused hys authoritie and reproued them, but now ye shall see the multitude. There were (by the Iustices report) 36 whiche offred vp vnto hum theyr names (which was a much to saye, as that they would haue periured them selues, if the iustice would haue put them to their othes) to testifie agaynst the Minister, that where he complayned of disorder, they to ye contrarie affirmed, that there was no disorder at all. And yet it was manifest that the same Sabboth day was shamefully prophaned, with bulbeatynges, boulynges, drunkennes, dauncynges, and such lyke, in so much as men could not keepe their seruauntes frome lyinge out of theyr owne houses the same Sabboth day at night.[12]

The Sabbath dancers challenged the minister's authority (and the church's teachings on godly behavior) by breaking the Sabbath and subsequently used civil authorities to protect themselves from discipline. Another example appears in the 1622 Acts of the Decanal Court in Madley, Herefordshire, where one William Foote is charged for saying "as he passed towarde y church in ye churchyard … he would daunce there in contempt & derogacion of ye churchwarden."[13] These dancers, like their medieval predecessors, committed what these sermons portray as a multileveled assault against the sacred and against authority: against God, against earthly ecclesiastical authorities, against sacred space, and against sacred time. And despite the very different chronological context of these sermons, they are underpinned by very medieval concerns about sacred space, sacred time, and clerical authority.[14] In short, ecclesiastical concern with these problematic parishioners still aligned dancers with sacrilege and the violation of sacred time.

While much of the evidence for the practice of dance in medieval church-yards comes from the repeated canon law prohibitions and sermon tales discussed in the previous chapter, evidence for repeated Sabbath dances

---

12 William Kethe, *A Sermon Made at Blanford Foru[m]* (At London: Printed by Iohn Daye, dwellyng ouer Aldersgate. Cum gratia & priuilegio Regiae Maiestatis, 1571), fol. C.iiii.v–r.

13 HCL, 1622 Acts of Decanal Court, fol. 112v. As transcribed and quoted in David N. Klausner, *REED Herefordshire, Worcestershire* (Toronto: University of Toronto Press, 1990), 153.

14 Another sermon records the lament of a minister struggling against those who dance on the Sabbath: "if we speak against gaming, dancing, and other prophana-tions of the Lords day, then they imagine that we allow Christians no manner of recreation. If we preach against any sin that they vse, then we preach of malice and against them." "VII Sermon," in Burton, *Ten Sermons Vpon the First, Second, Third and Fourth Verses of the Sixt of Matthew Containing Diuerse Necessary and Profitable Treatises , Viz. a Preseruative against the Poyson of Vaine-Glory in the 1 & 2, the Reward of Sincerity in the 3, the Vncasing of the Hypocrite in the 4, 5 and 6, the Reward of Hypocrisie in the 7 and 8, an Admonition to Left-Handed Christians in the 9 and 10*, 205.

Women, Dance and Parish Religion in England, 1300–1640

appears throughout early modern parish records. Visitation records often contained a query regarding whether churchyards have been kept clean and protected from profane activities like dance. In one of many examples, 1610 visitation articles for the diocese of Ely repeatedly asked:

> whether hath there beene any fighting, chiding, brawling, or quarrelling, any playes, feasts, temporall Courts or Leets, lay Iuries, Musters, or other prophane vsage in your Church or Churchyard, any bels superstitiously run on holy days or their Eeues, or at any other time, without good cause allowed by the Minister and Churchwardens: haue any trees been felled in your churchyard and by whome.[15]

Parish and diocesan records contain numerous accounts of dancers brought up on charges for skipping church services to attend dances on the Sabbath, sometimes even going as far as claiming illness and then travelling to the next village to dance in an attempt at avoiding detection.

Other cases show that protecting the minister and his authority, not just the churchyard, remained a priority in the sixteenth and seventeenth centuries. Such cases, like the one brought against John Knock before the Waterbeach, Cambridgeshire, Diocesan Court in 1602, far more deliberately challenged ministerial authority. John Knock not only danced in the churchyard on the Sabbath, but also, when criticized for this by his minister, "put on a blacke gowne and follow[ed] [the minister], leaping, daunceing, and reioycing in the defaceing of the ministerye."[16] In a letter from a vicar from New Windsor, Berkshire, another minister's plea for legal protection from his dancing parishioners mirrors the frustration that led the priest in the tale of the Kölbigk dancers to curse the dancers to a year of endless dancing. Minister John Marten appeals to a Master Jones to be his protector and to lodge a series of complaints in court against Thomas Hall, churchwarden of New Windsor. Among these complaints is that on "Ascension last past, when one of the morrice dauncers had leaped & daunced in the face of the miniser standing in his owne doore; [Hall] did before a great number of people revile and abuse the minister with these reporthfull speaches like the morrice dauncers should dance before his doore and before his face in spite of him."[17] The image of a

---

[15] Diocese of Ely, 1610, Bishop Lancelot Andrewe's Visitation Articles STC 10196, p. 2. As transcribed in *REED Cambridgeshire*, ed. Geck with Brannen (forthcoming 2022). See also Winerock, "Churchyard Capers," 242–243.

[16] Waterbeach, 1602, Diocesan Court Proceedings CUL, EDR B/2/18 (Waterbeach fols. 174v, 175, 179), fol. 174v. As transcribed in *REED Cambridgeshire*, ed. Geck with Brannen.

[17] Windsor, 1620, Oxfordshire History Centre, MS Oxon. Archd. Papers, Oxon.c.174. Letter of John Marten to Master Jones, fol. 1–1v. As transcribed in *REED Berkshire*, ed. Alexandra Johnston (REED Online: 2018), https://ereed.library.utoronto.ca/collections/berks/.

Dance and Disrupting Sacred Time

group of Morris dancers spitefully dancing around the minister's house after the minister's rebuke mirrors the direct flaunting of ecclesiastical authority of the medieval carolers. Like in the medieval *exempla*, rejection of religious authority remains the underlying concern with authority and sacred space present in early modern sermons and parish negotiations about dance.[18]

Ultimately, the central issue in the tale of the cursed dancing carolers is the interruption of the priest's mass; similarly, interruption of preaching or services, either by riotous noise or by non-attendance, plays a key role in discussions about dance and sacrilegious Sabbath behavior in these early modern sermons. This issue appears long before Sabbatarianism began as a movement, with an early sermon by Cranmer articulating "how great a sinne it is, not to sanctifye the [Sabbath]." Cranmer argued that this sin is committed:

> when we vpon the holye dayes do not heare with greate diligence and reuerence, sermons and the most frutefull woorde of God, when we do not gyue our myndes to prayer, and other Godly workes, but to idleness, eating, drynkynge, bankettynge, dauncynge, lechery, dicing, cardynge, backebytynge, slaunderyng, and other vngodly workes. For the which abuse of holy daies God is grieuously prouoked and punisheth vs greuouslye with dyuerse kyndes of plages, but specially with need and pouertie.[19]

Cranmer's sermon connected dance on the holy days with disrespect for God, for which God delivers punishment – an interpretation that far more prosaically conveys the central ideas at the heart of the tale of the cursed dancing carolers. A translation of Heinrich Bullinger's sermons, published in 1577, built on the point that sacrilege is committed both by disruption and by failure to attend services:

> Here therfore a haue to reckon vp the abuses of the sabboth day, or yt sinnes committed against this commaundement. They transgresse this commaundement, yt cease not from euil works, but abuse ye sabboths rest, to the prouoking of fleshly pleasures. For they keep the sabboth to God, but work to ye deuil, in dicing, in drinking in dauncing, and feeding their humors wt the vanities of this world, wherby we are no only drawn from ye companie of ye holy congregation, but do also defile our bodyes, which we ought rather to sanctifie and keepe holy.[20]

---

18 A number of other examples of dance in churchyards appear in Emily Winerock's study of churchyard dance. See Winerock, "Churchyard Capers."

19 "The Thirde Sermon," in Thomas Cranmer, *Catechismus* ([Imprynted at London: In S. Jhones strete by Nycolas Hyll. for] Gwalter Lynne, [dwellyng on Somers kaye by Byllynges gate], 1548), fol. xxxv.r.

20 "Of the Fourth Precept," in Heinrich Bullinger, *Fiftie Godlie and Learned Sermons*

Women, Dance and Parish Religion in England, 1300–1640

Likewise, Robert Wilkinson's 1602 sermon declared that "the Saboth is a day of holy rest, not of vnholy ryot ... but this is our corruption of nature, euery idle sporte prouokes vs to sacriledge, to rob God of his glory in his saboth."[21] In a lived example of this sermon rhetoric, a lengthy testimony from a defendant from Goodrich, one Thomas Williams, drew parallels between his accuser's hatred of God and love of dancing: "for the hatred of the said William Phillpot beareth to the exercise of the word of God which he desireth not oneline to interrupte but to prophane with dauncing Drinkinge and other Idle magames."[22] In both sermon and court-case rhetoric, dancing on the Sabbath represented service to the devil and defiled the bodies of the dancers, again bringing this disruption of sacred time back into discussion with the destruction of sacred space and bodies. Thus, although Sabbatarianism in its specific Reformation permutation may have been a discussion that emerged from the sixteenth century, the ideas to which violations of the Sabbath with dance were connected – rejection of the authority of the church and neglect of the honor of God – appeared in medieval discussions of dance and sacrilege as well.

The theme of Sabbath dance as dancing to the devil appears throughout the early modern sermons surveyed for this chapter, in another continuity with medieval discussions of dance. In the thirteenth-century *Liber Exemplorum*, an English priest watching a group of men and women dancing was horrified to notice that devils are controlling the movements of the dancers, acting as their puppeteers.[23] Similar to medieval sermon tales, some early modern sermons described devils dancing for joy at the sinful dancing of men and women. In a discussion about devils leading men away from God, a 1562 sermon by Hugh Latimer stated: "if [we] could see them [the devils], we shold see them to hoppe and dance vpon our heads for gladnes, because they haue done vnto vs a mischief."[24] Working to the devil is a fairly common phrase, appearing in other sermons such as this one, also from Latimer:

(Imprinted at London: By [Henry Middleton for] Ralphe Newberrie, dwelling in Fleet-streate a little aboue the Conduite, 1577), 142.

[21] The "idle sports" condemned in this sermon include "piping and dauncing," and this condemnation of Sabbath sacrilege is framed as disruption of services through non-attendance: "If lawfull businesses may not hinder our comming to the Church of God, then much lesse may idle sports and vnlawfull games detaine vs: if bargaininge and wiuing may not excuse vs, much lesse will piping and dauncing." Robert Wilkinson, *A Ievvell for the Eare* (London: printed for T. Pavier, 1602), fol. B.v.r.

[22] Star Chamber Answer of Defendant, PRO, STAC 8/234/10/Item 9, transcribed in *REED Herefordshire, Worcestershire*, ed. Klausner, 80.

[23] Arcangeli, "Dance and Punishment," 37.

[24] "Third Sermon," in Hugh Latimer, *27 Sermons Preached by the Ryght Reuerende Father* (Imprinted at London: By Iohn Day, dwelling ouer Aldersgate. Cum gratia & priuilegio Regi[a]e Maiestatis, 1562), fol. 79r.

Dance and Disrupting Sacred Time

God seeth all the whole holye dayes, to be spent miserablye in dronkennes, in glossing, in strife, in enuye, in daunsing, dicing, ydelnes and glottonye. He seeth al this, and threateneth punishment for it. He seeith it, which neither is deceyued in seeing, nore deceyueth when he threateneth. Thus men serue the Diuel, for God is not thus serued, al be it ye say, ye serue god. No the diuel hath more seruice done vnto hum on one holy day, then on many working daies.[25]

The metaphor of dancing after one's pipes is likewise used to discuss the actions of those who refused to dance to Christ and instead danced to the devil. Early modern sermon authors turn this heavenly dance into a hellish one, with dancers following after the devil rather than after Christ. In contrast to medieval depictions of Christ as the leader of the dance, a 1570 sermon by John Foxe used the voice of Christ on the cross to condemn the devil as "the master of these reuels, the ringleader of this daunce, the captaine of this crew."[26] A 1612 sermon by Francis Rollenson, when discussing the wicked, exhorts listeners to "marke the end of these men: the *Diuell* is their musitian, and they daunce afer his pipe so long, that at length he ensnares them, and caries their soules along with him into the bottomlesse pit, and into vtter darkenesse, where there is nothing but weeping and gnashing of teeth."[27] The dances that the wicked perform after the devil's pipes were often very specifically described and connected to especially controversial dances of the day. Thomas Adams's 1614 sermon "The Sinners Passing-Bell," in describing the fate of those who reject Christ, claims that "you shall runne after vs, as the Hinde on the barren Mountaines: but then you may daunce without a Pipe, and leape *Leuolto's* in Hell, that haue daunced the Deuils *Measures* on Earth."[28] Joseph Hall's 1622 sermon describes the end of the wicked in vivid terms:

Surely o God thou hast set them in slippery places, and castest them downe to desolation: how suddenly are they perished, and horribly consumed! Woe is me, they doe but dance a Galliard ouer the mouth of hell, that seemes now couered ouer with the greene sods of pleasure; the higher they leape, the more desperate is their lighting: oh wofull, wofull condition of those godlesse men, yea those epicurean Porkets, whose belly is their god,

---

25 Ibid., fol. ii.r.

26 John Foxe, *A Sermon of Christ Crucified* (At London: Imprinted by Iohn Daye, ouer Aldersgate, 1570), fols. 44r–45v.

27 Francis Rollenson, *Twelue Prophetical Legacies* (London: Imprinted by T[homas] C[reede] for Arthur Iohnson, dwelling at the signe of the white horse, by the great north doore of Paules, 1612), 285.

28 "The Sinners Passing-Bell," in Thomas Adams, *The Deuills Banket* (London: Printed by Thomas Snodham for Ralph Mab, and are to be sold in Paules Churchyard, at the signe of the Grayhound, 1614), 253.

Women, Dance and Parish Religion in England, 1300–1640

whose heauen is their pleasure, whose cursed iollity is but a feeding vp to an eternal slaughter.[29]

These sermons describe, in details that make the dances (lavoltas and galliards) recognizable to a contemporary audience, a dance led by the devil, performed both on earth and in hell and leading to eternal damnation. While it is obvious that this is at least partially a metaphor, the repeated connection between dance and damnation and realistic details about contemporary dance performance solidified the idea of contemporary dance as transgressive in the minds of listeners.[30]

As repeated charges against parishioners dancing on the Sabbath show, the Sabbatarian rhetoric of the sermons increasingly shaped parish discipline and practice, with citations becoming more frequent in the late sixteenth and especially the seventeenth century. In the records from Sussex alone, for example, there are charges laid specifically against Sabbath dancers in 1599, 1602, 1607, 1610, 1620, and 1623, with twenty-five men and nine women cited for the offense.[31] Many of these citations are relatively straightforward: dancers are charged for missing service to dance, fined or excommunicated, and then the record moves on. Other cases, however, reveal more about the interplay between sermon rhetoric and parish practice, revealing what exactly was at stake in some of these parish debates about dance and Sabbath practice. A 1611 debate in Salisbury between the mayor and the Tailors' Guild over dancing days reveals that in parish practice, the reasons for concern with Sabbath dancing do not always align with theological frameworks about the nature of the Sabbath (for example, very few devils show up in parish records).

---

[29] Joseph Hall, *A Sermon Preached before His Majestie at His Court of Thebalds* (London: Printed by I. Haviland for N. Butter, 1622), 30–31.

[30] Calvin, *Sermons ... Vpon the Fifth Booke of Moses Called Deuteronomie*, fol. B.iiiij.v–r; "A Sermon wherein all Christians are exhorted to flie from outward Idolatrie," in Jean Calvin, *Foure Sermons of Maister Iohn Caluin* (Imprinted at London: [By Thomas Dawson] for Thomas Man, dwelling in Pater Noster Rowe, at the signe of the Talbot, 1579), fol. 13.r. Similarly, other sermons portray sacrilegious individuals or unbelievers as leading the dance into hell. One sermon bluntly states that "hell was not made for nothing. The vantguard of that accursed departing rabble, the ringleaders of the crew that dance to hell, are vnbeleeuers." See Adams, *Mystical Bedlam*, 41; another sermon seems to tie dancing after other men's pipes to improper understandings of God's teaching, the same form of sacrilege used to condemn those who justify the dances of their day with scripture: "Let vs pray God too giue vs wisedome and discretion: and also let vs giue diligent eare to his woord, as whiche is able to strengthen vs against all Satans illusions, and let vs no more be led to daunce after other mennes pypes, as S. Paul warneth vs in the end of this Epistle." Jean Calvin, *Sermons of M. Iohn Caluine Vpon the Epistle of Saincte Paule to the Galathians* (Imprinted at London: By [Henrie Bynneman, for] Lucas Harison and George Bishop, 1574), fol. 251r.

[31] *REED Sussex*, ed. Louis 10–11, 21–23, 25, 27–28, 36–37, 39, 180–181.

Dance and Disrupting Sacred Time

A letter dated June 23, 1610, was sent from the mayor to the wardens and elders of the Tailors' Guild, the guild that was most closely associated with the dancing days. The mayor's letter read as follows:

> Forasmuch as heretofore the Lordes Sabbaoth day hath bene prophaned by some ydell and evill disposed persones with the Morrys dauncers and druommeres from the churches and in tyme of prayers, yt is thought fitt the same shold end and be forborne. These are therefore nowe to entreate youe and also to require youe that youe forebeare further to prophane the sabbath day as heretofore youe have donne eyther with drommes or Morris dauncers other then in your owne private howse.[32]

This letter is striking in what it reveals about the practice of dance in early modern Salisbury. The sermons focus on dance as an issue of sacrilege in and of itself, regardless of where it is performed. In contrast, while the mayor's letter clearly expresses a concern with the profanation of the Sabbath, its concern is not the offense against God but a concern about civil order and about maintaining the decorum of services. In the context of early modern parish discipline, sacrilege had been expanded as an offense to encompass assaults against governing authorities, not just divine or ecclesiastical ones.

The response of the dancing tailors clearly indicates that they saw the debate with the mayor in similar terms, although the dancing tailors saw sacrilege as an offense entirely different from rebelling against governing authorities. When, on June 26, the mayor attempted to have the wardens punished and imprisoned for profaning the Sabbath by continuing to hold dances in line with their "ancient custom," the tailors answered that "if they had offended therein they weare sorye for yt, but (as they tooke yt) that if they had prophaned the Sabbaoth the punishment therof it did not belong vnto [the mayor]."[33] The mayor's rebuttal to this moves away from a grounding in civil authority to a grounding in religious authority: "and who are the best [to judge], can you judge who are best? I am sure no man but will allowe of yt if they consider thoroughlye of hit for it is abomynable before god. And hell gapes for such ydle and prophane fellowes as delyght in [dancing]."[34] When

---

[32] Sarum 1610–1611 Instructions of the Corporation of Tailors Touching Their Wardens' Imprisonment, TNA, SP/14/64, fols. 1–2, 13 January 1611/12 to 11 January 1612/13. As transcribed in *REED Salisbury*, ed. Douglas; forthcoming with *REED Wiltshire*, ed. Hays and McGee.

[33] Sarum 1610–1611 Instructions of the Corporation of Tailors Touching Their Wardens' Imprisonment, TNA, SP/14/64, fols. 1–2, 13 January 1611/12 to 11 January 1612/13. As transcribed in *REED Salisbury*, ed. Douglas; forthcoming with *REED Wiltshire*, ed. Hays and McGee.

[34] Sarum 1610–1611 Instructions of the Corporation of Tailors Touching Their Wardens' Imprisonment, TNA, SP/14/64, fols. 1–2, 13 January 1611/12 to 11

Women, Dance and Parish Religion in England, 1300–1640

the mayor's authority was challenged, he pulled in more general rhetoric against dance from the sermons to buttress his position.

Part of this tension between mayor and guild (carried into debates about parish life and religious observation) clearly comes from the shifting function of the parish in the sixteenth century.[35] As noted in Chapter 1, in the changes brought about by the Reformations, parishes handed over much of their authority over things like roads and infrastructure to government officials, ultimately ceding some of their influence. But at the same time, the close interplay between church and state in the English Reformations meant that sixteenth-century parishes were also more political in nature than previously.[36] In the case of Salisbury, prior to the Reformations, parish guilds and trade guilds collaborated in staging the festive life of the parish. The boundaries of the city's three parishes roughly corresponded with the boundaries of the city's three wards, and the parishes and wards were established contemporaneously in the thirteenth century. These parishes seem to have been relatively heterogeneous in population, with members of multiple trades in each parish and a wide variety of occupations in each ward. By the sixteenth and seventeenth centuries, these parish and trade guilds had become more exclusive (with fewer women and poorer members) and more closely aligned with the elite of the parish.[37] Salisbury's receipt of a royal charter of incorporation in 1612 brought about another shift in parish and municipal relations, marking a definite step in the erosion of the power of the bishop. As Audrey Douglas argues, the changes enforced on the parish in the Reformations meant that civic identity overtook parish identity in importance, and "by the end of the sixteenth century mayor and council had achieved de facto control in areas of taxation, musters, execution of royal writs, and regulation of city markets, as well as episodic connection with commissions of justice."[38] For those who

---

January 1612/13. As transcribed in *REED Salisbury*, ed. Douglas; forthcoming with *REED Wiltshire*, ed. Hays and McGee.

[35] For some of the studies on the structures and functions of the parish during this transitional period, see Katherine L. French, Gary G. Gibbs, and Beat A. Kümin, *The Parish in English Life, 1400–1600* (Manchester: Manchester University Press, 1997); C. Burgess, "Pre-Reformation Churchwardens' Accounts and Parish Government: Lessons from London and Bristol," *The English Historical Review* 117, no. 471 (2002): 306–332; Sylvia Gill, "'Of Honest Conversation and Competently Learned': The Dissolution of the Chantries (1548) and Chantry Priests of the East and West Midlands," *Midland History* 44, no. 2 (2019): 205–221.

[36] Craig, "Co-Operation and Initiatives."

[37] Audrey Douglas, "'Parish' and 'City' – A Shifting Identity: Salisbury 1440–1600," *Early Theatre* 6, no. 1 (2003): 67–70; for more on the overlap between civic and parish identity in terms of festive culture, see Ernst Gerhardt, "'We Pray You All … to Drink Ere Ye Pass': Bann Criers, Parish Players, and the Henrician Reformation in England's Southeast," *Early Theatre* 11, no. 2 (2008): 64–69.

[38] Douglas, "'Parish' and 'City' – A Shifting Identity," 68.

Dance and Disrupting Sacred Time

had had more influence and power under the older models of parish life, this shift in community and function came with tension. It is perhaps not surprising that against this backdrop, the liturgical activities that once helped create community within and among the city's parishes instead led to tension between guild and mayor.[39]

Keeping in mind this background of tension between parish and civic authorities as we consider the interplay between sermons and parish conflicts, the extreme rhetoric in these early modern sermons seems meant to establish a position of moral authority that could be used for dealing with actual dance practices that challenged either religious or civic authority, a change from medieval theological frameworks which expressed concern only with dance's violation of ecclesiastical authority. In these early modern texts, the unyielding language provided support for one's authority (whether sacred or secular) but was invoked only when needed. A black-and-white position on dance such as that presented in the sermons left little room for congregational argument, providing a firm foundation for ecclesiastical and civil authority within the parish. We see this in the case of the Tailors' Guild, where the dancers were charged not because of the action of dancing itself but because of the rejection of authority that this dancing represented. The initial concern was not their dancing per se, but their disruption of sacred and civil order; only once the dancers blatantly flaunted the mayor's authority did the mayor's responses present dance itself as an issue of sacrilege and sin. This parallels with the sermons, which present dance as sacrilegious flaunting of authority and as a sin that both men and women can commit – but as a sin that is graver when committed by women for the double flaunting of spiritual and patriarchal authority.

In the face of lessening influence, religious authors and parish officials doubled down on the authority they could preserve by heightening the gendered rhetoric around problematic behavior. In short, religious, civic, and parish officials emphasized patriarchal authority as a way to reconcile competing claims for authority and supremacy from both parish and city. The fact that the issue was not dance itself, but rather power and control of sacred space, helps explain the apparent bifurcation between preaching and practice regarding dance and early modern parish practices, in which dance often endured alongside vitriolic sermons. The medieval tension between preaching and practice carried into the early modern debates about dance in sacred spaces, as did the locus of concern regarding dance. Despite shifts in what was sacrilege and in what true belief meant, debates around *adiaphora* like dance did not significantly shift but continued to move forward along the same trajectory set in the wake of Fourth Lateran. But the changed context for

---

[39] For a fuller discussion of these changes, particularly in Salisbury, see Douglas, "'Parish' and 'City' – A Shifting Identity."

Women, Dance and Parish Religion in England, 1300–1640

the theological rhetoric about dance and sacrilege meant that the application of models of dance as gendered and sacrilegious shifted, pushing beyond limiting parish dance and aspiring to end danced parish festivities altogether.

GENDERED SACRILEGE AND SACRED TIME

The Tailors' Guild discussed in the preceding section gives an example of ecclesiastical concern about challenges to ministerial authority from the men of the parish. But what about the women of the parish, the figures most involved in the medieval parish lights and guilds that formed the center of medieval parish dance? Thus far, from the sermons quoted in this discussion of dance and sacrilege, the connections between dance and sacrilege in the early modern era do not appear to be gendered like their medieval counter-parts, either in practice or in discourse. However, a closer examination reveals that the gendering of sacrilege in sermons and didactic literature continued apace during the sixteenth and seventeenth centuries. Explicit connections between women and sacrilegious dance appear both in repeated narratives about Hebrew women and dancing on the Sabbath and in one other lengthy discussion on Sabbath-breaking as one of the sins of England, a Paul's Cross sermon from 1593:

> Prophanation of the Sabaoth is another of the euident sinnes of England. We are willed to hallow our Sabaoth … and yet in all places, and of the greater part of the people of this land, the sabaoth is prophaned with dauncing, stage-playing, bearbayting, bowling, and with all manner of abhominations. And not onely the holy word of God, but the ancient fathers and the ciuill Law doo speake of the sanctification of the sabaoth. *Augustine* on the 32 psal. saith, it is better to digge than to daunce on the sabaoth. *Chrisostome* in his 48. homily saith, where wanton dauncing is, there no doubt the diuell is present: for God hath giuen vs these members not to daunce, but that we should walke modestly, and not to daunce impudently after the manner of Camels (for not only women but Camels daunce vndecently) but that we should stand in the companie of the Angells: and if the bodie bee deformed by dauncing, how much more is the soule? in these daunces the diuell daunceth: with these daunces they are deceiued of the ministers of the diuell.[40]

The author highlighted women in this analysis of Sabbath breaking, dance, and the devil. He connected profanation of the Sabbath to sin, named dancing

---

40 Adam Hill, *The Crie of England A Sermon Preached at Paules Crosse in September 1593* (London: Printed by Ed. Allde, for B. Norton, 1595), 16–17; for the lengthiest discussion of Sabbath-breaking and dance (and one that connects Salome to the women who dance on the Sabbath in sixteenth-century England), see John Walsall, *A Sermon Preached at Pauls Crosse by Iohn Walsall* (At London: Printed [by Henrie Middleton] for G. Byshop, 1578), fols. C.iii.r–C.iiii.r; C.vi.r.

Dance and Disrupting Sacred Time

as one of the specific acts that profane the Sabbath, and then, after pulling in patristic authorities to buttress this point, turned from discussing actions to gendered bodies, focusing on women and the destruction of holy bodies through dance. Here, dance is yet again a representative sacrilegious action that connects first to women's bodies and then to sacrilegious and deformed bodies and souls.

Women also sat at the center of a discourse that used dance to highlight a different form of sacrilege, one focused on false worship rather than abuse of sacred space. Early modern passages connecting dance on Sundays to serving the devil portray dance as a transgression similar to witchcraft (a topic to which we shall turn later in this chapter) in that both actions violate sacred services, disrespect God, and provide service to the devil. In these passages, when sermons used the metaphor "dancing after one's pipes," the authors often specified that the dancers were sinful women. These women were either dancing before their conversion (and thus did not know any better) or were dancing after the devil, refusing to repent and follow the voice of Christ. These sinful women, described as "the devil's camels," seem to have replaced Jacques de Vitry's description of "the devil's cows." The ideological connection between women and sacrilege established in the medieval period did not disappear with the advent of the Reformations, but instead seemed to strengthen. The sermons present a clear, black-and-white discourse in which dance is sinful and the key concerns are violation of clerical authority and sacrilege, both concerns discussed as actions committed most frequently and most problematically by women.

So much for the dancing women in early modern sermons. But what about dancing women in the early modern parish? Turning to gender and parish dance practice, at least in some English parishes, dancing still appeared more frequently as an approved part of parish life than as a transgressive action – and when parishes sponsored the dances, the dancers were often women. "Dancing days," similar in nature to the "maidens' lights" explored by Katherine French, appear throughout the ecclesiastical accounts of English parishes, particularly in the south.[41] And as Audrey Douglas notes, these processional dancing days served an important role in creating communal identity, both within the parish and extending beyond the parish, in the case of Rogation and Whitsun processions:

> Procession was crucial in defining the identity and consciousness of each parish; at the same time it provided a periodic ritual renewal of relation-ships with neighbouring parishes. Rogation and Whitsun processions

---

[41] As Audrey Douglas notes in her article on parish dance and procession in Salisbury, "the term 'dancing day' … is found in a parish context as early as the fifteenth century." Douglas, "'Owre Thanssynge Day,'" 600. See also French, *Good Women of the Parish*.

Women, Dance and Parish Religion in England, 1300–1640

are particularly significant, since they move outside the home parish. As prescribed in the Sarum sources, the Rogation litany procession proceeds from a central urban location to celebrate mass in three different churches: on Monday the procession goes from the choir through the south door to a church in the city or suburb and back the same way; on Tuesday, exiting the cathedral by the same door, leaving the city by its west gate to perambulate its north side (presumably outside or near the wall) and visit another church, thence returning through the city's east gate; on Wednesday, leaving by the city's east gate to go round the south side, visit a third church, and return by the west gate. Obviously the details of the processions were necessarily adapted to topographical circumstance. Nevertheless, the model of urban perambulation and blessing, with celebration of mass at stations on the overall circuit, provided an encompassing ritual that linked parish with parish, church with city and suburb.[42]

Like the tailors' dance, these danced processionals highlighted the close link between parish and civic identity in Salisbury, and women played a key role in them. This role was not unique to Salisbury: for example, at Wells, near Croscombe in Somerset, women danced in the May games, at Whitsuntide, and in a wives' dance.[43] Parish and diocesan records show that these "dancing days," parish-sanctioned celebrations used to raise funds, occurred with regularity across southern England from the fourteenth to seventeenth centuries.

Salisbury makes an ideal location for a case study looking at these ongoing parish festivities and the relation of preaching to practice, for its records are unusually complete and replete with references to parish dances. The records of both the parishes of St. Edmund's and St. Thomas's contain references to a "dancing day," usually held around Whitsun. Occasionally "procession day" is used in conjunction with "dancing day," indicating that the dance was not a circular dance, like the caroles discussed in the previous chapter, but one that moved intentionally throughout the parishes and city. References to Whitsun dances continue in the records for a number of years after references to

---

[42] Douglas, "'Parish' and 'City' – A Shifting Identity," 70; see also Christopher Wordsworth, *Ceremonies and Processions of the Cathedral Church of Salisbury: Ed. from the 15. Century Ms. No. 148 with Add. from the Cathedral Records and Wood Cuts from the Sarum Processionale of 1502. By C[Hristopher] Wordsworth. [8 Microfiches, 90 x 120 Mm, Pos.-Zug: Interdocumentation Co. 1974* (Cambridge: Cambridge University Press, 1901), 172–174; Terence Bailey, *The Processions of Sarum and the Western Church* (Toronto: Pontifical Institute of Mediaeval Studies, 1971), 25–26.

[43] For descriptions of this, see James (James David) Stokes and Robert Joseph Alexander, *Somerset Including Bath 2: Editorial Apparatus – Records of Early English Drama* (University of Toronto Press, 1996), 480–481, 484, 616; James Stokes and Robert Joseph Alexander, *Somerset Including Bath 1: The Records – Records of Early English Drama* (University of Toronto Press, 1996), 352, 384.

Dance and Disrupting Sacred Time

Whitsun processions cease, indicating that as time passed, the dance, rather than the processional, became the focus. Both sermons and these dances were sponsored by the church – so what does the juxtaposition of preaching and practice reveal about gender and the regulation of sacred space and time in early modern England?

First, the dancing days were a frequent occurrence, connected both to the guilds and parishes of the town. The Tailors' Guild Assembly Book records payments for dancers and minstrels each summer around the feast of St. John the Baptist as early as 1443 and continuing until 1624. Account books from the Masters of the Fabric record payments to the "wives of the parish of St. Thomas" for dancing each year at Pentecost, from 1477 to the 1510s. And churchwardens' accounts from St. Thomas's, St. Martin's, and St. Edmund's all record payments collected from danced processions performed by women and by children and payments made to select individuals who accompanied the processions (such as bell ringers) from 1517 to 1606. This highlights the second point about these processions and dances: a variety of parishes and civic organizations were involved in their production, making them not an isolated aberration but a widespread part of ecclesiastical and civic life. Finally, the entries are increasingly specific in detailing who is being paid to dance: while initially the entries list "women, children, and servants" as the individuals paid to dance, by 1522 the records are increasingly explicit about the gender, marital status, and age of the dancers. As the 1522 account of the Masters of the Fabric on expenses at Pentecost records, the individuals paid for dancing were "wives, servant girls, daughters, and young boys."[44] In the inverse of what one might expect from early modern sermons, women were the preferred dancers in church-sanctioned dances. And, as the gendered rhetoric against dancing women in early modern sermons escalated, the parish and civic records increasingly highlight rather than obscure the fact that it is women who are dancing in their festivities. It would thus initially seem that the gendered rhetoric of the sermons had little impact on actual parish practice in early modern England.

While the sermons consider profane female bodies to be at the heart of the embodied offenses of sacrilege and Sabbath-breaking, dance practices present a very different reality. This represents another continuity with medieval approaches to sacrilege and Sabbath-breaking: a greater concern with the bodies of women encountering or abusing the sacred, whether that concern was warranted or proportional based on parish practices or not. Although the rhetoric presented in early modern English sermons provides a gendered binary for determining dance's acceptability, records of dance

---

[44] Sarum 1522–1523, Accounts of the Masters of the Fabric on Receipts from St. Thomas, DCA: Press II. Single Sheet. (Expenses at Pentecost, 29 May). As transcribed in *REED Salisbury*, ed. Douglas; forthcoming with *REED Wiltshire*, ed. Hays and McGee.

Women, Dance and Parish Religion in England, 1300–1640

practice complicate this picture. In cases where parishioners are charged for Sabbath dancing, usually, the groups of dancers are composed entirely of men. Although occasionally a few women will join in, these women are often identified as the wives of some of the dancing men. And as noted earlier when discussing cases from Sussex, the number of men charged for Sabbath dancing outnumbers the number of women charged, not just in Sussex but in the records from each region surveyed. None of the several hundred cases of Sabbath dancers examined for this book involve only women.[45]

Ultimately, the sermons' discourses about dance did impact the daily lives of women in English parishes. The fact that the dancers in the Whitsun processions were increasingly chosen along gendered lines indicates that the concerns about men and women dancing together that appear throughout sermons are still in play, as the records made it increasingly clear that in these processions, men and women were dancing not together but separately. And other later sources likewise show a clear concern with mixed dancing. A 1626 account of an outbreak of plague in Salisbury attributes it to a dance held by a mixed group in the churchyard during a rushbearing, another form of ritual festivity common in early modern England. John Ivie, the author of the source, notes that he saw four men and a woman dancing together "amongst the Graves, singing Hie for more shoulder-work in a fearful manner, and when they saw me, they ran away. Shortly after one of them died, which put me to much care for another, for then the Plague did much increase, and in that summer died nine rush bearers."[46] While it appears that many of the transgressive dancers in Salisbury were men, dances involving women, such as the one mentioned above, are presented as having more deadly consequences because of the gender of the dancers. At the same time that the gendered rhetoric in sermons reached its peak, the danced processions of women come to a stop, replaced by sources like this 1626 description of a dance-driven plague.

While the dancing days disappear in the records of Salisbury in 1610, it appears that the official end of the dancing days came in April 1624, with the issuance of a justices' order banning Whitsun dancing from the cathedral and its cloister.[47] The end of the dancing days coincided with an economic depression and with concerns about not only dance but also the disorder it promoted. So, in the end, the reasons for abolishing the danced processions echo the medieval campaign against dancing in churchyards. The rhetoric

---

[45] Winerock's study of churchyard dancing notes a similar trend; all the dancers in her case studies are men. She does not, however, explore the significance of this. See Winerock, "Churchyard Capers."

[46] Sarum, 1626–1627, John Ivie's "Declaration," WSA, G23/1/276. As transcribed in *REED Salisbury*, ed. Douglas; forthcoming with *REED Wiltshire*, ed. Hays and McGee.

[47] Douglas, "'Owre Thanssynge Day,'" 609.

Dance and Disrupting Sacred Time

used in sermons had become increasingly gendered between then and the seventeenth century. But the underlying concern with maintaining clerical authority over sacred space and time remained. Gender was used as another weapon in the war over spiritual authority, and while the gendered composition of problematic dancers in the parish never fully reflected the gendered rhetoric of the sermons, the gender of the dancers did appear to be a point of increasing concern.

Perhaps the dancing days came to an end partially because the gendered "logic" of the sermons influenced parish community and governance. In the hotly contested liturgical and theological debates of the English Reformations, dance (or the cessation of dance) became another means of determining and enforcing "true religious practice" and separating gendered bodies. The reality of who was actually dancing in early modern England meant that the discourse tying sacrilegious and sinful dance to female bodies ultimately made little sense. Yet the discourse persisted nonetheless, and with each reiteration became more entrenched. The changing positionality of women in the Reformations may have impacted views on virginity or on marriage, and legislative changes certainly removed the ritual identity given to female groups in pre-Reformation parish practice.[48] But the discourse about women as innately sacrilegious continued across the Reformation divide, deepening rather than disappearing or shifting.

GENDERING TRANSGRESSION

The deepening embodiment of transgression in late medieval discussions about dance and sacrilege easily transitioned into an early modern discussion about sacrilege, dance, and gender that did not appear in medieval texts. This discussion helped to drive the early modern witchcraft trials, as discourses about gendered and embodied sin intertwined with discourses about the devil, dance, and sacrilege. As scholars have noted, witchcraft as a female transgression was often tied to economic concerns or to concerns about widows or single women who did not fit neatly within Protestant ideas of a rightly ordered society.[49] These same economic and social concerns helped

---

[48] Douglas, "'Parish' and 'City' – A Shifting Identity," 74.

[49] There is an extensive body of literature on witches and witch hunts in early modern Europe. For a few particularly relevant examples, see Robin Briggs, *Witches and Neighbours: The Social and Cultural Context of European Witchcraft* (Oxford: Blackwell, 2002); Stuart Clark, *Thinking with Demons: The Idea of Witchcraft in Early Modern Europe* (Oxford: Oxford University Press, 2005); Lyndal Roper, *Oedipus and the Devil: Witchcraft, Sexuality, and Religion in Early Modern Europe* (New York: Routledge, 1994); Merry E. Wiesner, *Witchcraft in Early Modern Europe* (Boston: Houghton Mifflin, 2007); Kallestrup and Toivo (eds.), *Contesting Orthodoxy in Medieval and Early Modern Europe*.

Women, Dance and Parish Religion in England, 1300–1640

bring sanctioned dancing within English parishes to an end, laying out an early connection between the communal dynamics of dance controversies and witchcraft. Building on this connection, witchcraft accusations, like dance controversies, revealed much about community dynamics: in both situations, the accusers and accused often came from the same parish and had often been at odds for significant lengths of time prior to any formal charges being made.[50] Orna Darr's work on legal standards of proof for witchcraft reveals the "social embeddedness of evidentiary techniques," the various ways in which witchcraft narratives exposed "various social groups [with] diverse goals and interests"; the same could be said for the dance conflicts like those with the spiteful Morris dancers taunting their minister, discussed earlier in this chapter.[51] Additionally, Peter Elmer's recent work shows that witchcraft accusations were inextricable from political and ecclesiastical politics that shaped other aspects of parish reform, particularly in the seventeenth century.[52] Like debates about dance, concerns about witchcraft were embedded within local communities and contexts but spurred by a broad rhetoric about sacrilege, dangerous bodies, and gender.[53] As the parish became more and more intertwined with national politics, witchcraft polemics emphasized witchcraft as an act of political and religious sacrilege: to quote Elmer, "rebellion against God and monarch [were] one and the same."[54] Playing out within the parish, as did debates about festive culture and female interest groups, the parallels between concerns about dance and concerns about witchcraft helped associate female bodies with the practice of witchcraft, a ramification from this discourse about dance with dire consequences for women.

For, indeed, it was the early modern connections of witchcraft to sacrilege, dance, and women that helped to bind these transgressions together, both rhetorically and in early modern communities. As Brian Levack notes, while the *Malleus maleficarum* spends little time discussing witches and the details of their heretical worship, other sources reveal that one of the greatest concerns regarding witches was their sacrilegious worship in the witches' Sabbath, "which included both naked dancing and cannibalistic infanticide."[55] Much

---

[50] Orna Alyagon Darr, *Marks of an Absolute Witch: Evidentiary Dilemmas in Early Modern England* (Farnham: Ashgate, 2011), 10.

[51] Ibid. See especially Ch. 11, "Searching for Reliable Testimony," for evidence of how legal theorists recognized and dealt with communal dynamics.

[52] Peter Elmer, *Witchcraft, Witch-Hunting, and Politics in Early Modern England* (Oxford: Oxford University Press, 2016).

[53] For a consideration of masculinity and witchcraft, also grounded in communal concerns and anxieties, see Erika Gasser, *Vexed with Devils: Manhood and Witchcraft in Old and New England* (New York: New York University Press, 2017).

[54] Elmer, *Witchcraft, Witch-Hunting, and Politics in Early Modern England*, 5.

[55] Brian P. Levack, *The Witch-Hunt in Early Modern Europe*, 2nd edn. (London; New York: Longman, 1995), 40; see also Michael David Bailey, *Battling Demons:*

Dance and Disrupting Sacred Time

like witchcraft, dance had become an activity that was increasingly defined as sacrilegious in nature throughout the medieval period, especially when performed by women, the individuals considered most likely to engage in witchcraft or in dancing. Further reinforcing the growing connection between witchcraft and dance, the dancing cults and dancing mania of the fourteenth and fifteenth centuries paralleled the growth of witchcraft during the same time period; the dancers in the dancing mania outbreaks throughout Europe during this period often called out the names of demons as they danced, reinforcing the connection between dance, sacrilege, and the demonic.[56]

Medieval sermon tales like one found in the thirteenth-century *Liber Exemplorum* laid the early groundwork for the development of witches' dances and for the connections between women and witchcraft. The *Liber Exemplorum* conveys the story of women who, "according to the evil custom of the country, wanted to perform their lewd dances," and made a straw man with which to dance lustfully. As they called out to the doll, asking it to sing with them, "the devil, who had power over the wretched women, replied in a fearsome voice, saying 'I shall sing.' And immediately he shouted – not the doll, that is, but the devil within it – and gave forth such a dread noise that several of the women fell down dead."[57] Tales like this did not initially use the word "witchcraft" to describe the actions of the dancing women in the text. But as the associations between sacrilege, dance, and women grew in the late Middle Ages, a parallel discourse about witchcraft grew as well.

Given these long-standing connections between dance and the devil, connecting dance to witchcraft seems a logical move for medieval and early modern thinkers for whom witchcraft had become increasingly about devil worship and heresy rather than malevolent actions (*maleficia*). Keith Thomas has noted that the late Middle Ages saw the origin of the idea of witchcraft as identified primarily through the creation of "a deliberate pact with the Devil."[58] Michael David Bailey argues that medieval witches were "accused of worshiping demons, renouncing their faith, and surrendering themselves completely to the service of the devil," a theological position that derived both from clerical authorities and from popular conceptions of magic.[59] By 1487, the appearance of the *Malleus maleficarum*, a witch-hunting manual that

---

Witchcraft, Heresy, and Reform in the Late Middle Ages (University Park: Pennsylvania State University Press, 2003); Gary K. Waite, *Heresy, Magic and Witchcraft in Early Modern Europe* (London: Palgrave, 2003).

[56] See J. F. C. Hecker, *The Dancing Mania of the Middle Ages* (New York: B. Franklin, 1970); Jeffrey Burton Russell, *Witchcraft in the Middle Ages* (Ithaca, NY: Cornell University Press, 1972), 201.

[57] Jones, *Friars' Tales*, 138.

[58] Keith Thomas, *Religion and the Decline of Magic* (New York: Scribner, 1971), 438.

[59] Bailey, *Battling Demons*, 4.

Women, Dance and Parish Religion in England, 1300–1640

created an image of witches as idolaters and apostates, helped to cement the primacy of this definition of witchcraft.[60]

This concept of witchcraft as a pact with the devil defined early modern ideas of witchcraft as well. Although slower to reach England, by 1650 this idea of witchcraft was the predominant one in England.[61] The differing language between the 1563 *Act Against Conjurations, Enchantments, and Witchcrafts* and the 1603 *Act Against Conjuration, Witchcraft, and Dealing with Evil and Wicked Spirits* clearly illustrates this: the 1563 act is concerned primarily with punishing *maleficia*, while the 1603 act is concerned with not only *maleficia* but also the relationship between the witch and the devil. Under the 1603 act, witnesses to the witch's interactions with evil spirits (or a confession from the witch) were all that was required for conviction, whereas in the earlier act, proof of evil actions was necessary.[62] And, as this 1627 sermon by Isaac Bargrave makes clear, this sin of relationship with the devil was idolatry and sacrilege: "disobedience to God and his Deputes, though it proceed from weakenesse, is a sinne. But if it swell to stubbornnesse and rebellion, it is a great sinne; great as *Idolatry*, which is the *worst* kinde of sinne; great as Witch-craft (which in blessed King Iames his phrase) is the *worst* kinde of Idolatry."[63] The sins associated with dancing – rebellion, sacrilege, idolatry – are also the sins of witchcraft. The female sinners associated with dancing are also those associated with witchcraft.

Very few scholarly works mention dance as an important defining charac-teristic of witchcraft. Levack mentions the late sixteenth-century belief that witches, in their gatherings, would "dance naked, and engage in sexual

---

[60] Ibid., 30. For the actual text of the *Malleus maleficarum* (which does not mention dance), see Heinrich Institoris, Jakob Sprenger, and Christopher S. Mackay, *Malleus maleficarum* (Cambridge: Cambridge University Press, 2006); Ankarloo and Clark note that the *Malleus maleficarum* was initially published under the title *Malleus maleficarum*, then later changed to the gender-inclusive *Malleus malefi-corum*, changing the meaning of the title from "The Hammer of Women Who Commit Maleficia" to "The Hammer of Men and Women Who Commit Maleficia." See Karen Louise Jolly et al., *Witchcraft and Magic in Europe: The Middle Ages* (Philadelphia: University of Pennsylvania Press, 2002), 239.

[61] Thomas, *Religion and the Decline of Magic*, 438. With this shifting definition came increased difficulty in handling witch trials in accordance with English law. For a full discussion of this topic, see Darr, *Marks of an Absolute Witch*.

[62] Excerpts from the text of both these acts is found in Marion Gibson (ed.), *Witchcraft and Society in England and America, 1550–1750* (Ithaca, NY: Cornell University Press, 2003), 3–7. The 1603 act was the most recent English legislation regarding witchcraft at the time of the Salem witch trials.

[63] Isaac Bargrave, *A Sermon Preached before King Charles, March 27. 1627* (London: Printed by Iohn Legatt, for Peter Paxton, and are to be sold at his shop at the Angell in Pauls Church-yard, 1627), A3.

Dance and Disrupting Sacred Time

intercourse with the Devil and the other witches,"[64] and Kathryn Dickason's recent book notes in passing that by the sixteenth century some authors associated dance with witchcraft.[65] But it is important to note that, as the discourse connecting dance, sacrilege, and female sin deepened in the late medieval period, dance started to become an action used to identify witchcraft. Dance's appearance in witchcraft trials helps to support this argument for consistent connection of witches with dance in late medieval and early modern thought. A 1353 trial before the Inquisition at Toulouse condemned sixty-eight witches for magic and heresy, with specific charges detailing that these witches had, as Jeffrey Burton Russell puts it, "done acts of sorcery, danced in a magic circle, and parodied the ceremonies of the church ... This is the first report of a ritual dance at the witch assembly."[66] Johan Nider's 1431 text on Joan of Arc references how "some good men [have] been deceived by sorceresses or witches," and in describing how the deception took place, mentions how a "certain maiden ... danced in dances with men, and was so given to feasting and drink that she seemed altogether to pass the bounds of her sex."[67] This woman was described as a witch, who, through her dancing, "showed all men openly by what spirit she was led."[68] One examinant quoted in Thomas Potts's 1612 *The Wonderfull Discoverie of Witches* notes that while she saw the three accused women carried over the Ribble by a black creature, she was on the other side of the water, and thus did not "see them eat or dance," implying that a dance was somehow involved in the nocturnal activities of the accused witches.[69] The more that dance was described as sacrilegious, the more it was connected to witchcraft, and the more both transgressions were connected to the female body.

Accounts of witches' dances were not the only place where male authors connected dance, witchcraft, and transgression to the female body. Several early modern sermons also connect dance to witchcraft. One of these sermons by Thomas Adams started with a verse from Matthew commonly used to justify dance, but quickly moved from dance to hell to witchcraft:

> Christ saith to vs, as once to the Iewes; We haue piped vnto you, the sweet tunes of the Gospell, but ye would not daunce in obedience: time will come, you shall runne after vs, as the Hinde on the barren Moutaines: but then you

---

64 Levack, *The Witch-Hunt in Early Modern Europe*, 27.

65 Dickason, *Ringleaders of Redemption*, 47, 233–234.

66 Russell, *Witchcraft in the Middle Ages*, 184.

67 C. G. Coulton (ed.), *Life in the Middle Ages* (New York: Macmillan, 1910), vol. I, pp. 210–213.

68 Ibid.

69 Thomas Potts, "The Wonderfull Discoverie of Witches," in Marion Gibson, *Early Modern Witches Witchcraft Cases in Contemporary Writing* (New York: Taylor and Francis, 2000), 221.

Women, Dance and Parish Religion in England, 1300–1640

may daunce without a Pipe, and leape Leuolto's in Hell, that haue daunced the Deuils Measures on Earth. This is the time, you shall hardly lay the spirit of ruine, which your sinnes haue raised. This World is a Witch, Sinne her circle, Temptation her charme, Satan the Spirit coiured up.[70]

Adams's dancers, like the witches of early modern accounts, dance not after Christ but after the devil, not to heaven but to hell. And although much of the passage avoids gendered language, its conclusion is particularly striking. The only gendered language in the passage is gendered female and is used to describe the witch of the world (a fairly common metaphor in early modern sermons referencing witches). The witch of the world, in Adams's passage, is performing a circular dance similar to the carole, the dance medieval authors often connected to the devil: "a ring-dance is a circle at whose center is the devil, and everyone is turning perversely."[71] Other sermons made the connections between dance, women, idolatry, and witchcraft even more strongly:

The third abomination is greater, women weeping for that monster that Devill of lust, or that devill of Idolatry, women shamelesse Idolaters. The devill had no other engine in Paradise but the woman, shee was the wheele to turne about all the world. Ahabs Iezebell is his instrument to slay the Prophets, Herodias daughter to strike of Iohn Baptist his head ... whether it be that women by their nature are more flexible, or by law lesse lyable to punishment (though very many of them haue beene holte worth Saints and Martyrs of God), yet many haue beene most faithfull servants to their infernall Master, they be the loadstones and loadstars in all evil, the Iesuit not more serviceable to the Pope then Idolatrous women to the devill ... these women, those idolatrous witches, should openly, even at the doore of the house of the Lord, mourne for that monster, whether it were the God of their corporall, or spiritual filthines, for both be sworne sisters and inseparable associats.[72]

The gendering of the sins of dance and witchcraft in this passage proved resilient and widespread in the early modern era, as sermon authors frequently presented witchcraft, like dance, as a gendered sin. Of the 169 printed English

---

[70] From "The Sinners Passing-Bell," in Thomas Adams, *The Deuills Banket Described in Foure Sermons [Brace], 1. The Banket Propounded, Begunne, 2. The Second Seruice, 3. The Breaking vp of the Feast, 4. The Shot or Reckoning, [and] The Sinners Passing-Bell, Together with Phisicke from Heauen*, 253.

[71] Stevens, *Words and Music in the Middle Ages*, 161. This quote is from the transcription and translation in Lecoy de la Marche, *La Chaire francaise au Moyen Age* (Paris, 1886).

[72] Price, *Spirituall Odours to the Memory of Prince Henry in Foure of the Last Sermons Preached in St James after His Highnesse Death, the Last Being the Sermon before the Body, the Day before the Funerall. By Daniel Price Then Chaplaine in Attendance*, 21–22.

100

Dance and Disrupting Sacred Time

sermons from 1473 to 1640 that mention witches, around sixty of these refer specifically to the witch of Endor.[73] Furthermore, sermons often held female witches up as comparisons to holy men to make their points about sin and virtue. Richard Greenham's 1595 sermon provides one example:

> the worlde through the hatred it beareth to them [men of God], dealeth with them as it doth with Witches and Phisitions: the Witch though she fayle in twentie thinges, yet if she do some one thing aright, though it be but small, the worlde loueth and commendeth her for a good and a wyse woman: but the Phisitian, though he worke fiue hundred cures, yet yf through the waywardnes of his patient, or for the punishment of his patientes sinnes, he fayle but in one, that one fayle, doth more turne to his discredite, then his manifolde, goodly, and notable cures, do get him praise.[74]

The sermon's male author contrasts the female witch with the male physician, the woman following the devil with the man living earnestly after Christ.

To say that the late medieval connections between dance, sacrilege, and women directly led to the gender imbalance in early modern witchcraft accusations is oversimplistic. But as sermons like these make clear, preexisting connections between dance and women simply helped to bind one more transgression – that of witchcraft – to the female form and certainly influenced the political, economic, and social factors that played into witchcraft trials. The gender imbalance in early modern witchcraft trials came not just from economic or social concerns or from rhetoric about female sexuality, but from discourses spanning back centuries connecting women and their bodies to the devil and to sacrilege. Dance helped to entrench these discourses in the popular consciousness, with the height of England's witchcraft trials coinciding with the disappearance of dancing days and parish processions.[75]

It is not coincidental that tensions related to both these sacrilegious activities – dance and witchcraft – peaked at the same time and played out in the same communities. For witchcraft polemicists and reformers like John Jewel (1522–1571), all sacrilege, whether Catholic or demonic, was related. In this

---

73 Statistics drawn from an EEBO search, with "witch" as the full text keyword, and with parameters limited to sermons originating in England and in English printed between the dates given. Search conducted in August 2019. Variant forms and variant spellings included.

74 Richard Greenham, *Two Learned and Godly Sermons* (London: Printed by Gabriel Simson and William White, for William Iones, dwelling neare Holborne condite at the signe of the Gunne: where they are to be solde, 1595), A7v–A8r.

75 Elmer notes that "historians of English witchcraft, however, are generally agreed that an initial surge in prosecutions in the period from about 1580 to 1620 was followed by a lull in the 1630s, a further spike in the years of civil war, followed by a rapidly accelerating decline after 1660." See Elmer, *Witchcraft, Witch-Hunting, and Politics in Early Modern England*, 2–3.

Women, Dance and Parish Religion in England, 1300–1640

framework, witchcraft grew out of Catholic rites and practices like the dancing days and processional ceremonies that featured women so heavily. Thus, the debates over parish traditions, like those in Salisbury explored earlier in this chapter, often occurred concurrently with accusations of witchcraft. For example, an attempted exorcism and witchcraft accusations in the parish of West Ham in the 1620s focused on three women – yet this witchcraft scare erupted only at the end of a long decade in which Puritan, nonconformist, and conformist factions within the parish fought over the parish's traditions and festivities, including inappropriate Sabbath behavior.[76] Another case, that of Margaret Wiseman in 1592 in Essex, grew out of the frustration of a small group within the port borough of Maldon with the ardent reformers and Puritans within their community. In Maldon, home of noted Puritan author George Gifford (c. 1548–1600), accusations of magic against Wiseman and against Edmund Hunt (a leading figure of the anti-Puritan faction in Maldon) seem to have acted as outgrowths of bitter parish conflicts over traditional parish festivities.[77] Witchcraft accusations and trials, like debates about the Sabbath, took place in specific localized contexts and surrounded by unique parochial tensions and personalities.

Yet, in the case of witchcraft as in the case of dance, the localized contexts often mask broader and significant theological similarities. As many scholars have noted, no clear correlation exists between nonconformity, Puritan convictions, and witch trials. In fact, many of the trials from England took place in communities that were decidedly conforming, and both "Puritan" and "Anglican" parishes accused and tried witches.[78] The connection between presentations of dance and witchcraft in sermons helps explain this: reformers of all convictions carried the treatment of both dance and women as sacrilegious into early modern sermons, creating comparable treatments of witchcraft across theological divides. Dance was sacrilegious and associated with women, and witches committed sacrilege, danced, and were often female: these were "facts" on which early modern sermon authors agreed because, despite differences in opinion over parish festivities, liturgy, and theology, the foundational concern with sacrilege, dance, and women remained unchanging. Against this inherited medieval theological backdrop and early modern parish tensions over sacrilege, belief, and practice, it is no surprise then that dance, already a mark of the sacrilegious woman, also became a mark of the witch.

---

[76] Essex Record Office, D/AEA/27, fols. 217v, 303; D/AEA/29, fol. 76v. Cited from Elmer, *Witchcraft, Witch-Hunting, and Politics in Early Modern England*, 39.

[77] For the prosecutions, see Alan MacFarlane, *Witchcraft in Tudor and Stuart England* (Hoboken: Taylor and Francis, 2012), 154n, 284, 291, 297.

[78] Elmer, *Witchcraft, Witch-Hunting, and Politics in Early Modern England*, 34.

Dance and Disrupting Sacred Time

CONCLUSION

"S. Hierome in his commentary vpon the words of Ieremie, Chap. 22.3. Execute yee uidgement and righteousnesse, doe no violence, nor shed innocent blood in this place; saith expressely, that the putting to death of homicids, witches, sacrilegious persons, is not effusion of blood, but execution of right."[79] This early modern sermon reflects clearly that for women, the consequences of the connections between sacrilege and gender were very real. The discourse about women, witchcraft, and sacrilege led to the prosecution and deaths of those accused of these transgressions. Despite a lack of basis in reality, the rhetoric connecting primarily women to dance and then to witchcraft had very real consequences, consequences highlighted in the records of the witchcraft accusations and trials of the sixteenth and seventeenth centuries.[80]

While early modern dancers were not executed, parish and ecclesiastical court records show they did often incur fines and punishment for dancing deemed transgressive. And while the late medieval discourse about both women and dance as sacrilegious increasingly centered around female bodies rather than actions, within the parish, the bodies of the dancers themselves did not reflect this rhetoric, for the problematic dancing bodies were often those of men. The rhetoric about women, sacrilege, and dance was defined by a discourse driven by male fears rather than the reality of dance practices. In closely linking these transgressions together, a rubric for gendered transgression with little connection to actual events slowly developed. The *adiaphora* of dance seemed far less peripheral to the issue of sacrilege once it became associated with witchcraft, and the consequences for both dance and women were thus far more dire.

---

[79] John Boys, *Remaines of That Reverend and Famous Postiller* (London: Printed by Aug: Math[ewes]: for Humphrey Robinson and are to bee solde at the three Pidgeons in Paules Church-yard, 1631), 185.

[80] For one of many examples, see Michael MacDonald et al. (eds.), *Witchcraft and Hysteria in Elizabethan London: Edward Jorden and the Mary Glover Case* (New York: Routledge, 2013).

CHAPTER 4

"SATAN DANCED IN THE PERSON OF THE DAMSEL"

Through a fixation on sacrilege – on protecting sacred spaces and times from profane bodies – vernacular authors shifted the status of both women and dance within the late medieval and early modern parish. Dance and women were both reframed as sacrilegious threats to true belief. But how and when did sexuality become the primary focal point of concern, as it had by the late sixteenth century? For indeed, as vernacular authors connected dance more closely to female bodies, the sexual potential of those bodies became more important. This sexualization of dance took place, like the transformation of dance into sacrilege, gradually. Yet it is important to note that the sexualization of dance, while always a secondary concern for religious authors, became a primary concern only after dance had become clearly defined (like women) as sacrilegious. The transformation of dance into sacrilege started in the eleventh and twelfth centuries; the sexualization of dance in the English parish began in the thirteenth and fourteenth centuries.

Perhaps the clearest example of this transformation from sacrilege to sex appears in the reworking of Salome, the young dancing girl mentioned in the biblical accounts of the death of John the Baptist. Embedded into the gospel accounts of Matthew and Mark, this brief episode is perhaps the best-known biblical narrative associated with dance, both in the Middle Ages and in the present. In the narrative, King Herod has taken his brother's wife as his own, an action for which John the Baptist rebukes him, in accordance with Levitical law. For this, Herod and his wife Herodias have John the Baptist arrested and thrown into prison. While John the Baptist is imprisoned, Herod holds a feast (according to medieval interpreters, a birthday feast for himself) at which his young stepdaughter (traditionally referred to as Salome, although unnamed in the biblical text) dances before the guests. Herod is so well pleased with her dance that he makes an oath: to give Salome whatever she asks, up to half his kingdom. Salome consults with her mother Herodias, who urges her to ask for the head of John the Baptist. Salome does so, and Herod, bound by his hasty oath, regretfully beheads John the Baptist, delivering the head to the girl on a dish.

Modern audiences might be familiar with this tale from Oscar Wilde's one-act play *Salomé*, in which Salome attempts to seduce John the Baptist before performing a dance of the seven veils before Herod, or from Richard

Strauss's retelling of Wilde's play in his opera of the same name.[1] In these modern interpretations, Salome's sexuality is at the fore. Yet, medieval audiences encountered this tale quite differently; for medieval lay audiences, the dance of Salome would have been presented primarily in sermons, with an emphasis not on sex but instead on other sins: on oath taking, on birthdays, on rash speech, or on adultery. Despite the role a dancing woman played in bringing about the death of John the Baptist, medieval authors did not use this narrative solely to talk about dance or sinful women. Instead, medieval authors focused much of their rhetoric against the sins committed by Herod rather than by the women of the text.

Even more striking than this medieval lack of focus on dance in this particularly infamous account of a biblical dancer are the ways in which medieval authors adapted and revised patristic commentary on the biblical text. Initially, patristic comments used in interpretations of Salome's dance were both positive and negative, with varying potential elucidations. While, as Kathryn Dickason's work notes, Salome was never a completely positive *exemplum* for dance in patristic exegesis – unlike her counterpart, the dancing David – these early interpretations did leave space for a sacred Salome, a Salome who danced to exalt Christ rather than to kill a saint. Yet, patristic authors such as Origen and Pseudo-Jerome who had seen the possibility for a positive allegorical interpretation for Salome's role gradually disappeared from late medieval interpretations. Later medieval authors chose to set aside these patristic interpretations and to present a Salome who was much less nuanced and far more culpable for the death of the saint.[2] A study of twelfth- to fifteenth-century Latinate glosses, vernacular English sermons, and other vernacular didactic texts reveals that later medieval theological texts countered any mention of positive allegorical dance with an emphasis on literal interpretation of the narrative, highlighting the sinfulness of the dancing daughter. At least in medieval Latinate texts, both potential Salomes – holy and harlot – appeared side-by-side, albeit with an ever-increased emphasis on Salome as sinner in fourteenth-century texts. But the laity encountered only the sinful Salome, for in vernacular presentations of the dance of Salome aimed at lay audiences, nuances in presentation of dance and dancing women never really existed: none of the positive patristic allegories made their way

---

[1] See, for reference, Oscar Wilde and Aubrey Beardsley, *Salomé*, 2021; Richard Strauss et al., *Salome*, 2020, accessed June 4, 2021, www.naxosmusiclibrary.com; for recent studies of the modern Salome, see Petra Dierkes-Thrun, *Salome's Modernity: Oscar Wilde and the Aesthetics of Transgression* (Ann Arbor: University of Michigan Press, 2014); Clair Rowden, *Performing Salome, Revealing Stories* (New York: Routledge, 2016).

[2] Dickason's study of Latinate texts provides a good overview of this late medieval Salome as a *saltatrix criminis* (a female dancer of crime). Dickason, *Ringleaders of Redemption*, 40–48.

"Satan Danced in the Person of the Damsel"

into sermons for ordinary men and women. At the same time that allegorical interpretations of Salome disappeared from Latinate glosses, for those in the ordinary English parish, dance was presented not as a positive allegory for the Christian life or as a means of salvation, but as an act tied to literal sexual sin and death.

Consistency in the scriptural text itself between the tenth and fourteenth centuries indicates that the changes in interpretations of Salome were not driven by textual change or retranslation. These changing interpretations in glosses and then in sermons were instead driven by the same shifting approaches to dance and to women that led to increasingly gendered presentations of the tale of the cursed dancing carolers. As seen in Chapter 2, as dance became more closely tied to sacrilege, it became more closely entwined with sin. And as sacrilege became more closely secured to the female body, the associations between dance, sex, and women deepened and expanded.

These connections were not new. As shown through even the earliest interpretations of Salome's narrative, the connections between sex, women, and dance were an omnipresent threat in the minds of religious theologians and authors from the patristic era forward. Furthermore, the danger of sex lurked in the background of many discussions of medieval dance. But as the past two chapters have shown, and as thirteenth- and fourteenth-century vernacular English sermons on Salome show, sex was not the primary concern of most medieval authors writing for the laity, at least in discussions of dance. Only once sacrilege had been firmly connected to dance and, more significantly, to women did discussions of dance become more sexualized. As transgression became further tied to the female body in discussions of *adiaphora* like dance or gossip, dialogues about sins became more centered on the sexualized female body. The changes in Salome's story in the fourteenth and fifteenth centuries show this shift in focus from the sins of both men and women to the sins of women, from sacrilege to sex.

THE TALE

Before turning to the glosses and sermons, it is important to look at the biblical text from which all these sources drew, for although the text itself remained consistent, its lack of emphasis on either dance or gender is significant for understanding the extent to which medieval interpreters added their own concerns. Salome's story appears in Matthew 14:1–12 and Mark 6:17–29. These two accounts differed in length and detail, but on Salome's role they agreed: Salome danced before King Herod, and, bringing him pleasure, received a promise that she would be granted whatever she might ask. Prepared by her mother, she asked for the head of John the Baptist. Thus, John the Baptist was beheaded, and his head given to Salome.

However, the two accounts vary slightly in their presentation of certain details. Mark states that it was Herodias who desired John's death, writing in

Women, Dance and Parish Religion in England, 1300–1640

the Vulgate that "Herodias laid snares for him: and was desirous to put him to death, and could not. For Herod feared John, knowing him to be a just and holy man: and kept him, and when he heard him, did many things: and he heard him willingly."[3] Matthew's version omitted this interaction between Herod and John, as well as the role of Herodias, simply writing, "Herod had apprehended John and bound him, and put him into prison, because of Herodias, his brother's wife. For John said to him: it is not lawful for thee to have her. And having a mind to put him to death, he feared the people: because they esteemed him as a prophet."[4] Mark's text presents an expanded list of the audience for Herod's dance, specifying that the audience was composed of "the princes, and tribunes, and chief men of Galilee," while Matthew's account simply mentions a birthday feast.[5] Mark's version also contains a more expanded quotation of Herod's oath and an exchange between Herodias and her daughter, which Matthew abbreviates or simply alludes to. Both accounts, however, note that Salome's request saddened Herod and that he was forced to fulfill his oath because it had been made in front of an audience. The accounts end with the same event, delivered almost verbatim: "And he sent,

---

3   Swift Edgar (ed.), *The Vulgate Bible: Douay-Rheims Translation* (Cambridge, MA: Harvard University Press, 2010). Mark 6:17–28. "Ipse enim Herodes misit, ac tenuit Joannem, et vinxit eum in carcere propter Herodiadem uxorem Philippi fratris sui, quia duxerat eam. Dicebat enim Joannes Herodi: Non licet tibi habere uxorem fratris tui. Herodias autem insidiabatur illi: et volebat occidere eum, nec poterat. Herodes enim metuebat Joannem, sciens eum virum justum et sanctum: et custodiebat eum, et audito eo multa faciebat, et libenter eum audiebat. Et cum dies opportunus accidisset, Herodes natalis sui coenam fecit principibus, et tribunis, et primis Galilaeae: Cumque introisset filia ipsius Herodiadis, et saltasset, et placuisset Herodi, simulque recombentibus, rex ait puellae: Pete a me quod vis, et dabo tibi: Et juravit illi: Quia quidquid petieris dabo tibi, licet dimidium regni mei. Quae cum exisset, dixit matri suae: Quid petam? At illa dixit: Caput Joannis Baptistae. Cumque introisset statim cum festinatione ad regem, petivit dicens: Volo ut pronus des mihi in disco caput Joannis Baptistae. Et contristatus est rex: propter jusjurandum, et propter simul discumbentes, noluit eam contristare: Sed misso speculatore praecepit afferri caput ejus in disco. Et decollavit eum in carcere, Et attulit caput ejus in disco: et dedit illud puellae, et puella dedit matri suae."

4   Ibid., Matthew 14:1–11. "In illo tempore audivit Herodes tetrarcha fama Jesu: Et ait pueris suis: Hic est Joannes Baptista: ipse surrexit a mortuis, et ideo virtutes operantus in eo. Herodes enim tenuit Joannem, et alligavit eum: et posuit in carcerem propter Herodiadem uxorem fratris sui. Dicebat enim illi Joannes: Non licet tibi habere eam. Et volens illum occidere, timuit populum: quia sicut prophetam eum habebant. Die autem natalis Herois saltavit filia Herodiadis in medio, et placuit Herodi: Unde cum juramento pollicitus est ei dare quodcumque postulasset ab eo. At illa praemonita a matre sua: Da mihi, inquit, hic in disco caput Joannis Baptistae. Et contristatus est rex: propter juramentum autem, et eos qui pariter recumbebant, jussit dari. Misitque et decollavit Joannem in carcere. Et allatum est caput ejus in disco, et datum es puellae, et attulit matri suae."

5   Edgar, *Douay-Rheims Bible.*

"Satan Danced in the Person of the Damsel"

and beheaded John in the prison. And his head was brought in a dish: and it was given to the damsel, and she brought it to her mother."[6]

All the scriptural quotes from the previous paragraph come from the Vulgate, the standard Latin translation used by medieval theologians and in interpretive texts like the twelfth-century *Glossa Ordinaria*, described by Lesley Smith as "the ubiquitous text of the central Middle Ages."[7] Wycliffe's translation, produced during the fourteenth century, might have also impacted the preparation of sermons on Salome's dance. Wycliffe's version of the biblical text made very few changes to the Vulgate's syntax and wording, simply presenting a vernacular version of the text. Herodias's desire for John's death appears in Wycliffe's translation of Mark, which states that "Herodias ledie aspies to him: and wolde sle him and my3te not/ And heroude dredde Jon: and knewe him a iust man and hooly and kepte him/ And heroude herde him: and he dide many þingis and gladly herde him."[8] The Wycliffite translator's version of Herod's role as described in Matthew placed more blame on Herod than did the Vulgate text: "For heroude hadde holden Jon: and bounde him/ and he puttied him into prisoun. For Herodias the wijf of his brother for Jon seide to him/ It is not leeful to þee: to haue hir/ and he willynge to sle him dredde the puple: for þei hadden him as a prophete."[9] The same descriptions of the audience for Salome's dance appeared, with the slight addition of the location of her dance in Matthew, which states that she "daunside in the myddil" of the guests.[10] Again, in this translation, Mark presents more detailed information regarding the exchange between Herodias and Salome than did Matthew, along with a lengthier version of Herod's oath. The Wycliffite accounts end in almost the same manner as the Vulgate: "and he sente: and bihedide ion in the prisoun/and his heed was brou3t in a dische: and it was 3oue to the damesel/ and sche bare it to hir modir."[11] Echoes of the wording of both the Vulgate and the Wycliffite translation appear throughout late medieval sermons, indicating the degree to which medieval preachers were familiar with the actual scriptural narratives and the importance of these two translations in late medieval England.[12]

---

6   Edgar, *Douay-Rheims Bible.*

7   Lesley Smith, *The Glossa Ordinaria: The Making of a Medieval Bible Commentary* (Leiden: Brill, 2009), 1.

8   John Wycliffe, *King Henry's Bible: MS Bodley 277: The Revised Version of the Wyclif Bible*, ed. Conrad Lindberg, Acta Universitatis Stockholmiensis, Stockholm Studies in English 89 (Stockholm: Almqvist & Wiksell, 1999), vol. IV, pp. 81–82.

9   Ibid., vol. IV, p. 52.

10   Ibid.

11   Ibid.

12   These descriptions of Salome's dance would have been influential in late medieval England; Dove noted that around 250 manuscripts (or partial manuscripts) of the Wycliffite Bible survive, indicating its broad circulation and its popularity during

Women, Dance and Parish Religion in England, 1300–1640

Within these two gospel accounts of the events of John the Baptist's death, Salome and her dance made only a brief appearance.[13] Yet, the placement of her dance at the center of events made this narrative one that could be interpreted as a warning against dance more broadly. The role of the two women, Herodias and Salome, in the text likewise made it a tale that could be used to discuss the dangers of women in general. The scriptural tale itself did not emphasize the dance or the dancer and did not provide a clear moral lesson. Thus, interpretations of Salome's dance focus on providing a moral framework within which to fit the tale. It is in these interpretations that the tale starts to revolve first around sacrilege and then around sexualized female transgression.

INTERPRETING SALOME IN THE GLOSSES

Any study of the medieval interpretations of Salome must begin with the glosses, the collections of patristic and theological commentaries of the high and late Middle Ages, for it is in these texts that the foundations for medieval sermons were laid. While most ordinary English parish priests would not have access to the glosses, which were expensive Latinate texts and less likely to be owned by smaller rural parishes, those in larger parishes and the Augustinian canons or mendicants composing sermon cycles would have likely utilized the glosses in choosing which authorities to quote in their preaching.[14] Thus, considering the glosses as a first step in bridging the gap between the biblical

---

the fifteenth century. Mary Dove, *The First English Bible: The Text and Context of the Wycliffite Versions* (Cambridge: Cambridge University Press, 2007), 1.

[13] Margarita Stocker, "Short Story, Maximal Imbroglio: Salome Ancient and Modern," in *From the Margins 2: Women of the New Testament and Their Afterlives*, ed. Christine E. Joynes and Christopher Rowland (Sheffield: Phoenix Press, 2009), 176.

[14] The importance of glosses in sermon preparation is discussed by scholars such as Karlfried Froehlich and Smith. Froehlich asserted that the *Glossa's* importance to medieval preachers is "strikingly demonstrated by the privileged place it held in the circles of one of the great preaching orders of the Middle Ages, the Dominicans." Karlfried Froehlich, "The *Glossa Ordinaria* and Medieval Preaching," in *Biblical Interpretation from the Church Fathers to the Reformation*, ed. Karlfried Froehlich (Farnham: Ashgate Variorum, 2010), 7–8. More than 3,000 manuscripts of the *Glossa* survive, pointing to its wide circulation and use in the preparation of sermon cycles. Smith's discussion of *Glossa* manuscripts in English monastic libraries shows the *Glossa's* extensive influence. Smith, *The Glossa Ordinaria*, 170. Direct evidence from other sources used in sermon composition also demonstrates the *Glossa's* influence on vernacular preaching. For example, *The Golden Legend* quoted from the *Glossa Ordinaria* directly, introducing one of Jerome's comments on Herod and Herodias by stating "likewise, Jerome in the Gloss ...." Furthermore, this same saint's tale quoted Chyrsostom exactly as Aquinas quoted him. Jacobus, *The Golden Legend: Readings on the Saints* (Princeton: Princeton University Press, 2012), vol. 2, pp. 133–134.

"Satan Danced in the Person of the Damsel"

text and lay audiences helps us to see the intentionality with which sermon authors constructed their cycles for laity along with change over time in treatments of dance.

The most influential gloss that presented interpretations of Salome's dance was arguably the *Glossa Ordinaria*, a twelfth-century gloss on the whole of scripture composed by multiple authors that served, as Frans van Liere put it, as "the standard commentary to the entire biblical text."[15] The *Glossa* was not composed of original theological interpretations but "largely drew on patristic traditions, filtered through the Carolingian commentaries" formed in the eleventh and twelfth centuries.[16] A compilation and synthesis of patristic and early medieval interpretations, the *Glossa* reflected its compilers' opinions about how to interpret scripture in its multiple senses. Another gloss composed simultaneously with some of the sermons and lay texts about Salome was Thomas Aquinas's *Catena Aurea*, a text that drew heavily upon the *Glossa Ordinaria*.[17] A final scriptural commentary of great importance during this period is Nicholas of Lyra's fourteenth-century *Postilla literalis*, composed between 1322 and 1331 and widely circulated during the late medieval period.[18] These three texts give an idea of the most prevalent theological interpretations of Salome's dance during the late medieval period, albeit interpretations confined to a Latin-literate audience and thus likely inaccessible to the ordinary men and women of most English parishes. Yet, in their shifting choice of patristic commentators and interpretations, these texts show the growing connections between dance and sacrilege in the twelfth and thirteenth centuries that then shaped the thirteenth- and fourteenth-century sermons presented to laity. The glosses marked a first step in interpreting Salome's narrative for contemporary audiences and concerns, one that would ultimately shape the lived theology of the parish.

The glosses presented a more complex version of Salome than most current scholarship has acknowledged.[19] The *Glossa Ordinaria* presented several allegorical interpretations of Salome's dance in its commentary on Matthew 14 and Mark 6. Its commentary on Mark's version of the tale, the more detailed of the scriptural versions, presented an extended positive allegorical interpretation, attributed to Bede. This positive allegorical Salome featured prominently in the *Glossa's* interpretation of Mark 6. In fact, an

---

15 Frans van Liere, *An Introduction to the Medieval Bible* (Cambridge: Cambridge University Press, 2014), 153.

16 Ibid. For a more in-depth exploration of the history and contents of the *Glossa*, see Smith, *The Glossa Ordinaria*.

17 Froehlich, "The *Glossa Ordinaria* and Medieval Preaching," 2.

18 van Liere, *An Introduction to the Medieval Bible*, 166.

19 Dickason's discussion of Salome, for example, pays little attention to these more positively framed allegorical interpretations. Dickason, *Ringleaders of Redemption*, 40–48.

Women, Dance and Parish Religion in England, 1300–1640

allegorical exegesis in which Salome played a positive role composed the *Glossa's* entire comment on the Mark passage's version of Salome's dance. In the *Glossa*, Bede was quoted as stating that the "head of the law is Christ" and that this head "was given to a girl of the Gentiles, that is, the Roman Church. The girl gave it to her adulterous mother, that is the synagogue ..." Bede continued the analogy to discuss how the law was buried and Christ, having been given to the church, was placed on the altar and honored. The *Glossa's* Bede then moves into a discussion of how John pointed to Christ and to Christ's ultimate exultation, just as the head (Christ) was honored after the law (the body) was buried.[20] The *Glossa Ordinaria* also presented a briefer version of this positive allegorical interpretation of the text in its commentary on Matthew 14, noting that "the death of John signifies the end of the law" and the merit of Christ, "who is the finish of the law to everyone that believes."[21] The *Glossa* did present a brief version of a negative allegory of the Salome narrative towards the end of its comments on Matthew 14, in which "Herod symbolizes the Jewish people" and Salome represented pleasure as the daughter of unbelief.[22] Far from centering transgressive dance and sinful women, the *Glossa's* interpretations instead highlight a dancing woman as an allegory for Christ's true church.

The Salome of the *Glossa Ordinaria* fits with the early medieval approach to Salome and to dance more generally, as shown in earlier discussions of dancing saints and dancing piety.[23] William Chester Jordan points out that "the medieval Salome, in western (Latin) Christian interpretation, has two faces." While the first face was the one which appears in the tales of her death, that of "the seductive woman who leads men away from virtue and into vice," the second face was "allegorical and develops a radically contrasting image in which the girl ... personates the hope of Christian salvation."[24] Jordan argues that this allegorical interpretation was "far more widely adopted" than a literal reading of Salome's narrative and was made possible by the "head–body

---

[20] Fulgensis Strabus and Nicholas of Lyra, *Bibliorum sacrorum cum glossa ordinaria*, ed. Paul Burgensus et al. (Venice: [s.n.], 1603), 544. Accessed November 16, 2015, http://archive.org/details/bibliorumsacroru05strauoft. Translations from Latin my own.

[21] Ibid., 253.

[22] Ibid., 254.

[23] Ela Nutu, "Reading Salome: Caravaggio and the Gospel Narratives," in *From the Margins 2: Women of the New Testament and Their Afterlives* (Sheffield: Phoenix Press, 2009), 210.

[24] William Chester Jordan, "Salome in the Middle Ages," *Jewish History* 26, no. 1/2 (May 2012): 8. Jordan's article draws upon a number of Latin hymns, some of which support the positive allegorical Salome, but most of which contribute towards a negative image of Salome as a sexually immoral conspirator.

"Satan Danced in the Person of the Damsel"

dichotomy" that enabled an allegory of the division of two things.[25] However, Jordan does not note that most of the authors who propagated this allegorical interpretation in exegesis and hymns wrote during the ninth and tenth centuries, indicating that the popularity of the positive allegorical view peaked before the creation of most of the glosses.[26] As dance became increasingly associated with sacrilege in the years following Fourth Lateran, a dancer could no longer be used to create positive allegories for the church.

This shift is apparent in Thomas Aquinas's thirteenth-century *Catena Aurea*. From the composition of the *Glossa Ordinaria* in the eleventh and twelfth centuries to Aquinas's thirteenth-century *Catena Aurea*, the use of Salome as an allegory for the church had become increasingly difficult within the context of church concerns about protecting sacred space from the dangers of dancing women. Accordingly, Aquinas shortened the allegory and placed it at the very end of his comments on the Mark text, after he had already presented several less positive interpretations of the dance. Aquinas attributed the interpretation to Jerome and explained that Jerome wrote that "the head of the law, which is Christ, is cut off from his own body, that is, the Jewish people, and is given to a Gentile damsel, that is, the Roman Church, and the damsel gives it to her adulterous mother, that is, to the synagogue, who in the end will believe. The body of John is buried, his head is put in a dish; thus the human Letter is covered over, the Spirit is honoured, and received on the altar."[27] Thus, in line with growing concern about dance as sacrilege, Aquinas's thirteenth-century gloss somewhat begrudgingly presented the view of Salome as an allegory for the church. Aquinas's briefer use of this positive allegory, and Nicholas of Lyra's complete omission of it in his fourteenth-century text, reflected this shift. Between the *Glossa* and Nicholas's gloss, dance had become so associated with sacrilege that to use a dancer (especially a female dancer) as an allegory for the church no longer resonated with most audiences.

In Aquinas's and Nicholas of Lyra's texts, Salome typically represented either hedonistic pleasure or false understanding of scriptures – sins that parallel the increased connections being drawn during the thirteenth and fourteenth centuries between dance, sacrilege, and bodies. Nicholas presented another brief version of the negative allegorical interpretation found in the *Glossa*'s commentary on Matthew 14. Nicholas, however, placed this allegorical interpretation in his commentary on Mark 6, replacing the allegory

---

25 Ibid., 11.

26 Jordan does not make this distinction; however, the authors he uses to support this argument are Pseudo-Jerome, Otfrid of Weissenburg (8th century), Paschasius Radbertus (9th century), and an unnamed eighth-century Irish commentator. See ibid., 11–12.

27 Thomas Aquinas, *Catena Aurea: Commentary on the Four Gospels Collected out of the Works of the Fathers*, ed. John Henry Newman and Aidan Nichols (London: Saint Austin Press, 1997), vol. 2, p. 118.

Women, Dance and Parish Religion in England, 1300–1640

of Salome as the true church with one in which Herodias "signifies luxury" and the "dancing girl signifies dissolute pleasure."[28] Aquinas left the interpretation in its original location in Matthew, expanding the commentary to give the fullest explanation of this allegory in which Salome symbolizes not a positive allegorical figure but a negative one. Aquinas quoted Hilary as stating:

> Mystically, John represents the Law; for the Law preached Christ, and John came of the Law, preaching Christ out of the Law. Herod is the Prince of the people, and the Prince of the people bears the name and the cause of the whole body put under him. John then warned Herod that he should not take to him his brother's wife. For there are and there were two people, of the circumcision, and of the Gentiles; and these are brethren ... the Law warned Israel that he should not take to him the works of the Gentiles and unbelief which was united to them as by the bond of conjugal love.[29]

Even in his treatment of Herod and John the Baptist, Aquinas showed how this narrative was gendered differently in this allegorical reading: two men played positive roles in the allegory, with Herod representing Israel. To be clear, Israel often strayed from righteousness throughout the scriptural narrative, but was nonetheless meant to be a righteous and godly character. Returning to the *Catena Aurea*, the very different treatment of the women in the narrative becomes apparent:

> On the birthday, that is amidst the enjoyments of the things of the body, the daughter of Herodias danced; for pleasure, as it were springing from unbelief, was carried in its alluring course throughout the whole of Israel, and the nation bound itself thereto as by an oath, for sin and worldly pleasures the Israelites sold the gifts of eternal life. She (Pleasure) at the suggestion of her mother Unbelief, begged that there should be given her the head of John, that is, the glory of the law ... so among the other gratifications of a debauched people the head of John is brought in in a dish, that is by the loss of the Law, the pleasures of the body, and worldly luxury is increased.[30]

The women (Herodias and Salome) represented transgression and sin, pleasure and unbelief respectively. This allegory in which Salome represented pleasure rather than the Latin Church connected more directly to ideas of dance as a sinful, sacrilegious, and sexual pursuit. This specific allegorical exegesis appeared in various forms in the *Glossa*, in Aquinas's *Catena Aurea*, and in Nicholas of Lyra's *Postilla literalis*, indicating that this gendered

---

[28] Strabus and Nicholas of Lyra, *Bibliorum sacrorum cum glossa ordinaria*, 544.

[29] Aquinas, *Catena Aurea*, vol. 1, pp. 528–529.

[30] Ibid.

"Satan Danced in the Person of the Damsel"

allegorical interpretation was the most prevalent negative allegorical interpretation of Salome.

But this was not the only negative allegorical interpretation of Salome's dance gaining prominence in the thirteenth century. Aquinas presented yet another interpretation of Salome's dance, attributed to Theophyl, in his commentary on Mark 6:

> In a mystical way, however, Herod, whose name means 'of skin' is the people of the Jews, and the wife to whom he was wedded means vain glory, whose daughter even now encircles the Jews with her dance, namely, a false understanding of the Scriptures; they indeed beheaded John, that is, the word of prophecy, and hold to him without Christ, his head.[31]

Aquinas's presentation of multiple negative allegorical interpretations of Salome highlights the change in late medieval approaches to dance, from a positive act that could represent worship or a holy performance to a highly transgressive action. And as these texts minimized or erased dance's sacred potential, they also started to blur the lines separating the dancer from the dance. Salome and Salome's body started to become the focus of the tale.

This focus on Salome as a transgressive figure was not confined to an allegorical sense. Although discussions of Salome as a transgressive figure in a literal sense do not appear within the *Glossa*, both Nicholas of Lyra and Aquinas treated Salome as a figure who demonstrated real individual transgressions as well. Nicholas remarked in his commentary on Matthew 14 that John was beheaded "at the petition of a dancer and the admonishment of her adulterous mother," placing the direct blame for John's death squarely on the women in the text.[32] However, he then noted that it was not probable that "it was for the dance of one girl" that Herod had made such an oath, and concluded that a desire for the death of John, not the dance, explained Herod's promise.[33] His commentary on Mark 6 also stated this view, noting that Herod used the girl's dancing as an excuse but also pointing out that her petition was vital to securing John's death without sparking political uprising.[34] While the body of the dancing girl bore the brunt of the blame for the death of the saint, the male actors in the tale were not yet absolved of blame or agency as they would be in early modern interpretations of Salome.

Aquinas's treatment of Salome was ultimately much less generous than Nicholas's, in which Herod received some of the blame. Aquinas quoted Remigius's comments to highlight for his reader Salome's sexual transgressiveness: "It should be known that it is customary not for rich only but for

---

[31] Aquinas, *Catena Aurea*, vol. 2, p. 118.
[32] Strabus and Nicholas of Lyra, *Bibliorum sacrorum cum glossa ordinaria*, 252.
[33] Ibid., 254.
[34] Ibid., 544.

Women, Dance and Parish Religion in England, 1300–1640

poor mothers also, to educate their daughters so chastely, that they are scarce so much as seen by strangers. But this unchaste woman had so brought up her daughter after the same manner, that she had taught her not chastity but dancing."[35] Dancing as the opposite of chastity: the sexualization of dance and dancers could not be much clearer. In his commentary on Matthew 14, he also included Jerome's description of Salome's request for the head of John as "a reward of blood worthy of the deed of the dancing," and gave Chrysostom's analysis of her petition: "Here is a twofold accusation against the damsel, that she danced, and that she chose to ask an execution as her reward."[36] Through choosing to quote both these patristic authors, Aquinas hammered home to his reader his point that dancing represented sin in not only an allegorical sense but also a literal sense. In Aquinas's gloss on Matthew, dance was connected to a sexually promiscuous damsel and to death, implicating both dance and the dancer as deeply transgressive and culpable for the death of the saint. Perhaps the most damning comment on Salome came yet again from Aquinas in his gloss of Mark 6, drawing upon Theophyl: "For during the banquet, Satan danced in the person of the damsel, and the wicked oath is completed."[37] Treatments of Salome as a literal figure factored little in the *Glossa's* study of the text yet dominated Aquinas's and Nicholas of Lyra's commentaries, indicating that theologically at least, dance by women had become a transgressive activity connected to sexual sin and sacrilege.

It is important to note here that this exclusively negative rhetorical portrayal of women's dance was not the only theologically viable option in the fourteenth century, particularly when considering lived piety alongside written theology. The parish dance practices noted in previous chapters involved large groups of women, and even English parish festivities centered on St. John the Baptist's nativity involved large numbers of female dancers.[38] Dance served as a form of devotion in multiple late medieval convents, with groups of nuns dancing along to the psalms in imitation of David's example (although in late medieval England this dancing was strictly confined to the cloister and had been prohibited entirely by the fifteenth century).[39] And

---

[35] Aquinas, *Catena Aurea*, vol. 1, p. 526.

[36] Ibid., vol. 1, p. 526.

[37] Ibid., vol. 2, p. 116.

[38] Kathryn A. Smith, "'A Lanterne of Lyght to the People': English Narrative Alabaster Images of John the Baptist in Their Visual, Religious, and Social Contexts," *Studies in Iconography* 42 (2021): 90–91; Pamela Allen Brown and Peter Parolin (eds.), *Women Players in England 1500–1660: Beyond the All-Male Stage* (Farnham: Ashgate, 2008), 30; H. F. Westlake, *The Parish Gilds of Mediæval England* (New York: Macmillan, 1919), 55; Andrew Prescott, "Men and Women in the Guild Returns," in *Gender and Fraternal Orders in Europe, 1300–2000*, ed. Máire Cross (Basingstoke: Palgrave Macmillan, 2010), 44.

[39] Kathryn Emily Dickason, "King David in the Medieval Archives," in *Futures of*

"Satan Danced in the Person of the Damsel"

on the continent, many of the fourteenth-century female mystics danced as a mark of their holiness.[40] Yet, when the dancer is a solitary one, in an English context, we see none of the holy dancing mystics of the continent. Solitary dancing women in fourteenth-century England were, like the Salome of Nicholas of Lyra's fourteenth-century gloss, problematic figures. English bishops and authors drew a firm line between communal dance under proper ecclesiastical supervision and solitary dancing women. Furthermore, sermon authors did not connect the presence of communal female dance in the English parish with any positive scriptural exemplars for dance, whether the allegorically sacred Salome, Miriam and her dancing women from Exodus, or the dancing King David.[41]

In fact, the sacred dances of Miriam and David make no appearances in vernacular English sermons. It was the fourteenth-century Salome, a solitary sexually transgressive dancing damsel, who featured most prominently in late medieval art, vernacular sermons, and theological commentary. Clerics treated her dance as a specific incident from the past that served as a general warning against dance, with no attempt to connect her dance to more specific late medieval rituals or activities.[42] While the Salome of the glosses, with her holy allegorical potential held in tension with transgressive action, gradually evolved in response to changing medieval approaches to dance, sacred space, and gender, this evolution may not have been apparent to the laity. The reforms and concerns of the thirteenth and fourteenth centuries shaped what material the glosses emphasized and likewise molded what made it from the glosses to

---

    Dance Studies, ed. Susan Manning, Janice Ross, and Rebecca Schneider (Madison: University of Wisconsin Press, 2020), 39; for an example of dancing English nuns and the careful restriction of their practices in the fifteenth century, see *REED Herefordshire, Worcestershire*, ed. Klausner, xliv, 88, 188, 355.

40 See Ch. 5, "Partnering Divinity: Mystical Dancers," in Dickason, *Ringleaders of Redemption*, 141–173.

41 Jansen notes that Mary Magdalen was also associated with dance in some contexts; see Katherine Ludwig Jansen, *The Making of the Magdalen: Preaching and Popular Devotion in the Later Middle Ages* (Princeton: Princeton University Press, 2000), 158.

42 For more on Salome in other sources in the medieval period, see Diane Apostolos-Cappadona, "Imagining Salome, or How La Sauterelle Became La Femme Fatale," in *From the Margins 2: Women of the New Testament and Their Afterlives*, ed. Christine E. Joynes and Christopher Rowland (Sheffield: Phoenix Press, 2009), 190–209; Stocker, "Short Story, Maximal Imbroglio: Salome Ancient and Modern"; Barbara Baert, *Revisiting Salome's Dance in Medieval and Early Modern Iconology* (Leuven: Peeters, 2016); Jane C. Long, "Dangerous Women: Observations on the Feast of Herod in Florentine Art of the Early Renaissance," *Renaissance Quarterly* 66, no. 4 (2013): 1153–1205; Willard Bohn, "Apollinaire, Salome and the Dance of Death," *French Studies* 57, no. 4 (2003): 491–500; Christiane Klapisch-Zuber and Susan Emanuel, "Salome's Dance," *Clio: Women, Gender, History*, no. 46 (2017): 186–197.

Women, Dance and Parish Religion in England, 1300–1640

vernacular sermons. And in line with the distinctions made between clergy and laity in regard to dancing during mass or as part of Easter services noted in Chapter 2, the Salome presented to ordinary men and women looked quite different from the tenth-century Latinate radiant representation of the true church. The Salome of medieval sermons instead bore a much stronger resemblance to the demon-possessed damsel mentioned in Aquinas and to the women caroling with devils in other medieval sermon tales, as her sacrilege in killing a saint led into her sexualization.

TEACHING SALOME FROM THE PULPIT

The Salome of the late Middle Ages was slowly dancing her way from saint to sinner, at least in the allegorical Latinate texts circulating among clergy and educated nobility. But how would her dance have appeared to laity in a late medieval English parish? Would it have appeared? The answer to the second question is simple: yes. As a part of an important saint's *vita* and as part of the gospel texts, the narrative of Salome's dance appeared frequently in sermon cycles based upon the liturgical calendar. The third Sunday of Advent, the Decollation of St. John the Baptist (August 29), and the Nativity of St. John the Baptist (June 24) were the occasions on which this narrative was most frequently preached. Furthermore, sermons would not have been the only context in which medieval laity encountered John the Baptist's martyrdom. Church art frequently depicted the event. As Kathryn Smith shows, in England, "altarpieces and individual narrative reliefs devoted to the Baptist appear to have outnumbered those associated with every other saint save the tremendously popular Catherine of Alexandria."[43] St. John's heads, reliefs depicting the Baptist's head on a dish or a plate, were a common and relatively inexpensive form of decoration, bringing to mind the martyrdom of the saint wherever they were displayed, often in the home.[44] Katherine French records, in just one of many examples of this practice, that a Southwark tailor kept a St. John's head by his bed.[45] Some churches even had St. John's heads incense

---

[43] Smith, "'A Lanterne of Lyght to the People,'" 61; Francis W. Cheetham, *Alabaster Images of Medieval England* (Woodbridge: Boydell Press, 2003), 46–52.

[44] For more on St. John's heads, see Francis W. Cheetham, *English Medieval Alabasters, with a Catalogue of the Collection in the Victoria and Albert Museum* (Oxford: Phaidon-Christie's, 1984); Paul Williamson and Fergus Cannan, *Object of Devotion: Medieval English Alabaster Sculpture from the Victoria and Albert Museum* (London: Art Services International, 2011); Barbara Baert and Sophia Rochmes (eds.), *Decapitation and Sacrifice: Saint John's Head in Interdisciplinary Perspectives: Text, Object, Medium* (Leuven: Peeters, 2017); Smith, "'A Lanterne of Lyght to the People.'"

[45] My thanks to Katherine French for letting me consult a pre-publication version of Ch. 7 for this reference and for her broader discussion of St. John's heads.

"Satan Danced in the Person of the Damsel"

burners, a visceral reminder of the saint's martyrdom interwoven within the practice of the mass.[46]

Perhaps most significantly, the feast of John the Baptist's birth, falling as it did near Midsummer's Eve, represented one of the peaks of parish festivity. In most English parishes, June 24 was surrounded with about ten days of bonfires, dances, and other parish festivities. The visual reminder of the saint's martyrdom continued in these festivities, as processional banners for the midsummer celebrations often featured images of John's head on a platter similar to the St. John's heads of the domestic sphere.[47] As one example from the records of the Guild of St. John Baptist in Baston, Lincolnshire, shows, this celebration was not considered optional. Records from 1388–1389 indicate that "(it was decided) that all the sisters of the said brotherhood, or someone in their name, shall come on St. John the Baptist's Day to dance with their sisters under pain of one measure of barley" and that "all the sisters of the aforesaid guild shall be present at vespers and at matins on St. John the Baptist's Eve carrying the light in their hands and also dancing on (St. John the Baptist's) Day, unless they are so old or in ill health or on pilgrimage or have been excused by the brotherhood for business of some kind, on pain of one measure of barley."[48] The 1443 Tailors' Guild Assembly Minute Book from Salisbury likewise provides a lengthy list of instructions for observing St. John's Day, with a procession, several masses, lights, a feast, and specified roles for men and women of the parish, with fines for non-participation.[49] In English parishes, John the Baptist's association with light, the burning of his

---

Katherine L. French, *Household Goods and Good Households in Late Medieval London: Consumption and Domesticity after the Plague* (Philadelphia: University of Pennsylvania Press, 2021), 193; 193–209.

[46] I am thankful to Taylor A. Sims for this reference. She told me of the existence of such an incense burner in Reading, mentioned as an item for repair in the Reading St. Laurence churchwardens' accounts, MS fol. 161. She uncovered this specific St. John's Head in work for her forthcoming doctoral dissertation, "Everyday Women and the English Reformation: Gender and Religion in the Diocese of Salisbury, 1450–1600" (University of Michigan).

[47] French, *Household Goods and Good Households*, 203–204.

[48] Baston 1388/1389, *Certificate of the Guild of St John Baptist*, TNA, PRO C/47/39/76, single sheet. As transcribed and recorded in *Records of Early English Drama: Lincolnshire*, ed. James Stokes, 2 vols. (Toronto: University of Toronto Press, 2009). Original Latin text: "tripidiare cum sororibus suis sub pena vnius modij ordei" and "Item quod omnes sorores predicte Gilde intersint versperis & ad matutinas in vigilia sancti Iohannis Baptiste lumen in manibus portantes aceciam in die tripidi-antes nisi sint ad talem senectutem redacte vel in infirmitate vel peregrinacione aut negocio aliquali fuerint per fraternitatem excusate sub pena vnius chori ordei" on 24–25; translation from 619.

[49] Sarum 1443 Tailors' Guild Assembly Minute Book, WSA, G23/1/251, 10 July Rules, Ordinances, and Constitutions, fols. 3–4v; see also Sarum 1477 Tailors' Guild Act and Memoranda Book, WSA, G32/1/250, fols. 0v–10*, 15 August. Both records

Women, Dance and Parish Religion in England, 1300–1640

bones, and the role of dance in his *vita* all played a role in parish observation of his saint's day.[50] In short, medieval audiences were intimately familiar with the way in which John the Baptist met his death at the hands of Herod, Herodias, and the unnamed daughter, a familiarity obtained through art, performance, and literary texts.

Several of these practices – like parish dances or St. John's heads – indicate a clear connection in lay theology between dance and narratives about John the Baptist. Yet, these parish practices leave little evidence to help interpret what meaning they held for laity. Sermons give the clearest indication as to what meaning religious figures wanted their parishioners to associate with the dance of Salome and with John the Baptist and provide valuable insight into what associations English laity may have used to understand Salome's dance. No late medieval vernacular sermons mention Salome by name, referring to her instead as a girl, wench, or maid. But a number of vernacular sermons mention her dance, always in conjunction with her mother Herodias and within the broader narrative surrounding her dance. The *Repertorium* mentions nine prose sermons that contain Herodias's name. These are the only English vernacular prose sermons that discuss the death of John the Baptist in any detail; they are found in sermon collections, specifically *Speculum Sacerdotale*, John Mirk's *Festial*, and the Wycliffite sermons. Verse sermons from the *Northern Homily Cycle*, from the *Manuel des péchés*, and from Robert Mannyng of Brunne's *Handlyng Synne* also present a version of Salome's dance. These sermons, along with the version of Salome's dance presented in the *Golden Legend*, a key reference text used in the composition of medieval sermons, form the basis of this analysis of medieval portrayals of Salome in texts aimed at the laity.[51] The medieval sermons span the period from the thirteenth century to the late fifteenth century, with the *Golden Legend* dating to the same time as the *Mirror* (Bodl. MS Holkham 40), and Mirk's *Festial* emerging simultaneously with the earliest of the other prose sermon texts.[52]

---

   transcribed and recorded in *REED Salisbury*, ed. Douglas; forthcoming with *REED Wiltshire*, ed. Hays and McGee.

[50] See R. T. Hampson, *Medii Ævi Kalendarium; or, Dates, Charters, and Customs of the Middle Ages, with Kalendars from the Tenth to the Fifteenth Century; and an Alphabetical Digest of Obsolete Names of Days: Forming a Glossary of the Dates of the Middle Ages* (London: Henry Kent Causton, 1841), vol. 1, pp. 299–305.

[51] Parts of the narrative contained in Matthew 14:1–12 and Mark 6:14–29 are referenced in four other prose sermons, according to the *Repertorium*. However, these sermons all referenced either Herod's unlawful taking of his brother's wife or his wicked oath and did not discuss the dancing daughter. Information taken from the extensive index of O'Mara and Paul, *A Repertorium of Middle English Prose Sermons*, vol. 4, pp. 2750, 2758, 2820. St. John the Baptist appears in a staggering 170 sermons. However, they do not all refer to the manner of his death.

[52] The dates of the sermon texts are as follows: Bodl. MS Holkham 40 from the thirteenth century; BL Add. MS 40672 from the late fourteenth or early fifteenth

"Satan Danced in the Person of the Damsel"

Within the sermons and other lay texts surveyed for this project, only BL Add. MS 40672 and BL MS Egerton 2820 represent Wycliffite thought, with all the other sermons appearing in officially orthodox sermon cycles. There appears to be no significant variation between orthodox and heterodox presentations of Salome, revealing resonance of this presentation of Salome and her dance as deadly and sexually transgressive.

It is perhaps no surprise that when teaching Salome in late medieval sermons, sermon authors emphasized sin rather than any possible redemptive interpretations of the tale. In these interpretations in vernacular sermons, the sin of sacrilege continued to play a significant role. A bifurcation between the sacred body of the saint and the profane bodies of Herod and Herodias dominates the sermons, deepening and reinforcing the boundary separating dance from the sacred. Yet, most of the medieval sermons presenting the narrative of the death of John the Baptist do not specifically mention dance or the dancer. The contrast between the profane and damned bodies of Herod and Herodias and the sacred body of John the Baptist, with its power for miraculous happenings, was the focus. The authors included dance only occasionally as one of the features of profane and damned bodies. Furthermore, in the sermons that do highlight the presence of dance in the narrative, dance was not initially singled out as the most sinful element. But as these sermons repeatedly connected dance to death and to the sins of the flesh, the role played by dance and by the female dancer expanded until, eventually, the body of the female dancer span into the center of the narrative frame.

As presented in sermons, discussions of Salome's dance did not reference heavenly dances for the saintly John the Baptist or parish practices commemorating the saint through dance. Sermon authors instead fixated on the death and destruction of the bodies of the physical earthly dancer and those associated with her sin. While John the Baptist's martyrdom was the central death in the narrative and connected directly to profane dancing bodies, his was not the only death that the sermons attributed to Salome's dance. The *Golden Legend* noted that "just as Herod was punished for beheading John ... so also Herodias was punished for instructing her daughter to ask for the head, and the girl for doing so."[53] In this text, Herod and Herodias were condemned to exile, where they eventually died in misery. The *Golden Legend* also mentioned that some sources claimed when "Herodias had the head in her hands and taunted it gleefully, by God's will the head breathed in her face and she expired." The *Golden Legend* likewise attributed Salome's

---

century; Longleat MS 4 from between 1409 and 1413; BL Add. MS 41321 from the first half of the fifteenth century; BL Add. MS 36791 (*Speculum Sacerdotale*) from the mid-fifteenth century; and Bodl. MS Greaves 54 from the mid-to-late fifteenth century. Dates taken from O'Mara and Paul, *A Repertorium of Middle English Prose Sermons*.

53 Jacobus, *The Golden Legend*, vol. 2, p. 138.

Women, Dance and Parish Religion in England, 1300–1640

death directly to her dance: "she was walking over an icy pond when the ice gave way under her and she was drowned, though one chronicle says that the earth swallowed her alive."[54] The *Golden Legend* appeared to be drawing from the same tradition as Nicephorus's slightly later *Ecclesiastical History*, which described Salome's death more explicitly as a display of "the dance of death":

> As [Salome] was journeying once in the winter time, and a frozen river had to be crossed on foot, the ice broke beneath her, not without the providence of God. Straightaway she sank down up to her neck. This made her dance and wriggle about with all the lower parts of her body, not on land, but in the water. Her wicked head was glazed with ice, and at length severed from her body by the sharp edges, not of iron, but of frozen water. Thus, in the very ice she displayed the dance of death, and furnished a spectacle to all who beheld it, which brought to mind what she had done.[55]

As Nicephorus reminded his audience, it was Salome's dance that led to St. John the Baptist's death, and the manner of her own death thus provided a graphic reminder of her dance of death which had cost John his head.[56] The bodies of dancers would meet the same deadly fate that they forced upon the saints.

The sermon in *Speculum* gave the clearest portrait of dance as deadly to all involved, and in this sermon, the deaths of Herod, Herodias, and Salome were also the immediate result of John's execution. In the sermon contained in *Speculum*, Herod was slowly killed by worms that infested him the moment he held John's head in his hands ("for alle his body spronge ful of woms and he was þeto dampned to anverlastyng peyne"). Herodias died when "at the virtue of God the hede 3af hire a blaste in hire visage that sche dyede wiþoute lenger delay." Salome's fate was just as immediate. As soon as Herod held John's head, "in the si3t of alle the peple the erþe swalowyd the wenche that hadde dawnsid, and sche sonke into an euel feste."[57] In this sermon, Salome's dance caused the death of John the Baptist; it then brought about the immediate deaths of the three conspirators and the destruction of their profane earthly bodies.

Each of these sermons described Salome's death in a way that connected her demise with her dancing. Regardless of whether she was described as dying immediately by sinking into the earth or dying later by dancing under the ice, the listener was left with no doubt that it was because of her dance that she died. The emphasis on the destruction of the profane body of the dancer was directly contrasted with the martyrdom of the saint, emphasizing a boundary

---

54 Ibid., vol. 2, pp. 138–139.

55 Blaise Hospodar, *Salome: Virgin or Prostitute?* (New York: Pageant Press, 1953), 49. Hospodar draws this quote from Cornelius a Lapide's version of Nicephorus's *Ecclesiastical History*, I:20.

56 Hospodar, *Salome*, 49.

57 *Speculum Sacerdotale*, ed. Edward H. Weatherly, EETS OS 200 (London: Oxford University Press, 1936), 195–196; BL Add. MS 36791, fol. 111r.

"Satan Danced in the Person of the Damsel"

between profane dancing bodies and sacred still ones. In parsing out sacred bodies from profane ones, discussions of Salome's dance as presented in sermons made it clear that dancing bodies could contaminate and profane the bodies of those around them, leading to death for all involved.

Looking beyond these Middle English sermons, it becomes clear that this idea of the dance of Salome as a contaminating and deadly disease was not confined to rhetorical overtures. It appeared in other settings, particularly in the connection of Salome with the disease of epilepsy and in the continental dancing mania of the fourteenth century, a phenomenon that loosely paralleled the Kölbigk dancers episode discussed in Chapter 2.[58] In these episodes, particularly those taking place in 1374, the alignment between the dance of Salome, female bodies, disease, and death showed how this rhetorical construction of dance played out in medieval understandings of danced death. Accounts of many of the 1374 episodes mention St. John the Baptist.[59] In the Chronicle of Cologne, for example, the dancers called out "St. John so, so, brisk and cheerful, St. John."[60] Yet, like the Salome of the vernacular English sermons, these dancers are not aligned with the saint, nor are they acting as allegorical dancers of salvation. Instead, ecclesiastical authorities are quick to align these dancers (described as primarily female) with sin, death, and damnation. Part of this is apparent in the records that claim the dancers shriek the names of demons; however, authors also make this connection by describing the dancers as descendants of Salome. The Dominican preacher Hugo of Constance, for example, claims that the dancers are women "born from Salome," who suffer a hereditary punishment for the death of the saint:

> I have seen with my very eyes, that all the women born from her [from Salome] have to come to Saint John's minster. And on the day before his day at vespers they all get struck by such an untold pain, that they cry and shout and clap their hands from the misery and affliction they suffer. And the pain is so strong, that two or three men cannot hold a woman. That continues until the next day at none when Mass is sung. In such a way our Lord has avenged Saint John.[61]

Other chronicle accounts note that "above a hundred unmarried women were seen raving about in consecrated and unconsecrated places, and the

---

[58] Smith, "'A Lanterne of Lyght to the People,'" 62.

[59] Gregor Rohmann, "Dancing on the Threshold: A Cultural Concept for Conditions of Being Far from Salvation," *Contributions to the History of Concepts* 10, no. 2 (2015): 48.

[60] "... here sent johan, so so, vrisch ind vro, here sent Johan." *Die Cronica van der hilliger Stat van Coellen* (Cologne, 1499), fol. 277. Also cites Cyr. Spangenberg, *Adels-Spiegel – Mirror of Nobility* (Schmalkalden, 1591), fol. 403.B. As translated and cited in Hecker, *The Dancing Mania of the Middle Ages*, 2.

[61] As translated and quoted in Rohmann, "Dancing on the Threshold," 64.

Women, Dance and Parish Religion in England, 1300–1640

consequences were soon perceived."[62] These accounts present quite a contrast with English parish practice, in which St. John's Day dances celebrated the birth of the saint with groups of dancing women; however, the dancing mania shows how shifting sermon rhetoric about Salome could be weaponized against women and communal dance practices. As eventually happened with the Kölbigk account, descriptions of the continuous dance aligned the dance with divine vengeance upon female sin, in violation of consecrated places and in disrespect for a saint. Sacrilege and gender intertwined, with contagious and deadly result.

Building on these rhetorical connections between Salome and sacrilege, the presentation in these sermons of Salome's own fate (swallowed by the earth) mirrored Old Testament judgments on the irredeemably sinful or on the sacrilegious. When discussing this account of Salome's death, the *Golden Legend* compared it to the death of the Egyptians in the Red Sea.[63] The sinking of a dancer into the earth also mirrored contemporary fates for dancers in *exempla* such as the tale of the cursed dancing carolers, discussed in Chapter 2, where the dancers underwent a living burial and were slowly swallowed by the earth. This *exemplum*, with its condemnation of dance in inappropriate times and places as a form of sacrilege, began to circulate around the same time as the use of Salome as an allegory for the church began to disappear.[64] In the Old Testament narratives hinted at in these punishments, such as the Exodus drowning of the Egyptians in the Red Sea or the more clearly parallel swallowing of Korah and his followers, the punishments are for direct assaults against God, his leaders, or his people, even for blasphemy.[65] In setting up dance as an offense punished by the same means, the sermon authors clearly underscore the connections between dance and sacrilege vital to shifting perceptions of dance. These medieval authors drew a direct connection between Salome's punishment and sacrilege. Connecting Salome, a figure referenced only by her gender ("girl") in the biblical text, to punishments for sacrilege was simply one more way of reinforcing the connections between dance, women, and sacrilege.

Medieval sermons clearly linked Salome's dance to death and to sacrilege. But what about the late medieval shift connecting dance and sinful bodies? The Salome narrative, framed as it is within the transgressions of lust and adultery, provided a clear route to connect dance to the sins of the body. Salome's dance was placed within the context of Herod and Herodias's adulterous relationship in a way that implied that dance could not only cause sinful behavior but often came out of sinful behavior as well. Some of the sermons such as Mirk's

---

[62] Hecker translating and quoting Schenk V. Granburg; Hecker, *The Dancing Mania of the Middle Ages*, 4.

[63] Jacobus, *The Golden Legend*, vol. 2, p. 139.

[64] Kemmler and Mannyng, *"Exempla" in Context*, 133.

[65] See, for example, Exodus 14 and Numbers 16.

"Satan Danced in the Person of the Damsel"

Festial presented an account very similar to the scriptural texts, with language echoing the text of the Vulgate: "Wherefore Herode made to don Iohn Baptiste in preson and schapute betwynne hym and hys wyf how Iohne mygh be do to dethe wythowte sturbans of þe pepul, for þe pepul lovyd Iohn. Than schapud Herode to make a grete fest of alle þe greate men of the cuntre."[66] However, other sermons such as the *Speculum* account expanded upon these details, placing more emphasis on the role that dance played in the plot. The author of *Speculum* stated:

> Þis Herode and Herodian confedrid togedre for his deth þat he schuld make a grete feste in þe day of his birthe, and in the worschip of þat day he schulde feede þe lords and þe elders of Galilee and alle his lords, and þat the damsel schuld play and dawnce afore hem in the best maner, and þat þe Herode schulde swere to ȝeue hire what þat sche askyd of hym, and þat hire askynge schulde be the hede of John, þe whiche he schuld graunte hire for loue of his oth.[67]

Speculum's author made sure to state that dance formed an integral part of the plot to kill John the Baptist, an emphasis that also appears in the *Golden Legend*'s account. The *Golden Legend* noted "both Herodias and Herod longed to find an opportunity to get rid of John, and they seem to have arranged secretly between themselves that Herod would invite the leading men of Galilee to a banquet in honor of his birthday, and would have Herodias's daughter dance for them."[68] The *Golden Legend* then placed more emphasis on the plot than on the dance's role in the plot, noting "that there had been this conspiracy and false pretense seems to be suggested by what the *Scholastic History* says: 'It is entirely credible that Herod and his wife had secretly plotted John's death on this occasion.' Likewise Jerome in the *Gloss*: 'He therefore swore to find an occasion to put John to death, because if the girl had asked for the death of her father or mother, Herod would not have yielded.'"[69] A final sermon that directly attributed John's death to a plot, the Wycliffite sermon on the narrative, noted that "it semeth that þis fraude was castun by þis woman and Eroude, or ellis he were to greet a fool to ȝyue half his rewme for lepyng of a strumpet."[70] In all these presentations of the plot, Herod and Herodias were cast as the primary actors driving John the Baptist's death. And in all but one of these texts, dance's role in the plot was also highlighted, hinting at the

---

66 John Mirk, *John Mirk's Festial: Edited from British Library MS Cotton Claudius A II*, ed. Susan Powell, EETS OS 334–335 (Oxford University Press, 2009), vol. 1, p. 169.

67 Weatherly, *Speculum Sacerdotale*, 195–196.

68 Jacobus, *The Golden Legend*, vol. 2, p. 133.

69 Ibid.

70 Anne Hudson (ed.), *English Wycliffite Sermons* (Oxford: Clarendon Press, 1983), vol. 2, p. 297.

125

Women, Dance and Parish Religion in England, 1300–1640

ways in which dance could easily grow out of sin and be used for evil means. Again, the bodies of all those associated with dance were marked as profane.

Because the transgressive dancer in the scriptural narrative was a woman, the medieval sermons inherently involved some discussion of gender. However, the extent to which authors highlighted the gender of the dancer as a part of the transgressions of the text varied. Late medieval verse sermons on Salome presented much less diverse accounts of her dance than do the prose sermons, with each verse sermon emphasizing the dance, the oath, and the death of the saint. *Handlyng Synne* described how the scripture "telleth that Eroud swore/ To here þat tymbled yn þe flore,/ þat what-aseuer she wuld aske to mede,/ he wuld fulfyl hyt here yn dede/ halfe hys kyndom/ ȝyf she wuld craue,/ haluyndele she shuld hyt haue. Eueyl he vosed, and swore hys oth,/ þer-for with hym ys now god wroth."[71] The *Northern Homily Cycle*'s version of the tale notes that the action originates with Herodias, whose "flesly liking" was hindered by John the Baptist. It then turns to the dance of Salome, describing how at the feast, "bifor him come a fair yong lasce,/ þat Herodiascs dohter was,/ and tumbeled sa wel for alle/ þat þar war gendered in þat halle."[72] A final verse sermon, found in BL MS Arundel 20, warned its audience to "be not hasty in avow making" and, recounting "how herrode avowyd in hys nadhed/ because his doughter tumbyled indid," concluded that it would have been better for him to break his oath than to "in so folysly to sle wiþout cause a man."[73] Although none of the verse sermons highlighted the dire fates of the dancer or the instigators of the plot, they did directly connect dance to the saint's death, to a woman, and to other forms of sin (adultery and false oaths). The prose sermons, similarly, highlighted the connections between dance, women, and death. The *Golden Legend*, rather matter-of-factly, stated that after Salome's dance and Herod's corresponding oath, "the headsman is dispatched, John loses his head, the head is given to the daughter and presented by the daughter to her adulterous mother."[74] It then echoed Chrysostom's lament, as given in the *Gloss*, "so great a one as this is given to an incestuous woman, betrayed to an adulteress, awarded to a dancing girl!"[75] Sermons like these laid the ideological foundations for later discussions and parish treatments of dance as a sin that instigates other sins, as we will see in Chapters 5 and 6.

These sermons also expanded on the connection between dance and the sexual sin of women, something else that starts to appear in later parish records. A number of these late medieval prose sermons connected Salome

---

[71] Mannyng, *Handlyng Synne*, 100.

[72] Anne B. Thompson, *The Northern Homily Cycle* (Kalamazoo, MI: Medieval Institute Publications, 2008), Homily 3.

[73] BL Add. MS 17013, fol. 54v, col. 2.

[74] Jacobus, *The Golden Legend*, vol. 2, p. 133.

[75] Ibid.

and her dance to other forms of sin, particularly sexual wrongdoing, in another form of embodied transgression that began to connect dance more closely to women. Mirk's *Festial* presented a brief version of events, noting how Herodias "sente into the halle hyr doghtyr to daunce and to tombul before þe gestes, and so pleased Herode þat he bade hur aske of hym whatte scheo wolde and scheo schulde haue it, and þerto swore a grete othe."[76] The dancing of Mirk's Salome was described as pleasing to Herod, with no mention made of the other guests; he did not specify a gender for the rest of Salome's audience, and implied that lustful Herod was the main individual affected by her dance. The *Golden Legend* noted that the girl's dance pleased everyone in attendance, but again did not gender the audience as exclusively male.[77] The sermon in *Speculum* took a slightly different approach by seeming to indicate that her dance was performed for an all-male audience: "þe mayde dawnswed, and sche plesid so wel to alle men."[78] Although this specification could simply be a use of male generic language, when considered alongside visual depictions of a sexualized Salome performing for men, this addition appears to be intended to highlight the sexual nature of Salome's dance. For, as Kathryn Smith's study of the iconography of John the Baptist in the thirteenth and fourteenth centuries points out, there is evidence that fourteenth-century English audiences would have associated John with chastity and Salome with sex: the man with chaste holiness and the woman with sexualized transgression.[79] Julian Luxford's analysis of a 1340 manuscript illumination owned by a monk of St. Augustine's, Canterbury, shows how the Baptist's chastity tramples Salome's sexuality underfoot, with his attire bringing to mind his asceticism and Salome's position as her arched body is trampled by the saint highlighting her pelvis and her thighs: her dance and her sex.[80]

Finally, the language in these sermons, particularly the use of the word "wench" in the sermon in *Speculum*, makes clear that the dance is one performed by a sexualized female body. As Carissa Harris's *Obscene Pedagogies* shows, the term "wench" carried a range of meanings, most of which were disparaging: "the 'wenche' is not only an object or commodity for men; she is also subjugated to other women, and frequently contrasted with the powerful 'lady' or the respectable 'wyf.'"[81] This linguistic sexualization of

---

[76] Mirk, *John Mirk's Festial: Edited from British Library MS Cotton Claudius A II*, vol. 1, p. 169.

[77] Jacobus, *The Golden Legend*, vol. 2, p. 133.

[78] Weatherly, *Speculum Sacerdotale*, 195–196.

[79] Smith, "'A Lanterne of Lyght to the People,'" 71.

[80] Julian M. Luxford, "Out of the Wilderness: A Fourteenth-Century English Drawing of John the Baptist," *Gesta* 49, no. 2 (2010): 140–141; for more on visual representations of dancing, see Gertsman, *The Dance of Death in the Middle Ages*.

[81] Carissa M. Harris, *Obscene Pedagogies: Transgressive Talk and Sexual Education in Late Medieval Britain* (Ithaca, NY: Cornell University Press, 2018), 34–35.

Salome is clearest in the Wycliffite sermon cycle, which likewise most clearly tied Salome's dance to sexual transgression. After quoting the scripture that stated that Salome was "plesude to Eroude and his gestus" the sermon added in the phrase "by tomblerys lepyng" making clear that it was her dance that brought pleasure. The sermon then referred to Salome throughout the rest of the text as a "lepyng strompat" or as a "wenche," explicitly connecting dance and sexual transgression.[82] The very language in which Salome was presented in some of these late medieval sermons implied illicit sexuality and a transgressive body where the biblical text did not. The occasional addition of phrases clarifying the gender of the audience and Salome's virtue revealed that the authors of most of these texts connected her dance with lust and expected their audiences to do the same.

The closest that any of these sermons come to an overt invective against dance was in their discussion of the ways (including dance) in which women can lead men into foolish, sinful oaths, as occurs in the Wycliffite sermon cycle, or in the connection between adultery and sacrilege, as in the Wycliffite sermon contained in BL MS Egerton 2820. Thus, in the clearest indictment of dance as sinful in these sermons, dance is bound to female bodies and female transgression. Egerton 2820 connected Herodias's "avoutrie" and "þe wicked will of þe curched woman" to the "apostasie and avowtrie" of the late medieval church.[83] The Wycliffite sermon cycles noted that the "doing of Eroude is not wiþoute blame, for he schulde not swere þus to a ʒong strumpat."[84] Ultimately, the key moral of the sermon seemed to focus on male transgression: "For who may denye þat ne lordis don aftur ladyus, or þat freris counseylon with ladyus, or myche synne is now vppe by werkis of lordis? And knyte alle these togeydere and freris ben drownd þerof, more sutyl and sinful þan þis lepyng strompat."[85] But a careful close reading of the sermon highlights implicit conclusions about dance as a female sin and women as transgressive threaded throughout, undercutting the seeming judgment that male sin was ultimately more responsible for the saint's death than a female dancer. The same Wycliffite sermon placed the greatest part of the blame on "þis false womman [Herodias]. For as wymmen where þei ben goode passon other creaturys, so wher þei ben turned to yuel, þei passon money other feendis."[86] It continued on to state that when women "mouen lordis herto as þes wymmen duden Eroude, þis synne is in þes proctouris, but more in þes lordis," nuancing the seeming condemnation of women within this sermon.[87] Given the gradual

---

[82]   Hudson, *English Wycliffite Sermons*, vol. 2, p. 297.

[83]   BL MS Egerton 2820, fols. 121r–122v.

[84]   Hudson, *English Wycliffite Sermons*, vol. 2, p. 297.

[85]   Ibid.

[86]   Ibid.

[87]   Ibid., p. 298.

"Satan Danced in the Person of the Damsel"

shifts in rhetorical constructions of dance, sin, and gender that took place over the thirteenth and fourteenth centuries, it is no surprise that in this early fifteenth-century sermon, the latest of the medieval sermons from this chapter, female transgression drove the narrative and moral interpretation, pointing to the gradual entrenchment of the view of the dance of Salome as an exemplar of female transgression and of dance itself as a particularly female form of sin.

CONCLUSION

In the biblical text, dance played a marginal part in the death of John the Baptist. The dancing girl, not even significant enough to be named, twirled through the margins of the narrative, eclipsed by the conflict between the saint, the king, and the queen. And in at least some late medieval texts, this outline remains the same. Dance is one of many sins in the narrative, the dancing girl one of many different individuals tied to the profane and to transgression. But therein lies a key difference between the scriptural narrative and the sermon texts: in the sermon texts, the dancer herself is classified as profane, surrounded by sin. At least rhetorically, dance is one of the sins separating the saints and the sinners, although this distinction had not yet made its way into parish practices, in which dance maintained its ambivalence and place in parish festivities.

Late medieval sermons did not explicitly reflect the negativity towards Salome herself articulated in the glosses of the Salome narrative. Instead, they implicitly connected Salome's dance with sin and murder by simply telling the narrative with little interpretation: Salome danced, Herod lusted (or, in language more accurate to the texts, was pleased), and John the Baptist died. This simplicity in presentation seems to have left no doubt in the minds of medieval listeners that when a woman danced, men lusted, and death followed for both men and women. The sermons and lay texts on Salome did not repeat the negative statements made about Salome in patristic writings and medieval glosses, yet they left their listeners with the clear impression that a dancing woman brought death to both herself and her audience, reinforcing a boundary between innocent male bodies and profane female ones. Taking a step back to consider biblical figures dancing in fourteenth-century English sermons more holistically emphasizes the ties between sexuality, female sin, and dance even more strongly, for Salome was the only dancing scriptural figure the men and women of the English parish would have heard about from the pulpit. These fourteenth-century sermons did not immediately change fourteenth- and fifteenth- century parish practices: yet, as the next chapter shows, the rhetorical construction of dance as a sacrilegious, sexualized sin did eventually play a part in bringing the parish festivities around St. John's Day to a close.

Women, Dance and Parish Religion in England, 1300–1640

It is this shift, from separating sacred and profane bodies to separating sacred male bodies from profane female ones, that proves to be most lasting and most significant. The initial focus on the sins of all prevented a complete focus on the bodies of the women in the text. But with the disappearance of positive allegorical roles for the women in the text, the emphasis on the literal bodies of the figures in the tale, and the connections between female bodies and the profane, bodies move more and more towards the center of the narrative. Dance's connection to sacrilege and to women helps narrow the focus to the female bodies in the narrative. Once the focus has become the body of the dancing woman, dance itself becomes more sexualized and feminized. In the fourteenth century, glosses, sermons, and art increasingly represented Salome as a sexualized sinner. Yet, these sources still portrayed her as a specific woman from a specific historical moment. And although the late medieval Salome remained frozen in these texts as a sinful and sexualized damsel, she was still just one dancer. Fourteenth- and fifteenth-century parish records do not yet reflect the application of models developed around Salome in their discussion of women and dance. However, as the vision of Salome as a sexualized, sacrilegious dancer took root in rhetoric in the late Middle Ages, it would then spread into perceptions and treatment of contemporary women in the sixteenth and seventeenth centuries. With the shift to framing dance as sacrilegious, sexualized, and female, the lessons drawn from Salome's dance began to be applied to all women, whether they danced or not.

CHAPTER 5

"IN HER DANCE SHE HAD NO REGARD UNTO GOD"

In John Lowin's 1609 pamphlet *Brief Conclusions of Dancers and Dancing*, Salome made several appearances: first, as an example of performing an "unlawfull" or "prophane" dance, and later on as the ultimate reason why Christians should forgo all dances. In the conclusion of his pamphlet, Lowin wrote that "mee thinketh it were enough, to make us leave and forsake the usage of such Dances ... to observe and consider with studius diligence ... how that through the meanes and occasion of a Dance St. John Baptist was put to death."[1] Lowin's order to his audience, to think on how dance led to the death of a saint and thus to stop all dancing, stands in stark contrast with the celebration of St. John's Day with parish dances in the fourteenth and fifteenth centuries. Sermons and commentaries from sixteenth- and seventeenth-century England consistently present Salome as Lowin portrayed her: as a transgressive woman, with emphasis placed on the sinfulness of her dance and its sexual nature. By the time Lowin wrote in 1609, no sign of Salome as a positive allegory appeared.

One reason for the disappearance of more positive patristic and medieval perspectives on Salome relates to changes in biblical exegesis brought about by the influence of the Reformations. However, these exegetical changes are not the sole cause behind the vanishing of these views of Salome. An altered vision of worship, combined with a new emphasis on orderliness as a sign of morality, also contributed to the changes in Salome's presentation.[2] Yet these changes only furthered the already evolving attitudes to Salome and to dance revealed in late medieval glosses and sermons. As the previous chapter showed, the real shift came in the solidification of the transition begun in the

---

[1] John Lowin, *Brief Conclusions of Dancers and Dancing: Condemning the Prophane Use Thereof and Commending the Excellencie of Such Persons Which Have from Age to Age, in All Solemne Feasts, and Victorious Triumphs, Used That (No Lesse) Honourable, Commendable, and Laudable Recreation: As Also True Physicall Observations for the Preservatoin of the Body in Health, by the Use of the Same Exercise* (London: For Iohn Orphinstrange, and are to bee sold at his shop by the Cocke and Katherine-wheel neere Holbourne bridge, 1609), Dii.

[2] Cameron, *The European Reformation*, 408.

131

Women, Dance and Parish Religion in England, 1300–1640

medieval sermons: from a focus on dance as a sin of sacrilegious action to a focus on dance as a sin of sexualized bodies.

This chapter follows these shifts to their end point, exploring the ways in which Salome's evolving presentation became used to condemn all dancers and all women. As shown in the previous chapter, Salome's transformation began in the Middle Ages, as authors connected her dance first to sacrilege and then to sex. The dance of Salome transformed from an allegory for the true church to the act of a literal demon-possessed woman. Moving into the early modern era, Salome's dance became the ultimate exemplar for why women dancing, in any time or circumstance, were transgressive and dangerous. Her dance provided a place for focused discussions about the dangers of dance in the audience's time, especially when performed by women. The shifts in which sins were emphasized in the narrative, in the interpretation of her dance, and in the exemplarity attributed to her dance indicate the strengthening of the discourse connecting dance and women to sin. Furthermore, these shifts meant that discussions of dance revolved more and more around the sexualized female body, a sexualized body still connected to sacrilege. Salome's dance reveals the ways in which connections of sacrilege with dance and women laid the foundation for a discourse connecting dance and women to sin in all forms. Dance, initially connected to sacrilege, became connected to specific sexualized women and then to all women and all sins. In short, rhetorical frameworks of dance again broadened out to encompass female sin in general.

Emerging comparisons between Salome's dance and David's dance, presented as exemplars of sin and of godliness, further emphasized the extent to which transgressive, sexualized, and sacrilegious dance had become a female offense. As dance became more clearly associated with transgression in the form of sacrilege, it also became more closely tied to the female body and thus to sexual transgression as well. Tying discourses about dance to conversations about sacrilege helped to tie dance to discussions about transgression more generally. Salome became scriptural proof for why women who danced were transgressive and the model for why contemporary women who danced were sinful. By the end of the sixteenth century, only a single possible interpretation of Salome's dance – as the act of a sinful and sexual woman – remained. And, as interpretations of Salome's dance narrowed, so did the parameters of holiness and the performance of gender.

THE TEXT

With the advent of the Reformations and the proliferation of vernacular scriptures, the number of biblical texts upon which preachers could draw increased exponentially, making another survey of the text of the scriptural narrative of the dance of Salome worthwhile. Did Salome's dance as conveyed in early modern bibles shift in translation, or did it remain consistent? In short, the

"In Her Dance She Had No Regard Unto God"

narrative remained consistent, both within Reformation-era translations and with its medieval predecessors. The Tyndale Bible, appearing in 1525, was the first Reformation-era English vernacular translation. It was followed by a long string of successive editions and new translations, including the Coverdale Bible, the Great Byble, the Taverner Bible, the Geneva Bible, and the Authorized Version.[3] The earliest of these, like the late medieval Wycliffite version, added to the emphasis on Herodias's role: "Herodias layd wate for him and wolde have killed him butt she coulde not. For Herode feared Jhon knowynge that he was juste and holy and gave him reverence. And when he herde him he did many thinges and herde him gladly."[4] Again, the text noted that the "doughter of the same Herodias cam and daunsed and pleased herode and them that sate att bourde also," leading to Herod's oath, his regret at her request, and the death of the saint.[5] Each of the early modern English translations presents the same text as Tyndale's 1525 version, and the wording of Tyndale's and subsequent translations parallels the medieval Wycliffite translation almost verbatim.

Thus, changes in Salome's presentation in early modern scriptures came not from variance in translation but from shifting extratextual interpretations in glosses, commentaries, and sermons. These extratextual apparatus used in conjunction with the scriptural text, especially marginalia and commentaries, were shaped by new approaches to exegesis developed during the Reformations of the sixteenth century. Theologians and commentators sought to place the text in its proper historical context, to clarify syntactical and linguistic issues, to elucidate the clear and straightforward meaning of scripture, and to connect it to broader moral truths.[6] These goals differed significantly from the purposes of the medieval glosses, which sought to collect relevant interpretative opinions into one location and to provide useful, often allegorical, interpretations of the passage. But the disappearance of the allegorical Salome from early modern commentaries demonstrates more than an exegetical shift or a shift in audience. As shown in the previous chapter, as early as the thirteenth century, medieval texts had already begun to emphasize the sinfulness of dance and to interpret the passage more literally.[7]

---

3 Translations and new editions appeared in 1535, 1537, 1538, 1539, 1541, 1542, 1543, 1544, 1545, 1546, 1547, 1548, 1549, 1550, 1583, 1610, 1611, 1612, and 1613.

4 F. Fry, *The First New Testament Printed in the English Language. 1525 or 1526. Translated from the Greek by William Tyndale Reproduced in Facsimilie with an Introduction by Francis Fry* (Bristol: Printed for the Editor, 1862), fol. lij.

5 Ibid.

6 Euan Cameron, "Calvin the Historian: Biblical Antiquity and Scriptural Exegesis," in *Calvin and the Book: The Evolution of the Printed Word in Reformed Protestantism*, ed. Karen E. Spierling (Göttingen: Vanderhoeck and Ruprecht, 2015), 77–82.

7 For more extensive discussions of medieval and Reformation interpretation, see Robert M. Grant and David Tracy, *A Short History of the Interpretation of the Bible,*

Women, Dance and Parish Religion in England, 1300–1640

Thus, although the exegetical changes of the sixteenth century did influence the narrowing of potential interpretations of Salome's dance, the Salome presented in these commentaries comes more from the continuation of a medieval shift in approaches to dance than from a change in interpretative paradigms.

As in the medieval glosses, in early modern bibles, the textual apparatus do the work of developing the gendered boundary between sacred and profane bodies. The Authorized Version of the bible, in its 1611, 1612, and 1613 editions, contained no textual marginalia for this passage in either Matthew or Mark. Katrin Ettenhuber notes that, in the Authorized Version in particular, marginalia were reserved for instances where a word or phrase could have a variety of interpretations; commentary, historical context, or interpretative guidelines were confined to prefatory material.[8] S. L. Greenslade adds that doctrinal notes were viewed suspiciously, as the normal preference of the Catholic church; thus, "Luther's New Testament had few notes, Tyndale's Worms quarto none."[9] Kevin Killeen, Helen Smith, and Rachel Willie's recent work similarly contends that "the King James Bible presents annotation as unnecessary. Individuals are able to understand the world of God without the intervention of (partisan) marginal glosses."[10] With such a suspicious approach to scriptural annotations, vernacular bibles only rarely included interpretive apparatus. Out of fifteen vernacular bibles, Christopher Barker's 1583 Bible and William Whittingham's 1610 Geneva Bible are the only two that added commentary on the passage. However, in both cases, the commentary highlighted the dance, sexual transgression, and the female body of the dancer.

The marginal comments on the Matthew 14 passage in Christopher Barker's 1583 text focused on the oath rather than on the dance. The comment on the Matthew passage notes that "the promes was wicked, but yet it was more

---

2nd edn. (Philadelphia: Fortress Press, 1984); James Atkinson and W. P. Stephens (eds.), *The Bible, the Reformation and the Church: Essays in Honour of James Atkinson* (Sheffield: Sheffield Academic Press, 1995); Karlfried Froehlich, *Biblical Interpretation from the Church Fathers to the Reformation* (Farnham: Ashgate Variorum, 2010).

8   Katrin Ettenhuber, "'A Comely Gate to so Rich and Glorious a Citie': The Paratextual Architecture of the Rheims New Testament and the King James Bible," in *The Oxford Handbook of the Bible in Early Modern England, c. 1530–1700*, ed. Kevin Killeen, Helen Smith, and Rachel Judith Willie (Oxford: Oxford University Press, 2015).

9   S. L. Greenslade, "English Versions of the Bible, 1525–1611," in *The Cambridge History of the Bible, Vol. 3: The West from the Reformation to the Present Day*, ed. S. L. Greenslade (Cambridge: Cambridge University Press, 1963), 146.

10 Kevin Killeen, Helen Smith, and Rachel Willie (eds.), *The Oxford Handbook of the Bible in Early Modern England, c. 1530–1700* (Oxford: Oxford University Press, 2015), Introduction to Part I.

"In Her Dance She Had No Regard Unto God"

vile to be obstinate in the same, that he might seem constant."[11] However, the marginal comments on the Mark passage are entirely different in focus, with two of the four comments on the sixteen verses focusing on the dance. Barker placed the first of these two comments on verse 22, which states that "the daughter of the same Herodias came in and daunced, and pleased herode and them that sate at table together." A mark next to "daunced" directed the reader's attention to the margin, to a cross-reference to Matthew 14:8 and the comment, "what inconvenience commeth by wanton dancing."[12] The second comment appeared next to verse 28, which describes how the head of John the Baptist was "brought in a charger, and gave ... to the maide." At this point, the note added that "Josephus calleth her name Salomen, the daughter of Philip and Herodias."[13] Barker's apparatus not only add historical context but also discuss dance as a step towards broader moral failure, something the medieval glosses failed to do. Furthermore, Barker connected dancing directly to sexual sin, a move rarely made in the medieval texts and one that indicates a growing concern with the gendered bodies of dancers rather than with the action of dancing itself.

William Whittingham's 1610 printing of the Geneva Bible included an even more extended commentary on the Matthew 14 passage. Introducing the text, the marginal annotation reads: "Here is in John, an example of an invincible courage, which al faithful ministers of Gods worde ought to follow: in Herod, an example of tyrannous vanitie, pride, and crueltie, and to be short, of a cowardly conscience, and of these miserable slaverie, which have once given themselves over to pleasures; in Herodias and her daughter, an example of whorelike wantonnesse, and womanly crueltie."[14] By using the individuals as exemplars, not allegories, Whittingham's text tied the transgressions more closely to real human figures and thus highlighted sexual transgression as female transgression. Herod, portrayed in medieval glosses as equally liable for the sexual transgression in the narrative, is not explicitly connected to sexual sin. In Whittingham's commentary, only the bodies of the women are blamed for sexual sin, with Herod's sins connected to actions or emotions and the sins of the women connected primarily to their bodies.

Whittingham's Salome, "an example of whorelike wantonnesse, and womanly crueltie," was the only one to appear in three early modern scripture commentaries printed in England: Thomas Tymme's 1570 translation of Augustin Marlorat's *Catholike and Ecclesiastical Exposition of the holy Gospel*

---

[11] Christopher Barker, *The Bible. Translated According to the Ebrew and Greeke* (Imprinted at London: by Christopher Barker, printer to the Queenes most excellent Maiestie, 1583), B.4.v.

[12] Ibid., D.5.v.

[13] Ibid.

[14] William Whittingham, *The Bible That Is, the Holy Scriptures* (Imprinted at London: By Robert Barker, printer to the Kings most excellent Maiestie, 1610), 494.

after St. Matthew, Christopher Fetherston's 1584 *Harmonie Upon the Three Evangelists, Matthew, Mark and Luke*, created from John Calvin's commentaries, and John Mayer's 1631 *Commentarie Upon the New Testament*. Each of these commentaries presented Salome similarly: each avoided allegorical interpretation, provided more information about genealogical and historical context, and connected her dance to broader moral lessons. All these changes stemmed from the transformations in exegesis and approach to scripture that grew out of the Reformations.

Of the three commentaries, Fetherston's translation of John Calvin's *Harmonie* presents the greatest break with the style of medieval exegesis. However, despite the drastic break in exegetical approach and in style, many of the same themes appear. Fetherston's translation of Calvin still touched on the evils of feasting and of improper birthday celebrations, yet spent less time on these evils and on false oaths than do the medieval texts. In line with the shifting priorities in discussions of dance, Fetherston's text instead expanded the treatment of the dance of Salome:

> So it came to passe that herode meaning to entertayne his guests sumptuously, suffred his wifes daughter to dance. Hereby it also appeareth what the discipline of that court was: for though many gaue themselues liberty then to dance, yet it was a vile note of whorish wantonnes for a damsel marriageable to dance. But filthy Herodias had so framed her daughter Salome after her own maners, least she should shame her. And what followed then? Namely the ungodly slaughter of the godly Prophet: for the heat of wine in Herod so flamed; that he forgetting grauity and wisdom, promised that he would gue to a dauncing damsel even to the one halfe of his kingdome. Truly a shamefull example, that a drunken king doth not only abide to upon with favourable eyes so shamefull a shew of his household, but also promiseth so great a rewarde. Wherfore let us learn carefully to resist the deuill, lest he intrap us in such snares.[15]

While the medieval glosses that dealt with Salome literally and not allegorically focused on her dance as a singular event, this passage connected her dance to a larger moral lesson for the audience: dancing damsels in any situation were transgressive and played key roles in the devil's snares for the godly. Fetherston transferred agency from Satan to the damsel, and the largest share of blame moves from drunken Herod, with his foolish oath, to the whorish wanton women of the text. In the process of moving from a focus on her dance as a single event to a broadly applicable moral interpretation, the focus shifted from a focus on the action of dancing to a focus on the sexualized female body of the dancer.

---

[15] Jean Calvin, *A Harmonie Vpon the the Three Euangelists, Matthew, Mark and Luke*, ed. Fetherston (Londini: [Printed by Thomas Dawson] impensis Geor. Bishop, 1610), 421.

"In Her Dance She Had No Regard Unto God"

Thomas Tymme's translation of Marlorate's *Exposition* draws on standard patristic figures such as Augustine, Jerome, Chrysostom, and Josephus as well as on reformers such as Bucer, Calvin, and Melancthon.[16] Tymme presented the same aforementioned excerpt from Calvin, highlighting the prevalence of that interpretation. Yet, Tymme added other, more specific moral lessons to his interpretation of the text. One such lesson was directed to the parents in his audience and pointed to Salome as an example of a youth ruined by ungodly parents, something hinted at in Fetherston's reference to how "filthy Herodias" framed her daughter but more fully expanded in Tymme's work:

> In this daunsing damsel, we have an example of the euyll instructionge and bringing up of youthe, and howe great a matter the good or euvill behauioure of the parentes is. The wicked, lasciuiouse, adulterouse, and cruell mother, is not contented with her owne rashenesse and ungodly behauiour, but shee seeke the also to frame the chylde or younge impe after her owne bente and disposition: that by the daughter a man may knowe what the moder is. And truely the damsel sheweth her selfe to apte and ready to be taught in following and fulfilling, the sonde mynde of her frantike mother.[17]

Fetherston focused on Salome's dance as an example of the immorality and wantonness of dancers, while Tymme used dance as an example of evil instruction and wickedness more generally. The connections between changes in approach to dance and theological conceptions of gender and the household will be a topic for the next chapter, but it is worth noting here that the sexualized sin at the heart of Tymme's and Fetherston's analysis is connected to the moral failure of the mother. Furthermore, Tymme's condemnation of Salome's dance even clarified which styles of dance were transgressive: "She daunced not rudely as do the common sort with leapynge, but she daunced with a comely gesture with measure."[18] This description of Salome's dance made clear that her dance was not like the "animal-like" wedding dances condemned by early modern reformers, but rather a stately, courtly, controlled

---

16 Tymme's text is composed in much the same style as the medieval glosses, with the text of the verse followed by notes on the interpretation of the text. However, in line with shifting priorities for paratextual apparatus, notes on translation and grammatical features also play a prominent role in this commentary. See Molekamp's essay in Killeen et al., *The Oxford Handbook of the Bible in Early Modern England*, 41, along with Ettenhuber's introduction to Part 1. Hall, "Biblical Scholarship: Editions and Commentaries," 76–80.

17 Augustin Marlorat, *A Catholike and Ecclesiastical Exposition of the Holy Gospel after St. Matthew, Gathered out of All the Singular and Approved Divines*, trans. Thomas Tymme (Imprinted at London: In Fletestreate neare vnto S. Dunstones churche, by Thomas Marshe, 1570), 311.

18 Ibid., 310.

Women, Dance and Parish Religion in England, 1300–1640

performance.[19] Yet Tymme insisted that even a comely, measured dance, in which passion or madness did not overtake the dancer, was immoral and an example of ungodly behavior. Tymme's interpretation left the reader with no doubts regarding the status of dance: "For there is no man that hath any care or respect of honest grauytie, that wyl commende or allowe daunsing, specially in a mayde."[20] Again, gender played the largest role in defining the boundaries laid out in this commentary, and again, a sexualized female body was placed at the center of the transgressions of the tale.

In the latest of these commentaries, the boundary separating profane dancing female bodies from holy male ones is most apparent. Mayer's commentary began by quoting Chrysostom, in a section with the marginal note "against dancing":

> In this meeting were many sinnes concurring: 1. Hot and unlawfull delights. 2. Libertie to speake, doe, or heare any thing. 3. A maid coming forth openly to dance, and exceeding all harlots in impudency. 4. The unfitnesse of the time being his birthday, wherein he should have praysed God, and for joy rather have let loose his prisoner. Heare this (yee maids and marryed women, which feare not to dance at marriages, and so to shame the whole sexe of women).[21]

Mayer thus emphasized the dance's "unlawful delights," the depth of the maid's sexual transgression, and the unholy nature of dance at celebrations meant to honor God, such as birthdays and weddings. While in Aquinas's

---

[19] Susan Karant-Nunn provides a lengthy discussion of wedding dances and their criticism in early modern Germany in Karant-Nunn, *The Reformation of Ritual*, 27–40.

[20] Marlorat, *A Catholike and Ecclesiastical Exposition of the Holy Gospel after St. Matthew, Gathered out of All the Singular and Approved Divines*, 310.

[21] John Mayer, *A Commentarie Vpon the Nevv Testament* ... (London: printed by Thomas Cotes, for Iohn Bellamie [and John Haviland for John Grismond], and are to be sold at his shoppe in Cornehill, at the signe of the three Golden Lyons, neere the Royall Exchange [and at Grismond's shop in Ivie lane at the signe of the Gun], n.d.), 199. After a lengthy analysis of the historicity of the text and the genealogy of Herod and his family, Mayer included comments on the wickedness of birthday celebrations and of Herod's oath. However, both these transgressions received only a sentence or two, and were then followed by another comment on Salome's dance. "We reade that Flaminius, a Captaine of the Romanes, in anger causing a man to be beheaded at a feast ... was by the censors banished from the Court, because he had mingled the banquet with blood, and had killed a man, though guiltie, to delight others. How much more wicked was Herod, and Herodias and his daughter, requiring John Baptist's head as the price of her dancing, that they might have the tongue in their power, which spake against their wickednesse?" (p. 200). While the medieval glosses address Salome's dance but spend more time discussing the sins of oath taking and dissembling, of the sins addressed in Mayer's commentary, dancing receives the most time and the only interpretive marginal note of the passage.

"In Her Dance She Had No Regard Unto God"

use of Chrysostom, the focus was on condemning the dancer in the biblical text and dancing in general, Mayer drew on paraphrased commentary from Chrysostom as a launching point for condemning contemporary dancers, dancers all gendered female. Like Fetherston and Tymme, he connected the biblical dance to customs from his time, again adding a level of directness in his condemnation of dance that is absent from the medieval texts. And, although there are sacred and profane male bodies in his discussion of the passage, the only bodies associated with dance are female ones, and no sacred counterpart to the profane dancing woman is offered.

Mayer's emphasis on wedding dancing provides insight into a change in parish treatments of dance, which, like the commentaries, broadened in focus from a concern with sacrilege to a concern with sin more generally: whereas most church court presentations of problematic dancers from 1300 onwards are of parishioners dancing on Sunday or during the time of prayers, wedding dances also start to appear in the records with more regularity in the seventeenth century. Some wedding dances are only hinted at through discussions of payments for minstrels who played at weddings, like a 1633 discussion of pay rates for musicians in York.[22] But other records, particularly from the 1620s onwards, indicate specifically that wedding dances were becoming problematic in the eyes of ecclesiastical authorities. Some of this concern connects to the now-familiar anxiety about churchyards and spaces; a 1634 report by the Bishop of Bath and Wells on East Coker Chapel noted with some alarm that "this Chappell hath beene prophan'd diverse ways, and at diverse times heretofore, by weddinge dinners kept there, and by dancing in the Chappell at those weddings."[23] Another record from Somerset, dated 1623, contained a deposition of one Walter Willis against Henrie Botwell, with the main concern being the timing of a wedding dance: "after dynner was ended the detected Henrie Botwell & other companie being att the said wedding did daunce, some times one parte of the companie & some times an other all or the greatest part of the after noone, but [Walter Willis] cannot expresselie saie that the said Botwell did daunce in the verie time of evening prayer."[24]

---

22 "... noe free brother of the said Arte shall serve att any freeman of Citizens weddinge without sufficient waiges vnder any pretence whatsoever, by which the saide Arte may be impaired or hindered, but that whosoever is disposed to have Musicke shall pay twelve pence att the elast to every Musitian that shall soe serve at his weddinge as their waiges due & accustomed vpon payne of every one offending herein to forfeit vj s viij d to bee paid & disposed to thuse aforesaid." York, 1633, Housebooks Y:B35, fols. 223–224 (31 October), in Alexandra F. Johnston and Margaret Rogerson (eds.), *Records of Early English Drama: York* (University of Toronto Press, 1979), 591.

23 1634 Report of Bishop of Bath and Wells on East Coker Chapel, PRO, SP16/535, fols. 3v–4. As transcribed in *REED Somerset Including Bath 1*, ed. Stokes with Alexander, 113.

24 Bishop's Court Deposition Book, SRO, D/D/Cd 58, fol. 8. As transcribed in *REED*

Women, Dance and Parish Religion in England, 1300–1640

Although Mayer's comment about wedding dancers did not target the timing of dances, in the parish, concerns about sacrilege clearly remained in play. But another case shows that the early modern concern about wedding dances reflected in Mayer's comment about "maids and marryed women, which feare not to dance at marriages," was connected not just to time or occasion but also to the behavior and sexuality of women. A 1624 deposition from Dulcote in Somerset indicates that in this case, wedding dancing led to multiple women (both maids and wives) staying out until almost two in the morning, with the dancing, the lateness of the hour, and mixed company leading to concern about possible sexual misbehavior.[25] Aligning Salome with early modern wedding dancers made the commentators' interpretations of Salome's dance far more pointed and far more connected to early modern parish behavior.

Thus, significant changes in approach to exegesis and scriptural interpretation during the Reformations did not affect the trajectory of interpretations of Salome and of dance. As early as the fourteenth century, interpretations of Salome as a literal, transgressive woman had already begun to replace the allegorical interpretations of her dance that were most prevalent in earlier glosses and texts, and the boundary between male and female bodies had begun to become the most important boundary in defining dance's acceptable parameters. Sixteenth-century authors, although less dependent on the church fathers than their predecessors, still drew heavily upon patristic opinions when crafting their commentaries.[26] The minimization of allegorical interpretation in the sixteenth century merely pushed this shifting perspective on Salome to an end point, in which the literal interpretation became not simply the preferred interpretation, but the only interpretation, of Salome's dance. This limitation of interpretative choices served to reinforce the status of dance as an act that could only be transgressive and was usually closely tied to female transgression. The greater emphasis that these early modern commentaries placed on the act of dancing in all contexts, as well as on the inappropriateness of women dancing, highlights the prevalence of this perception of dance and the ways in which dance had become tied to transgression not merely in

---

Somerset Including Bath 1, ed. Stokes with Alexander, 203.

[25] In this specific case, the detected individual was a married woman, Elizabeth Eliner Iefferies, and the depositions were meant to establish at what time she returned home to her husband. The maid under examination, Joane Gooddenow, complained that Elizabeth promised Joane and several other maids that she would stay after the wedding supper and dance if they did. Joane thus stayed until 2 a.m., while Elizabeth left shortly after midnight, leading Joane to complain that she had been badly used by being left at a dance with only maids and men. This latter complaint seems to imply concern about damage to her own sexual reputation. Account from a 1624 Bishop's Court Deposition Book, SRO, D/D/Cd 58, fols. 35–36. As transcribed in *REED Somerset Including Bath 1*, ed. Stokes with Alexander, 99.

[26] Weatherly, *Speculum Sacerdotale*, 196; Jacobus, *The Golden Legend*, vol. 2, p. 133.

"In Her Dance She Had No Regard Unto God"

sacred space but in all contexts. Furthermore, the added emphasis on drawing broad moral lessons from scriptural narratives helped to begin reifying this view of dance as transgressive and female into guidelines for Christian moral conduct. As parishioners heard more about Salome as representative of sinful sexualized dance, they started to pay closer attention to the sexual reputations of women who danced in their own contexts.

SINS, SEX, AND SALOME

The early modern sermons, like their medieval predecessors, presented a kaleidoscope of transgressions clustered around Salome's dance. Occasionally, dance was not explicitly identified as a sin but was portrayed as the action that enabled sin. More frequently, though, Salome's dance was identified as sinful, as one sin among many sins. However, in a change from the medieval sermons, her dance did not usually appear in straightforward discussions of the biblical narrative, but instead featured in thematic sermons addressing topics such as death, mourning, vanities, righteousness, idolatry, contentment, and kingship as well as in sermons on assorted scripture passages, including Ecclesiastes, Ezekiel, Judges, and Matthew 6.[27] This change is significant. Medieval sermons like those discussed in the previous chapter primarily addressed Salome's dance as a specific problematic action that occurred in the past and was performed by an individual in a specific narrative. Early modern sermons about Salome, however, use her dance as a broad representation of why dance itself is inherently problematic and sinful, a driving force that propels women (and the men around them) into committing multiple

---

[27] The sermons explored in this section come from an extensive search of EEBO. In this search, I found sixteen sermons that mention Salome or her dance; another fifty-one do not mention dance but allude to dance in discussing Herodias. These fifty-one sermons focus primarily on one's favorite sin, on unrepentant sin, on adultery, on oaths, and on manslaughter. One final clarification: several of the sixteen sermons on Salome refer to her as Herodias. The early modern authors appear to have broken with Josephus and instead assume that, as Herodias's daughter, the dancing damsel shares the same name. The sermons termed "early modern" in this chapter range from 1537 to 1640. Because the goal of this chapter is to create a collage that reveals larger religio-cultural trends rather than to explore sectarian differences, I am not dwelling on the exact chronological order of the sermons, nor on the specific religious affiliations of their authors. Change over time is being considered broadly as the change between medieval and early modern Christianity. Although I am not considering sectarian divisions in this chapter, I do think it is important to note that out of the sixty-seven early modern sermons (taken from EEBO) that mention Herodias and the sixteen that discuss dance specifically, there is little to no variance in how her dance is used or interpreted. Despite this consistency, the theological positions of the authors range broadly, from Catholic to puritan and everywhere in-between.

141

Women, Dance and Parish Religion in England, 1300–1640

other sins. In these early modern sermons, dance plays a more important role in differentiating sacred from profane bodies, indicating the gradual entrenchment of this boundary between the two, a boundary with dancing bodies on only one side of the dichotomy. And in a concrete example of the conflation of Salome with all women, these early modern sermons do not necessarily preserve the distinct female characters within the narrative: the dancing girl is referred to sometimes as Salome, sometimes as Herodias, and sometimes as Herodias's daughter. All the women in the tale collapse into one sinful sexual female body.[28]

Like the medieval sermons, some of the early modern sermons emphasized the connections between dance and death, for both the dancer and the saint. One Easter sermon drawn from John Day's 1615 *Festivals* discussed the death of Salome, noting that so that:

> they might knowe that wherewith a man sinneth, by the same also shall hee bee punished ... thus the daughter of Herodias, that by her Daucing had bereaued Iohn Baptist of his Head, was her selfe as she went on the Yce, bereaued of her owne Head, which seavered from the Body, daunced, as saith Nicephorus, vpon the selfe same Yce.[29]

Gilbert Primrose's 1625 sermon on the *Righteous Man's Evils* recorded, in a discussion of God's judgments upon persecutors and the deliverance of the church, that "Herodes Antypas, who beheaded Iohn Baptist, was relegated to Lion with his incestuous wife Herodias, and ended there his wicked life, by a wretched and miserable death."[30] A second sermon from Primrose's collection turned from the fates of the unrighteous to the martyrdom of the righteous, again connecting dance to death, albeit to the martyrdom of the godly: "Is it not better to feast with Herod, and to dance with Herodias daughter, than to fast, to lye in prison, and to lose the head for righteousnesse sake, with Iohn Baptist? The world doth so, because the world judgeth so."[31] Robert Willan's 1630 sermon *Eliah's Wish*, on death and Christian perspectives on death, stated that "Herodias heeles trip't off Iohn Baptists head," attributing direct causation for the saint's death to the dancer.[32] Becon's 1566 *New Postil* elaborated on these themes of martyrdom and the death of the righteous through the sin

---

[28] For clarity's sake, I will continue to refer to the dancer as Salome, although some of the sermons that I analyze in this section call her Herodias.

[29] John Day, *Day's Festiuals* (Printed at Oxford: By Ioseph Barnes, 1615), 331.

[30] Gilbert Primrose, *The Righteous Mans Euils* (London: Printed by H. L[ownes] for Nathanael Newberry, and are to be sold at the signe of the Starre in Popes-head Alley, Anno 1625), 219.

[31] Ibid., 20.

[32] Robert Willan, *Eliah's Vvish a Prayer for Death* (Printed at London: [By Thomas Cotes] for I. S[pencer] hypo-bibliothecary of Syon Colledge, and are to be sold by Richard Royston, at his shoppe in Iuie-lane, 1630), 12.

"In Her Dance She Had No Regard Unto God"

of the ungodly, contrasting the mourning of Christians with the frolicking of sinners.[33] More so than in the medieval sermons, the figures in these sermon narratives were split into two groups: the ungodly dancers, associated with sin and death, and the righteous John, martyred by a sinful dance and an example of Christian forbearance. In other words, the individuals in the narrative were split into profane and sacred bodies, represented by the body of the dancer and the body of the saint and seen as complete opposites. While these sermons continued to emphasize the connections between death and dance, they more clearly connected the dancer and the instigators of the dance to the ungodly, while John the Baptist became a clear parallel for sixteenth-century believers.

Similar divides between dancing sinners and motionless holy saints appear in early modern parish and court records. The records from Herefordshire, for example, contain long lists of parishioners charged not just for dancing during services but also simply for dancing.[34] And in a number of these cases, like in the 1622 case of one William Foote from Madley, persistent dancers are not simply fined but also excommunicated for their unrepentant dancing.[35] Dancing becomes a means of separating the body of Christ from the world, the sheep from the goats. And, like in the sermons, the dancers sometimes end up dead. Henry Burton's 1636 *Divine Tragedie* contains an account of one such dancer:

> At Hellingsby 5. Or 6. Miles from Ason in Sussex, the booke being read on the Lords day, in the Church by the Minister, on the next day being Munday, an honest man, one Tomkins being on his way, a neighbour overtakes him, and scoffingly askes him, if hee would goe daunce with him the next Sunday; to whom the man answered, take heed that thou bee not daunting in hell before that day come, or before it be long; By the next weeke Gods hand fell on the scoffer, that himself and two more of his family dyed.[36]

Tomkins's response to his dancing friend did not necessarily address the man's neglect of Sunday services, although the context certainly continued the Sabbatarian critique of Chapter 3. Tomkins's response instead focused on the action of dancing, not the action of skipping church, and Burton's retelling implied that those who dance will die. As in the early modern sermons, dance served as a means of separating the godly from the ungodly.

---

33 Thomas Becon, *A New Postil Conteinyng Most Godly and Learned Sermons* (Imprinted at London: In Flete-strete nere to S. Dunstons church, by Thomas Marshe [and John Kingston], M.D.LXVI, 1566), 266–267.

34 See, for a few of many examples, *REED Herefordshire, Worcestershire*, ed. Klausner, 63, 65, 70–71, 73, 139–140.

35 HCL, 1622 Acts of Decanal Court, fols. 112v, 116v. Transcribed in *Reed Herefordshire, Worcestershire*, ed. Klausner, 153–154.

36 *REED Sussex*, ed. Louis, 28.

143

Women, Dance and Parish Religion in England, 1300–1640

Like their medieval counterparts, early modern English sermons connected the narrative of Salome's dance to multiple transgressions, with dance not generally presented as the main sin in the text but seen rather as an action facilitating other transgressions. Thomas Jackson's sermon *An Helpe to the Best Bargaine* gives an example of the multiple sins connected to the narrative:

> He, that wittingly and willingly transgresseth any one, will (if occasion serue) breake euery one: wee see that in Herod, though he did many things, yet he made no conscience to breake the seauenth command; he, hauing occasion, made no conscience of the third, but sware to a wanton Dancer to giue what shee should aske, though to the halfe of his kingdome: yea, made no conscience of the sixt command, but most cruelly, for his faithfull dealing, persecuted to the death Iohn the Baptist.[37]

Jackson's sermon explicitly identified adultery, false oaths, and murder as the sins of the narrative, with a "wanton Dancer" playing a role in the breaking of two of the three commandments. Other sermons focused on the breaking of each commandment individually, concentrating on sexual transgression, murder, oaths, or idolatry rather than attempting to connect all three. Although dance was rarely condemned explicitly, its constant appearance alongside transgression served to connect it to sin. Much like occurred in the tale of the cursed dancing carolers, these sermon authors implicitly censured dance through its constant proximity to transgression. More importantly, dance was denounced for its constant proximity to female transgression specifically.

One transgression given far less prominence in the early modern sermons is that of the plot between Herod and Herodias. Whereas the medieval sermon authors tended to emphasize the agency of Herodias in setting up the events of the narrative, the early modern sermon authors focused instead on the actions of the dancer and of Herod. However, Herodias, as the adulterous wife, still played a vital role in tying the transgressions of the narrative to female bodies. The adulterous wife pointed to one of the transgressions most often in proximity to dance in this narrative – that of sexual transgression. As multiple sermons noted, sexual transgression set up the narrative, for it was the adultery of Herod and Herodias that led to John's rebuke of the king and set in motion the events leading to his death.[38] Other sermons, such as Richard Rogers's 1615 *Commentary Upon the Whole Booke of Judges*, extended the sexually transgressive behavior to specifically include the dancer as well:

> So the whorish daughter of an whorish mother, Herodias I meane, being so farre admitted as to dance before Herod the King, and being permitted to demand what recompence she listed, euen to the halfe of his kingdome,

---

[37] Thomas Jackson, *An Helpe to the Best Bargaine* (London: Printed by Nich. Okes, for Mat. Walbanke, and are to be sold in Grais-Inne Gate, 1624), 46–47.

[38] Bond, *Certain Sermons or Homilies (1547)*, 176–177.

"In Her Dance She Had No Regard Unto God"

shamed not to aske the head of Iohn Baptist: whom not onely all the people, but euen Herod himself reuerenced and stood in feare of.[39]

In this sermon, the "whorishness" of the women led Herod into sin and brought about the death of the saint. Another sermon, from Thomas Gibson in 1614, focused on good kingship and condemned the proxy rule of harlots such as the dancer from the tale, again attributing the root of the transgressions in the narrative to the female dancer:

> What a shame is it to be called Rulers and gouernours, and yet to be seruants and slaues to sinne? Yea, to as many sinnes as doe rule and raigne in them? Diogines had wont to say, that harlots were as Rulers, and Queenes to Kings; because they might command what they would; and that they would denie nothing to them as they did to their subjects. Of this there is example in Herod, who graunted to Herodias, a wanton dauncing Damsell, halfe of his kingdome.[40]

According to Gibson, female transgression, typified by sexual sin and dancing, led to the sins of Herod and to the murder of John the Baptist. Women's bodies overpowered men, leading to destruction and death. A final sermon from 1607 expanded upon this narrative to show how sexual sin, driven by the behavior of women and by dancing women in particular, led to the ruin of many men:

> may we well conclude, that the vntamed flesh of vs vnbridled men, will forcibly and with violence misleade our soules from the way of life ... in most of vs the flesh extinguisheth the spirit ... the temple of the holy Ghost was by lust made the member of a harlot ... this is that dancing daughter of Herodias, that cutteth of the head (the good beginnings) of many a Iohn Baptist.[41]

Dancing women brought about the death of godliness, both within the scriptural text and the present day, and therefore maintaining a boundary between profane female bodies and sacred male bodies was vital for ensuring the preservation of godliness.

---

[39] From the eighty-third sermon. Richard Rogers, *A Commentary Vpon the Vvhole Booke of Iudges* (London: Imprinted by Felix Kyngston for Thomas Man, and are to be sold at his shop in Pater-noster Row, at the signe of the Talbot, 1615), 739.

[40] "Sixth Sermon," in Thomas Gibson, *The Blessing of a Good King Deliuered in Eight Sermons* (At London: Printed by Tho: Creede [and N. Okes], for Arthur Iohnson, dwelling at the signe of the white Horse in Pauls Church-yard, 1614), 314–315. Lavater's sermon makes a similar move, connecting the sexual sin of the dancer to Herod's sins. Ludwig Lavater, *Three Christian Sermons* (London: Printed by Thomas Creede, 1596), 26.

[41] George Bury, *The Narrovv Vvay* (London: Printed [by R. Field] for Matthew Lownes, 1607), 40–41.

Women, Dance and Parish Religion in England, 1300–1640

Importantly, while men in the texts committed a wide variety of sins, women primarily committed sins closely tied to their bodies, a framing that parallels the medieval connections between the mere presence of women and the committing of sacrilege mentioned in Chapter 2.[42] Although ecclesiastical court records contain few cases where men or women are fined for dancing and sexual sin simultaneously, some of the cases in which early modern parishioners are fined for dancing alone reflect this concern with the mere presence of sinful women's bodies. One example appears in the records from Herefordshire, which contain abundant references to Morris dancing. While prosecutions of both men and women for Morris dancing are frequent, the charges laid against women are more ambiguous than those laid against men. Both men and women are charged for the timing of the dances (often on Sundays), and men are charged for performing the Morris dance. The single occasion on which women are charged explicitly for Morris dancing in the Herefordshire records, though, occurs in 1602. In this case from the consistory court of Hereford Cathedral, the consistory court cited and fined a group of men for dancing a Morris dance during divine service on Sunday. The court simultaneously charged one Elizabeth Wiett and several other women with "being at" a Morris dance.[43] David Klausner discusses this case as an example of the ambiguity as to the performance of the Morris dances, questioning whether or not women ever performed in them.[44] However, whether the women danced in the Morris is perhaps not the most important thing this episode reveals. The ambiguity about the women's behavior in this case shows that parish concerns about dance dovetailed with rhetorical concerns from these Salome sermons: the mere presence of the bodies of women at a dance was problematic. For these ecclesiastical authors and authorities, the issue was the existence of women.

Returning to the constellation of sins surrounding dancing bodies, what other sins did early modern sermon authors think dancing women (or the presence of women at a dance) could lead men into? Foolish oaths or words remained a paramount concern of early modern sermon authors, as multiple sermons mention Salome's dance in the context of condemning Herod's hasty oath. The 1547 *Certain Sermons* contains one such instance in its sermon against swearing and perjury:

> Thus doth God shewe plainly how muche he abhorreth breakers of honeste promises confirmed by an othe made in his name. And of them that make

---

[42] Chapters 3 and 4 in Bronach Kane's work on popular memory and gender in the medieval parish give good insight into how this dynamic played out in church courts more broadly. See Kane, *Popular Memory and Gender in Medieval England*, 81–136.

[43] 1602/3, Archdeaconry of Hereford Acts of Office, HRO, Box 21, vol. 80, pt. 4, p. 21. Transcribed in *REED Herefordshire, Worcestershire*, ed. Klausner, 171–172.

[44] Ibid., 14.

"In Her Dance She Had No Regard Unto God"

wicked promises by an othe and wil perfourme the same, wee have example in the Scripture chiefly of Herode, of the wicked Jewes, and of Jephthah. Herode promised by an othe unto the damosel whiche daunsed before hym to geve unto her whatsoever she should aske, when she was instructed before of her wicked mother to aske the hedde of Sainct Jhon Baptist. Herod, as he toke a wicked oth, so he more wickedly performed the same and cruelly slewe the mooste holy prophete.[45]

The sermon's author made clear that the dance acted as the catalyst for transgression but does not explicitly condemn the dance itself as sinful. George Gifford's 1589 sermon made a similar move, condemning the rash vow that came about because of the daughter's dance.[46] Both these sermons treat the transgressions in the text in a way that echoes medieval sermons – they focus on the oath, but acknowledge the role dance played in bringing about the larger sins of the story. However, sermons with this focus are far fewer in number during the early modern period than during the thirteenth and fourteenth centuries. Whereas late medieval sermons noted the dangers of a dancing woman but focused on the oath made by a man, early modern sermons only briefly mentioned the issues with the foolish oath made by Herod before focusing instead on the sexual sins of the women in the text, highlighting the gendering and embodying of transgression that had occurred over the elapsing centuries.

Other early modern sermons use both Herod's oath and Salome's dance as examples of false religion. The extent to which women feature in these discussions of false religion highlights the end result of medieval associations of women with sacrilege. A 1585 sermon by Edwin Sandys began by discussing how "Herode without all reason and iudgement promised to his daunsing daughter whatsoeuer shee should demaund, and his keeping of promise was euen as vnaduised." It then moved on to discuss how Herod was an example of those who:

forsake the freshe liuing springes, and drinke of a puddell, tat contemne the sauing word of God, and bee altogether addicted to mans vaine and deceitfull doctrine, that forsake christs merits by sticking to their owne. They want iudgement that call vpon dead Saints, when they may and should call only vpon the liuing God; who hath promised when we crie both to heare and to helpe vs. They are destitute both of reason and iudgement who vowe that which lieth not in their power to performe.[47]

---

45 Bond, *Certain Sermons or Homilies (1547)*, 132.

46 Eighth sermon in Gifford, *Eight Sermons, Vpon the First Foure Chapters, and Part of the Fift, of Ecclesiastes Preached at Mauldon*, 139.

47 Edwin Sandys, *Sermons Made by the Most Reuerende Father in God* (At London: Printed by Henrie Midleton, for Thomas Charde, 1585), 194–195.

Women, Dance and Parish Religion in England, 1300–1640

Herod and his dancing daughter, both of whom lacked discernment or godliness, were thus connected not simply to sexual sin and foolish oaths, but also to idolatry in the form of medieval religion and to "vain and deceitful doctrine." Laurence Humphrey's 1588 sermon on the "Romish Hydra" similarly juxtaposed false oaths with Catholic "idolatry" and with the sins of Herod and Salome:

> A peece and a part of this religion is a Vow, not of forced chastity, but of voluntary cruelty, which the Pope giueth presumptuously, and the Popelings take foolishly ... Is not their owne Law contrary to this? Is not there forbidden euery oth that is the hande of iniquity? And is it not an vniust band when wee sweare the spoile of Princely blood? ... No wise man will allowe the rash vowe perfourmed by Herode for the beheading of Iohn Baptist at the motiue of a dauncing damsel the Daughter of Herodias.[48]

The emergence of connections between this scriptural narrative, centered on a dance, and idolatry indicate the success of the medieval attempts to brand dance, especially by women, as sacrilegious and sinful.[49] Furthermore, while the medieval sermons do not present the medieval glossed interpretation of Satan dancing in the person of Salome, at least one early modern sermon explicitly mentions Salome as the tool of the devil in its discussion of idolatry: the same sermon referenced in Chapter 3 that connected Salome, witchcraft, idolatry, and women.[50] Salome's dance had shifted from one sin among many

[48] Laurence Humphrey, *A View of the Romish Hydra and Monster, Traison* (At Oxford: Printed by Ioseph Barnes, and are to be solde [by T. Cooke, London] in Paules Church-yearde at the signe of the Tygershead, 1588), 23.

[49] Several other sermons use the Salome narrative to discuss idolatry and the role of women in causing and sustaining false religion without specifically mentioning dance. These sermons include Bond, *Certain Sermons or Homilies (1547)*, 176–177; Samuel Ward, *A Coal from the Altar* (At London: Printed by H[umphrey] L[ownes] for Samuell Macham; and are to be sould at his shop in Pauls-church-yard, at the signe of the Buls-head, 1615), 25–26; Thomas Sutton, *Englands First and Second Summons* (London: Printed by Nicholas Okes for Matthevv Lavv, and are to be sold at his shop in Pauls Church-yard at the signe of the Fox, 1616), 142; Jeremiah Dyke, *Divers Select Sermons on Severall Texts* (London: printed by Tho. Paine, for L. Fawne and S. Gellibrand, at the sign of the brazen Serpent, in Pauls Church-yard, 1640), 343–344.

[50] As a reminder, the text of that sermon reads thus: "The third abomination is greater, women weeping for that monster that Devill of lust, or that devil of Idolatry, women shamelesse idolaters. The devil had no other engine in Paradise but the woman, she was the wheele to turne about all the world. Ahabs Iezebell is his instrument to slay the Prophets, Herodias daughter to strike of Iohn Baptist his head ... whether it be that women by their nature are more flexible, or by law lesse lyable to punishment (though very many of them haue beene holte worthy Saints and Martyrs of God), yet many haue beene most faithfull servants to their infernall Master, they be the loadstones and loadstars in all evill, the Iesuit not

"In Her Dance She Had No Regard Unto God"

to the sin that drove all other sins, from a sin primarily of sacrilege to a sin of sexual transgression, from a sin of action to a sin of the body. To early modern ecclesiastical authors and courts, dance was simply one way in which the devil utilized women as his tools, and dance was simply one means of revealing the status of women's bodies as profane rather than sacred.

DAVID AND SALOME

The extent to which dance had become a transgression centered on the sexualized female body by the sixteenth century is clearest in sermons that paired Salome's dance with David's dance before the Lord. Contrasting a godly dancing body – gendered male – with a profane dancing body – gendered female – effectively demonstrated and enforced an understanding of dance as a gendered action. Henry Smith's sermon placed its comparison of Salome and David in the midst of a long passage on vanities:

> *Turne away my eies* (saith the Prophet Dauid) *and my eares, & my heart too from vanitie.* Trie and proue thou no longer, for *Salomon* hath proued for thee, it is better to beleeue him than trie with him. Therefore now it remaineth that as they brought forth their vaine bookes ofter *Pauls* preaching, & cast them into the fire: so ye should cast out all your vanities this day, and sacrifice them to God, for they haue been your Idols, there|fore burie them as *Iacob* did the Idols, that neuer man saw them after. And as God gaue *Iob* other children, so they will giue you o|ther pleasures, feare not that your ioyes will goe way with your vanities, as many thinke they shall neuer bee merry againe, if they should be co~uerted to religion. But as *Dauid* daunced before the Arke as merily as *Hero|dias* daunced before the King: so knowe vn|doubtedlie that the righteous finde more ioy in goodnes, than euer the wicked found in filthines.[51]

Smith presented dance as performed by David as a Christian joy and contrasted that masculine dance with the sinful vanity of Salome's dance (and it is worth noting that Smith conflated Salome with Herodias, collapsing all the women in the passage into a single sinful figure). Although this passage highlighted the tension between dance as biblically justifiable and dance as dangerous, a second passage in this sermon made clear that dances such as David's were not typical and that a more standard fate for dancers was not praise but damnation: "What faith or feare haue they, that go dauncing and leaping to this fire, as it were to a banquet, like a foole which runneth to the

---

more serviceable to the Pope then Idolatrous women to the deuill." Price, *Spirituall Odours to the Memory of Prince Henry*, 21.

51 Smith, *The Sermons of Maister Henrie Smith Gathered into One Volume. Printed According to His Corrected Copies in His Life Time*, 845.

149

Women, Dance and Parish Religion in England, 1300–1640

stocks?"[52] Smith paired Salome and David but then added another image, that of sinners dancing to hell. Although Smith's sermon offered the potential for a form of dance which could be acceptable and a model for Christians, he made clear that it was a noble and male body that performed this sacred dance, and that the normal destination of dancers was not heaven but hell.

Other pairings of Salome and David appeared in sermons by Thomas Playfere and Michael Birkenhead, on the meaning of mourning and on the birth of Christ. Although the key text for his sermon was Luke 23:28, Playfere began his 1596 sermon with the reference to dance from Ecclesiastes 3 before moving on to discuss how a Christian should reflect upon the "honorable passion, and gladsome resurrection of Christ":

> And then though thou wert neuer so much afflicted, with ioy unspeakeable and glorious. Daunce now, not as Herodias did, but as Dauid did. Leap vp in affection, as high as heauen. Where thou shalt heare one rapt vp to the third heauen, saying, to himself, God forbid that I shoulde reioyce, reioyce in any thinge, but in the crosse of Christ; and to vs, reioycc in the Lord always, and againe, I say, reioyce.[53]

Playfere presented dancing as an appropriate response to the resurrection of Christ – but was clear that the sort of dancing he described was not that of Herodias. A similar theme appeared in Birkenhead's 1602 *Recoverie of Paradise*, which called its audience to:

> List vp they head, plucke vp a good courage; celebrate with ioy the Natiuity of they Sauiour; daunce now and be merry, not as Herodias did, but as Dauid did, leape vp in affection as high as heauen, where they Sauiour now sitteth, not in the lap of his mother, but on the right hand of his father in all glory and maiestie. Come then, my brethren, let vs sing vnto the Lord, let vs hartely reioyce in the strength of our Saluation. Let Israel reioyce in him that made him, and let the children of Sion be ioyfull in their King: Praise his name in the daunce, sing praises vnto him with Tabret and Harpe: yong men and maidens old men and children, praise the name of the Lord, sing Iustily vnto him with a good courage.[54]

Even more so than Playfere's sermon, Birkenhead drew upon dance as an expression of joy at the saving work of Christ, this time displayed in his

---

52 Ibid., 847–848. This sermon also appears in Henry Smith, *The Preachers Proclamacion* (Imprinted at London: By [E. Allde? for] William Kearney dwelling within Creeple-gate, 1591), 19–20.

53 Thomas Playfere, *The Meane in Mourning* (At London: Printed by the Widow Orwin for Andrew Wise, dwelling in Paules Church yeard, at the sign of the Angel, 1596), 111–112.

54 Michael Birkenhead, *The Recoverie of Paradise* ([London]: Printed for Nicholas Ling and Thomas Bushel, and are by them to be sold, 1602), 61–62.

"In Her Dance She Had No Regard Unto God"

birth. Furthermore, Playfere added in an allusion to Psalm 150, in which he referenced young men and maidens, old men and children. This is by far the most positive allusion to dance in early modern English sermons and is an outlier. Only these two sermons actually utilized the pairing of Salome and David to transition to a discussion of positive uses of dance, and both did so in reference to a response to one's salvation through the birth and death of Christ.

However, even in these sermons that serve as outliers, a closer examination reveals that the pairing of Herodias and David was done not to mitigate harsh views of dance by providing a sacred counterpoint, but to highlight the gendered nature of sinful dance. If the references to dance are allegorical rather than literal, it is significant that an allegory based on the dance of a man has replaced the earlier allegory for the true church, based on a woman. If these allusions refer to literal, physical dancing, using David's dance as an example of Christian joy provided an example of a noble man dancing, not a woman or ordinary parishioner. Yet, this was the only instance in these sermons in which dance was cited as acceptable. Salome and David were presented as opposites meant to provide clearer guidelines for congregational behavior and to illustrate the same lesson as the other sermons: dancing, when performed by a woman, was dangerous, sinful, and associated with false religion. Furthermore, even though maidens are mentioned in Birkenhead's reference to the psalms, maidens (women with no sexual experience) and children are the only female figures listed in his call to dance, whereas men of all ages, even old men who have presumably been married and have sexual experience, are called to dance. Thus, even the seeming contradictions presented in these few sermons that pair David and Salome as contrasting figures lend support to the growing prevalence of a view of dance as a gendered activity. By the sixteenth century, at least according to sermon authors, all dance performed by women was sinful. Dance by men, however, could be situationally justifiable.

Further support for this gendering of dance comes through considering early modern sermons about Miriam. Miriam, according to the Old Testament account, led a dance of joy in praise of God and provides a close parallel to David. Both are Old Testament figures utilizing dance as a form of rejoicing and worship. However, whereas forty-six early modern sermons discuss David's dance before the Lord, using the word "dance" to describe his actions, out of the fourteen sermons that mention Miriam's dance, only three English sermons actually use the word "dance." The other eleven replace "dance" with either "song" or "singing." These three outliers either connect her dance to old and outdated religious customs, or utilize it as a parallel for angels dancing for joy at Christ's birth, or see it as an example of the rejoicing of the church after Christ's return. None of these three examples presents Miriam's dance as something imitable by

Women, Dance and Parish Religion in England, 1300–1640

contemporary believers or present Miriam as, like David, an example of Christian rejoicing.[55]

Turning back to Salome and David, clearly, social status played a role in this rhetorical construction of dance: David's status as king helped validate his dance. But each of these sermons conveniently forgot to mention that Salome is likewise of the nobility, as the daughter of a king and queen. Nonetheless, this distinction between the dances of the aristocracy and of the peasantry had little meaning within most English parishes, which were composed of ordinary people. Its rhetorical importance appears only when records of courtly dance, which soared in popularity under the Stuart monarchs, are compared to records of parish dance practices.[56] The gendered distinction between dancing men and dancing women, however, shaped which festive parish practices survived the longest. The Morris dances and hobby horse dances, performed primarily if not exclusively by men, survived longer than the lights and processionals performed primarily by women. John Forrest's thorough study of the Morris dance ends in 1750, well after other forms of late medieval parish festivity had disappeared from both practice and memory.[57] As the clerical alignment of dancing men with David and dancing women with Salome became better known, gender influenced the levels of acceptability of dance. Previously, parish dances by groups of men or groups of women were equally acceptable, assuming the dances took place at the right time and in the right space. As the seventeenth century opened, the gender of the group of dancers also became part of the rubric for evaluating dance's acceptability.

These three sermons that pair David and Salome represent one interpretative move not appearing in the medieval sermons; a second interpretation

---

[55] The three sermons which act as outliers are Humphrey Sydenham, *Sermons Vpon Solemne Occasions* (London: Printed by Iohn Beale, for Humphrey Robinson, and are to be sold at the signe of the Three Pigeons in Pauls Church-yard, 1637), 12; John Wall, *Alae Seraphicae The Seraphins Vvings* (London: Printed by G[eorge] M[iller] for Robert Allot, and are to be sold at his shop in Pauls Churchyard at the signe of the Blacke Beare, 1627), 128; Smith, *The Sermons of Maister Henrie Smith Gathered into One Volume*, 496.

[56] See, for more on courtly dance, Skiles Howard, *The Politics of Courtly Dancing in Early Modern England* (Amherst: University of Massachusetts Press, 1998); B. Ravelhofer, *The Early Stuart Masque: Dance, Costume, and Music* (Oxford: Oxford University Press, 2009); Clare McManus, *Women on the Renaissance Stage: Anna of Denmark and Female Masquing in the Stuart Court (1590–1619)* (Manchester: Manchester University Press, 2002). For early modern courtly dance more broadly, see Jennifer Nevile, *Dance, Spectacle, and the Body Politick, 1250–1750* (Bloomington: Indiana University Press, 2008).

[57] Forrest, *The History of Morris Dancing, 1438–1750*; for a broader picture of when some of these festive traditions ended, see Hutton, *The Rise and Fall of Merry England*.

"In Her Dance She Had No Regard Unto God"

that is not present in the medieval sermons appears in two other early modern sermons. These two sermons directly condemn dance and women. Like the early modern commentaries, both use Salome's narrative as a starting point for a direct condemnation of all dance and repeatedly connect all dance to women. Thomas Baughe's 1614 *Summons to Judgment* warned its audience that "if like Herodias you loue to daunce, and striue, rather to keepe measure in your footing, then your liuing: if you more regard a glittering, and garish suite, then a gracious, and godly soule: if you more weigh a light feather, then the Law of your heauenly Father, here is a Quid facietis for you, what will you doe when you shall be excluded from God your father?"[58] Like the medieval glosses and early modern commentaries, Baughe used Salome (again conflated with the adulterous Herodias) as the ultimate example of a sinful dancer. Baughe then connected all who dance to Salome and asserted that measured Christian living is incompatible with dancing. William Holbrooke's 1609 sermon addressing discontentment and ungodliness similarly connected the dancing daughter to contemporary dance practices and to sin:

> Answerable vnto which, is that place, of the damsels dauncing before Herod, which was like, to the wanton, and artificiall dauncing, so much vsed, and practiced in these daies, as I take it, that is left vpon Record, to the dispraise of her, and then not to be imitated: shee did it to please Herod, without any thought, of Iohns head, vntill Herod made so large a proffer, and she consulted with her diuellish mother. And truly, the wanton dancing of our daies, is only to please men, abominable, as the effects thereof do shew. For what doth it bring forth, but wantonnes in action, wanton behauiour after? And often hereby, are affections drawne to marriage, to the after griefe of the parties, dishonoring of God, and vexation of parents. Hereby, is our land and nation iustly taxed of this sin, by being said, to be the New-fangledest nation vnder the heauens.[59]

Whereas Baughe's sermon drew a direct parallel between Salome and dancers, Holbrooke's sermon connected Salome to dance more generally, expanding his condemnation to include all dances of his day. More so than any of the medieval sermons, these two early modern sermons use the dance of Salome as indicative of the sinfulness of dancing. By discussing only a female dancer prior to shifting to broader condemnations of dancers and dance, Holbrooke and Baughe hammered home the nature of dance as a gendered transgression.

---

[58] Thomas Baughe, *A Summons to Iudgement* (London: Printed by G. Eld, for William Iones, and are to bee sold at his shop neere Holborne Conduit, at the signe of the Gunne, 1614), 49.

[59] William Holbrooke, *A Sermon Preached at Saint Buttolphs* (At London: Imprinted by Felix Kyngston, for Elizabeth Burby, dwelling in Pauls Churchyard at the signe of the Swan, 1609), 38–39.

Women, Dance and Parish Religion in England, 1300–1640

In these early modern sermons, the end result of the gradual association of dance with women and of women with sacrilege becomes apparent, as discussions of dance increasingly revolve around sin and gendered bodies. When a positive approach to dance did appear in the early modern sermons, it used Salome as a contrast to David, with Salome providing the example of evil and David that of godliness. This pairing of a transgressive female dancer with an acceptable (if not imitable) male dancer highlighted the increased conflation of transgressive dance with transgressive women. These sermons might still be willing to assign some of the blame to lustful Herod with his foolish oath, but Salome and Herodias were held more responsible for John's death. Portrayals of dance that did not treat dance as a female sin were gradually replaced by increasingly condemnatory presentations of the women involved in the text, and dance, particularly when performed by women, quietly moved closer to the forefront of the transgressions occurring in the narrative.

CONCLUSION

The early modern Salome presented quite a different face from her scriptural precursor or from her medieval predecessor. She still performed for a rash king whose hasty oath did not escape condemnation. But her dance was reframed as the sin that spurred the oath. Her body was conflated with that of her adulterous mother, and her dance was turned into an early modern wedding dance, used to trap godly men and lead them away from the faith. In early modern tellings of the dance of Salome, the body of each character – whether male or female – defined their potential for holiness.

This use of gender to separate saints from sinners becomes even clearer when examining the pairings of David and Salome, an interpretive pairing not extant in medieval vernacular sermons. David's holy male body provided the direct contrast to Salome's sacrilegious sinful one. True faith was contrasted with sexualized sacrilege, holy men with sinful women. In these early modern sermons, there were certainly still sinful men, but as the next chapter shows, early modern religious figures often assumed that the blame for men's sins could be, like Herod's oath, traced back to the actions of a woman. Transgression as a whole was not gendered female, but the action of dancing certainly was.

Perhaps because of this gendering of dance, dance itself was increasingly rendered as almost inherently sinful. None of the medieval glosses or sermons used Salome's dance as a starting point for criticizing dance in general. The early modern texts, with only a few exceptions, used Salome's dance to condemn not only all dancers but also contemporary dance practices, such as dancing at weddings. During the late medieval period, Satan might have danced in the person of one specific damsel. By the end of the sixteenth century, the conclusion appeared to be that the devil danced

"In Her Dance She Had No Regard Unto God"

not merely in Salome, but in every dancing damsel. Indeed, as Thomas Hall put it in a 1658 pamphlet, "who say to God depart from us, but those that dance?"[60]

---

[60] Thomas Hall, *A Practical and Polemical Commentary or Exposition upon the Third and Fourth Chapters of the Latter Epistle of Saint Paul to Timothy* (London: Printed by E. Tyler, for John Starkey, at the Miter at the North door of the middle Exchange in Saint Pauls Churchyard, 1658).

CHAPTER 6

PERFORMING DANCE, SIN, AND GENDER

"The foote is an vnhappy member, and carries a man to much wickednesse … There is a foote of pride, Psal. 26, a sawcie foote, that dares presumptuously enter vpon Gods free-hold. There is a foote of rebellion, that with an apostate malice kickes at God. There is a dauncing foote, that paceth the measures of circular wickednesse."[1] In a stark contrast with medieval exhortations to "dance to God," most early modern sermons focused on dance as a profane action, and on "dancing to hell." Roger Edgeworth's 1557 sermon is one such example: "most of part people … will not walke in the streyght way that bringeth a man to heauen, but had leauer keepe the brode waye of pleasure, easelye hopping and dauncing to hell, and therefore to them heauen is a wilderness."[2] Many similar sermons asserted that for dancers, heaven was a wilderness that could never be conquered, as does this sermon from 1589:

> I know not surely how we practise now a daies to get heauen by violence, vnlesse eating and drinking, banqueting and sporting, daunsing and vising, swearing, and staring, bee violence. If this violence, or the like kinde would get heauen, perhaps a number should come to Heauen, who for vsing the

---

[1] All sermons cited in this chapter are simply representative examples of trends that appear, unless noted otherwise, in multiple sermons. Sermons not directly cited but listed for further reference in the footnotes throughout are not the only other examples but simply particularly relevant ones. Sermons were found through a full text key word search on the word "dance" in Early English Books Online, with all variant boxes checked. Searches on "danc" and "daunc" and "dauns" all returned the same number of hits. The search was limited to sermons in English and sorted by earliest publication first; in a search of sermons 1473–1642 using the same search parameters, 685 hits in 307 records were pulled up. EEBO searches were run between November 2016 and March 2017; any changes in EEBO's search metrics and engines since then have not been accounted for. For this specific quote, see "The Taming of the Tongue," in Thomas Adams, *The Sacrifice of Thankefulnesse* (London: Printed by Thomas Purfoot, for Clement Knight, and are to be sold at his shop in Pauls Church-yard, at the signe of the Holy Lambe, 1616), 33.

[2] Roger Edgeworth, *Sermons Very Fruitfull, Godly, and Learned, Preached* (Excusum Londini: In aedibus Roberti Caly, Tipographi, 1557), fol. c.xxxxii.r.

Women, Dance and Parish Religion in England, 1300–1640

same shall bee assured neuer to come there, but violently to bee thrust into hel where they shal remaine and abide for euermore.[3]

Dance, according to Anthony Tyrrell, could not be a spiritual practice, and dance ensured not entry into heaven but entry into hell.

These three sermons, with their negative presentations of dance and dancers, represent just a sample of over three hundred early modern sermons about dance. These sermons range in topic and in audience, with some presenting lengthy discussions of dance and others simply remarking upon dance in passing. Like their medieval predecessors, very few of these homilies take as their main text a passage that references dance specifically, instead drawing in references to dance to support their larger points and confirming the late medieval theology of dance almost accidentally. Many of these sermons were printed in London; almost as many were preached in London, and on the whole, these sermons are the products of Oxbridge-educated clerics known for their erudition and eloquence. However, given the wide circulation of printed materials during this period, it is likely that these sermons may have also been circulated and preached in more rural parishes as well. And, despite the chronological span of these sermons and the differing denominational positions of their authors (with Church of England, separatist, and Catholic clergy represented), almost all of them present a remarkably consistent message about dance.[4] Again and again, dancers are portrayed as dancing to the devil's pipes, straight into eternal damnation.

While early modern sermon authors bewailed the evils of dance, they simultaneously lamented the death of neighborliness and community within early modern parishes. John Day, cited in the previous chapter as one of the early modern voices discussing Salome, wrote in another sermon from the same collection about the decay of neighborliness: "Witnesse those many Quarrels now a foot between Neighbour & Neighbour, especially in the Country. Witnesse that multiplying of Lawyers in our Age more than ever in former times. Witnesse that Thryving of them in our dayes, and those super-lative Purchases which they make in Lands, and Lordships."[5] George Gifford, the author of one of the sermons considered in Chapter 1, mourned that while the ancestors of his parishioners had "lived in friendshippe, and made merrie together, nowe there is no good neighbourhoode: nowe every man for himself,

---

3 Anthony Tyrrell, *A Fruitfull Sermon Preached in Christs-Church the 13. of Iulie. Anno 1589* (At London: Printed by Iohn Windet, and are to be sold at the signe of the Sun in Pauls church-yard by Abraham Kitson, 1589), fol. C.vii.v.

4 For the differing perspectives of the sermon authors considered in this chapter, see the appendix. For an overview of the complexities of religious divisions in the English Reformation as pertain specifically to dance, see the excellent historio-graphical work done in Winerock, "Reformation and Revelry," 6–13.

5 Day, *Day's Festiuals*, 346.

Performing Dance, Sin, and Gender

and are readie to pull one another by the throate."[6] Yet while sermon authors lamented the death of neighborliness, their parishioners also lamented the death of the festivities and dances that made neighborly feeling possible. Andy Wood's recent book *Faith, Hope, and Charity: English Neighbourhoods, 1500–1640*, shows clearly how sixteenth- and seventeenth-century individuals (both clerics and laity) felt that their parish and neighborhood were disintegrating under economic and religious pressures.[7] However, while laity often identified the Protestant and Puritan pressure on their parish festivities as the cause of rising parish tensions, their clerics and pastors did not necessarily connect the two trends. Many early modern sermon authors who bewailed the loss of community, like Day or Gifford, also preached strongly against dance and dancers, seeing no contradiction between concern with communal tensions and communal festivities. And it is important to note that these two concerns with community were not necessarily confined to specific theological movements; evangelicals, Catholics, and Puritans alike were all concerned with the decline of charity and community, and simultaneously were more concerned with dance than their medieval predecessors.

If dance was one of the practices binding community together, as the laity involved in some of the controversies explored by Wood clearly believed, how did a concern with the destruction of community and a push to stop communal dancing coexist so neatly in early modern sermons and parishes?[8] I argue that it is this very contradiction and tension that shows how far rhetorical constructions of dance have come since Langton's thirteenth-century call to dance after God, arm-in-arm with one's neighbors. By the time these early modern sermons were composed, clerical ideas about dance as sacrilege and then as sex had become a fully fledged theology of gender and dance in which sacrilege and sex inextricably intertwined. Rhetorically at least, religious authors now treated dancers exclusively as sinful and problematic, with a focus on their bodies and sexuality as indications of their sacrilegious spiritual status. There was thus no contradiction between calling for an end to danced parish festivities and calling for the restoration of traditional communal relations within the parish. Early modern sermons presented dance not as a communal activity that only crossed boundaries when performed in the

---

6   George Gifford (b. 1547 or 1548; d. 1600), *A Briefe Discourse of Certaine Points of the Religion Which Is among the Commō Sort of Christians, Which May Bee Termed the Countrie Diuinitie with a Manifest Confutation of the Same, after the Order of a Dialogue / Compiled by George Gifforde* (London, For Toby Cook, dwelling at the Tigres head in Paules churchyard, and are there to bee solde, 1582), fol. 5r.

7   Andy Wood, *Faith, Hope and Charity: English Neighbourhoods, 1500–1640* (Cambridge: Cambridge University Press, 2020).

8   For a few examples in Wood's recent study, see the section in Ch. 2 titled "Festivity, Play and the Celebration of Neighbourhood," Wood, *Faith, Hope and Charity*, 74–80.

Women, Dance and Parish Religion in England, 1300–1640

wrong place or time but as an individual pastime that disrupted community, gender, and holiness. Clerics framed dance within neatly defined binaries, setting sacred and profane bodies, gendered male and female respectively, as opposing poles. Both in sermons and in parishes, dance's acceptability was determined by the gender of the performer.

As the acceptability of dance was determined by the gendered body of the performer, so the gender of the dancer was increasingly indicated by the dance performance itself. As shown in the previous chapter, sermons and didactic texts presented dance as a sin tied to the female body; thus, male dancing bodies were increasingly discussed as effeminate, as malformed, and as unmanly. Discussions of dance initially used gendered bodies as a way to separate dancers: men could dance with men and women with women without transgression and within the confines of acceptable practice. But dance became a way to separate gendered bodies: to determine who was a man and who was a woman. The long transformation of discussions of dance produced not only a rubric for the performance of holiness but also a rubric for the performance of gender. The ideology developed through discussions of dance helped to crystallize standards for properly performing one's gender and had ramifications for what it meant to be a woman (or a man) in the early modern world. The collision of the two discourses tied to dance in English texts – discourses about sacrilege and about sex – culminated in a broadly negative perspective on dance as a sexualized, sacrilegious sin that could be used to separate holy male bodies from sinful female ones.

This rhetoric about gendered dancers and gendered sin, like earlier medieval rhetoric about dance as primarily sacrilege, moved from the pulpit to the parish, with the rhetoric again used as a tool for parish discipline. Turning to the parish, then, what was the end point of these gradual theological transformations and their according impact on lived parish experience? As hinted at in the earlier discussion of dance and witchcraft, one of the first notable shifts was in an emphasis on individual dancers and individual sin, in line with the sexualization of dance and connection of dance to individual bodies. Yet while witchcraft accusations were an extreme application of this shift, this emphasis on individual sinners played a role in the more normative setting of parish discipline as well. It contributed to the breakdown of the communal image of medieval dancers, performing charity arm in arm, and fundamentally shifted the dynamics of the early modern parish. The disappearance of communal dance practices occurred in the midst of the larger loss of communal festivity, and to some degree, the shift from communal to individual emphasis led to a loss of communal accountability.

Alongside this change, however, came an even more significant one: a change in attributions of agency and blame for transgression within the early modern parish, with women serving as the focal point for all sins, whether their own or the sins of the men around them. Fourteenth-century authors had blamed clerical failure and sacrilege on the mere presence of women, but

Performing Dance, Sin, and Gender

women could still participate in communal parish festivity and worship in the late medieval church. Their presence was primarily problematic within sacred space, not in general. In the early modern parish, the mere existence of women – in their houses, outside their houses, or in public spaces – was treated as a likely gateway to sin, both in sermons and in ecclesiastical courts. Parishioners and preachers alike might lament the death of parish neighborliness and community that they ascribed to their modern age. But without an identification of the rhetorical reasons behind that shift, the recovery of community as they remembered it would prove impossible, not because of government regulations or puritanical tendencies as early modern parishioners assumed, but because of the slow changes in consideration of sacrilege and gender that underpinned a variety of early modern theological positions.

THE DEVIL IN ALL WOMEN

By the sixteenth century, discussions of dance and transgression revolved not around specific female sinners but around all women. This broader, more condemnatory approach applied not only to dance but to a variety of other gendered transgressions as well. When the devil consorted with not just individual women but all women, then sins closely tied to the devil, whether dancing, witchcraft, gossip, or sacrilege, were likewise associated with all women. The avenues for religious and public engagement available to women increasingly narrowed as the pathways to holiness became more proscribed and masculine. The early modern parish was increasingly hostile towards women, despite the potential inherent in the Protestant adherence to salvation through individual professions of faith.

This increased hostility appears throughout early modern sermons connecting dance, women, and sin. One of the most blatant examples of this is the invention of transgressive biblical dancing women. Salome represents one of only a few actual biblical women explicitly associated with dance, and few of the other biblical dancing women join her in early modern homilies. For instance, Miriam and Jephthah's daughter, two of the other dancing women from the canonical scriptural text, were rarely if ever discussed, especially in early modern sermons. However, other biblical women not associated with dance in the biblical narrative suddenly dance through these early modern sermons. Women considered sinful often had dance added to their scriptural narratives. One 1619 sermon claimed that "Sampson, by the deceipt of daucing Dalilah, may haue his head cut, haire shorne, and strength goe from him."[9] Another sermon preached at Paul's Cross in 1613 gave a list of sinful women, connecting all three women to unbalanced and ungodly living:

---

[9] John Barlow, *The True Guide to Glory* (London: Printed by Thomas Snodham, for

Women, Dance and Parish Religion in England, 1300–1640

If like *Thamar* you sit in the way for to ensnare, or like *Dalila* you offer a bosome but to murther: if like *Herodias* you loue to daunce, and striue, rather to keep measure in your footing, then your liuing: if you more regard a glittering, and garish suite, then a gracious, and godly soule: if you more weigh a light feather, then the Law of your heauenly Father, here is a *Quid facietis* for you, what will you doe when you shall be excluded from God your Father?[10]

By listing dance as a sin equivalent to murder or sexual entrapment and by adding dance into scriptural narratives about transgression, these sermons reinforced the associations between dance, women, and sin. Whether the sins actually appeared in the scriptural text seems to have carried less weight than the rhetorical points these lists were intended to teach. This connection between dance, women, and sin was once again hammered home in a 1602 sermon connecting Michal, David, and Salome: "Michol was neuer such a scoffer at the zeale of Dauid her Lord and husband, as they would be: Herods minicing minion, and daunceing damsel did neuer so trip it as they would trippe it."[11] The sins of the text were connected to a woman and then eventually back to Salome, the early modern paradigmatic figure for sinful dancing. Given the growing importance afforded the biblical text during the Reformations, these associations between sinful biblical women and dance and oft-repeated lists of sinful women held increasing weight with audiences.

Salome's archetypal status points to another key theme in early modern theological treatments of dance. David was a dancing anomaly, while Salome was the rule proved by all women. The differing representativeness assigned to dancing men and women also demonstrates the increased emphasis on dance as a gendered transgression apparent in these early modern sermons. While discussions of men and dance either focused on specific scriptural narratives or on a specific group of men (clergy or noblemen), discussions of women and dance in these sermons were far more general, condemning all dancing women. Oftentimes, these condemnations began by associating the women of the day with transgressive women from scripture, as in the case of a sermon from February of 1609, which associated both Jezebel and Salome with the wanton women and dancing of the author's time:

Here againe commeth to be reproued, and to be charged deeply with this fault and sin, the painted *Iezabels* of our daies, who only, not being content

---

Nathaniel Newberry, and are to be sold at his shop vnder Saint Peters Church in Cornehill, 1619), 10.

[10] Baughe, *A Summons to Iudgement*, 49.

[11] "I Sermon," in Burton, *Ten Sermons Vpon the First, Second, Third and Fourth Verses of the Sixt of Matthew*, 9; for a second sermon that makes a similar rhetorical move by having "nature," a woman, criticize David's dance, see Joseph Hall, *The Great Impostor Laid Open* (London: Printed by J. Haviland for Nath. Butter, 1623), 33–34.

Performing Dance, Sin, and Gender

with that feature, and face, God (who is only wise) hath giuen them, must needs, and doe, digge vnto themselues, cisternes of their owne inuentions. A fearefull sinne it is, and most vsed, where sin should be least countenanced. For the confutation whereof, I will aske but this question: whether those words [*Iezabel the whore, that painted her selfe*] were spoken to the praise of her, or dispraise? If to the dispraise, whether to be imitated or no? answerable vnto which, is that place, of the damsels dauncing before *Herod*, which was like, to the wanton, and artificiall dauncing, so much vsed, and practised in these daies, as I take it, that is left vpon Record, to the dispraise of her, and then not to be imitated.[12]

Within this one discussion, Holbrooke rhetorically collapsed time to bring the sins of Jezebel into the present and to make these sins comparable to the actions of contemporary women. Dancing and "painting oneself" were likewise collapsed into generic female transgressions, transgressions that defined the absolute moral character of women in both the past and present. This association of contemporary people with transgressive individuals in scripture was not seen in discussions of men and dance, but it was common to discussions of women and dance, as shown in the discussions of presentations of Salome in the previous chapter. Notably, these compressions of time and action both focused on the same group: women and their sins.

Indeed, these sermons made clear that dance, particularly when performed by women, could connect to any number of transgressions. To quote from one 1621 sermon, in which the transgressions were all gendered female: "there are two Nations of finnes, eternall foes to the people of God, like *Moab* and *Ammon*, begotten of those two base Daughters of Health in their Fathers forgetfulnesse, Drunkennesse and Lust: of eyther of them may be said that of *Ambrose* concerning her dauncing, *How many faults were in that one Wickednesse?*"[13] In these early modern sermons, dancing women and their bodies were connected to multiple sins like vanity, lust, and drunkenness. The idea that dance was a sin of female vanity appears in several early modern sermons, like this 1566 sermon which contrasted worldly and foolish dancing with diligent and godly care for the household and obedience to God:

If then God doth so much praise this in a floure what a great renoume is this thynkest thou, for a man to be founde in the commaundement and obedience of God? The maydens are decked to daunce, it is but a toy and a trifle. For this is her cheif renoume, when she aplieth her worke and vocation, seeth diligentlye to her maysters chyldren, and to such other

---

12 Holbrooke, *A Sermon Preached at Saint Buttolphs*, 38–39.
13 John Reading, *A Faire Vvarning Declaring the Comfortable vse Both of Sicknesse and Health* (London: Printed by Bernard Alsop, for Iohn Hodgets, 1621), 22.

163

Women, Dance and Parish Religion in England, 1300–1640

seruice … he then, that walketh in Gods commaundement, walketh in the very honour of God.[14]

This is the most positive interpretation afforded to dances performed by women in these sermons – as vain actions with no lasting impact, used as a contrast with a virtuous and godly life. Other sermons are more aggressive in their connection of sin to women, such as the following sermon from 1616:

> Ye wanton *Dames*, that are in your ful-blowne pride, looke vpon *this Woman*. Saint *Chrysostome* saies, that when yee are hoyting, and dancing, *the Deuill dances among you*; and *Cyprian* tels you, that this *Pargetting of faces*, is *Opus Diaboli, the worke of the Deuill*. Shortly shall you finde, that your outward hue is but momentanie, and when the floure is gone, your selues may not abide the stalke.[15]

Women who array themselves to dance are aligned with the work of the devil and meet a sinister end. A 1607 sermon touching on this theme of women, dance, and vanity made the fate of these women clear:

> And sometime wee must come among women, and tell them as the Prophet *Esay* doth, of many prettie superfluities, and sinnes of supererogation; as for the example, their stretching and casting out their neckes, as if they were in distresse and gasping for aire; their minsing and shuffling, and tinkling with their feete, as if they were still meditating and practising to daunce; for euen for these things the Prophet threateneth desolation vpon them, as Christ for each idle word conuenteth to the day of iudgement.[16]

Whereas early modern sermon authors vaguely associated most men who danced with "wickedness" and with wicked women, women who danced were tied to specific transgressions, diabolical intervention, and eternal judgment.

The collapsing of a scriptural past and an English present likewise appears in discussions of dance, women, and sexual transgression. Scriptural passages were tied to specific contemporary female transgressions, and anxieties about the bodies of women appeared throughout these sermons. Some of these anxieties revolved around the preservation of virtuous female bodies and the ways in which dance endangered female virtue. For example, at least two sermons associated dancing with rape and loss of chastity. One 1620 sermon asserted that there is "nothing so pernicious as the company

---

14 Becon, *A New Postil Conteinyng Most Godly and Learned Sermons*, fol. 119v–r.

15 William Worship, *The Patterne of an Inuincible Faith* (London: Printed by Nicholas Okes, for Matthew Law, and are to be sold at his shop in Pauls Churchyard at the signe of the Fox, 1616), 4.

16 Robert Wilkinson, *Lots Wife* (At London: Imprinted by Felix Kyngston, for Iohn Flasket, and are to be sold at his shop in Paules churchyard at the signe of the black Beare, 1607), 33–34.

Performing Dance, Sin, and Gender

of the wicked. If Dina had not haunted dancing, shee had preserued her chastity."[17] While the author added dance to Dinah's narrative to justify her rape, another sermon printed in 1612 drew on an actual scriptural narrative mentioning dance to likewise connect rape and dance. In this case, the sermon interpreted the Benjamites' seizure of wives as a result of the dancing of the women: "*In the morning hee shall deuoure the Preye, and at might hee shall diuide the spoyle ... Rabbi Salomon* saith, that hereby is signified the exploite of the *Beniamites*, in taking as a preye, the daughters of *Silo*, as they came forth to daunce, to be their wiues, which afterwards they distributed and diuided as a spoile amongst themselues."[18] These sermons implied that the women, by dancing, lost their chastity and encouraged the transgressions of men, an implication with tangible repercussions that will be discussed later in this chapter.[19] Furthermore, these sermons focused not just on dance but on the female body too. The action of dancing was directly correlated with the loss of physical virtue. Sin and its consequences were both presented as embodied acts.[20]

Several ecclesiastical court cases demonstrate this correlation of dancing women with loss of virtue. In one 1628 deposition, Margaret Usher, aged 68, claimed that one Margerie Safe, a witness in a case, is "a wooman of noe credit and reputation," largely because "when shee was a younge wooman shee behaued her self wantonlie [and w] in daunscing."[21] Margaret maintained that because of Margerie's dancing, it was widely known in the parish that she was a woman of no repute who could not be trusted to bear witness. Another case from Somerset even more directly correlated female dancing with the loss of female virtue. A 1604 charge against John Hooper in the consistory court accused him of keeping "evill order in his howse manie Sabaoth days

---

17 Pierre Du Moulin, *A Preparation Vnto Fasting and Repentance* (London: Printed by T. S[nodham] for Nathaniel Newbery, and are to be sould at the signe of the Starre vnder S. Peters Church in Cornehill, and in Popes head ally, 1620), 46.

18 "Twelfth Sermon of Beniamin," in Rollenson, *Twelue Prophetical Legacies*, 276.

19 Unrepentant cities are also represented as dancing women: "As while the Prophet continued piping, Tyre was content to daunce, so now hee beginns his mourning, shee may frame her selfe to weepe; it was sweet Musick in her eares to heare tell of her glory, it will be a sharpe corasiue, to her heart to heare mention of her iudgement." John Grent, *The Burthen of Tyre* (London: Printed [by A. Mathewes] for Richard Royston, 1627), 11.

20 As Baines discusses in her work, Dinah's narrative was increasingly prominent in early modern England, used to discuss the consequences for women who leave their households. See Barbara J. Baines, *Representing Rape in the English Early Modern Period* (Lewiston, NY: Edwin Mellen Press, 2003), 41–48. Both these themes – the household and rape – will be taken up later in the chapter.

21 1628/9, Bishop's Court Deposition Book, SRO, D/D/Cd 64, fol. 28, as transcribed in *REED Somerset Including Bath 1*, ed. Stokes with Alexander, 391–392. The 'and w' set here in square brackets is crossed out in the original.

165

Women, Dance and Parish Religion in England, 1300–1640

at night in assembling manie young persons to dauncing att vnseasonable tymes of the night, by whiche meanes theire daughter hath bin defiled, and wee feare yat somme other haue, or may bee corrupted." While the charge noted the improper timing of the dancing, the court's broader concern was that the dances were destroying the virtue of not just the unnamed daughter, but other maidens of the town as well. In fact, the conclusion of the charge noted that because of the dancing, "hee and his wife are commonlie suspected ... to keepe a howse of bawdry."[22] The framing of these cases made clear that a woman who danced was a woman of no repute, and daughters who danced lost their virtue. The rhetorical framing of dance as destructive to female virtue and reputations in sixteenth- and seventeenth-century sermons shaped parish practice, where dancing was again treated as reflecting the state of one's body and soul.

Considering these parish examples alongside early modern sermons on dance and sin highlights a few key changes. First, the rhetoric of these sermons connected women and dance to sin not just rhetorically but in the audience's contemporary reality. Dancing women moved from the page into the present. As they did so, they seemed to multiply in number; scriptural exemplars of transgressive dancing women became analogies for the entire sex, and representatives of female holiness were overwhelmed by figures of female sin. Early modern clerics presented anxieties about women, their bodies, and the transgression enabled and encouraged by dancing as tied both to true religion and to current situations, leaving their audiences with the impression that dance was sinful when connected to women – no matter who or when those women were, and without questioning the actual actions of these women, like John Hooper's daughter. She was present at a dance: that alone condemned her and her early modern contemporaries.

THE BEHEADING OF GODLY MEN

While sermons like the ones on Dinah's rape and cases like that against John Hooper expressed concern with the destruction of female virtue through dance, a more frequently voiced fear in early modern sermons and records was the destruction of male virtue through the female body. This was not a new anxiety. Patristic authors often expressed concern with the dangers of female bodies, and medieval authors reiterated the theme. But in these early modern texts, authors shifted the danger from a vague looming threat to a very present and very specific one, represented through dancing female contemporaries.

---

[22] 1604/5, Ex Officio Act Book, SRO, D/D/Ca 138, fol. 247v. As transcribed in *REED Somerset Including Bath 1*, ed. Stokes with Alexander.

Performing Dance, Sin, and Gender

Authors expressed the connection between women, sexual sin, and dance quite explicitly, with few alternative readings of the relationship between the three. Thomas Cranmer, for example, connected Christ's command against adultery to dancing in his 1548 catechism for children: "Therfore Christe sayth. He yt seeth a woman to lust after her, hath alredye committed adultery in hys harte. You must also diligently auoyde al occasions, by the whiche such vnlawfull lustes are prouoked as surfetyng, dronkenes, idleness, wanton daunsing and such like."[23] Another 1586 sermon expressed anxiety not only about the sexual power of dancing women, but also about collaborations between generations of women to use dance and sex to entrap men:

> For the falles of the saints ought to make vs more warie, and not to allue vs to sinne. There are olde women, who when they hope that by this meanes, they can make marriages between young men and virgins, they call them to night banquettes, talkes, and daunces, and sometime exhort them, that they should goe to bed together.[24]

Yet another sermon from 1595 again combines condemnation of women, dance, and sexual sin with concerns about women training each generation in transgression and entrapment: "*Ambrose* in his 3. booke of Virgins, thus writeth: what say ye, O holy women? you see what ye ought to teach and vnteach your daughters: she danceth, but the daughter of an harlot; for she that is chast and shamefast, teacheth her children religion, and not dauncing."[25] One 1607 sermon on Salome lamented how, through a dancing woman, the heads of many godly men were lopped off. To quote, "may we well conclude, that the vntamed flesh of vs vnbridled men, will forcibly and with violence misleade our soules from the way of life ... in most of vs the flesh extinguisheth the spirit ... the temple of the holy Ghost was by lust made the member of a harlot ... this is that dancing daughter of Herodias, that cutteth of the head (the good beginnings) of many a Iohn Baptist."[26] This sermon was not alone in its lament. Thomas Hall included the dance of Herodias's daughter in a long list of dangers in his 1658 text, warning his reader:

> Set a watch over the Eyes. The Devill gets into our hearts by these windows of the soul Eve by seeing the forbidden fruits, David by seeing Beethsheba, Sampson by seeing a Harlot, Potiphars wife by seeing Josephs beauty, and Herod by seeing Herodias dance, they were all ensnared, and caught.[27]

---

23 "The Syxte Sermon," in Cranmer, *Catechismus*, fol. l.xxi.v.

24 "16 Sermon," in Ludwig Lavater, *The Book of Ruth* (At London: Printed by Robert Walde-graue, dwelling without Temple-bar, 1586), 96v–r. See also the fifteenth and twenty-fourth sermons, pp. 89r and 142v.

25 Hill, *The Crie of England*, 16–17.

26 Bury, *The Narrovv Vvay*, 40–41.

27 Hall, *A Practical and Polemical Commentary*, 106.

167

Women, Dance and Parish Religion in England, 1300–1640

To these authors, women, particularly dancing ones, held the power to lead men into great sin. More so than in medieval sermons on dance, these early modern sermons ascribed the blame for the sins associated with dance to women alone, in a consequence of repeated connections of sacrilege and sexual sin to the female body.

The blaming of women's bodies for men's sins was not always blatant, and discussions of dance in early modern sermons highlight other more insidious ways in which authors accomplished this shift in responsibility. A subtle shifting of agency and blame appears in discussions of Job 21:11–12, a text with a dance reference that appears in at least nine early modern sermons. Presentations of this text emphasized the lifestyles of the wicked and their eventual fate. One 1602 sermon stated, "they send foorth their children like sheepe, and their sons daunce, they take their tabret and harpe, and reioyce in the sound of the organes: they spend their daies in wealth. There is one banquet past, now cometh in the reckening, and that is this: suddenly they go downe to the graue."[28] Another sermon from 1615 noted that: "it much perplexed *Iob* to see the wicked in such prosperity ... they sent forth their children in droues, and their sonnes in dances ... yet when he saw how suddenly they dropped down to hell, hee knew their hauing was no heauen."[29] This passage, one of the most frequently cited scriptures that references dance in early modern sermons, clearly aligned dance with the actions and damnation of the wicked, an action that marked unrepentant behavior on earth and led to eternal condemnation.

Upon first glance, these early modern presentations of the Job passage appear to align dance with the transgressions of sons. But in considering this text as an example of the gendering of transgression and the shifting of blame to women, there are a few interesting twists. Medieval versions of this passage focused on the wicked as a gender-inclusive group, noting how "in a poynt of a wynk of an eyze they gon down to helle."[30] The King James Version of the text likewise utilizes gender-inclusive language, reading: "They send forth their little ones like a flock, and their children dance. They take the timbrel and harp, and rejoice at the sound of the organ." Some early modern sermons adopted this gender-inclusive language and discussed how the children of the wicked dance.[31] However, most sixteenth- and seventeenth-century authors changed "children" to "sons." This move might at first appear

---

28 "X Sermon," in Burton, *Ten Sermons Vpon the First, Second, Third and Fourth Verses of the Sixt of Matthew*, 242.

29 William Leigh, *Dauids Palme and Cedar* (London: Printed by Thomas Creede for Arthur Iohnson, and are to be sold at his shop in Paules churchyard, 1615), 46.

30 Longleat MS 4, fol. 53v.

31 "His Peremptory Asseveration," in Vase, *Ionah's Contestation about His Gourd*, 38; John Hoskin, *A Sermon Vpon the Parable of the King* (At London: Printed by G. E[ld] for Iohn Wright, 1609), fol. C.6.r.

Performing Dance, Sin, and Gender

to undermine the argument that dance had become a transgression associated with women.[32] Yet, these authors ultimately implicate women as the reason for the sons' transgressive and wicked dancing. One specific example of how female transgression remained at the center of this narrative, despite male-centric language, appears in a sermon titled *Huvsbands and Vvives* by John Day, printed in 1615: "As for the Vngodly saith the Prophet, it is not so with them: nor is it so indeed with Foolish Women ... nay it may be that the Houses in that kind [material houses] may stand strongly enough, and yet their Mistresses destroy them too."[33] While Day's sermon used the gender-neutral "children" in its actual reference to dance, these three lines which preface his quote of the Job passage clearly connected the dancing of the sons with the wickedness of their mothers and the wickedness of households with the failures of their mistresses.[34] In these texts, it was because of the failure of women that the households have become wicked and produced wicked sons. Despite the biblical text attributing fault to the men in this passage, these authors still blame women for the sin rather than men.

The explanation of sin as a failure of the household in interpretations of this passage from Job fits within the increasingly influential model of the household as the origin of virtue and rightly ordered society, in which

---

[32] Four other sermons that reference the Job passage and utilize "sons" instead of children are Barlow, *The True Guide to Glory*, 3; "The Trial of True Religion," in Robert Abbot, *A Hand of Fellovvship, to Helpe Keepe out Sinne* (London: Printed by Iohn Haviland for Nathaniel Butter, 1623), 266; "The Short Prosperity," in Richard Eedes, *Three Sermons* (London: Printed by G. M. for Philemon Stephens and Christopher Meredith, and are to be sold at the Golden Lyon in Pauls Churchyard, 1627), 86; John Chardon, *A Sermon Preached in S. Peters Church* (Imprinted at London: At the three Cranes in the Vintree, by Thomas Dawson, 1580), fols. C.2.r–C.3.v.

[33] "Huvsbands and Vvives," in Day, *Day's Festiuals*, 212–213.

[34] Another sermon references the sexual sin associated with dance in connection to the Job passage: "We see at this day that they whiche vse musike doo swell with poyson agaynste God, they become hardharted, they wil haue their songes, yea and what manner of songs? full of all villanie and ribauldrie. And afterward they fall to dauncing, which is the cheefest mischeefe of all. For there is always such vnchaste behauiour in dauncing: that of it selfe and as they abuse it (to speake the truth at one worde,) it is nothing else but an enticement to whoredome. So then it is not without a cause, that Ioh intending to declare that the children of this worlde, and the despizers of God doo passe measure in their reioycings, speaketh of the sounde of the taboret, of the flute, and of other instrumentes of musike." See "The lxxx Sermon," in Calvin, *Sermons of Master Iohn Calvin, Vpon the Booke of Iob*, 409. For other sermons connecting women, dance, and sexual sin to transgressive dancing by men, see "The xxxiiii Sermon," in Calvin, *Sermons of M. Iohn Caluine Vpon the Epistle of Saincte Paule to the Galathians*, fols. 242v, 244v–r; "The Second Sermon," in Pierre Merlin, *A Most Plaine and Profitable Exposition* (London: Printed by Thomas Creed, 1599), 40.

169

Women, Dance and Parish Religion in England, 1300–1640

much of the responsibility for the virtue of the household lay with women. Lyndal Roper's *Holy Household* provides an in-depth study of this "reformed moralism" centered in the early modern home.[35] The Reformation, according to Roper, was increasingly a domestic movement "accomplished through a politics of reinscribing women within the 'family.'"[36] And despite the many differences separating the Reformations in England from their continental counterparts, in this specific aspect of reform, England's trajectory paralleled that of the continent.[37] As Patricia Crawford noted in her study of women and religion in early modern England, the changes brought about by Reformation theology meant that women gained spiritual influence in the household, as their role as models of virtue was shifted more firmly into the private sphere.[38] Thus, a wicked or ungodly mistress sent her sons out dancing to their destruction, or destroyed the chastity of her daughters through teaching them dance, or even danced herself.

It is then perhaps no surprise to find that behind the fear of sinful dancing women in the streets was a desire to encourage the presence of women in the household. Virtue (or lack thereof) was tied to actions, to bodies, and to place. In one continental example of this dichotomy, the Lutheran pastor Caspar Huberinus discussed how the Virgin Mary herself was an example of the relationship between household and virtue. The angel approached Mary when she was inside her home, "not in the streets or at a dance."[39] An English sermon from 1633 made a similar point, noting that sin is compounded when "the wife of the house becommeth a brawling woman in the house of society, as the Hebrew phrase is, Prov. 21:9."[40] In a lengthier explication, another sermon printed in 1657 asserted:

> The woman is to preserve and enlarge that her husband hath provided; the domesticall duty of preserving the house and household pertaineth to her, as it is in *Proverbs* 31.21. She should be of the property of the Snail, still at

---

[35] Lyndal Roper, *The Holy Household: Women and Morals in Reformation Augsburg* (Oxford: Oxford University Press, 2001).

[36] Ibid., 3.

[37] Carlson's work highlights some of the differences, as well as provides a closer study of marriage in the English Reformations. See Eric Josef Carlson, *Marriage and the English Reformation* (Oxford; Cambridge, MA: Blackwell, 1994).

[38] See Patricia Crawford, *Women and Religion in England, 1500–1720* (London; New York: Routledge, 1993); see also Don Herzog, *Household Politics: Conflict in Early Modern England* (New Haven, CT: Yale University Press, 2013).

[39] Quoted and translated in Bridget Heal, *The Cult of the Virgin Mary in Early Modern Germany: Protestant and Catholic Piety, 1500–1648* (Cambridge: Cambridge University Press, 2007), 286.

[40] Bartholomew Parsons, *Boaz and Ruth Blessed* (Oxford: Printed by Iohn Lichfield, for William Webbe, 1633), 24. The citation from the sermon is to Prov. 21:9, although this is likely intended to be a reference to Prov. 31.

Performing Dance, Sin, and Gender

home … the house in holy Scripture is taken for the Children, whom she must bear and bring up in the fear of God; *The Wife through bearing of Children shall be saved*, saith *Paul*, 1. *Tim.* 2.15.[41]

The message is clear: for the creation of a virtuous society, women needed to remain inside their proper role within the house; to create a sinful society, women need only enter the streets or attend a dance. This message also appeared in what Andy Wood describes as a heightened concern with women's sociability and festive culture, with specific prohibitions in 1567 and 1575 of festive gatherings after women's churchings.[42] The sixteenth- and seventeenth-century focus on public women's gatherings and the use of masculine language to describe the dancers in the Job passage indicates that regardless of who was dancing, the blame ultimately fell to women. The repeated implication of women as the root cause of sinful dancing – in this case, as the individuals responsible for the failures of their households – places them back at the center of the discussion. The Protestant shift towards domesticity gave sermon authors another way to justify women's responsibility for male sin in the public sphere, foreshadowing later ideas about virtue and domesticity. But this was only one part of a much larger ideological shift that had already made women and their bodies bear the primary responsibility for men's transgressions.

This emphasis on domesticity and on the proper space for holy women had another set of implications, implications that again made women responsible for men's actions. Numerous English sermons highlight the dangers of venturing outside the home for holiness, often utilizing the example of Dinah, the woman mentioned earlier held responsible for her own rape. One 1599 sermon, in a discussion of John 21:22, warned audiences to keep check on their eyes, lest their eyes wander abroad and admit sin into their souls. Dinah, "whose eyes were no house-doues, but must needs be gadding out," provides the example of vanity leading to sin.[43] In speaking about guarding one's heart from sin, another sermon from 1615 admonished its listeners to "let it not stray from this home, lest like Dinah it be defloured."[44] Discussions of Dinah, used as a way to condemn women who dance, also provided an opportunity

---

[41] Lancelot Andrewes, *Apospasmatia Sacra* (London: Printed by R. Hodgkinsonne for H. Moseley, A. Crooke, D. Pakeman, L. Fawne, R. Royston, and N. Ekins, 1657), 235.

[42] The council decrees mentioned are from Leicester and Essex; a third decree from 1541 in Chester restricts churching feasts to a small number of women (the midwife and female relatives) and mandates that the feasts be held in the house. See Wood, *Faith, Hope and Charity*, 78.

[43] Lawrence Barker, *Christs Checke to S. Peter* (At London: Printed by P. S[hort] for Cuthbert Burbie, and Thomas Gosson, 1599), 3.

[44] "The Vessel Itself The Heart," in Adams, *Mystical Bedlam*, 15.

Women, Dance and Parish Religion in England, 1300–1640

to condemn women who wandered outside of the home for their own assaults: to again make women responsible for the sins of men.

Many of the cases against dancing women from sixteenth- and seventeenth-century records reflect this emphasis on holy women in the house, sinful women in the streets. One case from a 1636 quarter sessions role accuses one Mary Butcher of "sittinge in Marke Streat vpon a horse" talking to a man before attending a Morris dance (again in the street). When the dance ended, Mary Butcher, referred to as a "prety wench" (with all the sexual connotations of the word) went into an alehouse and drank with a group of men, the sole woman in the gathering.[45] In another case from 1606, charges were brought against John George (alias Cole) and Elizabeth Davyes, the wife of Christopher Davyes, for "[John George] vseth to call her in the nighte tyme out of her howse from her husband & to carry her to dauncing & other sportes and mearymentes."[46] A whole series of depositions against Katherine Bendle and Thomas Houlder focused on the fact that these two individuals "went to wedmore togeathers to make meare and yat they continewed theare all or the most part of that night att dauncing and then came home [either that night or] the next day togeathers." Each of the three deposed witnesses dwelt on the accusation that Thomas and Katherine had "of a long tyme haunted eache to thothers companie early and late, abroade at dauncing, and at home at her fathers howse in westburie aforesaid offensively to theire neighbores, by reason yat hee is a marryed man, and shee a single woman." The conclusion of the witnesses was that "Katherine Bendle hath bin of a long tyme and is a lewde idle huswief, a common resorter to alehowses & [ot] other places wheare dauncing is."[47] The individual circumstances of these and other similar cases varied widely, but in each instance, the wording and framing of the records highlighted a series of sins: women leaving their houses and loitering in male-dominated spaces, dancing, and then engaging in questionable activities with men, to the ruin of their reputations.[48] Despite the fact that the men in these cases were equally culpable for what seem to be mutually pursued pastimes, it was the women who had declarations about their character or virtue made in the record. In most of these cases, women were not the ones initiating the dancing, but the framework of the charges highlighted their responsibility for the sexual sin. Like in the case involving Margerie Safe, the women who left

---

[45] 1636/7, Quarter Sessions Role, SRO, Q/SR 76, pt. 2, fol. 118 as transcribed in *REED Somerset Including Bath 1*, ed. Stokes with Alexander, 162.

[46] Ex Officio Act Book, SRO, D/D/Ca 146, fol. 42 as transcribed in *REED Somerset Including Bath 1*, ed. Stokes with Alexander, 121.

[47] Deposition Book for Dean's Peculiar, SRO, D/D/Cd 28, n.f. as transcribed in *REED Somerset Including Bath 1*, ed. Stokes with Alexander, 233–235.

[48] Several of the cases Wood discusses in his third chapter also emphasize the problematic nature of women's presence and speech in public places. See Wood, *Faith, Hope and Charity*, 81–89.

Performing Dance, Sin, and Gender

their houses and danced were treated as responsible for their own sins and as catalysts for the sins of men.

Condemning women, their bodies, and their failure to fulfill their divinely given roles for the sins of men was not an innovation of the early modern era. But, using dance as a lens for closer examination, it becomes apparent that the attributions of agency and blame shifted between the medieval and early modern eras. Medieval discussions of dance highlighted the dangers female bodies posed to true worship and to sacred space, occasionally emphasizing the sexual sin associated with dance as well. But in these works, both men and women shared the blame for the sins that dance ultimately led them to commit. As discussions of women and sacrilege increasingly focused on keeping men safe from female bodies, the responsibility for sin shifted from both men and women to women alone. The discourse was no longer simply about the dangers posed by some women's bodies to men and the responsibility of both men and women to mitigate that danger; it was now about the dangers posed by all female bodies to an extent that almost completely absolved men of responsibility for sin if women were involved.

This rhetoric, developed gradually throughout the late Middle Ages through discussions of issues like dance, applied to the exercise of agency and blame for sin in other contexts as well. And in the midst of what Merry Wiesner-Hanks has referred to as the "criminalization of sin" in the early modern era, the impact of this rhetoric on the treatment of women tied to rape or prostitution was substantial.[49] Most women were held responsible for their rapes, in a tangible result of the cultural understandings of female sexuality developed partially through literary culture and ballads such as those explored by Carissa Harris. As Harris puts it in a discussion of one of the rape lyrics she examines, "if a woman can be characterized as 'asking for it,' a conclusion that rape culture is set up to produce, then the law is useless to her."[50] And, as this chapter has shown, simply by living in a female body, according to early modern sermons and authors, women were asking for it.

The increasing attention to the female body rather than to actions developed through discussions of sacrilege, pollution, and dance left early modern women with little space for agency or defense. Cristine M. Varholy's study of sexual assault cases in early modern London highlights the impact of this culture through its careful examination of the language used in these cases. She points out that the courts hold women responsible for all sexual activity involving their bodies, including in cases of assault.[51] Despite what Varholy refers to as "strong moral and legal rhetoric denouncing rape," there remains,

---

[49] Merry E. Wiesner, *Christianity and Sexuality in the Early Modern World: Regulating Desire, Reforming Practice* (New York: Routledge, 2005), 120, 318.

[50] Harris, *Obscene Pedagogies*, 207.

[51] Cristine M. Varholy, "'But She Woulde Not Consent': Women's Narratives of Sexual Assault and Compulsion in Early Modern London," in *Violence, Politics,*

Women, Dance and Parish Religion in England, 1300–1640

as Barbara J. Baines notes, "a great disparity between the text of the law and legal practice, that is to say, between the severity of the laws and the will to apply them."[52] Women attempting to protect themselves from charges of extra-marital sexual activity, or to obtain justice for assault, had to work against the assumption that women were always complicit in sex.[53] Pastourelles, scripture translations, and court cases from this period all suggest that rape counted as an assault only when it occurred in an isolated setting; in cases of urban rape victims and attackers were held equally responsible.[54] All too often, the result was punishment of the women involved for sexual promiscuity, despite their testimony and despite the presence of compelling evidence that, outside this discursive framework, would have pointed towards their innocence. The rhetoric about female bodies as the bearers of transgression, as responsible for both their own destruction and the destruction of godly men, bore fruit in the increased emphasis on female culpability and minimization of male agency that characterized early modern court cases. As the mid-seventeenth-century legal authority Matthew Hale explained when discussing this rhetoric, the charge of rape could easily destroy the life of an innocent man, and women's voices, tied as they were to problematic female bodies, should be heard only with extreme caution.[55]

PERFORMING ONE'S GENDER

So, godly men could be beheaded, like John the Baptist, by dancing women. But, according to some early modern sermons, godly men could also be unmanned by dancing. It is this concern – that besides making a godly man sinful, dance could also make any man effeminate – that highlights the extent to which dance had become a woman's sin in the early modern era. Dance was not only a sin committed most often by women, but a sin that made men into women via the extreme application of the association of dance with the female body.

Concern with the potential danger posed to male bodies through female ones took multiple forms between 1300 and 1600. Discussions about clerical

---

    and Gender in Early Modern England, ed. Joseph P. Ward (New York: Palgrave Macmillan, 2008), 45.

[52] Ibid., 46; Baines, *Representing Rape in the English Early Modern Period*, 2.

[53] Varholy, "'But She Woulde Not Consent,'" 61; see also Martin Ingram, *Carnal Knowledge: Regulating Sex in England, 1470–1600* (Cambridge: Cambridge University Press, 2017).

[54] Harris, *Obscene Pedagogies*, 116–117.

[55] Matthew Hale, *Historia Placitorum Coronae: The History of the Pleas of the Crown*, 2 vols. (1736; reprint, London: Professional Books, 1971), I:635. As referenced in Baines, *Representing Rape in the English Early Modern Period*, 10, 24.

Performing Dance, Sin, and Gender

purity were one manifestation.[56] Worries about how excessive sex could weaken men, sapping their virility and potency through repeated encounters with toxic female bodies, represented another facet.[57] In the face of redefinitions of masculinity and holiness in the sixteenth and seventeenth centuries, concerns like these intensified. As scholars like Alexandra Shepard, Mark Breitenberg, and others have noted, masculinity in early modern England was a fragile and fraught construct. Even as gender became increasingly polarized into a rhetorical dichotomy in sermons, the actual experience and performance of gender in the parish was complex. Breitenberg's work points to this anxiety as revealing of the weaknesses in patriarchal systems and as enabling the continuity of patriarchy highlighted by scholars like Judith Bennett.[58] This patriarchal system was by no means as simple as the natural order that sermon authors liked to lay out and expound upon. As Shepard put it, in early modern England, "stark hierarchies of age, social status, and marital status were deeply ingrained, interacting with gender hierarchies to produce a complex multidimensional map of power relations which by no means privileged all men or subordinated all women."[59] Dance, associated most often with youthful individuals, played a role in this complex map and in defining gendered performance. Shepard explores the feasting, drinking, and youthful rioting with which dance was so often associated as a means of contesting patriarchal notions of manhood. In the process, she highlights the brevity of this phase, beset as it was with concerns about male intimacy and the effeminacy it might imply.[60] However, digging more fully into the rhetoric surrounding the performance of masculinity through the framework of dance serves to highlight the ways in which men's discussions of masculinity centered not on the male body but rather on the female body, not simply as a touchstone for the "other" but also as a means of the destruction of masculinity. In tracing out concerns with dancing men and effeminacy, the extent of the gendering of sin and holiness and the ramifications for the performance of one's gender become strikingly clear.

[56] See Jennifer D. Thibodeaux, *The Manly Priest: Clerical Celibacy, Masculinity, and Reform in England and Normandy, 1066–1300* (Philadelphia: University of Pennsylvania Press, 2015); Elliott, *Fallen Bodies*; Ruth Mazo Karras, *From Boys to Men: Formations of Masculinity in Late Medieval Europe* (University of Pennsylvania Press, 2003).

[57] See Ch. 2, "'With a Cunt': Obscene Misogyny and Masculine Pedagogical Community in the Middle Scots Flyting," in Harris, *Obscene Pedagogies*.

[58] Mark Breitenberg, *Anxious Masculinity in Early Modern England* (Cambridge: Cambridge University Press, 1996), 2; Bennett, *History Matters*.

[59] Alexandra Shepard, *Meanings of Manhood in Early Modern England* (Oxford; New York: Oxford University Press, 2006), 3.

[60] See Ch. 4 in Shepard, *Meanings of Manhood in Early Modern England*.

Women, Dance and Parish Religion in England, 1300–1640

The rhetorical concern with effeminacy as a side effect of dancing first appeared in sermons against dancing clergymen, condemning them as worldly gallants rather than true men of God. Such discourse does not immediately begin by tying dancing clergymen to effeminacy. Authors instead start by connecting dancing clergymen to transgression and false religion, paralleling the connections between dancing women and false religion. One sermon printed in 1562 set out on an invective "against our cleargye menne, whiche goe so galluntlye nowe adayes. I heare saye, that somme of theym weare veluette shooes, and veluet: such felowes are more meete to daunce the morrice daunce, then to bee admitted to preache. I praye God amende suche worldelye felowes, for they bee not meete to be preachers."[61] Another sermon from 1557 argued that, according to Paul, new converts who were "yesterday at dice and cardes, and all vnthriftye games, and to daye to turne and reade the holy bokes of the scriptures, or the holy masse boke, yesterday to dauncying and daliing, and to daie to consecrate priestes, wydowes or virgyns" should not be promoted to preachers or ministers, for fear that they "wold sone forget themselues and their callinge."[62] A final 1620 sermon, somewhat less harsh but still condemnatory of dancing ministers, wished that "those paineful and zealous Preachers, which see so dearely to tender the instruction of the people, would for a time forbeare these May-poles and Morrice-dances, and other such trifles, vpon which they spend too much of their strength; and would presse this point of Obedience more closely to the Consciences of people," lest by their dancing example they lead the weak into sin.[63] Although parishioners certainly complained if their minister interfered with their dancing, some parish records also echo this disapproval of dancing ministers, as shown in cases like the proceedings against one Swankin, accused of going "vnto the howse of George Talbott, & being druncken putt of his ministers coate, & putt on a tawnie coate of one Oliver Iames of welles aforesaid, and the said Iames putt on the said Swankins, and theare they in that manner did daunce the more part of that after noone to the greate infamie & disgrace of his function & calling."[64] The picture of ministers who dance in early modern sermons and

---

[61] Latimer, *27 Sermons Preached by the Ryght Reuerende Father*, fol. 149.r.

[62] "Xviii Treatise or Sermon," in Edgeworth, *Sermons Very Fruitfull, Godly, and Learned*, fols. cclxxxvii.r–cclxxxviii.v.

[63] Samuel Burton, *A Sermon Preached at the Generall Assises in Warwicke* (London: Printed by W. Stansby for Nathaniel Butter, 1620), 13; for another example of condemnations of clergy failing to prevent ungodly dancing through improperly performing their duties, see Samuel Hieron, *Aarons Bells A-Sounding* ([Holland?: s.n.], 1623), 20–21.

[64] 1612–1613 Ex Officio Act Book, SRO, D/D/Ca 174, fols. 82v–83 as transcribed in *REED Somerset Including Bath 1*, ed. Stokes with Alexander, 372; for complaints against ministers who interfered with parish festivities, see Wood, *Faith, Hope and Charity*, 157–178.

Performing Dance, Sin, and Gender

parish records is of lapsed or negligent Christians at worst, and of weak or indifferent ones at best. And importantly, this picture of dancing preachers is remarkably similar to depictions of dancing sacrilegious women or Catholics.

From this starting point – portraying dancing ministers as false Christians – it seems that the parallels between sacrilegious women and sacrilegious preachers allowed for a condemnation of the dancing preacher's performance of godly masculinity. Again, early modern sermons arrive at this condemnation through a series of subtle moves, pulling on the associations between dance, gender, and sin built throughout the late Middle Ages and traced out in earlier chapters. Drawing on the idea that pastors should call their flocks to weep, not to dance, some sermons like Samuel Ward's 1615 sermon criticized preaching that focused on a "sound of preaching" rather than "sound preaching" of doctrine, "tickling mens eares, like a tinkling cymbal ... spoyling the plaine song, with descant and diuision: what is this but to shew our owne leuitie and want of true art; indeed affecting such a dauncing, piperly and effeminate eloquence (as *Tully, Demosthenes*, or any Masculine Orator would scorne) instead of that diuine powerful deliuery, which becommeth him, that speaks the Oracles of God."[65] Ward portrayed a "dancing, piperly and effeminate eloquence" as the opposite of divine powerful godliness and completed the move from condemning dancing pastors to portraying dancing pastors as ungodly and unmanly in this brief but complex passage. A dancing man could not be a godly man, at least according to these sermons. John Lowin, the author of one of the most extensive early modern analyses of dance and godliness, was apparently not alone in his conclusion in his 1609 *Conclusions Vpon Dances* that "by the Histories of daunces contained in the holy Scripture, it seemeth unto the consideration of many godly persons, that the practice of Dancing is more becoming unto women, than unto men."[66] With the notable exception of David, discussed later in this section, sermons authors presented dance as destructive not only to male holiness but to masculinity in general.

A number of early modern sermons elaborate upon this theme of the destruction of masculinity and the dangers that feminine actions like dance pose to godly men. One 1611 sermon referred to men who habitually dance as hermaphrodites, describing their response to worldly music like dance songs in the following manner:

> Let any of our *Hermophrodites*, effoeminate and wanton chamberers heare them, and they wil presently begin to be as mad-merrie as the *Tabareni*, of whom *Pomponious Mela* writes, which doe nothing all day long but make merrie, pipe and daunce: but of the contrary part, the *Regenerate* whose eares are circumcised; they heare *Christs* voice, and they know his heart.[67]

---

[65] Ward, *A Coal from the Altar*, 68–69.

[66] John Lowin, *Conclusions Vpon Dances*, 20.

[67] "The Bridegromes Banqvet," in Francis Rollenson, *Sermons Preached before His*

Women, Dance and Parish Religion in England, 1300–1640

The author presented men who dance as of questionable sex, unregenerate and unrepentant. A second sermon from 1621 expounded further upon this theme:

> *Vse not the company of a woman that is a singer and a dancer, neither hear her, lest thou bee taken by her craftinessei, Ecclus. 9.4.* To which purpose it was not unfitly spoken by the Roman Historian touching *Sempronia* a gentlewoman of Rome, that shee was taught *psallere & saltare elegantious quam modestam decebat,* to sing and dance more gracefully then became a modest woman. Besides, these amorous and wanton songs and sonnets, as they serve the Divels turn to convay poinson into the minde: so doo they abate the edge of the masculine vigour thereof, bending and turning it by degrees from a manly martiall disposition to an effeminate softness.[68]

This sermon displays all the many ways in which early modern authors presented dance as a sin connected inextricably with women's bodies. Scripture was retranslated to connect dance and women in a way that the actual text did not. Dance was connected to vanity, sexual sin, generations of female sin, and the devil. Finally, men who dance were presented as both wicked and effeminate.

The theme of effeminacy as tied to sins gendered female – like dance, vanity, and sacrilege – ran throughout early modern sermons concerned about the lack of godly men in English churches. For some, this decay of masculinity denoted the "evils of the age." For instance, to quote one such sermon from 1622, through the sins of the present age, "our women [are] turnd into the shapes of men, our men and especially they of the gallants ranke growne effeminate."[69] This is perhaps not just a rhetorical imagined evil, as a 1620 case from West Thorney, Sussex shows. In this case, a group of parishioners laid out a litany of complaints before the court of the archdeaconry, including complaints about dogs in the churchyard, absent parishioners, gossiping parishioners who will not come in to service, uncatechized youth, and "certeyne maydens [who] did daunce in mans apparel & young men in maydes clothes."[70] The sense of catastrophe the complainants convey fits with the tone of the sermons and their association of the turning of men into women through vanity, sacrilege, and dance with both the evils of the age and the end of times. The same sense of impending evil and destruction appears in

---

Maiestie (At London: Printed by T. Snodham for Robert Iackson, and are to be solde at his shop in Fleet-streete, ouer against the Conduit, 1611), 19.

[68] George Hakewill, *King Dauids Vow for Reformation* (London: Printed [by Humphrey Lownes] for Mathew Lownes, 1621), 12–13.

[69] Roger Ley, *The Bruising of the Serpents Head* (London: Printed by Iohn Dawson for Nicholas Bourne, and are to be sold at his shop at the Royall Exchange, 1622), 12.

[70] 1620/1, Archdeaconry of Chichester Detection Book, West Sussex Record Office, Ep. 1/17/19, fol. 118, as transcribed in *REED Sussex*, ed. Louis, 179–180.

Performing Dance, Sin, and Gender

this sermon printed in 1561 on Revelation, which ties the Antichrist and his followers to Catholicism and papists:

> And they had heere, like the heere of wemen: by the which similitude he noteth theyr wantonnesse, Idlenes, whorisshe apparel, and effeminate minds. For they be commed and piked, and very finely appareled, delightyng in wemens Iewels, wearing costely garments, especially in the church, where they ought moste of all to shewe humilitie and frugalitie. Whiche of the Apostles went euer so decked (or rather disguised) in the Temple or without the temple? The excesse and costelines of apparel of Priestes and Monkes geueth no place to the costely arraye of the Persian Kinges. Againe the thing it selfe speaketh S. Austen in an homelie vpon the seuenth of the Apocalipse, in the heere, sayeth he, he wold vnderstand and shewe, not only an effeminate or womanly sexe, but also eyther or both sexes.[71]

The intertwining of sacrilege, false religion, and bodies was again used to mark the ungodly, although in this case it was not ungodly women but men inhabiting ungodly, womanly bodies.

Effeminacy was not only made a marker of the followers of the Antichrist and of recusants and papists. It was also tied to sexual transgression and then, yet again, to the problematic bodies of women. Robert Abbott's 1625 sermon on *The Danger of Popery* explained this as it considered what it meant to take pleasure in unrighteousness: "the giuing of our hearts to the pleasing entice-ments of *Antichrist*, as effeminate persons giue themselues to the pleasing enticements of harlots."[72] According to other sermons, like this sermon from 1616, these enticements were traps of the devil, laid through the bodies of women to pull men from godliness:

> The deuill then hath his ginne and his trappe, for all kinds of men, for he knoweth the manners of men, and to what vice they are most prone, and layeth that baite before their eyes to which hee knoweth their minde will bee most easily inclined: as to effeminate, ioyfull, and delicate men, the bait of lechery, and vaine-glory ... so the deuill hath his gard, hath his hunters to take soules. For what else shall wee call the whoorish woman, the fraud-ulent friend, the alluring companion, him that keepeth a house of play and baudry, but the diuels Huntsmen?[73]

---

71 Heinrich Bullinger, *A Hundred Sermons* ([Impkinted [*sic*] at at [*sic*] London: By Iohn Day, dwelling ouer Aldersgate, beneath Saincte Martins. ... These bokes are to be sold at his shoppe ouer the gate], 1561), 162.

72 Robert Abbot, *The Danger of Popery* (London: Printed by I. L[egat] for Philemon Stephens, and Christopher Meredith and are to be sold at the Golden Lyon in Paules Church-yard, 1625), 7.

73 William Est, *The Right Rule of a Religious Life* (London: Printed by Nicholas Okes, and are to bee sold by Richard Lea at his shop on the North entry of the Royall Exchange, 1616), 148–149.

The complex interweaving of discourses about the alliance between women and the devil and the dangers women's bodies posed to men, along with the increased risk of effeminacy through dance and sacrilege, appears again in this passage. And while the passage's condemnation of whorish women (and dancers) as traps of the devil is quite clear, the full weight of each of these condemnations – of dance, of women, and of effeminate men – is only clear when read within the context of the broader discourses about sacrilege, gender, and dance outlined in the Middle Ages and quite literally fleshed out in the embodied focus of early modern texts. These discourses culminated in early modern sermons like this final example from 1628: "in Israels effeminate follie with the daughters of Moah, ioyning (as sinne seldome goes alone to hell) idolatry to adultery, by the pestilent plot of Balaam, Zimri and Cosbe, an Israelitish Prince and a Moabitish Princesse led the dance to destruction."[74] Idolatry was joined with sexual transgression, and women's bodies became the tools utilized to emasculate and behead godly men before leading the way to hell.

Against this rhetorical context, the repeated appearance and punishment of groups of dancing men in parish records in early modern England gains new significance. In one example, groups of men were presented in diocesan courts for dancing the Morris dance, usually on the Sabbath day during the time of service.[75] In another, one Thomas Oliver, of Parson Drove in Cambridgeshire, was first cited for being "very euill geauen in Daunceinge amonst mens [and] {serv}ant{es} and Children at vlawfull tymes" in April 1595. When confronted about his actions, Oliver "made a tushe at [the officers] in scorning," and was subsequently forced to publicly confess his actions before the congregation and to repent for offending almighty God and setting an evil example through his dance.[76] Within the context of the early modern sermons condemning dancing men as effeminate, these punishments aimed at dancing men are perhaps driven by multiple motivations. Oliver's case (and indeed, many of the cases in the records) are quite clear in specifying that he danced with other men; perhaps the unspoken concern behind his punishment was that his

---

[74] Stephen Jerome, *The Haughty Heart Humbled* (London: Printed [by Miles Flesher] for Richard More, and are to be sold at his shop in Saint Dunstanes Church-yard in Fleetstreet, 1628), 52.

[75] For a few of many examples, see Stretchworth 1603 Diocesan Court Proceedings CUL, EDR B/2/18 (Stretchworth fol. 238–238v), or Stretham 1596 Diocesan Court Proceedings CUL, EDR B/2/14 (Stretham repro. of fols. 213–213v, + 1 unid.). Both as transcribed and recorded in *REED Cambridgeshire*, ed. Geck with Brannen (forthcoming 2022). Examples from Salisbury discussed in Chapter 3.

[76] Parson Drove 1595 Diocesan Court Proceedings CUL, EDR B/2/15 (Parson Drove repro. of fols. 54, 118), and Parson Drove 1595 Dean's Papers CUL, Add. MS 6605 (Parson Drove repro of fol. 207–207v). Both as transcribed and recorded in *REED Cambridgeshire*, ed. Geck with Brannen (forthcoming 2022).

Performing Dance, Sin, and Gender

dance was "evil" and threatening to godliness not simply because of its performance on the Sabbath but also because of his company. If the concern with dance and effeminacy carried into treatments of dancers in parish records, the number of cases punishing groups of male dancers might not be linked only to the styles and timing of dances, but also to this broader and less obvious concern with male sexuality.

The concern with effeminate recusant clergy likewise carries into the records in a series of cases against early modern ministers. In each case, the pastor is cited for a list of sins: indecent apparel, ungodly conversation, failure to properly perform services, and dancing. A case from Moremonkton in Yorkshire West Riding against one John Birkbie complains of his "vndecent apparel," before accusing Birkbie of being "a notable fornicator" who:

> hath divers times in the night time bene taken abroade in the towne of Rippon by the wakema{n} and other officers w{i}th Lewde women. and he vseth to Daunce verie offencivelie at alehowses and mariag{es} in the presence of Com{m}on people to the verie evell example of others and the greate Slaunder of the ministerie.[77]

Another case from Yorkshire West Riding, from Rufforth, accuses one Tristram Tildsley of a number of sins and offenses against his office as cleric. Despite being a minister of God's word in the parishes of Rufford and Marstone, Tildsley:

> not having the feare of god before his eyes, very vnmodestly and to the great sclaunder of the m{in}istrye ... hath vpon sondais or hollidais hath daunced emongest light youthfull companie both men & women at wedding{es} drynking{es} & Rishbearing{es} or wedding drinking or Rishbearing in the p{ar}ishe of Rufforth & the p{ar}ishe of marstone & other p{ar}ishes therabout{es} & especiallie vpon one sonday or holliday w{i}thin one of the said yer{es} in his dauncing or after wantonlye & dissolutelye he kissed a mayd or yong woman then a dauncer in his companie, wherat diu{er}s p{er}sons were offended & so sore greved that ther was wepons drawne & great dissention arose or was lyke to aryse thervpon to the great disquietnes of god{es} peace & the Quene ma{ies}ties to the great p{er}il & daunger of his soull & to the great sclaunder & offence of a multitude then present & to the pernicious & wicked example especiallye of yong people then & ther assembled together.

Furthermore, the account continues:

---

[77] Moremonkton, York, Borthwick Institute V: Visitation Court Book 1567–1568, fols. 104v–105. As transcribed and recorded in *REED Yorkshire West Riding*, ed. Sylvia Thomas with C. E. McGee (Toronto: REED Online, forthcoming).

Women, Dance and Parish Religion in England, 1300–1640

the said Tristram by all the said tyme or some one yere of the said tyme hathe bene & yet is vicar or curet of Rufforth wher vpon a sonday or holliday w{i}thin the said tyme he did not onely p{er}mit & suffer a Rishbearing w{i}thin the church & churchyard of Rufforth wherat was vsed much lewde light & vnsemelye dauncing{es} & gestures very vnfit for thes plac{es} but also he hym selselve at the said Rishbearing very vnsemelye did Daunce skip leape & hoighe gallantlye as he thought in his owne folishe & lewde concepte in the said churchyard emongest a great multituld of people wher he was derided flowted & laughed at toe the great sclaunder of the m{in}istry.

Because of these sins – his dancing (in a churchyard no less), his lascivious behavior while dancing, and his gallantry, Tildsley was "greatlie & vehementlie suspectd to be a papist or mislyker of religion now established w{i}thin this Realme."[78] Concerns about dancing men and dancing ministers, read from both the parish records and sermons, revolve around sacrilege and ungodliness, traits of special concern when sacrilege remained a mark of effeminacy and sexual transgression.

To be clear, the sermons do not present all masculine dancing as ungodly. A number of early modern sermons mention David's dance before the Lord, always in approving terms. But the authors of these sermons carefully qualify his dance. According to early modern sermons, David's dance grew out of his internal joy and the "excitations of his soul." It was both devout and obedient to God. This description also included an important caveat: David's dance took place "in the Christian posteritie of the Heathen."[79] David's dance, in these sermons, was acknowledged as both fully godly and sacred but also grounded in the past; for Christians hearing the sermon, the encouragement was to mirror the worship, not the motion, a reading that continued a common medieval way of reading potentially problematic Old Testament passages.[80] One 1624 sermon, after a description of David's dance, reminded listeners that "cheere of the countenance, gestures of the body, leaping and dauncing are but dumbe shewes, the best Interpretour of the minde is the tongue, the glory of man, and glorifier of God."[81] Sermons on David's dance are also clear that he is a pious man of inimitable status: a king. One 1583 sermon pointed

---

[78] Rufforth, York, Borthwick Institute, GB 193, Cause Paper, Diocesan Court of the Archbishopric of York 1300–1858, MS CP. G. 3306 (1581), fols. 1–5. As transcribed and recorded in *REED Yorkshire West Riding*, ed. Thomas with McGee, forthcoming.

[79] Barten Holyday, *A Sermon Preached at Pauls Crosse* (London: Printed by William Stansby for Nathaniell Butter, and are to be sold at his shop at Saint Austines Gate in Pauls Church-yard, 1626), 14.

[80] For more detail on this, see Henri de Lubac, *Medieval Exegesis: The Four Senses of Scripture*, ed. and trans. Mark Sebanc and E. M. Macierowski (Grand Rapids, MI: W. B. Eerdmans; T. & T. Clark, 1998).

[81] Samuel Ward, *A Peace-Offring to God* (London: Printed by A[ugustine] Math[ewes]

Performing Dance, Sin, and Gender

out that "when the Arke of God was restored home, *Dauid* being King, played the chiefest part: *Dauid* being King, daunced before the Arke: and being king, set the Bishops and Priests in order. And for this cause they are kings, euen to serue ye Lord. And therefore they doe not wel that deuide common weales in two, and deuise two heads, the one for the spirituality, the other for the laitie."[82] Through presenting David as a man of unusual piety and status, the sermons negotiate the scriptural exemplar of holy dancing masculinity and create space for courtly dance as practiced by nobles. For men, dance retained its potentiality – sons of the wicked dancing to hell appeared alongside the holy king David, leaping up as high as heaven. Yet the sermons are also quite clear that unless a man were David – a righteous and noble king – a dancing man was counted among the wicked, as a sacrilegious, effeminate idolater dancing into damnation.

CONCLUSION

In 1607, one John Hole from Wells in Somerset lodged a complaint against a group of twenty-six of his neighbors and "divers others vnknowne" for, at a time of rebellion against the king in May and June of the previous year, his neighbors had:

> Assemble[d] themselues together in the Citty of Welles then armed with vnlawfull weapons and drums & then & there acted not only many disordered Maygames Morice daunces long daunces men in weamens apparall new deuised lords and ladyes and Churchales ... to faction & great disturbaunce of your highness subiects ... and by that meanes drewe many people then from the church & divine service & sermon there.[83]

Hole went on to describe the dancers' contempt for religious, civic, and royal officials, as well as their violent defiance of attempts to intervene, further cross-dressing and festivities, and other forms of disruption and destruction. Throughout the bill of complaint, descriptions of dance and festivity alternate with scenes of rebellion and destruction. And in the witness depositions that followed this complaint in the case of Hole v. White et al., a number of the questions posed to the witnesses focused on the dancing and cross-dressing that Hole's testimony emphasized.[84] At least in this specific case,

---

for Iohn Marriot, and Iohn Grismand, and are to be sold at their shops in St. Dunstons Churchyard, and in Pauls Alley at the signe of the Gunne, 1624), 10, 12.

[82] John Jewel, *Certaine Sermons* (Imprinted at London: By Christopher Barker, printer to the Queenes most excellent Maiestie, 1583), 51.

[83] 1607–8, Bill of Complaint in Hole v. White et al., PRO, STAC 8/161/1, sheet 219, as transcribed in *REED Somerset Including Bath 1*, ed. Stokes with Alexander, 261–262.

[84] The documents associated with this case are extensive, spanning over 100 pages

Women, Dance and Parish Religion in England, 1300–1640

no sign of dance as a means of performing and marking out community appears. Instead, dance acts as a wedge that drives various groups within the community apart; its loud, physical performance provokes frustrated responses from groups within the community, responses met with more dancing and with violence. It is the dancing (and associated transgression of gender norms that accompany it) that helps identify the dancing rebels as threats to church, town, and crown. It is perhaps no surprise then that most early modern authors were concerned both with neighborliness and with the cessation of dance, for if dance could cause controversies like this one, it would certainly be better to stop dancing altogether.

In framing his account of the rebellion so closely around dance, Hole perhaps drew on sermon appeals similar to this one, from 1636: "I appeale vnto our owne daylie experience, Whether many who led the *dance* in the *morning* haue not fallen foule, and beene blasted in the euening." Both early modern sermons and court cases highlight this concern with the antithetical natures of dance and godliness. Whether it be women dancing to the destruction of their virtue and the death of godly men or men dancing to the destruction of their gender and the state, dancers ultimately numbered among the wicked and would lament the loss of their worldly pleasures in the end. To quote from the same 1636 funeral sermon, "where now is our gay and gorgeous apparel? … Our effeminate songs? Our melodious musicke? Our lascivious dancing? Our amorous imbracings? All these things are vanished like shadowes; but our sorrowes come upon us thicke and threefold: all our joyes, delights, and comforts are withered at the root; but our terrours, hearts griefe and torments grow on us more and more, and shall till time shall be no more."[85] A dire end for dancers like the Wells rebels, to say the least. And a dire end for the parish community once held together partially through danced festivity. The extensive controversy explored in Hole v. White et al. is exceptional in its divisiveness, and most dances did not lead to actual armed rebellions. Yet, the conflict in the Wells community appears on a smaller scale in other parishes and communities, as the battle for parish reform and decorum raged.

Threaded throughout the Wells case and other parish records is an early modern concern with order, one often tied to alcohol and festive culture more broadly.[86] Yet, as shown in the concern with cross-dressing, effeminate

---

in the REED transcription. See *REED Somerset Including Bath 1*, ed. Stokes with Alexander, 261–364.

[85] Daniel Featley, *Clavis Mystica* (London: Printed by R[obert] Y[oung] for Nicolas Bourne, at the south entrance of the royall Exchange, 1636), 288.

[86] Alcohol and drinking in relation to parish culture and festivity is a topic that is beyond the scope of this book, yet often intersecting with dance. The following works provide a sense of possible directions for research on the connections between parish festivity, drink, and changing frameworks for gender and trans-gression. B. Ann Tlusty, *Alcohol in the Early Modern World: A Cultural History*

Performing Dance, Sin, and Gender

songs, lascivious dancing, and amorous embracings, each condemnation of dance (and ultimately, most early modern concerns with dance) references the proper performance of gender and the regulation of gendered bodies. Dance's ability to destroy virtue and masculinity underpins each presentation of dance, even as the concern with false worship and sacrilege remains present. One final example taken from court records, the case of Sir John Yorke, accused of recusancy in the Star Chamber Proceedings at Ripon, brings these discussions of dance, sacrilege, and the proper performance of godly masculinity back together. Testimony delivered against Yorke claimed that:

> the said Sir John Yorke is popishlie affected in Religion as concerning Comyng to the Church and receving the Sacrament ... diuers of the said Sir Iohn Yorkes Servantes and Tenantes wolde sometymes on the Saboath day haive a piper with theme, nere to the Church yarde, And there with theire piping, and Revelling, wolde make such a noyse in tyme of praier, as the Mynyster colde not well be harde. And that he was forced at one tyme when he was Christnyng a childe to goe furth in his Surplus to bidd them be quiet.[87]

Yorke's failure to prevent the dancing (implied through the piping and reveling mentioned in the court case) of those under his care was presented as a sign of his papist leanings. And in this case, with its minister admonishing dancing parishioners to be quiet and still, discussions of dance have come full circle. Dance remained, as in the tale of the cursed dancing carolers, a marker of sacrilege. But dance now also displayed the proper performance of gender, bound to the performance of holiness.

(New York: Bloomsbury, 2021); Beat A. Kümin, *Drinking Matters: Public Houses and Social Exchange in Early Modern Central Europe* (London: Palgrave Macmillan, 2007); Judith M. Bennett, *Ale, Beer and Brewsters in England: Women's Work in a Changing World, 1300–1600* (Oxford: Oxford University Press, 1996); Albrecht Classen, *Pleasure and Leisure in the Middle Ages and Early Modern Age: Cultural-Historical Perspectives on Toys, Games, and Entertainment* (Philadelphia: University of Pennsylvania Press, 2019); Rebecca Lemon, *Addiction and Devotion in Early Modern England* (Philadelphia: University of Pennsylvania Press, 2018).

[87] Star Chamber Proceedings London, PRO, STAC 8/19/10; 1612–1614 (131 folios), January 1613/1614, at Ripon, fol. 40. As transcribed and recorded in *REED Yorkshire West Riding*, ed. Thomas with McGee, forthcoming.

CONCLUSIONS

In Berkshire in 1599, a parishioner was presented in the court of the Archdeacon for having an illegitimate child. In the midst of this trial, the examinant got up and, rather than denying fault or the child, pointed at the accusers, accusing them of the following:

> The Chirchwardens of Coxwell aforesaid have left other matters that are apparent and notorious vnpresented, viz that the chirch porch of the said Chirch is vtterly decayed in the Walles thereof, and that one Iohn Cotterill of Colshill played, as a mision or minstrell and the [d] tyme of divine service, at Evening prayer in the howse of one Thomas Ogborne in Coxwell vppon the Sunday before Alhollausday last, and that the day tyme and place aforesaid there were divers of the parish of Coxwell dauncing.[1]

The parishioner then started naming names, moving through the room and pointing out the dancers. At this point, the entire trial derailed as the scribe frantically tried to keep up with the list of names, recording around the list of cases for the day and overflowing the space he had allotted for what he had expected would be an open and shut case. The rest of the record for that day focuses on the dancers, determining who danced when and where and assessing fines against all those the examinant had listed, with the parishioner charged with fornication forgotten for the moment.

The reforms of Fourth Lateran and the other late medieval councils, with their emphasis on protecting sacred space and maintaining order within the church, are still apparent in this late sixteenth-century case. The fornicating examinant pointed to the churchwardens' neglect of the church fabric and to their permissive approach to dancing as indications of their failure in their offices. Those responsible with care of souls – whether clerics or church-wardens – were still expected to protect and preserve sacred space. But this case also highlights the changes in approach to dance that occurred over the time covered in this study. Comparing dancing during a service to having an

---

[1] Berkshire, Great Coxwell, 1599, Berkshire Record Office, Archdeaconry of Berkshire Act Book, fol. 153–153v. Taken from *REED Berkshire*, ed. Johnston. My thanks to Dr. Johnston for drawing my attention to this case. The 'd' set here in square brackets is crossed out in the original.

Women, Dance and Parish Religion in England, 1300–1640

illegitimate child – indeed, focusing on dancing rather than on the illegitimate child – highlights the extent to which dance was now treated as transgressive.

Yet, while in the Berkshire case those involved weighed the sins of sacrilege (displayed through dance) against fornication, a second case from 1617 in the parish of St. John's, Glastonbury, shows that for seventeenth-century individuals, sacrilege and dance could not be separated so easily from sexual transgression. Nicholas Ruddock and Katheren Chauker were brought before the Quarter Sessions to settle the matter of a "base childe begotten on the boddie of Katheren Chauker by Nicholas Ruddock." The first few items in the record settled the matter of the child's maintenance and future, arranging for payments from Nicholas to Katheren and for the creation of a parish fund by the overseers of the poor to fund the child's eventual apprenticeship. Then, however, the record takes a turn:

> Item it is further ordered That the said Nicholas Ruddock and Katheren Chauker shalbe both whipped through the Highe Streete of Glaston aforesaid vntill their boddies shalbe both bloody and that there shalbe during the time of their whipping two fiddles playeing before them in regard to make knowne their lewdnes in begetting the said base childe vppon the sabboth day coming from danceing.[2]

While the parishioner in the Berkshire case used sacrilegious dancing as a weapon against those who accused him of illicit sexual behavior, in the Glastonbury case, dancing on the Sabbath was a key part of the sexual transgression at the heart of the matter. Dance, sacrilege, and sex: the three transgressions were no longer separable, but related actions all connected to sexualized, sinful bodies.

Using dance as a lens to access late medieval and early modern ideas about bodies, sex, and the sacred highlights consistency in the focus of religious discourses on sacrilege and sex, consistency that remained over several centuries and across massive theological ruptures. Concern with sacrilege led to concern with sacrilegious bodies, and concern with sacrilegious bodies slipped into concern with sexualized female bodies. However, applying dance as a lens also highlights how discourses about dance and gender were themselves changed by these boundaries understood to protect pure Christian practice. As these boundaries meant to protect the sacred from the profane became more entrenched, dance's potentiality flattened out. No longer an action with a spectrum of possible uses, dance became, in the sermons, a gendered action. Dancers marked themselves as not only sinful but also responsible for the sins of others. More significantly, through the gendering

---

[2] Quarter Sessions Roll, SRO, Q/SR 27, pt. 1, fol. 79. As transcribed in *REED Somerset Including Bath 1*, ed. Stokes with Alexander, 133.

Conclusions

of sacrilege and dance, dancers transformed into profane women rather than godly men.

Each of the chapters in this book has traced out a different step in this transition. The tale of the cursed dancing carolers and accompanying sermon tales about sacrilege represent one major concern, the foundational concern that pushed the transformation of dance forward: the sacred (whether sacred space, time, or relics) must be protected from profane lay bodies. Early versions of this tale began by separating sacred and profane bodies and spaces, with an emphasis on clergy and laity, churchyard and village. However, gradually, the gender of the dancers became a key point of concern. As discussions about sacrilege increasingly revolved around female bodies, the boundaries of true faith and sacred practice increasingly excluded both the voices and the bodies of women. Early modern sermons on dance and sacrilege highlight this exclusion and its consequences. Partially because of the association between women, dance, and sacrilege developed during the thirteenth and fourteenth centuries, authors connected the much-feared sin of witchcraft almost exclusively to women, even as parish services and sermons were repeatedly disrupted by drunken and dancing men. This rhetorical construction of dance as sacrilege was weaponized not just against the festive culture of the parish, but also against women in particular through the gendering of sacrilege and dance.

The progression of dance into a gendered transgression and the development of a rhetorical treatment of female bodies as profane also appears in the transformation of Salome. Salome's journey from representation of the true church to representation of the most sinful and frivolous women of the day highlights the transformation of the dancing female body, from a body with the same potential as its male counterparts to one defined by its inherent transgression. The boundary utilized to separate sacred and profane bodies had become reliant primarily upon gender and increasingly focused on bodies rather than actions. With this focus on bodies came a degree of inescapability, for if holiness was defined by one's body rather than one's actions, what access to holiness could women, increasingly discussed solely as problematic bodies, hope for?

The ramifications of this become apparent in the final chapter. Despite the theological fractures of the sixteenth and seventeenth centuries, hundreds of sermons present essentially the same discourse about dance. Women appear only as transgressive figures, dancing to their own damnation and leading others astray. Ministers blamed women's bodies for the downfall of godly men and accused dancing men of effeminacy. With each redrawing of boundaries meant to maintain proper Christian behavior in the centuries following Fourth Lateran, these boundaries closed in on a single profane body: that of the dancing woman. Through the *adiaphora* of dance, a clear binary rubric for performing both gender and holiness developed. And while dance served to bind community together in the thirteenth and fourteenth centuries, with the

Women, Dance and Parish Religion in England, 1300–1640

calcification of this theological construct of dance as gendered and sexualized sacrilege, dance instead served to rip communities apart, particularly through conflicts over what place (if any) dance could hold in a parish, increasingly the domain of men.

So, let us now return to the court cases with which this conclusion began. Given the discourses and implications that this book has traced, it makes sense that dance is now discussed as a transgression on par with having an illegitimate child and that dancing on the Sabbath is given equal weight in these court cases. By insistently presenting the action of dancing as a sacrilegious action performed by profane female bodies, dance itself became more transgressive and a gendered action. The balance of the always somewhat fraught relationship between dance and Christianity shifted.

This shift contributed to a culture in which early modern individuals consistently blamed women and their bodies for the transgressions of men. In early presentations of Salome's narrative, clerical authors held each individual – Herod, Herodias, and Salome – equally responsible for their actions. If clerics placed more blame on any one person, it was on Herod, considered the one who actually killed the saint. However, as these connections between dance, profane bodies, and transgression became increasingly gendered ones, blame shifted to Salome herself. Early modern sermons on Salome and on dance blame women for the sins of men and for men's failing to properly perform their gender. Thus, it is perhaps not surprising that the gendered dichotomy created around dance also held women liable for the sins commonly associated with dancing. The influence of this shift on parish life should not be understated: while the rhetorical transformation was slow, it was steady. The gendering of sinful dance provided ammunition for those seeking to control and confine women's bodies in the name of the good of the parish, resulting in smaller and less visible roles for early modern women. It was not just the Protestant shift towards domesticity and marriage that removed women from public processions and pushed them into their houses.

A third and final look at the Berkshire court case from the beginning of this chapter reframes the discourses covered in this book in ways that make their implications even more apparent. In the 1599 court case, the examinant was one Robert Ricottes; the individuals accused of dancing were John Cotterill, Thomas Ogborne, Edward Perkins, John Coates, and Katherine Jackson. Despite the persistent rhetoric connecting dance and female sin in sermons, this court case centers on the sins of men. In fact, almost all visitation records or ecclesiastical court cases that mention dance involve more men than women. This is not because women are not brought up in these cases; cases indicting women for other forms of transgression appear throughout the holdings, and clearly, as the second court case from Somerset shows, women who danced did not escape the notice of ecclesiastical courts.

But throughout the sixteenth and seventeenth centuries in particular, men repeatedly appear as the ones who are dancing, often on the Sabbath. To

Conclusions

mention only a few examples, a 1596 case presents seven men for dancing on the Sabbath day; a 1608 case presents three men for dancing on the Sabbath, along with one of their wives for dancing and another for watching; a 1593 case against churchwardens Blase Lee and Richard Johnson indicts them for going to a nearby dance during the service itself.[3] However, not a single entry records charges against a group comprised of only women for dancing on the Sabbath, and women appeared less frequently in the lists of dancers charged in ecclesiastical courts. When women do appear, it is often as participants at dances held by their husbands in their homes. In the sermons, it was women who were tied to sinful dance and damnation. In reality, women were more likely sitting in the service listening to the sermons while their husbands, often the very individuals charged with maintaining church spaces and proper order, held raucous dances during Sunday services. The sermons treated dance as a woman's sin; the parish was full of dancing, rebellious men. Why this break between preaching and practice? What further significance does this dichotomy reveal?

Ann Braude argued that the narratives presented in sermons and histories of American Christianity reveal not the reality of historical events or religious practice, but instead "historians' and churchmen's anxieties about the role of religion in American society, anxieties closely tied to women's numerical dominance in churches, synagogues, and temples."[4] I contend that, similarly, these discourses about dance in premodern England are more about what clerics feared than about a reality, more about perceived problems and concerns than problematic practices. Sermons against dance may inadvertently reveal certain realities of dance performance, but they do not accurately represent the reality of parish community and practice. But, because religious authors repeated this association of women, dance, and sin so persistently and so consistently – across centuries, denominational fractures, and geographic range – clerical fears came to define the reality

---

3   Stretham, 1596, Diocesan Court Proceedings, CUL, EDR B/2/14, fol. 213. From *REED Cambridgeshire*, ed. Geck (forthcoming). Sutton, 1608, Diocesan Court Proceedings, CUL, EDR B/2/29 9, fol. 142 av. From *REED Cambridgeshire*, ed. Geck (forthcoming). Streatley, 1593, Berkshire Record Office, Archdeaconry of Berkshire Act Book, D/A2/C32, fol. 93. From *REED Berkshire*, ed. Johnston. See also *REED Salisbury*, ed. Douglas (forthcoming with *REED Wiltshire*, ed. Hays and McGee); *REED Yorkshire North Riding*, ed. David N. Klausner (forthcoming); *REED Yorkshire West Riding*, ed. Thomas with McGee (forthcoming); *REED Yorkshire East Riding*, ed. Diana Wyatt (forthcoming); *REED York*, ed. Johnston and Rogerson; *REED Ecclesiastical London*, ed. Mary Erler (Toronto: University of Toronto Press, 2008); *REED Lincolnshire*, ed. Stokes; *REED Civic London to 1558*, ed. Anne Lancashire with David J. Parkinson (Cambridge: D. S. Brewer, 2015).

4   Ann Braude, "Women's History Is American Religious History," in *Retelling U.S. Religious History*, ed. Thomas A. Tweed (Berkeley: University of California Press, 1997), 87.

Women, Dance and Parish Religion in England, 1300–1640

moving forward. Whether women who danced actually led to sin became irrelevant. What shaped the reality of Anglo-Protestant approaches to dance moving forward was the fear of the consequences if women's bodies were not carefully monitored and controlled.

This creation of an ideology based on imagined sinners rather than the actual events of the parish likewise helps explain why – despite controversy, theological, political, and economic change – parish festive culture between 1300 and 1600 displays more continuities than differences. Similarly, the experience of women within the parish did not dramatically change until well into the seventeenth century. While the lived experience of the parish for women remained consistent, the rhetorical status of both dance and women slowly shifted as a result of clerical anxiety and fear, heightened in the turmoil of the early modern Reformations. It is this ultimately far-reaching change in rhetorical framing and status that enabled the dramatic changes in parish culture and in women's experiences of the seventeenth century. Concerns about sacrilege and about rightly practiced faith did indeed drive the transformation of the parish, but these concerns developed out of medieval concerns about gender and women's bodies, not just out of concerns about changing Reformation theology.

The desire to control and confine women's bodies, to keep them at a safe distance from sacred objects and from men, is not a new phenomenon. The tension between the egalitarian language in Galatians 3:28 ("there is neither Jew nor Greek, there is neither bond nor free, there is neither male nor female; for ye are all one in Christ Jesus") and concern about the dangers presented by sexualized and corrupting female bodies is a running theme throughout the history of the church. Similarly, the relationship between dance and the church has always been one defined by tension: either one is David, dancing to praise the Lord, or one is Salome, dancing to kill a saint. But the persistent connection of dance, women, and sin from the thirteenth century on reveals one way in which the careful compartmentalizing of women's bodies on an issue widely acknowledged to be *adiaphora* had very real and much larger implications for the relationship between Christianity and women – and, indeed, Christianity and the proper performance of gender for both men and women – moving forward.

Dance itself might be a minor issue, a point of concern that warranted warnings but not significant enough to receive extended theological treatment. But the gradual development of a concept of dance as a gendered transgression and the associated focus on women's culpability for men's sins led to extremely significant patterns of rhetoric that shaped treatments of women into the modern era, rhetoric weaponized as a mechanism of misogyny and used to perpetuate patriarchal structures, despite theological, social, and cultural changes. The nineteenth-century Anglican cleric Stewart Headlam repeatedly clashed with his bishops and superiors over whether dancers could be considered Christians or not. His arguments that dance could have

Conclusions

sacred potential led critics to condemn him as full of "too much balletolatry."[5] Victorian clerics condemned the sexual immorality of ballet dancers and lamented their influence on innocent young men.[6] Critics of the 1920s dance hall bemoaned the decay of society's morality through dance; American evangelicals in the 1950s condemned square dancing as a "gateway dance" that led to evil. In Henryetta, Oklahoma, a law against dancing within 500 feet of a church was lifted no less recently than February 2017.[7] Alongside each of these religious condemnations of dance came suspicion of women's bodies, motives, and presence.

Dance's role as a mechanism of misogyny highlights why we need to pay attention to what theological and ideological assumptions underpinned teachings about lived faith for the laity and to how these assumptions challenge traditional periodization based on major theological breaks. For ordinary men and women, teachings about daily life and about how to live their faith were perhaps more influential than formal theological doctrines. Because these issues were not the focus of full theological treatises, change occurred slowly and almost imperceptibly. This makes these discourses all the more dangerous, for without dramatic change, it is difficult to notice or to challenge the underlying assumptions driving that transformation. For women, this meant a slow entrenchment of misogyny and narrowing of their agency or space. It is in the weaponizing of minor issues that the most damage can be done, both rhetorically and to the lived experience of the marginalized.

Christian presentations of dance as sinful and connected to lascivious women and sexual sin slowly developed out of broader theological and cultural movements that redefined the relationship between women and sacred space, dance and worship. It was the reforms of the late medieval period that drew these boundaries separating both women and dance from sacred space. The gendering of dance that began in the thirteenth century with concerns about female bodies, dance, and sacred space culminated in this more binary early modern approach to dance, gender, and transgression. This discourse presenting dance as a gendered transgression connected to profane female bodies was, by the sixteenth century, so entrenched that it provided a

---

5 John M. Berry and Frances Panchok, "Church and Theater," *U.S. Catholic Historian* 6, no. 2/3 (n.d.): 103; for more on Headlam, dance, and gender, see Lynneth J. Miller Renberg, "An Outward and Visible Sign of an Inward and Spiritual Grace: Stewart Headlam on the Ballet," *Church History and Religious Culture* 99, no. 2 (August 12, 2019): 248–269.

6 John Orens, *Stewart Headlam's Radical Anglicanism: The Mass, the Masses, and the Music Hall* (Champaign-Urbana: University of Illinois Press, 2003), 63.

7 See www.usatoday.com/story/news/nation-now/2017/02/08/oklahoma-valentines-day-dance-canceled-after-ordinance-bans-dancing-near-church/97653088/ and www.cbsnews.com/news/henryetta-oklahoma-town-discards-decades-old-dancing-ban/

Women, Dance and Parish Religion in England, 1300–1640

foundation for Protestant ideas about dance and about women for centuries to come. Thus, by the end of England's long Reformation, Satan danced not in one specific damsel, but in every woman. Christians might still dance to heaven rather than to hell – but not if they were women, or "womanly" men.

APPENDIX

This appendix contains a list of English early modern sermon authors and brief biographical information about each one, taken from the *Oxford Dictionary of National Biography*. These authors wrote the more than three hundred early modern sermons that mention dance that this monograph consulted and analyzed. As is apparent from this table, authors who held roughly comparable positions on dance lived over a wide array of years and held quite different theological positions; to claim that opponents of dance were simply Puritans or opponents of tradition misses the broad consensus on dance as a rhetorical and theological concept that marked the sixteenth and seventeenth centuries. Authors are arranged in alphabetical order by last name. While a number of translations of sermons by prominent authors from the continental Reformations, such as Martin Luther or John Calvin, were printed in London and are cited in some chapters of this book, these continental authors have been omitted under the assumption that most readers are familiar with the basic outlines of their background. Their sermons can be found in the bibliography, along with the specific sermons cited from each of these authors.

Author	Biographical Information
Robert Abbot	1589–1652 Church of England clergyman and religious writer; conformist, concerned about both Catholicism and Puritanism
Thomas Adams	1583–1652 Church of England clergyman, esteemed as an excellent preacher; Calvinist Episcopalian, Sabbatarian, known for vehement invective against Catholics, but strongly in favor of maintaining the established episcopacy
Anthony Anderson	d. 1593 Church of England clergyman and theological writer
Bartimaeus Andrewes	1550/51–1616 Church of England clergyman, conformist

Appendix

Author	Biographical Information
Lancelot Andrewes	1555–1626 English bishop and scholar; oversaw translation of Authorized Version of the Bible under James I; conformist and moderate
John Baker	1531–1604/6
John Barlow	*no information*
Thomas Baughe	*no information*
Paul Baynes	1573–1617 "godly divine," moderate Puritan and firmly against separatists
Thomas Becon	1512/13–1567 Theologian and Church of England clergyman; early evangelical, Marian exile; last works are decidedly Zwinglian
Henry Bedel	1536–1537 Church of England clergyman, conformist
Sebastian Benefield	1568/9–1630 Church of England clergyman and divine, Calvinist, some accusations of separatism
Thomas Bentham	1513/14–1579 Bishop, Protestant, Marian exile, conformist
Michael Birkenhead	*no information*
James Bisse	*no information*
Nicholas Bownd	d. 1613 Church of England clergyman and religious writer, Sabbatarian, Puritan tendencies but remained conformist, early member of the classis movement
John Bradford	1510–1555 The ODNB contains several John Bradfords; the best fit for the sermons cited here appears to be John Bradford, evangelical preacher and Protestant martyr
Thomas Broad	*no information*
Samuel Burton	*no information*
William Burton	1545–1616 Church of England clergyman, Puritan
George Bury	*no information*

Appendix

Author	Biographical Information
John Carpenter	d. 1621 Church of England clergyman and author
Richard Carpenter	1575–1627 Church of England clergyman; noted preacher, moderate Puritan who distanced himself from nonconformists
John Carter	1554–1635 Church of England clergyman, avowed Puritan
Thomas Cartwright	1534/5–1603 Theologian and religious controversialist; radical critic of the ecclesiastical *status quo*; Presbyterian and Puritan, eventually exiled to the continent and placed on trial upon his return to England
William Case	*no information*
John Chardon	1548–1601 Church of Ireland, Bishop of Down and Connor
Henoch Clapham	1585–1614 Writer on theology and preacher; committed Presbyterian, rejected government of Church of England as antichristian
Samuel Collins	1576–1651 Moderate Calvinist; Regius Professor of Divinity at Cambridge, eventually charged with ceremonialism and removed from his position
Richard Crakanthorpe	bap. 1568, d. 1624 Puritan; religious controversialist who wrote particularly intense invective against Roman Catholics
Thomas Cranmer	1489–1556 Archbishop of Canterbury; evangelical reformer
Samuel Crook	*No information*
Richard Curteys	1532–1582 Bishop of Chichester; conformist and involved in conflict with Puritan factions during vestiarian controversy
Lancelot Dawes	1579/80–1655 Church of England clergyman; conformist
John Day	1566–1628 Aristotelian scholar and Church of England clergyman; moderate Calvinist who sought to refute Catholic apologists, skilled in speaking both to lay and scholarly audiences

Appendix

Author	Biographical Information
Laurence Deios	d. 1618 Church of England clergyman; conformist and anti-Puritan
John Denison	1569/70–1629 Church of England clergyman; Calvinist and conformist
John Dod	1550–1645 Church of England clergyman; committed Puritan, forced into hiding under James I, semi-separatist
Marco Antonio De Dominis	1560–1624 Archbishop of Spalato and ecumenist; member of Society of Jesus, critic of papacy, saw papal claims of supremacy as cause for the schisms in the church
Thomas Drant	1540–1578 Church of England clergyman
Roger Edgeworth	1488–1559/60 Church of England clergyman and religious controversialist
Richard Eedes	*no information*
Edward Elton	1569–1624 Church of England clergyman; Puritan but not separatist
Edward Evans	b. 1573/4 Church of England clergyman; conformist and in favor of ceremonial
Martin Fotherby	1560–1620 Bishop of Salisbury; conformist and orthodox
John Foxe	1516/17–1587 Martyrologist; Protestant
John Frewen	1558–1628 Church of England clergyman; nonconformist, Calvinist
William Fulke	1536/7–1589 Theologian and college head; strongly Protestant
Richard Gardiner	1590/91–1670 Church of England clergyman; outspoken defender of religious festivals and of Charles I, outspoken opponent of sectarism
Thomas Gataker	1574–1654 Church of England clergyman and scholar; favored a judicious mixture of episcopacy and Presbyterianism

Appendix

Author	Biographical Information
John Gee	1595/6–1639 Church of England clergyman and religious controversialist; perhaps held clandestine Catholic marriages in an attempt to improve his financial position and was thus suspended; sympathetic to recusants; the sermon in which he discusses dance is his recantation sermon after he was brought up on charges of recusancy
Thomas Gibson	*no information*
George Gifford	1547/5–1600 Church of England clergyman and author; nonconformist
Richard Greenham	early 1540s–1594 Church of England clergyman; nonconformist but strongly against separatists
John Grent	*no information*
Roger Hacket	1559–1621 Church of England clergyman; conformist with sensitivity to Puritan scruples
George Hakewill	bap. 1578, d. 1649 Church of England clergyman and author; fiercely anti-Catholic Calvinist, but also conformist
Joseph Hall	1574–1656 Bishop of Norwich, religious writer, and satirist; adhered to Calvinist theology but not an advocate of separatism or Presbyterianism; represented the Anglican church as an ideal mean between the extremes of radical nonconformity and Roman Catholicism
Robert Harris	1580/81–1658 Replaced John Dod when Dod was forced from his post in 1607; nonconformist and Puritan, but more moderate than Dod
William Harrison	1553–1621 Roman Catholic archpriest; seems to have been imprisoned for his faith at one point
Christoph Hegendorph	*no information*

Appendix

Author	Biographical Information
Samuel Hieron	bap. 1572, d. 1617 Church of England clergyman and devotional writer; considered to have laid the foundation for a vigorous tradition of Puritan nonconformity in south Devon; nonconformist but against separatism
Adam Hill	1548–1595 Church of England clergyman, trained by John Jewel, defends religious orthodoxy, ecclesiastical authority
William Holbrooke	*no information*
Barten Holyday	1593–1661 Church of England clergyman and poet; royalist, but allowed to continue writing and publishing for the remainder of the Civil War; noted and important scholar
Richard Hooker	1554–1600 Theologian and philosopher, conformist and opposed to Puritanism and Presbyterianism
Robert Horne	1564/5–1640 Church of England clergyman; nonconformist Puritan
John Hoskins	1581–1631 (Hoskins the younger) Church of England clergyman and author
John Howson	1556/7–1632 Bishop of Durham; conformist who was in support of liturgy and ceremonial and thus consistently embroiled in conflict
Laurence Humphrey	1525/27–1589 Committed Protestant, Marian exile, nonconformist tendencies, particularly in vestiarian controversy
Robert Humpston	d. 1606 Church of Ireland bishop of Down and Connor; Calvinist leanings
Thomas Ingmethorpe	bap. 1564, d. 1638 Schoolmaster; imprisoned and then resigned over a sermon in which he spoke against his employers at Durham School
Thomas Jackson	1570/71- 1646 Church of England clergyman; conformist and orthodox

Appendix

Author	Biographical Information
Stephen Jerome	fl. 1604–1650 Writer and Church of England clergyman; Puritan, career marred by sexual scandal
John Jewel	1522–1571 Bishop of Salisbury; reformer, Marian exile, strict conformist
Philip Jones	*no information*
William Kethe	d. 1594 Religious polemicist and translator; reformer with Puritan tendencies, associated with Calvin
Hugh Latimer	1485–1555 Bishop of Worcester; preacher, Protestant martyr
Ludwig Lavater	*no information*
Richard Leake	*no information*
William Leigh	1550–1639 Church of England clergyman; Puritan and conformist, led campaigns and trials against recusancy and witchcraft
Roger Ley	1593/4–1668 Church of England clergyman and author
William Loe	d. 1645 Church of England clergyman; protested against Laud's policies, Puritan but conformist
Thomas Lupset	1495–1530 Ecclesiastic and scholar; close to Erasmus and Reginald Pole
George Macey	*no information*
Francis Mason	1565/6–1621 Church of England clergyman and religious controversialist; sought to maintain conformity and to vigorously defend the Church of England against Roman Catholicism and sectarianism
Anthony Maxey	d. 1618 Dean of Windsor; conformist, but perhaps sympathized with nonconformists

Appendix

Author	Biographical Information
John Mayer	bap. 1583, d. 1664 Biblical commentator; flouted convention of publishing biblical commentaries in Latin in order that laity become as well versed in church fathers as the clergy; determined opponent both of popery and of Protestant extremism
John K. Mayo	*no information*
George Meriton	d. 1624 Dean of York; conformist and vehement defender of the ceremonies of the Church of England
Pierre Merlin	*no information*
Pierre Du Moulin	1568–1658 Reformed minister and religious controversialist; fiercely anti-Catholic, leading voice of French Protestantism
Gervase Nid	*no information*
Thomas Paynell	d. 1564? Canon of Merton Priory, Surrey; chaplain to Henry VIII, orator to Mary and Elizabeth; Erasmian who accommodated himself to Tudor regimes
William Perkins	1558–1602 Theologian and Church of England clergyman; moderate Puritan and advocate of Calvinist doctrine
Thomas Pestell	bap. 1586, d. 1667 Church of England clergyman and poet; controversial figure accused of ecclesiastical irregularities, but maintaining some degree of conformity
Elias Petley	*no information*
Edward Philips	*no information*
Thomas Playfere	1562–1609 Church of England clergyman; reputed to be a brilliant orator and preacher (albeit sometimes criticized for excessive use of rhetorical devices, thematic imagery, and allegory); Calvinist
Barnaby Potter	bap. 1577, d. 1642 Bishop of Carlisle; Puritan, but nonconfrontational; remained in good favor with Charles I and maintained good relations with Catholic recusants
Richard Preston	*no information*

Appendix

Author	Biographical Information
Daniel Price	1581–1631 Dean of Hereford; reputed to be a remarkable preacher, particularly against Catholics; evangelical Calvinist
Sampson Price	1585/6–1630 Church of England clergyman and religious writer; Calvinist, but conformist; vehemently anti-Catholic, anti-atheist, anti-Puritan
John Prideaux	1578–1650 Bishop of Worcester; Calvinist in theology but rejected the label, supported episcopacy but did not mandate it
Gilbert Primrose	1566/7–1642 Reformed minister, born in Scotland and tied to Church of Scotland; active theological controversialist, active in cause of French Huguenots
Samuel Purchas	bap. 1577, d. 1626 Church of England clergyman; vehemently anti-Catholic, Calvinist but not separatist; wrote militantly theological travel narratives
John Reading	Church of England clergyman and religious controversialist; "severe Calvinist" and Puritan, but also a royalist and against separatism
Thomas Reeve	1593/4–1672 Church of England clergyman; imprisoned in November 1642 for maligning and deriding the proceedings of Parliament; royalist but not an active delinquent
William Ressold	*no information*
Richard Rogers	1551–1618 Church of England clergyman and author; Presbyterian and Puritan, but not separatist
Francis Rollenson	*no information*
Anthony Rudd	1548/9–1615 Bishop of St. David's; conformist and moderate
Robert Sanderson	1587–1663 Bishop of Lincoln; doctrinal Calvinist, but rejected Puritan arguments against ceremonies and sought to preserve Protestant unity against Rome

Appendix

Author	Biographical Information
Edwin Sandys	1519–1588 Archbishop of York; Protestant, Marian exile, reputation for precipitate and misguided zeal, although not a nonconformist
Abraham Scultetus	*no information*
Richard Senhouse	d. 1626 Bishop of Carlisle; preached in a "prophetic, anti-Catholic vein"
Henry Smith	1560–1591 Church of England clergyman referred to as the "Silver-Tongued Preacher"; evangelical who objected to Church of England ceremonial, but remained in conformity with the church through a compromise of conscience
Humphrey Sydenham	1591–1650 Church of England clergyman and religious controversialist; very anti-Puritan and strongly pro-ceremony
Richard Taverner	1505–1575 Translator and evangelical reformer; served as Cromwell's principal propagandist for religious reform
Thomas Taylor	1576–1632 Church of England clergyman; moderate Puritan, opposed to separatism and antinomianism
Willem Teellinck	*no information*
Edward Topsell	baptized 1572, d. 1625 Church of England clergyman and author
Thomas Tuke	1580/81–1657 Church of England clergyman, moderate Puritan
Richard Turnbull	*no information*
Anthony Tyrrell	1552–1615 Roman Catholic priest and Church of England clergyman; continually flipped between Catholicism and Protestantism
John Udall	1560–1592/3 Religious controversialist, reformer
Robert Vase	*no information*
Pietro Martire Vermigli	1499–1562 Italian theologian turned evangelical reformer

Appendix

Author	Biographical Information
John Wall	1588–1666 Church of England clergyman; sermons characterized by Christocentricity and by a scorn of separatists and of Roman Catholics
John Walsall	*no information*
Samuel Ward	1577–1640 Preacher; Puritan, imprisoned because of controversy over an image that showed Spain in conference with the devil at the time that a match between Charles, Prince of Wales, and the Spanish Infanta was being negotiated; encouraged separatist immigration and was himself a separatist
Richard Webb	*no information*
William Westerman	*no information*
William Whateley	1583–1639 Church of England clergyman and Puritan preacher; moderate scholarly Puritan, persuasive preacher
Francis White	1563/4–1638 Bishop of Ely; anti-Catholic polemicist, part of group of Arminians who questioned Calvinist opinions, gave greater place to sacraments and ceremonies than to preaching, defended Charles I on issue of Sabbatarianism
John White	1570–1615 Church of England clergyman; polemicist against the Church of Rome and Calvinist
Thomas White	1550–1624 Benefactor of Sion College, London; vicar of St. Dunstan-in-the-West, London, associated with St. Paul's School; Protestant, conformist
Robert Wilkinson	*no information*
John Wing	*no information*
William Worship	*no information*
William Yonger	*no information*

TIMELINE

1015	Purported dating of the Kölbigk dancers
1140	Approximate date of compilation of Gratian's *Decretum*, with its prohibitions on women in sacred space
1209	Council of Avignon prohibits dance during sacred services and on sacred ground
1215	Fourth Lateran Council
1216	Accession of Henry III
1217–19	Richard Poore, Bishop of Salisbury, drives the creation of English synodal statutes meant to transmit Fourth Lateran's canons into English contexts
1250s–70s	Compilation of the *Manuel des péchés*
1259–66	Likely compilation of Jacobus de Voragine's *Legenda Aurea*, a widely circulated collection of saints' lives
1272	Accession of Edward I
1275–79	Compilation of the *Liber Exemplorum* as a reference for priests developing sermons to meet the new requirements established after Fourth Lateran
1280	Creation of *South English Legendary* as a reference guide for sermon development in England
1281	Council of Lambeth convened under John Peckham, Archbishop of Canterbury, resulting in the Constitutions of Lambeth, which created a mandatory list of teachings parish priests must cover each year; Synod of Oxford convened under Robert Grosseteste, Bishop of Lincoln, to further forward the implementation of certain provisions of Fourth Lateran
1295–1306	Composition of early version of the *Northern Homily Cycle*
1303	Robert Mannyng of Brunne begins to compose *Handlyng Synne*
1307	Accession of Edward II
1327	Accession of Edward III

Timeline

1348–49	First outbreak of the Black Death in England
1377	Start of the Hundred Years' War; accession of Richard II
1378	John Wycliffe's reforms and writings spark the Lollard movement
1381	Peasants' Revolt
1380s	John Mirk's *Festial* likely composed and enters circulation
1380s–90s	Composition of *Of Shrifte and Penance*, a Middle English translation of the *Manuel des péchés*
1382	Early publications of the Wycliffite Bible; works of Wycliffe officially condemned
1399	Accession of Henry IV
1401	Henry IV passes *De heretic comburendo*, aimed against Lollardy and giving bishops power to arrest and examine those suspected of Lollard beliefs
1409	Thomas Arundel, Archbishop of Canterbury, issues his *Constitutions*, condemning Wycliffe's translation of Scripture and prohibiting new vernacular writing and theology in an attempt to suppress the Lollard movement
1413	Accession of Henry V
1422	First accession of Henry VI
1445–50	Peter Idley's *Instructions to His Son* composed
1453	England loses the last of its holdings in France, bringing an end to the Hundred Years' War
1455	The start of the Wars of the Roses, a dynastic dispute over the English throne
1461	First accession of Edward IV
1470	Second accession of Henry VI
1471	Second accession of Edward IV
1483	Accession of Edward V, followed shortly by the accessoin of Richard III
1485	Accession of Henry VII, first Tudor monarch; his accession brings an end to the conflict of the Wars of the Roses
1509	Accession of Henry VIII
1526	Publication of William Tyndale's second edition of the New Testament, after his attempt at a 1525 edition was cut short

Timeline

1529	The Reformation parliament starts to put in place the framework for an eventual break with Rome
1533–56	Thomas Cranmer serves as Archbishop of Canterbury
1534	Act of Supremacy under Henry VIII establishes the English monarch as the head of the English church
1535	Miles Coverdale publishes his compilation of the Bible, the first complete modern English translation of the Bible
1536	Thomas Cromwell issues a set of *Injunctions* for clergy and his *10 Articles*, which rejects four of the seven Catholic sacraments
1536–41	Dissolution of the English monasteries
1539	Act of Six Articles argues against clerical marriage and for transubstantiation; publication of the Great Bible, the first authorized edition of the Bible in English developed to be read aloud in the services of the Church of England; publication of the Taverner Bible
1547	Accession of Edward VI; publication of Thomas Cranmer's Book of Homilies; Chantries Act begins the dissolution of the chantries
1549	Institution of the first *Book of Common Prayer*, made compulsory by the Act of Uniformity
1553	Accession of Mary I; Thomas Cranmer produces his *42 Articles*, eventually formalized as the core doctrinal statements of the Church of England as the *39 Articles* in 1563; First Act of Repeal reverses all the religiously aimed legislation from the reign of Edward VI
1555	Second Act of Repeal abolishes all legislation on religious matters from 1529 onwards
1557	Publication of the New Testament of the Geneva Bible
1558	Accession of Elizabeth I
1559–63	Elizabethan Settlement, attained with a new Act of Supremacy, Act of Uniformity, Royal Injunctions, and revised Book of Common Prayer
1560	Completion of the Geneva Bible with the publication of the Old Testament
1563	Ratification of the *39 Articles* as the basic summary of belief for the Church of England
1603	Accession of James I

Timeline

1611	Publication of the Authorized Version of the Bible
1618	*Book of Sports* published, including a controversial statement in support of dancing and related activities like bowling on Sunday afternoons
1625	Accession of Charles I
1633	Charles I reissues a slightly updated version of the *Book of Sports*, with continued support for Sunday afternoon dances and like activities
1633–45	William Laud serves as Archbishop of Canterbury, heading the Laudian Reforms and working against Puritans to strengthen the Anglican church
1642–51	English Civil Wars

BIBLIOGRAPHY

ARCHIVES AND ARCHIVAL SOURCES

Cambridge

Cambridge University Library

CUL Additional MS 8335
CUL MS Dd.I.1
CUL MS Ee.I.20
CUL MS Gg.5.31
CUL MS Gg.6.16
CUL MS Gg.I.1
CUL MS Ii.4.9
CUL MS Mm.6.4

Parker Library

Corpus Christi College MS 278
Corpus Christi College MS 357
Corpus Christi College MS 387

Pepys Library

Magdalene College MS Pepys 2125
Magdalene College MS Pepys 2498

Sidney Sussex College

Sidney Sussex College MS 89

St. John's College

St. John's College MS F.30
St. John's College MS G.30

Trinity College

Trinity College Cambridge MS B.5.25

Bibliography

Dublin

Trinity College

Trinity College Dublin MS 69
Trinity College Dublin MS 70
Trinity College Dublin MS 71
Trinity College Dublin MS 72
Trinity College Dublin MS 83
Trinity College Dublin MS 3

London

British Library

Additional MS 17013
Additional MS 10046
Additional MS 17376
Additional MS 22283 (Simeon)
Additional MS 30358
Additional MS 35284
Additional MS 36791
Additional MS 37677
Additional MS 38010
Additional MS 40671
Additional MS 40769
Additional MS 74953
MS Arundel 20
MS Arundel 158
MS Arundel 288
MS Arundel 372
MS Cotton Vespasian D.VII
MS Cotton Tiberius E VII
MS Egerton 614
MS Egerton 2820
MS Harley 273
MS Harley 1770
MS Harley 1806
MS Harley 1896
MS Harley 2247
MS Harley 2391
MS Harley 2398
MS Harley 3860
MS Harley 4196
MS Harley 4657
MS Harley 4971

Bibliography

MS Royal 18 A XVII
MS Royal 18 B XXIII
MS Royal 18 B XXV
MS Royal 18 C XXVI
MS Royal 18 D.I
MS Royal 20 B XIV

Lambeth Palace Archives

Lambeth Palace MS 34
Lambeth Palace MS 260

Oxford

Bodleian Library

Bodl. MS 30526 (Engl. Poet. c.3).
Bodl. MS 3440 (Seldon Supra 52)
Bodl. MS 31791 (Eng. Poet. c.4)
Bodl. MS Ashmole 42
Bodl. MS Ashmole 61
Bodl. MS Bodley 288
Bodl. MS Bodley 415
Bodl. MS Bodley 425
Bodl. MS Bodley 467
Bodl. MS Bodley 554
Bodl. MS Bodley 806
Bodl. MS Bodley 877
Bodl. MS Bodley 921
Bodl. MS Bodley 953
Bodl. MS Douce 258
Bodl. MS E. Musaeo 180
Bodl. MS Eng. Poet. a.1 (the Vernon Manuscript)
Bodl. MS Eng. Th. F. 39
Bodl. MS Hatton 12
Bodl. MS Hatton 57
Bodl. MS Hatton 96
Bodl. MS Hatton 99
Bodl. MS Holkham Misc. 40
Bodl. MS Lat. Misc. b. 17
Bodl. MS Laud 524
Bodl. MS Laud Misc. 286
Bodl. MS Laud Misc. 321
Bodl. MS Laud Misc. 448
Bodl. MS Rawl. Poet 241
Bodl. MS Tanner 1

Bibliography

Bodl. MS Tanner 16
MS University College 56 D
MS University College 64
MS University College 74 C
MS University College 97 E

Magdalen College

Magdalen College MS Lat 52

Merton College

Merton College MS 94

New College

New College MS 320

Wiltshire

Longleat House

Longleat MS 4

York

York Minster

York MS XVI.K.7
York MS XVI.K.13

RECORDS OF EARLY ENGLISH DRAMA VOLUMES

Douglas, Audrey, ed. *Records of Early English Drama: Salisbury.* Toronto: REED Online. Forthcoming with *Records of Early English Drama: Wiltshire,* ed. Roslyn Hays and C. E. McGee.

Erler, Mary, ed. *Records of Early English Drama: Ecclesiastical London.* Toronto: University of Toronto Press, 2008.

Geck, John, and Anne Brannen, eds. *Records of Early English Drama: Cambridgeshire.* Toronto: REED Online, forthcoming 2022.

Greenfield, Peter, and Jane Cowling, eds. *Records of Early English Drama: Hampshire.* Toronto: REED Online, 2020. https://ereed.library.utoronto.ca/collections/hamps/.

Johnston, Alexandra F., ed. *Records of Early English Drama: Berkshire.* Toronto: REED Online, 2018. https://ereed.library.utoronto.ca/collections/berks/.

———. *Records of Early English Drama: Oxfordshire.* Toronto: REED Online, forthcoming.

———, and Mary Rogerson, eds. *Records of Early English Drama: York.* 2 vols. Toronto: University of Toronto Press, 1979.

Bibliography

Klausner, David N., ed. *Records of Early English Drama: Herefordshire, Worcestershire.* Toronto: University of Toronto Press, 1990.

———. *Records of Early English Drama: Yorkshire North Riding.* Toronto: REED Online, 2021. https://ereed.library.utoronto.ca/collections/yksnr/

Lancashire, Anne, ed., with David J. Parkinson, asst. ed. *Records of Early English Drama: Civic London.* 3 vols. Cambridge: D. S. Brewer, 2015.

Louis, Cameron, ed. *Records of Early English Drama: Sussex.* Toronto: University of Toronto Press, 2000.

Nelson, Alan H., ed. *Records of Early English Drama: Cambridge.* 2 vols. Toronto: University of Toronto Press, 1989.

———, and John R. Elliott Jr., eds. *Records of Early English Dram: Inns of Court.* 3 vols. Cambridge: D. S. Brewer, 2010.

Stokes, James, ed. *Records of Early English Drama: Lincolnshire.* 2 vols. Toronto: University of Toronto Press, 2009.

———, with Robert J. Alexander, eds. *Records of Early English Drama: Somerset, Including Bath.* 2 vols. Toronto: University of Toronto Press, 1996.

Thomas, Sylvia, with C. E. McGee, eds. *Records of Early English Drama: Yorkshire West Riding.* Toronto: REED Online, forthcoming.

Wyatt, Diana, ed. *Records of Early English Drama: Yorkshire East Riding.* Toronto: REED Online, forthcoming.

EARLY MODERN PRINTED PRIMARY SOURCES

Abbot, Robert. *The Danger of Popery: Or, A Sermon Preached at a Visitation at Ashford in Kent Vpon 2. Thess. 2.12. Wherein the Marks of Antichristianisme and Signes of Truth Are Opened and Applied, and the Question of the Sauing and Damning of Thos. That Follow Antichrist Is Explanted by the Scriptures. By Robert Abbott, Preacher of the Word of God at Cranebrooke in Kent.* EEBO / 864:07. London: Printed by I. L[egat] for Philemon Stephens, and Christopher Meredith and are to be sold at the Golden Lyon in Paules Church-yard, 1625.

———. *A Hand of Fellovvship, to Helpe Keepe out Sinne and Antichrist In Certaine Sermons Preached Vpon Seuerall Occasions.* EEBO / 864:08. London: Printed by Iohn Haviland for Nathaniel Butter, 1623.

Adams, Thomas. *The Deuills Banket Described in Foure Sermons [Brace], 1. The Banket Propounded, Begunne, 2. The Second Seruice, 3. The Breaking vp of the Feast, 4. The Shot or Reckoning, [and] The Sinners Passing-Bell, Together with Phisicke from Heauen.* EEBO / 1699:05. London: Printed by Thomas Snodham for Ralph Mab, and are to be sold in Paules Churchyard, at the signe of the Grayhound, 1614.

———. *Mystical Bedlam, or the Vvorld of Mad-Men.* EEBO / 818:01. London: Printed by George Purslowe for Clement Knight, and are to be sold at his shoppe in Paules Church-yard at the signe of the Holy Lambe, 1615.

———. *The Sacrifice of Thankefulnesse A Sermon Preached at Pauls Crosse, the Third of December, Being the First Aduentuall Sunday.* EEBO / 649:08. London:

Bibliography

Printed by Thomas Purfoot, for Clement Knight, and are to be sold at his shop in Pauls Church-yard, at the signe of the Holy Lambe, 1616.

———. *The Temple A Sermon Preached at Pauls Crosse the Fifth of August.* EEBO / 818:03. London: Printed by A. Mathewes for Iohn Grismand, and are to bee sold at his shop in Pauls Alley at the signe of the Gunne, 1624.

Andrewes, Lancelot. *Apospasmatia Sacra, or, A Collection of Posthumous and Orphan Lectures Delivered at St. Pauls and St. Giles His Church / by the Right Honourable and Reverend Father in God, Lancelot Andrews ...* London: Printed by R. Hodgkinsonne for H. Moseley, A. Crooke, D. Pakeman, L. Fawne, R. Royston, and N. Ekins, 1657., n.d.

Augustine, Saint, Bishop of Hippo. *Certaine Sermons of Sainte Augustines Translated out of Latyn, into Englishe, by Thomas Paynell.* Translated by Thomas Paynell. EEBO / 1762:09. London: J. Cawood, 1557.

Baker, John. *Lectures of I.B. Vpon the Xii. Articles of Our Christian Faith Briefely Set Forth for the Comfort of the Godly, and the Better Instruction of the Simple and Ignorant. Also Hereunto Is Annexed a Briefe and Cleare Confession of the Christian Faith, Conteining an Hundreth Articles, According to the Order of the Creede of the Apostles. Written by That Learned [and] Godly Martyr I.H. Sometime Bishop of Glocester in His Life Time.* Edited by John Hooper and Jean Garnier. EEBO / 195:13. Imprinted at London: By C. Barker, 1581.

Bargrave, Isaac. *A Sermon Preached before King Charles, March 27. 1627. Being the Anniuersary of His Maiesties Inauguration: By Isacc [Sic] Bargraue, Doctor in Diuinity, Then Chaplaine to His Maiestie in Attendance: And Deane of Canterbury: By His Maiesties Speciall Command.* EEBO / 1019:05. London: Printed by Iohn Legatt, for Peter Paxton, and are to be sold at his shop at the Angell in Pauls Church-yard, 1627.

Barker, Christopher. *The Bible. Translated According to the Ebrew and Greeke, and Conferred with the Best Translations in Diuers Languages. With Most Profitable Annotations Vpon All the Hard Places, and Other Things of Great Importance, as May Appeare in the Epistle to the Reader.* EEBO / 1472:02. Imprinted at London: by Christopher Barker, printer to the Queenes most excellent Maiestie, 1583.

Barker, Lawrence. *Christs Checke to S. Peter for His Curious Question out of Those Words in Saint Iohn: Quid Ad Te? Begun in Paules Church on S. Iohns Day the Euangelist. 1597. out of Part of the Gospel Appointed for That Day, and Prosecuted the Same Day This Yeare 1598. in the Same Place, and Else Where at Other Times the Six Seueral Sermons.* EEBO / 410:04. At London: Printed by P. S[hort] for Cuthbert Burbie, and Thomas Gosson, 1599.

Barlow, John. *The True Guide to Glory A Sermon Preached at Plympton-Mary in Deuon.* EEBO / 824:02. London: Printed by Thomas Snodham, for Nathaniel Newberry, and are to be sold at his shop vnder Saint Peters Church in Cornehill, 1619.

Barnes, Robert. *A Sermon Preached at Henly at the Visitation on the 27. of Aprill, 1626 Vpon Those Words of the 9. Psalme, Vers. 16.* EEBO / 695:09. Oxford: Printed by I. L[ichfield] and W. T[urner], 1626.

Bibliography

Baughe, Thomas. *A Summons to Iudgement. Or a Sermon Appointed for the Crosse, but Deliuered Vpon Occasion in the Cathedrall Church of S. Paul London the 6. Day of Iune, 1613. Beeing the First Sunday of Midsommer Terme. By Thomas Baughe, Student of Christ-Church in Oxford.* EEBO / 826:09. London: Printed by G. Eld, for William Iones, and are to bee sold at his shop neere Holborne Conduit, at the signe of the Gunne, 1614.

Becon, Thomas. *A New Postil Conteinyng Most Godly and Learned Sermons Vpon All the Sonday Gospelles, That Be Redde in the Church Thorowout the Yeare.* EEBO / 173:01. Imprinted at London: In Flete-strete nere to S. Dunstons church, by Thomas Marshe [and John Kingston], M.D.LXVI, 1566.

Bentham, Thomas. *A Notable and Comfortable Exposition, Vpon the Fourth of Mathevv; Concerning the Tentations of Christ Preached in S.Peters Church, in Oxenford; By Thomas Bentham, Fellovv Ov Magdalin Colledge and Afterwards Vyshop of Liechfeeld and Coventrie.* EEBO / 173:05. At London: Printed by Robert Walde-graue, dwelling in Foster-Lane, ouer against Goldsmiths Hall, 1583.

Birkenhead, Michael. *The Recoverie of Paradise. A Sermon, on the Incarnation and Birth of Our Sauior Christ. By Michael Birkhed.* EEBO / 2059:05. [London]: Printed for Nicholas Ling and Thomas Bushel, and are by them to be sold, 1602.

Boys, John. *Remaines of That Reverend and Famous Postiller, Iohn Boys, Doctor in Divinitie, and Late Deane of Canterburie Containing Sundry Sermons; Partly, on Some Proper Lessons Vsed in Our English Liturgie: And Partly, on Other Select Portions of Holy Scripture.* EEBO / 702:02. London: Printed by Aug: Math[ewes]: for Humphrey Robinson and are to bee solde at the three Pidgeons in Paules Church-yard, 1631.

Bradford, John. *A Double Summons the One, to Vnfained Repentance. The Other, to the Worthie Receiuing of the Lords Supper.* EEBO / 1540:15. London: Printed by George Purslowe, 1617.

Bullinger, Heinrich. *A hundred sermons vpo[n] the Apocalips of Iesu Christe reueiled in dede by thangell of the Lorde: but seen or receyued and written by thapostle and Eua[n]gelist. S. Iohn: compiled by the famous and godly learned man, Henry Bullinger.* EEBO/184:02 [impkinted [sic] at at [sic] London: By Iohn Day, dwelling ouer Aldersgate, beneath Saincte Martins … These bokes are to be sold at his shoppe ouer the gate, 1561.

———. *Fiftie Godlie and Learned Sermons Diuided into Fiue Decades, Conteyning the Chiefe and Principall Pointes of Christian Religion.* Translated by H. I. EEBO / 183:03. Imprinted at London: By [Henry Middleton for] Ralphe Newberrie, dwelling in Fleet-streate a little aboue the Conduite, 1577.

Burton, Samuel. *A Sermon Preached at the Generall Assises in Warwicke, the Third of March, Being the First Friday in Lent. 1619. By Samuel Burton, Archdeacon of Gloucester. Seene and Allowed by Authoritie.* EEBO / 1371:12. London: Printed by W. Stansby for Nathaniel Butter, 1620.

Bibliography

Burton, William. *The Rowsing of the Sluggard, in 7. Sermons Published at the Request of Diuers Godlie and Well Affected. By W.B. Minister of the Word of God at Reading in Barkeshire*. EEBO / 876:08. At London: Printed by the Widow Orwin for Thomas Man, 1595.

———. *Ten Sermons Vpon the First, Second, Third and Fourth Verses of the Sixt of Matthew Containing Diuerse Necessary and Profitable Treatises , Viz. a Preseruatiue against the Poyson of Vaine-Glory in the 1 & 2, the Reward of Sincerity in the 3, the Vncasing of the Hypocrite in the 4, 5 and 6, the Reward of Hypocrisie in the 7 and 8, an Admonition to Left-Handed Christians in the 9 and 10: Whereunto Is Annexed Another Treatise Called The Anatomie of Belial, Set Foorth in Ten Sermons Vpon the 12, 13, 14, 15 Verses of the 6 Chapter of the Prouerbs of Salomon*. EEBO / 1747:32. Imprinted at London: By Richard Field for Thomas Man, 1602.

Bury, George. *The Narrovv Vvay, and the Last Iudgement Deliuered in Two Sermons: The First at Pauls Crosse, the Other Elsewhere*. EEBO / 869:14. London: Printed [by R. Field] for Matthew Lownes, 1607.

Calvin, Jean. *Foure Godlye Sermons Agaynst the Pollution of Idolatries Comforting Men in Persecutions, and Teachyng Them What Commodities Thei Shal Find in Christes Church, Which Were Preached in French by the Moste Famous Clarke Ihon Caluyne, and Translated Fyrst into Latine and Afterward into Englishe by Diuers Godly Learned Men*. EEBO / 490:05. Printed at London: By Rouland Hall, dwelling in Golding lane at the signe of the thre arrowes, 1561.

———. *Foure Sermons of Maister Iohn Caluin Entreating of Matters Very Profitable for Our Time, as May Bee Seene by the Preface: With a Briefe Exposition of the LXXXVII. Psalme. Translated out of Frenche into Englishe by Iohn Fielde*. EEBO / 416:02. Imprinted at London: [By Thomas Dawson] for Thomas Man, dwelling in Pater Noster Rowe, at the signe of the Talbot, 1579.

———. *A Harmonie Vpon the the Three Euangelists, Matthew, Mark and Luke with the Commentarie of M. Iohn Caluine: Faithfully Translated out of Latine into English, by E.P. Whereunto Is Also Added a Commentarie Vpon the Euangelist S. Iohn, by the Same Authour*. Edited by Christopher Fetherston. EEBO / 1370:15. Londini: [Printed by Thomas Dawson] impensis Geor. Bishop, 1610.

———. *Sermons ... Vpon the Fifth Booke of Moses Called Deuteronomie*. London: Printed by Henry Middleton for George Bishop, 1583.

———. *Sermons of M. Iohn Caluine Vpon the Epistle of Saincte Paule to the Galathians*. EEBO / 200:02. Imprinted at London: By [Henrie Bynneman, for] Lucas Harison and George Bishop, 1574.

———. *Sermons of Master Iohn Calvin, Vpon the Booke of Iob*. London: Imprinted by Henry Bynneman, 1574.

Carpenter, John. *Remember Lots Wife Two Godly and Fruitfull Sermons Verie Conuenient for This Our Time: Lately Preached on a Sunday in the Cathedral Church of S. Peters, in Excester: The One, in the Forenoone: The Other, in the Afternoone the Same Day*. EEBO / 311:05. At London: Printed by Thomas

Bibliography

Orwin, and are to be solde by Edward White at the litle North-doore of S. Paules, at the signe of the Gunne, 1588.

Cartwright, Thomas. *A Commentary Vpon the Epistle of Saint Paule Written to the Colossians. Preached by Thomas Cartwright, and Now Published for the Further vse of the Church of God.* EEBO / 1229:04. London: Printed by Nicholas Okes, and are to be sold by George Norton, dwelling neere Temple-barre, 1612.

Chardon, John. *A Sermon Preached in S. Peters Church in Exeter the 6. Day of December Last Wherin Is Intreated of the Second Commming of Christ Vnto Iudgement, & of the End of the World. By Iohn Chardon Maister of Art, and Preacher of the Word of God.* EEBO / 952:11. Imprinted at London: At the three Cranes in the Vintree, by Thomas Dawson, 1580.

Cranmer, Thomas. *Catechismus, That Is to Say, a Shorte Instruction into Christian Religion for the Synguler Commoditie and Profyte of Childre[n] and Yong People. Set Forth by the Mooste Reuerende Father in God Thomas Archbyshop of Canterbury, Primate of All England and Metropolitane.* EEBO / 33:07. [Imprynted at London: In S. Jhones strete by Nycolas Hyll. for] Gwalter Lynne, [dwellyng on Somers kaye by Byllynges gate], 1548.

———. *Certayne Sermons, or Homelies Appoynted by the Kynges Maiestie, to Be Declared and Redde, by All Persones, Vicars, or Curates, Euery Sondaye in Their Churches, Where They Haue Cure.* EEBO / 48:03. [Imprinted at London: The laste daie of Iulii, in the first yere of the reigne of our souereigne lord Kyng Edvvard the. VI: by Rychard Grafton printer to his moste royall Maiestie, 1547.

Curteys, Richard. *Two Sermons Preached by the Reuerend Father in God the Bishop of Chichester the First at Paules Crosse. The Second at Westminster before the Queenes Maiestie.* EEBO / 1601:07. London: Printed by T. Man, and W. Brome, 1584.

Day, John. *Day's Festiuals or, Twelve of His Sermons Deliuered by Him at Seueral Times to the Parishioners of St Maryes in Oxford, on the Three Chiefe Festivals of the Yeere, Christmas, Easter, and Whit-Sontide.* EEBO / 1200:02. Printed at Oxford: By Ioseph Barnes, 1615.

Denison, John. *The Heauenly Banquet: Or The Doctrine of the Lords Supper Set Forth in Seuen Sermons. With Two Prayers before and after the Receiuing. And a Iustification of Kneeling in the Act of Receiuing.* EEBO / 1410:05. London: Printed by E[lizabeth] A[llde] for Robert Allot, and are to bee sold [by W. Brooks?] within the Turning-Stile in Holborne, 1631.

Dod, John, and Robert Cleaver. *Three Godlie and Fruitful Sermons; the Two First Preached by Maister Iohn Dod: The Last by Maister Robert Cleauer.* EEBO / 1234:13. London: Printed [by N. Okes and F. Kingston] for William Welby, and are to be sold at his shop in Pauls Church-yard, at the signe of the white Swan, 1610.

Dyke, Jeremiah. *Divers Select Sermons on Severall Texts Viz. 1. Of Quenchiug [Sic] the Spirit. I Thessalon. 5.16. 2. Of the Sinners Suite for Pardon. 2 Sam. 24.10. 3. Of Eating and Digesting the Word. Ier. 15.16. 4. Of Buying and Keeping the Truth.*

Bibliography

Prov. 23.23. EEBO / 1956:01. London: printed by Tho. Paine, for L. Fawne and S. Gellibrand, at the sign of the brazen Serpent, in Pauls Church-yard, 1640.

Edgeworth, Roger. *Sermons Very Fruitfull, Godly, and Learned, Preached and Sette Foorth by Maister Roger Edgeworth, Doctoure of Diuinitie, Canon of the Cathedrall Churches of Sarisburie, Welles and Bristow, Residentiary in the Cathedrall Churche of Welles, and Chauncellour of the Same Churche: With a Repertorie or Table, Directing to Many Notable Matters Expressed in the Same Sermons.* EEBO / 219:02. Excusum Londini: In aedibus Roberti Caly, Tipographi, 1557.

Eedes, Richard. *Three Sermons Preached by That Learned and Reuerend Diuine, Doctor Eedes, Sometimes Dean of Worcester, for Their Fitnesse Vnto the Present Time.* EEBO / 643:18 ; EEBO / 1943:06. London: Printed by G.M. for Philemon Stephens and Christopher Meredith, and are to be sold at the Golden Lyon in Pauls Churchyard, 1627.

Elton, Edward. *An Exposition of the Epistle of St Paule to the Colossians Deliuered in Sundry Sermons, Preached by Edvvard Elton Minister of Gods Word at St Mary Magdalens Bermondsey Neare London.* EEBO / 883:10. London: Printed by Edward Griffin for Ralph Mab and are to be sold at his shop, at the signe of the Grey-hound, in Pauls-Church-yard, 1615.

Est, William. *The Right Rule of a Religious Life: Or, The Glasse of Godlinesse Wherein Euery Man May Behold His Imperfections, How Farre Hee Is out of the Way of True Godlinesse, and Learne to Reduce His Wandring Steppes into the Pathes of True Pietie. In Certaine Lectures Vpon the First Chapter of the Epistle of S. Iames. The First Part. By William Est Preacher of Gods Word.* EEBO / 884:21. London: Printed by Nicholas Okes, and are to bee sold by Richard Lea at his shop on the North entry of the Royall Exchange, 1616.

Featley, Daniel. *Clavis Mystica a Key Opening Divers Difficult and Mysterious Texts of Holy Scripture; Handled in Seventy Sermons, Preached at Solemn and Most Celebrious Assemblies, upon Speciall Occasions, in England and France. By Daniel Featley, D.D.* London: Printed by R[obert] Y[oung] for Nicolas Bourne, at the south entrance of the royall Exchange, an. Dom., 1636.

Fotherby, Martin. *Foure Sermons, Lately Preached, by Martin Fotherby Doctor in Diuinity, and Chaplain Vnto the Kings Maiestie.* EEBO / 1306:03. At London: Printed by Henry Ballard, for C. K[night] and W. C[otton], 1608.

Foxe, John. *A Sermon of Christ Crucified, Preached at Paules Crosse the Friday before Easter, Commonly Called Goodfryday Written and Dedicated to All Such as Labour and Be Heavy Laden in Conscience, to Be Read for Their Spirituall Comfort.* EEBO / 543:04 ; EEBO / 1896:04. At London: Imprinted by Iohn Daye, ouer Aldersgate, 1570.

Frewen, John. *Certaine Sermons Vpon the 2, 3, 4, 5, 6, 7, and 8. Verses of the Eleuenth Chapter of S. Paule His Epistle to the Romanes Preached in the Parish Church of Northiham, in the County of Sussex.* EEBO / 1306:07 ; EEBO / 1987:01. London: printed for Richard Bankworth, dwelling at the signe of the Sunne in Paules Church-yard, 1612.

Bibliography

Gataker, Thomas. *Two Sermons Tending to Direction for Christian Cariage [Sic] Both in Afflictions Incumbent, and in Judgements Imminent: The Former on Psalm 13.1, the Latter on Hebr. 11.7.* EEBO / 1066:10 ; EEBO / 1945:16. London: Printed by Iohn Haviland, 1623.

Gee, John. *Hold Fast a Sermon Preached at Pauls Crosse Vpon Sunday Being the Xxxi. of October, Anno Domini 1624.* EEBO / 1099:14. London: Printed by A. M[athewes] and I. N[orton] for Robert Mylbourne, and are to be sold at his shop at the great south doore of Pauls, 1624.

Gibson, Thomas. *The Blessing of a Good King Deliuered in Eight Sermons Vpon the Storie of the Queene of the South, Her Words to Salomon, Magnifying the Gouernment of His Familie and Kingdome.* EEBO / 1067:06. At London: Printed by Tho: Creede [and N. Okes], for Arthur Iohnson, dwelling at the signe of the white Horse in Pauls Church-yard, 1614.

Gifford, George. *A Briefe Discourse of Certaine Points of the Religion which is among the Commō Sort of Christians, which may Bee Termed the Countrie Diuinitie with a Manifest Confutation of the Same, After the Order of a Dialogue / Compiled by George Gifforde.* EEBO/ 1946:05. London, For Toby Cook, dwelling at the Tigres head in Paules churchyard, and are there to bee solde, 1582.

———. *Eight Sermons, Vpon the First Foure Chapters, and Part of the Fift, of Ecclesiastes Preached at Mauldon.* EEBO / 709:13. At London: Printed by Iohn Windet for Toby Cooke, at the Tygers head in Paules Church-yard, 1589.

Greenham, Richard. *Paramythion Tvvo Treatises of the Comforting of an Afflicted Conscience, Written by M. Richard Greenham, with Certaine Epistles of the Same Argument. Heereunto Are Added Two Sermons, with Certaine Graue and Wise Counsells and Answeres of the Same Author and Argument.* EEBO / 298:10. Imprinted at London: By Richard Bradocke, for Robert Dexter, and are to be solde at the signe of the Brasen Serpent in Paules Churchyard, 1598.

———. *Two Learned and Godly Sermons, Preached by That Reuerende and Zelous Man M. Richard Greenham: On These Partes of Scripture Folowing. The First Sermon on This Text. A Good Name Is to Be Desired Aboue Great Riches, and Louing Fauour Aboue Siluer and Golde. Pro. 22, I. The Second Sermon on This Text. Quench Not the Spirit. I. Thessa. 5, 19.* EEBO / 710:02. London: Printed by Gabriel Simson and William White, for William Iones, dwelling neare Holborne condite at the signe of the Gunne: where they are to be solde, 1595.

———. *The Workes of the Reuerend and Faithfull Seruant Af Iesus Christ M. Richard Greenham, Minister and Preacher of the Word of God Collected into One Volume: Reuised, Corrected, and Published, for the Further Building of All Such as Loue the Truth, and Desire to Know the Power of Godlinesse. By H.H.* Edited by Henry Holland and Robert Hill. EEBO / 1174:05. London: Printed [by Thomas Snodham and Thomas Creede] for VVilliam VVelby, and are to be solde at his shop in Paules Church-yard, at the signe of the Swanne, 1612.

Bibliography

Grent, John. *The Burthen of Tyre A Sermon Preach'd at Pauls Crosse, by Iohn Grent, Then Fellow of New Colledge in Oxford.* EEBO / 888:15. London: Printed [by A. Mathewes] for Richard Royston, 1627.

Gwalther, Rudolf. *The Homilies or Familiar Sermons of M. Rodolph Gualther Tigurine Vpon the Prophet Ioel. Translated from Latine into Englishe, by Iohn Ludham Vicar of Withersfielde.* EEBO / 1613:16. Imprinted in London: [By Thomas Dawson] for William Ponsonnby, 1582.

Hacket, Roger. *A Learned Sermon Handling the Question of Ceremonies, Controuerted in Our Church: By Roger Hacket Doctor in Diuinitie.* EEBO / 1103:13. At London: Printed by Felix Kyngston, for Cuthbert Burbie, and are to be sold at his shop at the signe of the Swan in Pauls Churchyard, 1605.

Hakewill, George. *King Dauids Vow for Reformation of Himselfe. His Family. His Kingdome Deliuered in Twelue Sermons before the Prince His Highnesse Vpon Psalm 101.* Edited by Renold Elstracke. EEBO / 1239:16. London: Printed [by Humphrey Lownes] for Mathew Lownes, 1621.

Hall, Joseph. *The Great Impostor Laid Open in a Sermon at Grayes Inne, Febr. 2.1623. By Ios. Hall D.D.* EEBO / 1104:01. London: Printed by J. Haviland for Nath. Butter, 1623.

———. *A Sermon Preached before His Majestie at His Court of Thebalds, on Sunday, Sept. 15. 1622 In the Ordinary Course of Attendance. By Ios. Hall D.D.* Early English Books, 1475–1640 / 714:07. London: Printed by I. Haviland for N. Butter, 1622.

Hall, Thomas. *A Practical and Polemical Commentary or Exposition upon the Third and Fourth Chapters of the Latter Epistle of Saint Paul to Timothy.* London: Printed by E. Tyler, for John Starkey, at the Miter at the North door of the middle Exchange in Saint Pauls Churchyard, 1658.

Harrison, William. *Deaths Aduantage Little Regarded, and The Soules Solace against Sorrow Preached in Two Funerall Sermons at Childwal in Lancashire at the Buriall of Mistris Katherin Brettergh the Third of Iune. 1601. The One by William Harrison, One of the Preachers Appointed by Her. Maiestie for the Countie Palatine of Lancaster, the Other by William Leygh, Bachelor of Diuinitie, and Pastor of Standish. Whereunto Is Annexed, the Christian Life and Godly Death of the Said Gentlevvoman.* Edited by William Leigh. EEBO / 1142:24. At London: Imprinted by Felix Kyngston, 1602.

Hieron, Samuel. *Aarons Bells A-Sounding In a Sermon, Tending Cheiftly [Sic] to Admonish the Ministerie, of Their Charge, & Duty. Preached by M. Samuel Hieron at a General Visitation Neere Bristow. And Now Published by Them to Whom His Coppy Was Entrusted after His Death.* EEBO / 1382:04. [Holland?: s.n.], 1623.

Hill, Adam. *The Crie of England A Sermon Preached at Paules Crosse in September 1593 by Adam Hill Doctor of Diuinitie, & Published at the Request of the Then Lord Maior of the Citie of London, and Others the Aldermen His Brethren.* EEBO / 1275:02. London: Printed by Ed. Allde, for B. Norton, 1595.

Bibliography

Holbrooke, William. *A Sermon Preached at Saint Buttolphs Neare Aldersgate, the 26. of Februarie, 1609. By William Holbrooke. Entitled No Gaine to This.* EEBO / 1072:01. At London: Imprinted by Felix Kyngston, for Elizabeth Burby, dwelling in Pauls Churchyard at the signe of the Swan, 1609.

Holyday, Barten. *A Sermon Preached at Pauls Crosse, August the 5. 1623. By Barten Holyday, Now Archdeacon of Oxford.* EEBO / 1107:03. London: Printed by William Stansby for Nathaniell Butter, and are to be sold at his shop at Saint Austines Gate in Pauls Church-yard, 1626.

Hoskin, John. *A sermon vpon the parable of the King that taketh an accompt of his seruants Math. 18. 23. Wherein is declared, the iustice, mercy, and seueritie of God: the crueltie of man, and his reward for the same. Rising vpon St. Peters question to Christ, viz. How oft shall I forgiue my brother? seauen times? 21. vers. [...] By Iohn Hoskin, minister of Gods holy word, student in Diuinitie.* EEBO / 1208:16. At London: Printed by G. E[ld] for Iohn Wright, 1609.

———. *Sermons Preached at Pauls Crosse and Else-Where, by Iohn Hoskins, Sometimes Fellow of New-Colledge in Oxford, Minister and Doctor of Law.* EEBO / 1177:05. London: Printed by William Stansby for Nathaniel Butter, and are to be sold at his shop at Saint Austens gate, 1615.

Howson, John. *A Sermon Preached at St. Maries in Oxford, the 17. Day of November, 1602. in Defence of the Festivities of the Church of England, and Namely That of Her Maiesties Coronation.* EEBO / 1072:10. At Oxford: Printed by Joseph Barnes, and are to be sold in [London in] Fleete-streete at the signe of the Turkes head by Iohn Barnes, 1602.

Humphrey, Laurence. *A View of the Romish Hydra and Monster, Traison, against the Lords Annointed: Condemned by Dauid, I. Sam. 26. and Nowe Confuted in Seuen Sermons to Perswade Obedience to Princes, Concord among Our Selues, and a Generall Reformation and Repentaunce in All States.* EEBO / 571:06. At Oxford: Printed by Ioseph Barnes, and are to be solde [by T. Cooke, London] in Paules Church-yearde at the signe of the Tygershead, 1588.

Humpston, Robert. *A Sermon Preached at Reyfham in the Countie of Norff. the 22. of September.* EEBO / 549:04. London: Printed by Iohn Wolfe for Edward Aggas, 1589.

Jackson, Thomas. *An Helpe to the Best Bargaine a Sermon on Mat. 13–16. Preached on Sunday, the 20. of Octob. 1623. in the Cathedrall Church of Christ, Canterbury.* EEBO / 992:02. London: Printed by Nich. Okes, for Mat. Walbanke, and are to be sold in Grais-Inne Gate, 1624.

Jerome, Stephen. *The Haughty Heart Humbled: Or, The Penitents Practice: In the Regall Patterne of King Ezekiah Directory and Consolatory to All the Mourners in Sion, to Sow in Teares, and to Reape in Ioy. By S.I. Preacher of Gods Word.* EEBO / 1277:07. London: Printed [by Miles Flesher] for Richard More, and are to be sold at his shop in Saint Dunstanes Church-yard in Fleetstreet, 1628.

———. *Moses His Sight of Canaan with Simeon His Dying-Song. Directing How to Liue Holily and Dye Happily.* EEBO / 1353:07. London: Printed [by T.

Bibliography

Snodham] for Roger Iackson, and are to be solde at his shop, neare to the conduit in Fleetstreete, 1614.

Jewel, John. *Certaine Sermons Preached before the Queenes Maiestie, and at Paules Crosse, by the Reuerend Father Iohn Ievvel Late Bishop of Salisburie. Whereunto Is Added a Short Treatise of the Sacraments, Gathered out of Other His Sermons, Made Vpon That Matter, in His Cathedrall Church at Salisburie.* Edited by John Garbrand. EEBO / 423:08. Imprinted at London: By Christopher Barker, printer to the Queenes most excellent Maiestie, 1583.

Jones, Philip. *Certaine Sermons Preached of Late at Ciceter, in the Countie of Glocester Vpon a Portion of the First Chapter of the Epistle of Iames: Wherein the Two Seueral States, of the Riche and Poore Man Are Compared and Examined, the Differences in Quality, and Duety Betwixt Them Shewed, Both Directed to Such Christian Parts and Offices, as the Sufficiencie of the One May, and Ought to Performe, and the Wants of the Other Do Necessarily Require.* EEBO / 1384:22. Imprinted at London: By T. D[awson] for Thomas Butter, 1588.

Kethe, William. *A Sermon Made at Blanford Foru[m] in the Countie of Dorset on Wensday the 17. of Ianuarij Last Past at the Session Holden There, before the Honorable and the Worshyppefull of That Shyre.* EEBO / 472:07. At London: Printed by Iohn Daye, dwellyng ouer Aldersgate. Cum gratia & priuilegio Regiae Maiestatis, 1571.

Latimer, Hugh. *27 Sermons Preached by the Ryght Reuerende Father in God and Constant Matir [Sic] of Iesus Christe, Maister Hugh Latimer, as Well Such as in Tymes Past Haue Bene Printed, as Certayne Other Commyng to Our Handes of Late, Whych Were yet Neuer Set Forth in Print. Faithfully Perused [and] Allowed Accordying to the Order Appoynted in the Quenes Maiesties Iniunctions. 1. Hys Sermon Ad Clerum. 2. Hys Fourth Sermon Vpon the Plough. 3. Hys. 7. Sermons before Kyng Edward. 4 Hys Sermon at Stamforde. 5. Hys Last Sermon before Kyng Edward. 6. Hys. 7. Sermons Vpon the Lordes Prayer. 7. Hys Other. 9. Sermons Vpon Certayne Gospels and Epistles.* Edited by Augustine Bernher. EEBO / 258:04. Imprinted at London: By Iohn Day, dwelling ouer Aldersgate. Cum gratia & priuilegio Regi[a]e Maiestatis, 1562.

———. *A Notable Sermo[n] of Ye Reuerende Father Maister Hughe Latemer Whiche He Preached in Ye Shrouds at Paules Churche in Londo[N].* EEBO / 82:01 ; EEBO / 103:08. Imprinted at London: By Ihon Day, dwellynge at Aldersgate, and Wylliam Seres, dwellyng in Peter Colledge. These bokes are to be sold at the new shop by the lytle Conduyte in Chepesyde, 1548.

———. *The Seconde [Seventh] Sermon of Maister Hughe Latimer Which He Preached before the Kynges Maiestie [with?]In His Graces Palayce at Westminster.* EEBO / 1900:04. Jmprinted at London: By Jhon Day, dwellynge at Aldersgate, and Wylliam Seres, dwellyng in Peter Colledge … to be solde at the new shop by the [sp--e?] Conduyte in Chepesyde, 1549.

Lavater, Ludwig. *The Book of Ruth Expounded in Twenty Eight Sermons, by Levves Lauaterus of Tygurine, and by Hym Published in Latine, and Now Translated into Englishe by Ephraim Pagitt, a Childe of Eleuen Yeares of Age.* Edited by

Bibliography

Ephraim Pagitt. EEBO / 1278:05. London: Printed by Robert Walde-graue, dwelling without Temple-bar, 1586.

———. *Three Christian Sermons, Made by Lodouike Lauatere, Minister of Zuricke in Heluetia, of Famine and Dearth of Victuals: And Translated into English, as Being Verie Fit for This Time of Our Dearth.* EEBO / 473:11. London: Printed by Thomas Creede, 1596.

Leigh, William. *Dauids Palme and Cedar Shewing the Reward of the Righteous. In a Sermon Preached at Eccleston Church in Lancashire; Iuly, 25. 1614. Being the Day of Dedication of Heskine Schoole: Founded by Sir Iames Pemberton Knight, Late Alderman and Citizen of London.* EEBO / 715:13. London: Printed by Thomas Creede for Arthur Iohnson, and are to be sold at his shop in Paules churchyard, 1615.

Ley, Roger. *The Bruising of the Serpents Head A Sermon Preached at Pauls Crosse September 9. 1621. By Roger Ley Maister of Arts, and Minister of Gods Word in Shoreditch.* EEBO / 843:11. London: Printed by Iohn Dawson for Nicholas Bourne, and are to be sold at his shop at the Royall Exchange, 1622.

Lowin, John. *Brief Conclusions of Dancers and Dancing Condemning the Prophane vse Thereof; and Commending the Excellencie of Such Persons Which Haue from Age to Age, in All Solemne Feasts, and Victorious Triumphs, Vsed That (No Lesse) Honourable, Commendable and Laudable Recreation: As Also True Physicall Obseruations for the Preseruation of the Body in Health, by the vse of the Same Exercise.* London: For Iohn Orphinstrange, and are to bee sold at his shop by the Cocke and Katherine-wheel neere Holbourne bridge, 1609.

Marlorat, Augustin. *A Catholike and Ecclesiastical Exposition of the Holy Gospel after St. Matthew, Gathered out of All the Singular and Approved Divines.* Translated by Thomas Tymme. Imprinted at London: In Fletestreate neare vnto S. Dunstones churche, by Thomas Marshe, 1570.

Maxey, Anthony. *An Other Sermon Preached before the King at Greenewich on Tuesday before Easter, Being the 26. of March. 1605. By Anthonie Maxey, Bachelar in Diuinity, and Chaplaine to His Maiesty. The Points Herein Handled Are These. 1. That There Is an Hardening. 2. That God Hardeneth Not. 3. How Men Become Hardened. 4. The Meanes to Auoid It.* EEBO / 580:06. At London: Printed by George Snowdon and Lionell Snowdon, for Clement Knight, and are to be sould at his shoppe, in Paules Church-yard, at the signe of the Holy Lambe, 1605.

Mayer, John. *A Commentarie Vpon the Nevv Testament Representing the Divers Expositions Thereof, out of the Workes of the Most Learned, Both Ancient Fathers, and Moderne Writers: And Hereby Sifting out the True Sense of Every Passage, for the Benefit of All That Desire to Reade with Understanding. The First Volumne upon the Foure Evangelists and the Acts of the Apostles. Wherein the Places More Difficult Going under the Name of Texts, Are More Largely; the Lesse Difficult, More Briefly Expounded.* EEBO / 1998:03. London: printed by Thomas Cotes, for Iohn Bellamie [and John Haviland for John Grismond], and are to be sold at his shoppe in Cornehill, at the signe of the three Golden

Bibliography

Lyons, neere the Royall Exchange [and at Grismond's shop in Ivie lane at the signe of the Gun], n.d.

Meriton, George. *A Sermon Preached before the Generall Assembly at Glascoe in the Kingdome of Scotland, the Tenth Day of Iune, 1610. By George Meriton Doctor of Diuinitie, and One of His Maiesties Chaplaines.* EEBO / 1354:17. London: Printed by William Stansby for Henry Featherstone, 1611.

Merlin, Pierre. *A Most Plaine and Profitable Exposition of the Book of Ester Deliuered in 26. Sermons. By Peter Merlin, One of the Ministers of the Church of Garnezey: And Now Translated in English, for the Helpe of Those Who Wanting the Knowledge of the Tongues, Are yet Desirous of the Vnderstanding of the Scriptures and True Godlinesse. With a Table of the Principall Points of Doctrine Contained Therein.* EEBO / 854:02. London: Printed by Thomas Creed, 1599.

Moulin, Pierre Du. *A Preparation Vnto Fasting and Repentance. By Peter Moulin, and Translated by I.B.* EEBO / 643:15. London: Printed by T. S[nodham] for Nathaniel Newbery, and are to be sould at the signe of the Starre vnder S. Peters Church in Cornehill, and in Popes head ally, 1620.

Parsons, Bartholomew. *Boaz and Ruth Blessed: Or A Sacred Contract Honoured with a Solemne Benediction By Bartholomew Parsons B. of Divinity and Rector of Ludgershall in the County of Wiltes.* EEBO / 1180:21. Oxford: Printed by Iohn Lichfield, for William Webbe, 1633.

Philips, Edward. *Certain Godly and Learned Sermons, Preached by That Worthy Seruant of Christ M. Ed. Philips in S. Sauiors in Southwarke: Vpon the Whole Four First Chapters of Matthew, Luc. 11. Vers. 24. 25. 26. Rom. 8. the Whole, 1. Thess. 5. 19. Tit. 2. 11. 12. Iames 2. from the 20. to the 26. and 1. Ioh. 3. 9. 10. And Were Taken by the Pen of H. Yeluerton of Grayes Inne Gentleman.* EEBO / 662:06 ; EEBO / 1976:04. London: Printed by Arn. Hatfield for Elizabeth Burbie widow, and are to be sold at her shop in Pauls Church-yard at the signe of the Swanne,1607.

Playfere, Thomas. *The Meane in Mourning. A Sermon Preached at Saint Maryes Spittle in London on Tuesday in Easter Weeke. 1595. / By Thomas Playfere Doctor of Diuinitie.* EEBO / 2124:06. At London: Printed by the Widow Orwin for Andrew Wise, dwelling in Paules Church yeard, at the sign of the Angel, 1596.

———. *The Pathway to Perfection A Sermon Preached at Saint Maryes Spittle in London on VVednesday in Easter Weeke. 1593. By Thomas Playfere, Doctor of Diuinitie.* EEBO / 1608:03. At London: Printed by Iames Roberts for Andrew VVise, dwelling in Paules church-yard, at the signe of the Angel, 1597.

Price, Daniel. *Spirituall Odours to the Memory of Prince Henry in Foure of the Last Sermons Preached in St James after His Highnesse Death, the Last Being the Sermon before the Body, the Day before the Funerall. By Daniel Price Then Chaplaine in Attendance.* EEBO / 970:24 ; EEBO / 1580:17. At Oxford: Printed by Ioseph Barnes and are to be sold by Iohn Barnes dwelling neere Holborne Conduit [, London], 1613.

Bibliography

Price, Sampson. *The Beauty of Holines: Or The Consecration of a House of Prayer, by the Example of Our Sauiour A Sermon Preached in the Chappell at the Free-Schoole in Shrewsbury. the 10. Day of September, Anno Dom. 1617. At the Consecration of the Chappell, by the Right Reuerend Father in God, the Lord Bishop of Couentrey and Lichfield. By Sampson Price, Doctor in Diuinity, and Chapleine in Ordinary to His Maiesty.* EEBO / 1183:11. London: Imprinted by B[ernard]: A[lsop]: for Richard Meighen, and are to be solde at his shop neere S. Clements Church without Temple-Barre, 1618.

———. *Ephesus Vvarning before Her Woe A Sermon Preached at Pauls Crosse on Passion Sunday, the 17. of March Last. By Sampson Price, Bachelour of Diuinity, of Exeter Colledge in Oxford: And Lecturer at S. Olaus.* EEBO / 1555:03. Imprinted at London: By G. Eld for Iohn Barnes, dwelling in Hosier lane, neere Holborne Conduit, 1616., 1618.

Prideaux, John. *Eight Sermons, Preached by Iohn Prideaux, Doctor of Diuinity, Regius Professor, Vice-Chancellor of the Vniuersity of Oxford, and Rector of Exeter Colledge. The Severall Texts and Titles of the Sermons, Follow in the next Leafe.* EEBO / 1668:10. Imprinted at London: by Felix Kyngston, for Iohn Budge, and are to be sold at his shop in Pauls Church-yard, at the signe of the greene Dragon, 1621.

Primrose, Gilbert. *The Righteous Mans Euils, and the Lords Deliuerances. By Gilbert Primerose, Minister of the French Church in London.* EEBO / 1580:22. London: Printed by H. L[ownes] for Nathanael Newberry, and are to be sold at the signe of the Starre in Popes-head Alley, 1625.

Reading, John. *A Faire Vvarning Declaring the Comfortable vse Both of Sicknesse and Health. Deliuered in Seuerall Sermons at Saint Maries in Douer.* EEBO / 1253:20. London: Printed by Bernard Alsop, for Iohn Hodgets, 1621.

Ressold, William. *Foure Sermons Viz. I. Sinnes Contagion, or the Sicknesse of the Soule. II. The Description of a Christian. III. The Blindnesse of a Wilfull Sinner. IV. A Race to Heaven.* EEBO / 1286:10. London: Printed by H. L[ownes] for George Lathum, at the Bishops head in Pauls Church-yard, 1627.

Rogers, Richard. *A Commentary Vpon the Vvhole Booke of Iudges Preached First and Deliuered in Sundrie Lectures; since Collected, and Diligently Perused, and Now Published. For the Benefit Generally of All Such as Desire to Grow in Faith and Repentance, and Especially of Them, Who Would More Cleerely Vnderstand and Make vse of the Worthie Examples of the Saints, Recorded in Diuine History.* EEBO / 1186:07. London: Imprinted by Felix Kyngston for Thomas Man, and are to be sold at his shop in Pater-noster Row, at the signe of the Talbot, 1615.

Rollenson, Francis. *Sermons Preached before His Maiestie 1. The Bridegromes Banquet. 2. The Triumph of Constancie. 3. The Banishment of Dogges.* EEBO / 1582:09. At London: Printed by T. Snodham for Robert Iackson, and are to be solde at his shop in Fleet-streete, ouer against the Conduit, 1611.

———. *Twelue prophetical legacies. Or Twelue sermons vpon Iacobs last will and testament recorded by Moses, in the 49. chapt. of Genesis: containing his bequests and blessings, bestowed vpon his twelue sonnes.* EEBO / 1288:03. London:

Bibliography

Imprinted by T[homas] C[reede] for Arthur Iohnson, dwelling at the signe of the white horse, by the great north doore of Paules, 1612.

Rudd, Anthony. *A Sermon Preached at Greenwich before the Kings Maiestie Vpon Tuesday in VVhitson Weeke Being the 14. of Iune. 1603.* EEBO / 1582:26. London: Imprinted by I. H[arrison] for Thomas Man and Clement Knight, 1603.

Sandys, Edwin. *Sermons Made by the Most Reuerende Father in God, Edwin, Archbishop of Yorke, Primate of England and Metropolitane.* EEBO / 352:11. At London: Printed by Henrie Midleton, for Thomas Charde, 1585.

Scultetus, Abraham. *A Secular Sermon Concerning the Doctrine of the Gospell by the Goodnes and Power of God Restored in the Fifteenth Age from the Birth of Our Lord Iesus Christ. Made by the Reuerend and Worthy Precher Mr. Abraham Scultetus, in the High-Dutch Tongue. After by Another Translated into Latin, and Now out of Latin into English.* EEBO / 1334:16. London: Printed by William Iones, dwelling in Red-crosse streete neare S. Giles Church, 1618.

Smith, Henry. *A Preparatiue to Mariage The Summe Whereof Was Spoken at a Contract, and Inlarged after. Whereunto Is Annexed a Treatise of the Lords Supper, and Another of Vsurie.* EEBO / 939:14 (part 3 only) ; EEBO / 1395:05. Imprinted at London: By Thomas Orwin for Thomas Man, dwelling in Paternoster row at the signe of the Talbot, 1591.

———. *The Preachers Proclamacion Discoursing the Vanity of All Earthly Things, and Proouing That There Is No Contentation to a Christian Minde, but Onely in the Feare of God.* EEBO / 1693:04. Imprinted at London: By[E. Allde? for] William Kearney dwelling within Creeple-gate, 1591.

———. *The Sermons of Maister Henrie Smith Gathered into One Volume. Printed According to His Corrected Copies in His Life Time.* EEBO / 398:07. At London: Printed by Richard Field [, T. Orwin, and R. Robinson] for Thomas Man, dwelling in Pater Noster row, at the signe of the Talbot, 1593.

———. *Six Sermons Preached by Maister Henry Smith at Clement Danes Church without Temple Barre. VVith Tvvo Prayers of the Same Author Hereunto Annexed.* Edited by W. S. EEBO / 2085:04. Imprinted at London: by R[ichard]. F[ield]. for Robert Dexter, dwelling at the Brasen serpent in Paules Church-yard, 1592.

Sutton, Thomas. *Englands First and Second Summons Two Sermons Preached at Paules Crosse, the One the Third of Ianuarie 1612; the Other the Fifth of Februarie, 1615.* EEBO / 940:04. London: Printed by Nicholas Okes for Matthevv Lavv, and are to be sold at his shop in Pauls Church-yard at the signe of the Fox, 1616.

Sydenham, Humphrey. *Sermons Vpon Solemne Occasions Preached in Severall Auditories. By Humphrey Sydenham, Rector of Pokington in Somerset.* EEBO / 1397:01 ; EEBO / 1672:16. London: Printed by Iohn Beale, for Humphrey Robinson, and are to be sold at the signe of the Three Pigeons in Pauls Church-yard, 1637.

Taverner, Richard. *The Epistles and Gospelles with a Brief Postil Vpon the Same from after Easter Tyll Aduent, Which Is the Somer Parte Set Forth for the Singuler*

Bibliography

Co[m]Moditie of All Good Christen Men and Namely of Prestes and Curates. EEBO / 1772:05. Imprinted at London: By Richarde Bankes, and are to be solde in Fletestrete at the sygne of the Whyte Harte, 1540.

Taylor, Thomas. *A Mappe of Rome Liuely Exhibiting Her Mercilesse Meeknesse, and Cruell Mercies to the Church of God: Preached in Fiue Sermons, on Occasion of the Gunpowder Treason, by T.T. and Now Published by W.I. Minister. 1. The Romish Furnace. 2. The Romish Edom. 3. The Romish Fowler. 4. The Romish Conception. To Which Is Added, 5. The English Gratulation.* Edited by William Jemmat. EEBO / 1366:08. At London: Imprinted by Felix Kyngston, for Iohn Bartlet, and are to be sould [by Thomas Man] at the signe of the Talbot in Pater-noster Row, 1620.

Topsell, Edward. *Times Lamentation: Or An Exposition on the Prophet Ioel, in Sundry Sermons or Meditations.* EEBO / 361:04. At London: Printed by Edm. Bollifant, for George Potter, 1599.

Tyrrell, Anthony. *A Fruitfull Sermon Preached in Christs-Church the 13. of Iulie. Anno 1589. By Anthony Tyrell Sometime a Seminarie Priest. But by the Great Mercie of God Made a True Professor of the Gospel, and Preacher of His Holy Word: Conteining an Admonition Vnto Vertue, and a Dehortation from Vice.* EEBO / 552:09. At London: Printed by Iohn Windet, and are to be sold at the signe of the Sun in Pauls church-yard by Abraham Kitson, 1589.

Udall, John. *The Combate Betwixt Christ and the Deuill Foure Sermons Vpon the Temptations of Christ in the Wildrenes by Sathan, Wherein Are to Be Sene the Subtle Sleightes That the Tempter Vseth Agaynst the Children of God, and the Meanes That God Hath Appointed to Resiste Him, Sanctified to Our vse in the Example of Our Sauiour Iesus Christ.* EEBO / 1696:15. At London: Printed by Robert Walde-graue, for Thomas Man, and William Brome, 1588.

Vase, Robert. *Ionah's Contestation about His Gourd In a Sermon Deliuered at Pauls Crosse. Septemb. 19. 1624.* EEBO / 1042:07. London: Printed by I[ohn] L[egat] for Robert Bird, and are to be sold at his shoppe, at the signe of the Bible in Cheape-side, 1625.

Wall, John. *Alae Seraphicae The Seraphins Vvings to Raise Us unto Heauen. Deliuered in Six Sermons, Partly at Saint Peters in Westminster, Partly at S. Aldates in Oxford. 1623.* EEBO / 1014:14. London: Printed by G[eorge] M[iller] for Robert Allot, and are to be sold at his shop in Pauls Churchyard at the signe of the Blacke Beare, 1627.

Walsall, John. *A Sermon Preached at Pauls Crosse by Iohn Walsal, One of the Preachers of Christ His Church in Canterburie. 5. October. 1578. And Published at the Earnest Request of Certeine Godlie Londoners and Others.* EEBO / 1121:06. At London: Printed [by Henrie Middleton] for G. Byshop, 1578.

Ward, Samuel. *A Coal from the Altar, to Kindle the Holy Fire of Zeale In a Sermon Preached at a Generall Visitation at Ipswich. By Samuell Ward, Bach. of Diuinity.* Edited by Ambrose Wood. EEBO / 1160:03. At London: Printed by H[umphrey] L[ownes] for Samuell Macham; and are to be sould at his shop in Pauls-church-yard, at the signe of the Buls-head, 1615.

229

Bibliography

———. *A Peace-Offring to God for the Blessings We Enioy Vnder His Maiesties Reigne with a Thanksgiuing for the Princes Safe Returne on Sunday the 5. of October. 1623. In a Sermon Preached at Manitree in Essex.* EEBO / 1045:06. London: Printed by A[ugustine] Math[ewes] for Iohn Marriot, and Iohn Grismand, and are to be sold at their shops in St. Dunstons Churchyard, and in Pauls Alley at the signe of the Gunne, 1624.

Webb, Richard. *Christs Kingdome Described in Seuen Fruitfull Sermons Vpon the Second Psalme. By Richard Web Preacher of Gods Word. The Contents Whereof Follows after the Epistles.* EEBO / 2087:12. London: printed by Nicholas Okes for Henry Rockit, and are to be sold at his shop in the Poultry, vnder S. Mildreds Diall, 1611.

White, Thomas. *A Sermon Preached at Paules Crosse the 17. of Nouember An. 1589 Inioyfull Remembrance and Thanksgiuing Vnto God, for the Peaceable Yeres of Her Maiesties Most Gratious Raigne Ouer Vs.* EEBO / 1048:07. [London]: Printed by [H. Bynneman for] Robert Robinson and Thomas Newman, 1589.

———. *A Sermo[n] Preached at Pawles Crosse on Sunday the Thirde of Nouember 1577. in the Time of the Plague.* EEBO / 384:03. Imprinted at London: By [Henry Bynneman for] Francis Coldock, 1578.

Whittingham, William. *The Bible That Is, the Holy Scriptures Contained in the Old and New Testament. Translated According to the Ebrew and Greeke, and Conferred with the Best Translations in Diuers Languages. With Most Profitable Annotations Vpon All the Hard Places, and Other Things of Great Importance.* Edited by Anthony Gilby and Thomas Sampson. EEBO / 1594:04. Imprinted at London: By Robert Barker, printer to the Kings most excellent Maiestie, 1610.

Wilkinson, Robert. *A Ievvell for the Eare.* EEBO / 2088:06. London: printed for T. Pavier, 1602.

———. *Lots Wife A Sermon Preached at Paules Crosse.* EEBO / 1225:06. At London: Imprinted by Felix Kyngston, for Iohn Flasket, and are to be sold at his shop in Paules churchyard at the signe of the black Beare, 1607.

———. *A Paire of Sermons Successiuely Preacht to a Paire of Peereles and Succeeding Princes The Former as an Ante-Funerall to the Late Prince Henry, Anno Dom. 1612. October 25. The First Day of His Last and Fatall Sicknesse. The Latter Preacht This Present Yeere 1614. Ianuar. 16. to the Now Liuing Prince Charles, as a Preseruer of His Life, and Life to His Soule.* EEBO / 1563:11. At London: Imprinted by Felix Kyngston, for VVilliam Aspley, 1614.

Willan, Robert. *Eliah's Vvish a Prayer for Death. A Sermon Preached at the Funerall of the Right Honourable Viscount Sudbury, Lord Bayning.* Edited by John Spencer. EEBO / 1049:10. Printed at London: [By Thomas Cotes] for I. S[pencer] hypo-bibliothecary of Syon Colledge, and are to be sold by Richard Royston, at his shoppe in Iuie-lane, 1630.

Worship, William. *The Patterne of an Inuincible Faith A Sermon Preached at Paules Crosse, the First Sunday after Trinity, Being the 2d. of Iune. 1616.* EEBO / 583:11. London: Printed by Nicholas Okes, for Matthew Law, and are to be sold at his shop in Pauls Churchyard at the signe of the Fox, 1616.

Bibliography

EDITED PRIMARY SOURCES

Aquinas, Thomas. *Catena Aurea: Commentary on the Four Gospels Collected out of the Works of the Fathers*. Edited by John Henry Newman and Aidan Nichols. London: Saint Austin Press, 1997.

The Books of Job, Psalms, Proverbs, Ecclesiastes, and the Song of Solomon According to the Wycliffite Version. Edited by John Purvey, Josiah Forshall, Frederic Madden, and Walter W. Skeat. Oxford: Clarendon Press, 1881.

The Catholic Doctrine of the Church of England: An Exposition of the Thirty-Nine Articles. Edited by Thomas Rogers. University Press, 1854.

Ceremonies and Processions of the Cathedral Church of Salisbury: Ed. from the 15. Century Ms. No. 148 with Add. from the Cathedral Records and Wood Cuts from the Sarum Processionale of 1502. By C[hristopher] Wordsworth. [8 Microfiches, 90 × 120 Mm, Pos.-Zug: Interdocumentation Co. 1974. Edited by Christopher Wordsworth. Cambridge: Cambridge University Press, 1901.

Certain Sermons or Homilies (1547): And, A Homily against Disobedience and Wilful Rebellion (1570): A Critical Edition. Edited by Ronald B. Bond. Toronto: University of Toronto Press, 1987.

Councils and Ecclesiastical Documents Relating to Great Britain and Ireland. Edited by Arthur West Haddan and William Stubbs. Oxford: Clarendon Press, 1869.

English Wycliffite Sermons. Edited by Anne Hudson. Oxford: Clarendon Press, 1983.

The First New Testament Printed in the English Language. 1525 or 1526. Translated from the Greek by William Tyndale Reproduced in Facsimilie with an Introduction by Francis Fry. Edited by Francis Fry. Bristol: Printed for the Editor, 1862.

Friars' Tales: Thirteenth-Century Exempla from the British Isles. Edited by David Jones. Manchester: Manchester University Press, 2011.

Idley, Peter. *Instructions to His Son*. Edited by Charlotte D'Evelyn. Boston; London: D. C. Heath and Co.; Oxford University Press, 1935.

Innocent III. *Between God and Man*. Edited by Corinne J. Vause. Washington, DC: Catholic University Press, 2004.

Institoris, Heinrich, and Jakob Sprenger. *Malleus Maleficarum*. Edited by Christopher S. Mackay. Cambridge: Cambridge University Press, 2006.

Jacobus. *The Golden Legend: Readings on the Saints*. Translated by William Granger Ryan. Princeton: Princeton University Press, 2012.

Kempe, Margery. *The Book of Margery Kempe: An Abridged Translation*. Translated by Liz Herbert McAvoy. Cambridge: D. S. Brewer, 2003.

A Late Fifteenth-Century Dominical Sermon Cycle. Edited by Stephen Morrison. EETS OS 337–338. Oxford: Oxford University Press, 2012.

The Lay Folks Mass Book or the Manner of Hearing Mass with Rubrics and Devotions for the People in Four Texts and Offices in English. Edited by Thomas Frederick Simmons. London: Oxford University Press, 1968.

Mannyng, Robert. "An Edition of Robert Mannyng's Handlyng Synne." Edited by Betty Marie VanderSchaff. Ph.D. diss., University of Iowa, 1978.

Bibliography

———. *Handlyng Synne*. Edited by Idelle Sullens. Binghamton, NY: Medieval & Renaissance Texts & Studies, 1983.

———. *Robert of Brunne's "Handlyng Synne," A.D. 1303, with Those Parts of the Anglo-French Treaties on Which It Was Founded, William of Wadington's "Manuel Des Pechiez.*" Edited by Frederick James Furnivall. EETS OS 119, 123. London: K. Paul, Trench, Trübner & Co., 1901.

The Middle English Glossed Prose Psalter: Edited from Cambridge, Magdalene College, MS Pepys 2498. Edited by Robert Ray Black, Raymond St.-Jacques, and J. J. Smith. Heidelberg: Universitätsverlag Winter, 2012.

Mirk, John. *John Mirk's Festial: Edited from British Library MS Cotton Claudius A.II*. Edited by Susan Powell. EETS OS 334–335. Oxford; New York: Oxford University Press, 2009.

———. *Mirk's Festial: A Collection of Homilies*. Edited by Theodor Erbe. EETS ES 96. London: K. Paul, Trench, Trübner & Co., 1905.

Missale Ad Usum Ecclesiae Eboracensis: A Translation of the Order of Holy Communion According to the Use of York. Edited by Adam Gaunt, Catherine Button, and Richard Bimsom. Durham: The editors, 2001.

The Northern Homily Cycle. Edited by Anne B. Thompson. Kalamazoo, MI: Medieval Institute Publications, 2008.

Of Shrifte and Penance: The ME Prose Translation of Le Manuel des péchés. Edited by Klaus Bitterling. Heidelberg: C. Winter, 1998.

Rolle, Richard. *Two Revisions of Rolle's English Psalter Commentary and the Related Canticles*. Edited by Anne Hudson. New York; Oxford: Oxford University Press, 2012.

Saints Edith and Æthelthryth: Princesses, Miracle Workers, and their Late Medieval Audience: The Wilton Chronicle and the Wilton Life of St Æthelthryth. Edited by Mary Dockray-Miller. Turnhout: Brepols, 2009.

Simeon of Durham. *A History of the Church of Durham*. In *Women's Lives in Medieval Europe: A Sourcebook*. Edited by Emilie Amt. New York: Taylor and Francis, 2013.

Speculum Sacerdotale. Edited by Edward H. Weatherly. EETS OS 200. London: H. Milford, Oxford University Press, 1936 (for 1935).

The Statutes of the Fourth General Council of Lateran. Edited by J. Evans, 1843.

Strabus, Fulgensis, and Nicholas of Lyra. *Bibliorum sacrorum cum glossa ordinaria*. Edited by Paul Burgensus, Matthias Toringus, François Feuardent, Jean Dadré, and Jacques de Cuilly. Venice: [s.n.], 1603.

A Thirteenth-Century Preacher's Handbook: Studies in MS Laud Misc. 511. Edited by Mary E. O'Carroll. Toronto: Pontifical Institute of Mediaeval Studies, 1997.

Vitry, Jacques de. *The Exempla Or Illustrative Stories from the Sermones Vulgares of Jacques de Vitry*. London: Folklore Society, 1890.

The Vulgate Bible: Douay-Rheims Translation. Edited by Swift Edgar. Cambridge, MA: Harvard University Press, 2010.

Witchcraft and Society in England and America, 1550–1750. Edited by Marion Gibson. Ithaca, NY: Cornell University Press, 2003.

Bibliography

Wycliffe, John. *King Henry's Bible: MS Bodley 277: The Revised Version of the Wyclif Bible*. Edited by Conrad Lindberg. Stockholm: Almqvist & Wiksell, 1999.

SECONDARY SOURCES

Apostolos-Cappadona, Diane. "Imagining Salome, or How La Sauterelle Became La Femme Fatale." In *From the Margins 2: Women of the New Testament and Their Afterlives*. Edited by Christine E. Joynes and Christopher Rowland. Sheffield: Phoenix Press, 2009.

Arcangeli, Alessandro. *Carnival in Medieval Sermons*. Turnhout: Brepols, 1997.

———. *The Confessor and the Theatre*. Barcelona: Institut del Teatre, 1996.

———. "Dance and Health: The Renaissance Physicians' View." *Dance Research* 18, no. 1 (2000): 3–30.

———. *Dance and Law*. Ghent: The Institute for Historical Dance Practice, 2000.

———. "Dance and Punishment." *Dance Research* 10, no. 2 (1992): 30–42.

———. "Dance under Trial: The Moral Debate, 1200–1600." *Dance Research* 12, no. 2 (1994): 127–155.

———. *Danse et sociabilité dans le miroir du discours théologique*. Paris: Anthropos, 1998.

———. *Davide o Salomè?: Il dibattito europeo sulla danza nella prima età moderna*. Rome; Treviso: Viella; Fondazione Benetton Studi Ricerche, 2000.

———. "Moral Views on Dance." In *Dance, Spectacle, and the Body Politick, 1250–1750*. Bloomington: Indiana University Press, 2008.

———. *Recreation in the Renaissance: Attitudes Towards Leisure and Pastimes in European Culture, 1350–1700*. Basingstoke: Palgrave Macmillan, 2003.

Archambo, Shelley Batt. "The Development of the English Carol through the Fifteenth Century." *The Choral Journal* 27, no. 3 (October 1986): 28–31.

Aston, Margaret. "Segregation in Church." In *Women in the Church*. Edited by W. J. Sheils and Diana Wood. Oxford: Blackwell Publishers, 1990.

Atkinson, James, and W. P. Stephens, eds. *The Bible, the Reformation and the Church: Essays in Honour of James Atkinson*. Sheffield: Sheffield Academic Press, 1995.

Backman, E. Louis. *Religious Dances in the Christian Church and in Popular Medicine*. London: Allen & Unwin, 1952.

Baert, Barbara. *Revisiting Salome's Dance in Medieval and Early Modern Iconology*. Leuven: Peeters, 2016.

———, and Sophia Rochmes, eds. *Decapitation and Sacrifice: Saint John's Head in Interdisciplinary Perspectives: Text, Object, Medium*, Leuven: Peeters, 2017.

Bagchi, David V. N., and David Curtis Steinmetz. *The Cambridge Companion to Reformation Theology*. Cambridge; New York: Cambridge University Press, 2004.

Bailey, Michael David. *Battling Demons: Witchcraft, Heresy, and Reform in the Late Middle Ages*. University Park: Pennsylvania State University Press, 2003.

Bibliography

Bailey, Terence. *The Processions of Sarum and the Western Church*. Toronto: Pontifical Institute of Mediaeval Studies, 1971.

Baines, Barbara J. *Representing Rape in the English Early Modern Period*. Lewiston, NY: Edwin Mellen Press, 2003.

Bardsley, Sandy. *Venomous Tongues: Speech and Gender in Late Medieval England*. Philadelphia: University of Pennsylvania Press, 2006.

Barr, Beth Allison. "'He Is Bothyn Modyr, Broþyr, & Syster vn-to Me': Women and the Bible in Late Medieval and Early Modern English Sermons." *Church History and Religious Culture* 94, no. 3 (2014): 297–315.

———. "Medieval Sermons and Audience Appeal after the Black Death." *History Compass* 16, no. 9 (2018).

———. *The Pastoral Care of Women in Late Medieval England*. Woodbridge: Boydell Press, 2008.

———. "'Sche Hungryd Ryth Sor Aftyr Goddys Word': Female Piety and the Legacy of the Pastoral Programme in the Late Medieval English Sermons of Bodleian Library MS Greaves 54." *Journal of Religious History* 39, no. 1 (2015): 31–50.

Bennett, Judith. *Ale, Beer and Brewsters in England: Women's Work in a Changing World, 1300–1600*. New York: Oxford University Press, 1996.

———. *History Matters: Patriarchy and the Challenge of Feminism*. Philadelphia: University of Pennsylvania Press, 2006.

———. "Ventriloquisms: When Maidens Speak in English Songs, c. 1300–1550." In *Medieval Woman's Song: Cross-Cultural Approaches*. Edited by Anne Klinck and Anne Marie Rasmussen. Philadelphia: University of Pennsylvania Press, 2002.

Berlioz, Jacques, and Marie Anne Polo de Beaulieu. "Exempla: A Discussion and a Case Study." In *Medieval Women and the Sources of Medieval History*. Edited by Joel T. Rosenthal. Athens, GA: University of Georgia Press, 1990.

Berry, John M., and Frances Panchok. "Church and Theater." *U.S. Catholic Historian* 6, no. 2/3 (n.d.): 151–179.

Blamires, Alcuin. "The Limits of Bible Study for Medieval Women." In *Women, the Book, and the Godly*. Edited by Lesley Smith and Jane H. M. Taylor. Cambridge: D. S. Brewer, 1995.

———, and C. W. Marx. "Woman Not to Preach: A Disputation in MS Harley 31." *The Journal of Medieval Latin* 03 (1993): 34–63.

Bohn, Willard. "Apollinaire, Salome and the Dance of Death." *French Studies* 57, no. 4 (2003): 491–500.

Boulton, Maureen B. M. *Literary Echoes of the Fourth Lateran Council in England and France, 1215–1405*. Toronto: Pontifical Institute / Brepols, 2019.

Braude, Ann. "Women's History Is American Religious History." In *Retelling U.S. Religious History*. Edited by Thomas A. Tweed. Berkeley, CA: University of California Press, 1997.

Breitenberg, Mark. *Anxious Masculinity in Early Modern England*. Cambridge: Cambridge University Press, 1996.

Bibliography

Briggs, Robin. *Witches and Neighbours: The Social and Cultural Context of European Witchcraft*. Oxford: Blackwell, 2002.

Brown, Pamela Allen, and Peter Parolin, eds. *Women Players in England 1500–1660: Beyond the All-Male Stage*. Farnham: Ashgate, 2008.

Burgess, C. "Pre-Reformation Churchwardens' Accounts and Parish Government: Lessons from London and Bristol." *The English Historical Review* 117, no. 471 (2002): 306–332.

Burnett, Amy Nelson. *Teaching the Reformation: Ministers and Their Message in Basel, 1529–1629*. Oxford: Oxford University Press, 2006.

Butler, Judith. "Performative Acts and Gender Constitution: An Essay in Phenomenology and Feminist Theory." *Theatre Journal* 40, no. 4 (December 1988): 519–531.

Bynum, Caroline Walker. *Christian Materiality: An Essay on Religion in Late Medieval Europe*. New York; Cambridge, MA: Zone Books, 2011.

———. *Fragmentation and Redemption: Essays on Gender and the Human Body in Medieval Religion*. New York; Cambridge, MA: Zone Books, 1991.

———. *Holy Feast and Holy Fast*. Oakland: University of California Press, 1987.

Caciola, Nancy. *Afterlives: The Return of the Dead in the Middle Ages*. Ithaca, NY: Cornell University Press, 2017.

Cameron, Euan. "Calvin the Historian: Biblical Antiquity and Scriptural Exegesis." In *Calvin and the Book: The Evolution of the Printed Word in Reformed Protestantism*. Edited by Karen E. Spierling. Bristol, CT: Vanderhoeck and Ruprecht, 2015.

———. *Enchanted Europe: Superstition, Reason, and Religion 1250–1750*. New York; Oxford: Oxford University Press, 2010.

———. *The European Reformation*. Oxford: Oxford University Press, 2012.

Campbell, William H. *The Landscape of Pastoral Care in 13th-Century England*. Cambridge: Cambridge University Press, 2018.

Carlson, Eric Josef. "The Boring of the Ear: Shaping the Pastoral Vision of Preaching in England, 1540–1640." In *Preachers and People in the Reformations and Early Modern Period*. Edited by Larissa Taylor. Leiden: Brill, 2001.

———. *Marriage and the English Reformation*. Oxford; Cambridge, MA: Blackwell, 1994.

Chaganti, Seeta. *Strange Footing: Poetic Form and Dance in the Late Middle Ages*. Chicago: University of Chicago Press, 2019.

Chapman, Ann C. "Sacred Movement in the High and Late Middle Ages." Unpublished thesis. ProQuest, 2009.

Chappell, Julie, and Kaley A. Kramer, eds. *Women during the English Reformations: Renegotiating Gender and Religious Identity*. New York: Palgrave Macmillan, 2014.

Cheetham, Francis W. *Alabaster Images of Medieval England*. Woodbridge: Boydell Press, 2003.

———. *English Medieval Alabasters: With a Catalogue of the Collection in the Victoria and Albert Museum*. Oxford: Phaidon-Christie's, 1984.

Bibliography

Clark, Stuart. *Thinking with Demons: The Idea of Witchcraft in Early Modern Europe*. Oxford; New York: Oxford University Press, 2005.

Classen, Albrecht. *Pleasure and Leisure in the Middle Ages and Early Modern Age: Cultural-Historical Perspectives on Toys, Games, and Entertainment*. Philadelphia: University of Pennsylvania Press, 2019.

Clopper, Lawrence M. *Drama, Play, and Game: English Festive Culture in the Medieval and Early Modern Period*. Chicago: University of Chicago Press, 2001.

Coletti, Theresa. *Mary Magdalene and the Drama of Saints: Theater, Gender, and Religion in Late Medieval England*. Philadelphia: University of Pennsylvania Press, 2004.

Coulton, C. G., ed. *Life in the Middle Ages*. New York: Macmillan, 1910.

Craig, J. S. "Co-Operation and Initiatives: Elizabethan Churchwardens and the Parish Accounts of Mildenhall." *Social History* 18, no. 3 (1993): 357–380.

Crane, T. F. "Mediaeval Sermon-Books and Stories." *Proceedings of the American Philosophical Society* 21, no. 114 (March 1883): 49–78.

Crawford, Patricia. *Women and Religion in England, 1500–1720*. London; New York: Routledge, 1993.

Cressy, David. *Birth, Marriage, and Death: Ritual, Religion, and the Life-Cycle in Tudor and Stuart England*. Oxford; New York: Oxford University Press, 1997.

———. *Travesties and Transgressions in Tudor and Stuart England: Tales of Discord and Dissension*. Oxford: Oxford University Press, 2000.

Cummings, Brian, and James Simpson. *Cultural Reformations: Medieval and Renaissance in Literary History*. Oxford: Oxford University Press, 2016.

Daniels, Marilyn. *The Dance in Christianity*. New York: Paulist Press, 1981.

Darr, Orna Alyagon. *Marks of an Absolute Witch: Evidentiary Dilemmas in Early Modern England*. Farnham: Ashgate, 2011.

D'Avray, D. L. *The Preaching of the Friars: Sermons Diffused from Paris before 1300*. New York: ACLS History E-Book Project, 2005.

Dennison, James T. *The Market Day of the Soul: The Puritan Doctrine of the Sabbath in England, 1532–1700*. Kentwood, MI: Reformation Heritage Books, 2001.

Dickason, Kathryn Emily. "Caroling like Clockwork: Technologies of the Medieval Dancing Body in Dante's Paradiso." *Dance Chronicle* 41, no. 3 (2018): 303–334.

———. "Decadance in the Late Middle Ages: The Case of Choreomania." In *Medieval Theatre Performance: Actors, Dancers, Automata and Their Audiences*. Edited by Philip Butterworth and Katie Normington. Cambridge: D. S. Brewer, 2017.

———. "King David in the Medieval Archives." In *Futures of Dance Studies*. Edited by Susan Manning, Janice Ross, and Rebecca Schneider. Madison: University of Wisconsin Press, 2020.

———. *Ringleaders of Redemption: How Medieval Dance Became Sacred*. Oxford; New York: Oxford University Press, 2021.

Dickens, A. G. *The English Reformation*. University Park: Pennsylvania State University Press, 1991.

Bibliography

Dierkes-Thrun, Petra. *Salome's Modernity: Oscar Wilde and the Aesthetics of Transgression*. Ann Arbor: University of Michigan Press, 2014.

Douglas, Audrey. "'Owre Thanssynge Day': Parish Dance and Procession in Salisbury." *Folk Music Journal* 6, no. 5 (1994): 600–616.

———. "'Parish' and 'City' – A Shifting Identity: Salisbury 1440–1600." *Early Theatre* 6, no. 1 (2003): 67–91.

Dove, Mary. *The First English Bible: The Text and Context of the Wycliffite Versions*. Cambridge: Cambridge University Press, 2007.

Drescher, Elizabeth. "Practicing Church: Vernacular Ecclesiologies in Late Medieval England." Ph.D. diss., Berkeley, 2008.

Duffy, Eamon. *Saints, Sacrilege and Sedition: Religion and Conflict in the Tudor Reformations*. London; New York: Bloomsbury, 2012.

———. *The Stripping of the Altars: Traditional Religion in England, 1400–1580*. 2nd edn. New Haven, CT; London: Yale University Press, 2005.

———. *The Voices of Morebath: Reformation and Rebellion in an English Village*. New Haven, CT: Yale University Press, 2001.

Dunn, Leslie C., and Katherine Rebecca Larson, eds. *Gender and Song in Early Modern England*. New York: Routledge, 2014.

Ehrenreich, Barbara. *Dancing in the Streets: A History of Collective Joy*. New York: Macmillan, 2007.

Eire, Carlos M. N. *Reformations: The Early Modern World, 1450–1650*. New Haven, CT: Yale University Press, 2016.

———. *War against the Idols: The Reformation of Worship from Erasmus to Calvin*. Cambridge: Cambridge University Press, 1989.

Elliott, Dyan. *The Bride of Christ Goes to Hell: Metaphor and Embodiment in the Lives of Pious Women, 200–1500*. Philadelphia: University of Pennsylvania Press, 2012.

———. *Fallen Bodies: Pollution, Sexuality, and Demonology in the Middle Ages*. Philadelphia: University of Pennsylvania Press, 1999.

Elmer, Peter. *Witchcraft, Witch-Hunting, and Politics in Early Modern England*. Oxford: Oxford University Press, 2016.

Ettenhuber, Katrin. "'A Comely Gate to so Rich and Glorious a Citie': The Paratextual Architecture of the Rheims New Testament and the King James Bible." In *The Oxford Handbook of the Bible in Early Modern England, c. 1530–1700*. Edited by Kevin Killeen, Helen Smith, and Rachel Judith Willie. Oxford: Oxford University Press, 2015.

Evans, G. R. *A History of Pastoral Care*. London: A&C Black, 2000.

Fletcher, Alan J. *Late Medieval Popular Preaching in Britain and Ireland: Texts, Studies, and Interpretations*. Turnhout: Brepols, 2010.

Fletcher, Christopher. *Richard II: Manhood, Youth, and Politics 1377–99*. Oxford: Oxford University Press, 2008.

Ford, Judy Ann. *John Mirk's Festial: Orthodoxy, Lollardy and the Common People in Fourteenth-Century England*. Cambridge: D. S. Brewer, 2006.

Bibliography

Forrest, Ian. *Trustworthy Men: How Inequality and Faith Made the Medieval Church*. Princeton: Princeton University Press, 2020.

Forrest, John. *The History of Morris Dancing, 1438–1750*. Toronto: University of Toronto Press, 2016.

Frassetto, Michael. *Medieval Purity and Piety: Essays on Medieval Clerical Celibacy and Religious Reform*. London: Taylor & Francis, 1998.

French, Katherine L. *The Good Women of the Parish: Gender and Religion after the Black Death*. Philadelphia: University of Pennsylvania Press, 2008.

———. *Household Goods and Good Households in Late Medieval London: Consumption and Domesticity after the Plague*. Philadelphia: University of Pennsylvania Press, 2021.

———. "Maidens' Lights and Wives' Stores: Women's Parish Guilds in Late Medieval England." *The Sixteenth Century Journal* 29, no. 2 (July 1, 1998): 399–425.

———. *The People of the Parish: Community Life in a Late Medieval English Diocese*. Philadelphia: University of Pennsylvania Press, 2001.

———. "The Seat Under Our Lady: Gender and Seating in Late Medieval English Parish Churches." In *Women's Space: Patronage, Place, and Gender in the Medieval Church*. Edited by Virginia Chieffo Raguin and Sarah Stanbury. Albany: State University of New York Press, 2005.

———, Gary G. Gibbs, and Beat A. Kümin, eds. *The Parish in English Life, 1400–1600*. Manchester: Manchester University Press,1997.

Froehlich, Karlfried. *Biblical Interpretation from the Church Fathers to the Reformation*. Farnham: Ashgate Variorum, 2010.

———. "The *Glossa Ordinaria* and Medieval Preaching." In *Biblical Interpretation from the Church Fathers to the Reformation*. Edited by Karlfried Froehlich. Farnham: Ashgate Variorum, 2010.

Garrison, Jennifer. "Mediated Piety: Eucharistic Theology and Lay Devotion in Robert Mannyng's 'Handlyng Synne.'" *Speculum* 85 (2010): 894–922.

Gasser, Erika. *Vexed with Devils: Manhood and Witchcraft in Old and New England*. New York: New York University Press, 2017.

Gerhardt, Ernst. "'We Pray You All … to Drink Ere Ye Pass': Bann Criers, Parish Players, and the Henrician Reformation in England's Southeast." *Early Theatre* 11, no. 2 (2008): 57–88.

Gertsman, Elina. *The Dance of Death in the Middle Ages: Image, Text, Performance*. Turnhout: Brepols, 2010.

Gibbs, Gary G. *Five Parishes in Late Medieval and Tudor London: Communities and Reforms*. New York: Routledge, 2021.

Gibson, Marion, ed. *Early Modern Witches: Witchcraft Cases in Contemporary Writing*. Hoboken: Taylor and Francis, 2000.

———, ed. *Witchcraft and Society in England and America, 1550–1750*. Ithaca, NY: Cornell University Press, 2003.

Bibliography

Gill, Sylvia. "'Of Honest Conversation and Competently Learned': The Dissolution of the Chantries (1548) and Chantry Priests of the East and West Midlands." *Midland History* 44, no. 2 (2019): 205–221.

Gowing, Laura. *Common Bodies: Women, Touch, and Power in Seventeenth-Century England*. New Haven, CT: Yale University Press, 2003.

———. *Domestic Dangers: Women, Words, and Sex in Early Modern London*. Oxford; New York: Oxford University Press, 1996.

Grant, Robert M., and David Tracy. *A Short History of the Interpretation of the Bible*. 2nd edn. Philadelphia: Fortress Press, 1984.

Greenslade, S. L. "English Versions of the Bible, 1525–1611." In *The Cambridge History of the Bible, Vol. 3: The West from the Reformation to the Present Day*. Edited by S. L. Greenslade. Cambridge: Cambridge University Press, 1963.

Greenspan, Kate. "Lessons for the Priest, Lessons for the People: Robert Mannyng of Brunne's Audiences for *Handlyng Synne.*" *Essays in Medieval Studies* 21 (2004): 109–121.

Gunn, Cate, and Catherine Innes-Parker, eds. *Texts and Traditions of Medieval Pastoral Care: Essays in Honour of Bella Millett*. York: York Medieval Press, 2009.

Habermann, Ina. *Staging Slander and Gender in Early Modern England*. Aldershot, England; Burlington, VT: Ashgate, 2003.

Haigh, Christopher. *English Reformations: Religion, Politics, and Society under the Tudors*. Oxford; New York: Oxford University Press, 1993.

Hall, Basil. "Biblical Scholarship: Editions and Commentaries." In *The Cambridge History of the Bible, Vol. 3: The West from the Reformation to the Present Day*. Edited by S. L. Greenslade. Cambridge: Cambridge University Press, 1963.

Hampson, R. T. *Medii Ævi Kalendarium or, Dates, Charters, and Customs of the Middle Ages, with Kalendars from the Tenth to the Fifteenth Century; and an Alphabetical Digest of Obsolete Names of Days: Forming a Glossary of the Dates of the Middle Ages*. London: Henry Kent Causton, 1841.

Harper, Sally, P. S. Barnwell, and Magnus Williamson, eds. *Late Medieval Liturgies Enacted: The Experience of Worship in Cathedral and Parish Church*. Aldershot: Routledge, 2019.

Harris, Carissa M. *Obscene Pedagogies: Transgressive Talk and Sexual Education in Late Medieval Britain*. Ithaca, NY: Cornell University Press, 2018.

Harris, Max. *Christ on a Donkey: Palm Sunday, Triumphal Entries, and Blasphemous Pageants*. York: Arc Humanities Press, 2019.

———. *Sacred Folly: A New History of the Feast of Fools*. Ithaca, NY: Cornell University Press, 2011.

Harris, Victor. "Allegory to Analogy in the Interpretation of Scriptures." *Philological Quarterly* 45, no. 1 (January 1, 1966): 1–23.

Heal, Bridget. *The Cult of the Virgin Mary in Early Modern Germany: Protestant and Catholic Piety, 1500–1648*. Cambridge: Cambridge University Press, 2014.

Hecker, J. F. C. *The Dancing Mania of the Middle Ages*. New York: B. Franklin, 1970.

Bibliography

Hellsten, Laura. *Through the Bone and Marrow: Re-Examining Theological Encounters with Dance in Medieval Europe*. Turnhout: Brepols, 2021.

Heng, Geraldine. *The Invention of Race in the European Middle Ages*. Cambridge: Cambridge University Press, 2018.

Herzog, Don. *Household Politics: Conflict in Early Modern England*. New Haven, CT: Yale University Press, 2013.

Holmes, Jeremy. "Aquinas' *Lectura in Matthaeum*." In *Aquinas on Scripture: An Introduction to His Biblical Commentaries*. Edited by Thomas G. Weinandy, Daniel A. Keating, and John P. Yocum. London; New York: T. & T. Clark International, 2005.

Hospodar, Blaise. *Salome: Virgin or Prostitute?* New York: Pageant Press, 1953.

Houlbrooke, Ralph A. *Church Courts and the People during the English Reformation, 1520–1570*. Oxford; New York: Oxford University Press, 1979.

Howard, Skiles. *The Politics of Courtly Dancing in Early Modern England*. Amherst: University of Massachusetts Press, 1998.

Hunt, Arnold. *The Art of Hearing: English Preachers and Their Audiences, 1590–1640*. Cambridge; New York: Cambridge University Press, 2010.

Hutton, Ronald. *The Rise and Fall of Merry England: The Ritual Year, 1400–1700*. Oxford: Oxford University Press, 2001.

———. "Seasonal Festivity in Late Medieval England: Some Further Reflections." *The English Historical Review* 120, no. 485 (February 1, 2005): 66–79.

Ingram, Martin. *Carnal Knowledge: Regulating Sex in England, 1470–1600*. Cambridge: Cambridge University Press, 2017.

James, Mervyn. "Ritual, Drama and Social Body in the Late Medieval English Town." *Past & Present* 98, no. 1 (1983): 3–29.

Jansen, Katherine Ludwig. *The Making of the Magdalen: Preaching and Popular Devotion in the Later Middle Ages*. Princeton: Princeton University Press, 2000.

Jolly, Karen Louise, Edward Peters, Catharina Raudvere, Bengt Ankarloo, and Stuart Clark, eds. *Witchcraft and Magic in Europe: The Middle Ages*. Philadelphia: University of Pennsylvania Press, 2002.

Jordan, William Chester. "Salome in the Middle Ages." *Jewish History* 26, no. 1/2 (May 2012): 5–15.

Jütte, Daniel. "Sleeping in Church: Preaching, Boredom, and the Struggle for Attention in Medieval and Early Modern Europe." *The American Historical Review* 125, no. 4 (October 21, 2020): 1146–1174.

Kallestrup, Louise Nyholm, and Raisa Maria Toivo, eds. *Contesting Orthodoxy in Medieval and Early Modern Europe: Heresy, Magic and Witchcraft*. Cham: Springer International, 2017.

Kane, Bronach Christina. *Popular Memory and Gender in Medieval England: Men, Women and Testimony in the Church Courts, c.1200–1500*. Woodbridge: Boydell Press, 2019.

———, and Fiona Williamson, eds. *Women, Agency and the Law, 1300–1700*. London: Routledge, 2016.

Bibliography

Karant-Nunn, Susan C. *The Reformation of Feeling: Shaping the Religious Emotions in Early Modern Germany*. New York: Oxford University Press, 2010.

———. "The Reformation of Liturgy." In *The Oxford Handbook of the Protestant Reformations*. Edited by Ulinka Rublack. Oxford: Oxford Handbooks Online, December 2016.

———. *The Reformation of Ritual: An Interpretation of Early Modern Germany*. London; New York: Routledge, 1997.

Karras, Ruth Mazo. *Common Women: Prostitution and Sexuality in Medieval England*. New York: Oxford University Press, 1998.

———. *From Boys to Men: Formations of Masculinity in Late Medieval Europe*. Philadelphia: University of Pennsylvania Press, 2003.

———. "Gendered Sin and Misogyny in John of Bromyard's 'Summa Predicantium.'" *Traditio* 47 (1992): 233–257.

———. *Sexuality in Medieval Europe: Doing unto Others*. New York: Routledge, 2005.

Katz, David S. *Sabbath and Sectarianism in Seventeenth Century England*. Leiden: Brill, 1988.

Kemmler, Fritz. *"Exempla" in Context: A Historical and Critical Study of Robert Mannyng of Brunne's "Handlyng Synne."* Tübingen: Gunter Narr Verlag, 1984.

Kienzle, Beverly Mayne. *The Sermon*. Turnhout: Brepols, 2000.

Killeen, Kevin, Helen Smith, and Rachel Willie, eds. *The Oxford Handbook of the Bible in Early Modern England, c. 1530–1700*. Oxford: Oxford University Press, 2015.

Klapisch-Zuber, Christiane, and Susan Emanuel. "Salome's Dance." *Clio: Women, Gender, History*, no. 46 (2017): 186–197.

Kleinschmidt, Harald. *Perception and Action in Medieval Europe*. Woodbridge: Boydell Press, 2005.

Krey, Philip D. W., and Lesley Janette Smith. *Nicholas of Lyra: The Senses of Scripture*. Leiden: Brill, 2000.

Kümin, Beat A. *Drinking Matters: Public Houses and Social Exchange in Early Modern Central Europe*. Basingstoke [England]; New York: Palgrave Macmillan, 2007.

———. "Late Medieval Churchwardens' Accounts and Parish Government: Looking beyond London and Bristol." *The English Historical Review* 119, no. 480 (February 1, 2004): 87–100.

———. *The Shaping of a Community: The Rise and Reformation of the English Parish, c. 1400–1560*. Aldershot: Scholar, 1996.

Laird, Charlton G. *The Source of Robert Mannyng of Brunne's Handlyng Synne: A Study of the Extant Manuscripts of the Anglo-Norman Manuel des pechiez …* Stanford: Stanford University, 1940.

Lambert, Malcolm. *Medieval Heresy: Popular Movements from the Gregorian Reform to the Reformation*. 3rd edn. Oxford: Blackwell, 2002.

Langer, Susanne. "The Dynamic Image: Some Philosophical Reflections on Dance." *Salmagundi*, no. 33/34 (1976): 76–82.

Bibliography

Le Goff, Jacques, and Lydia G. Cochrane. *In Search of Sacred Time: Jacobus de Voragine and the Golden Legend*. Princeton: Princeton University Press, 2014.

Lemon, Rebecca. *Addiction and Devotion in Early Modern England*. Philadelphia: University of Pennsylvania Press, 2018.

Levack, Brian P. *The Witch-Hunt in Early Modern Europe*. 2nd edn. London; New York: Longman, 1995.

Lochrie, Karma. *Covert Operations: The Medieval Uses of Secrecy*. Philadelphia: University of Pennsylvania Press, 2012.

Long, Jane C. "Dangerous Women: Observations on the Feast of Herod in Florentine Art of the Early Renaissance." *Renaissance Quarterly* 66, no. 4 (2013): 1153–1205.

Lubac, Henri de. *Medieval Exegesis: The Four Senses of Scripture*. Edited and translated by Mark Sebanc, and E. M. Macierowski. Grand Rapids: W. B. Eerdmans; T. & T. Clark, 1998.

Luxford, Julian M. "Out of the Wilderness: A Fourteenth-Century English Drawing of John the Baptist." *Gesta* 49, no. 2 (2010): 137–150.

MacDonald, Michael, Stephen Bradwell, Edward Jorden, and John Swan, eds. *Witchcraft and Hysteria in Elizabethan London: Edward Jorden and the Mary Glover Case*. New York: Routledge, 2013.

MacFarlane, Alan. *Witchcraft in Tudor and Stuart England*. Hoboken: Taylor and Francis, 2012.

Madigan, Kevin. *Medieval Christianity: A New History*. New Haven, CT: Yale University Press, 2015.

Makowski, Elizabeth. *Canon Law and Cloistered Women: Periculoso and Its Commentators, 1298–1545*. Washington, DC: Catholic University of America Press, 1999.

———. *English Nuns and the Law in the Middle Ages: Cloistered Nuns and Their Lawyers, 1293–1540*. Woodbridge: Boydell Press, 2012.

Marsh, Christopher W. *Music and Society in Early Modern England*. Cambridge: Cambridge University Press, 2013.

———. *Popular Religion in Sixteenth-Century England: Holding Their Peace*. Basingstoke: Macmillan, 1998.

Marshall, Peter. *Heretics and Believers: A History of the English Reformation*. New Haven, CT: Yale University Press, 2018.

———. *Reformation England, 1480–1642*. Oxford: Oxford University Press, 2003.

McClendon, Muriel C. *The Quiet Reformation: Magistrates and the Emergence of Protestantism in Tudor Norwich*. Stanford: Stanford University Press, 1999.

McManus, Clare. *Women on the Renaissance Stage: Anna of Denmark and Female Masquing in the Stuart Court (1590–1619)*. Manchester; New York: Manchester University Press, 2002.

McSheffrey, Shannon. *Gender and Heresy: Women and Men in Lollard Communities, 1420–1530*. Philadelphia: University of Pennsylvania Press, 1995.

Bibliography

Miller, Lynneth J. "Divine Punishment or Disease? Medieval and Early Modern Approaches to the 1518 Strasbourg Dancing Plague." *Dance Research* 35, no. 2 (November 1, 2017): 149–164.

Miller, Mark. "Displaced Souls, Idle Talk, Spectacular Scenes: *Handlyng Synne* and the Perspective of Agency." *Speculum* 71, no. 3 (July 1996): 606–632.

Miller Renberg, Lynneth J. "An Outward and Visible Sign of an Inward and Spiritual Grace: Stewart Headlam on the Ballet." *Church History and Religious Culture* 99, no. 2 (August 12, 2019): 248–269.

———, and Bradley Phillis, eds. *The Cursed Carolers in Context*. New York: Routledge, 2021.

Minnis, A. J. "'De Impedimento Sexus': Women's Bodies and Medieval Impediments to Female Ordination." In *Medieval Theology and the Natural Body*. Edited by Peter Biller and Alastair J. Minnis. York: York Medieval Press, 1997.

———. *Translations of Authority in Medieval English Literature: Valuing the Vernacular*. Cambridge; New York: Cambridge University Press, 2009.

Moore, Robert Ian. *The Formation of a Persecuting Society: Authority and Deviance in Western Europe, 950–1250*. 2nd edn. Malden, MA; Oxford; Carlton: Blackwell, 2007.

———. *The War on Heresy*. Cambridge, MA: Harvard University Press, 2012.

Morrison, Susan Signe. *Women Pilgrims in Late Medieval England: Private Piety and Public Performance*. London; New York: Routledge, 2000.

Mosher, Joseph A. *The Exemplum in the Early Religious and Didactic Literature of England*. New York: AMS Press, 1966.

Muessig, Carolyn, ed. *Preacher, Sermon, and Audience in the Middle Ages*. Leiden; Boston: Brill, 2002.

Mullally, Robert. *The Carole: A Study of a Medieval Dance*. Farnham: Ashgate, 2011.

Mullin, Robert Evan. "The Exempla in *Handlyng Synne*." Thesis, Emporia Kansas State College, 1974.

Nevile, Jennifer. *Dance, Spectacle, and the Body Politick, 1250–1750*. Bloomington: Indiana University Press, 2008.

Normington, Katie. *Gender and Medieval Drama*. Cambridge: D. S. Brewer, 2004.

Null, Ashley. "Official Tudor Homilies." In *The Oxford Handbook of the Early Modern Sermon*. Edited by Peter McCullough, Hugh Adlington, and Emma Rhatigan. Oxford: Oxford University Press, 2011.

Nutu, Ela. "Reading Salome: Caravaggio and the Gospel Narratives." In *From the Margins 2: Women of the New Testament and Their Afterlives*. Edited by Christine E. Joynes and Christopher C. Rowland. Sheffield: Phoenix Press, 2009.

O'Carroll, Mary E. *A Thirteenth-Century Preacher's Handbook: Studies in MS Laud Misc. 511*. Toronto: Pontifical Institute of Mediaeval Studies, 1997.

O'Mara, Veronica, and Suzanne Paul, eds. *A Repertorium of Middle English Prose Sermons*. Turnhout: Brepols, 2007.

Bibliography

Orens, John. *Stewart Headlam's Radical Anglicanism: The Mass, the Masses, and the Music Hall*. Champaign-Urbana: University of Illinois Press, 2003.

Owen, Nancy H. "Thomas Wimbledon." *Mediaeval Studies* 24 (1962): 377–381.

———. "Thomas Wimbledon's Sermon: 'Redde Racionem Villicacionis Tue.'" *Mediaeval Studies* 28 (1966): 176–197.

Owst, G. R. *Literature and Pulpit in Medieval England: A Neglected Chapter in the History of English Letters & of the English People*. 2nd rev. edn. New York: Barnes & Noble, 1961.

———. *Preaching in Medieval England: An Introduction to Sermon Manuscripts of the Period c. 1350–1450*. Cambridge: Cambridge University Press, 2010.

Ozment, Steven E.. *The Age of Reform (1250–1550): An Intellectual and Religious History of Late Medieval and Reformation Europe*. New Haven, CT: Yale University Press, 1980.

Parker, Kenneth L. *The English Sabbath: A Study of Doctrine and Discipline from the Reformation to the Civil War*. Cambridge: Cambridge University Press, 2002.

———. "Thomas Rogers and the English Sabbath: The Case for a Reappraisal." *Church History* 53 (1984): 332–347.

Payer, Pierre J. *Sex and the New Medieval Literature of Confession, 1150–1300*. Studies and Texts 163. Toronto: Pontifical Institute of Mediaeval Studies, 2009.

Pearsall, Arlene Epp. *Johannes Pauli (1450–1520) on the Church and Clergy*. Lewiston, NY: E. Mellen Press, 1994.

———. "Johannes Pauli and the Strasbourg Dancers." *Franciscan Studies* 52 (1992): 203–214.

Peters, Christine. *Patterns of Piety: Women, Gender, and Religion in Later Mediaeval and Reformation England*. Cambridge: Cambridge University Press, 2002.

Phythian-Adams, Charles. "Ceremony and the Citizen: The Communal Year at Coventry 1450–1550." In *Crisis and Order in English Towns, 1500–1700*. Edited by Peter Clark and Paul Slack. New York: Routledge, 2013.

Plummer, Marjorie Elizabeth. *From Priest's Whore to Pastor's Wife: Clerical Marriage and the Process of Reform in the Early German Reformation*. Farnham: Ashgate, 2012.

Powell, Susan, Martha W. Driver, and V. M. O'Mara, eds. *Preaching the Word in Manuscript and Print in Late Medieval England: Essays in Honour of Susan Powell*. Turnhout: Brepols, 2013.

Prescott, Andrew. "Men and Women in the Guild Returns of 1389." In *Gender and Fraternal Orders in Europe: 1300–2000*. Edited by Máire Cross. Basingstoke: Palgrave Macmillan, 2010.

Ravelhofer, Barbara. *The Early Stuart Masque: Dance, Costume, and Music*. Oxford: Oxford University Press, 2009.

Reeves, Andrew. "'The Nourishment of God's Word': *Inter Caetera* (Canon 10) in England." In *Literary Echoes of the Fourth Lateran Council in England and France, 1215–1405*. Edited by Maureen B. M. Boulton. Toronto: Pontifical Institute/Brepols, 2019.

Bibliography

———. *Religious Education in Thirteenth-Century England: The Creed and Articles of Faith.* Leiden, Netherlands: Brill, 2015.

———. "Teaching the Creed and Articles of Faith in England: 1215–1281." In *A Companion to Pastoral Care in the Late Middle Ages, 1200–1500.* Edited by Ronald J. Stansbury. Leiden: Brill, 2010.

Rittgers, Ronald K. *The Reformation of Suffering: Pastoral Theology and Lay Piety in Late Medieval and Early Modern Germany.* Oxford: Oxford University Press, 2012.

Robertson, D. W. "The *Manuel des péchés* and an English Episcopal Decree." *Modern Language Notes* 60, no. 7 (1945): 439–447.

———. "A Study of Certain Aspects of the Cultural Tradition of Handlyng Synne." Ph.D. diss, University of North Carolina at Chapel Hill, 1945.

Rohmann, Gregor. "Dancing on the Threshold: A Cultural Concept for Conditions of Being Far from Salvation." *Contributions to the History of Concepts* 10, no. 2 (2015): 48–70.

———. "The Invention of Dancing Mania." *The Medieval History Journal* 12, no. 1 (2009): 13–45.

———. *Tanzwut: Kosmos, Kirche und Mensch in der Bedeutungsgeschichte eines mittelalterlichen Krankheitskonzepts.* Göttingen: Vandenhoeck & Ruprecht, 2013.

Roper, Lyndal. *The Holy Household: Women and Morals in Reformation Augsburg.* Oxford: Oxford University Press, 2001.

———. *Oedipus and the Devil: Witchcraft, Sexuality, and Religion in Early Modern Europe.* New York: Routledge, 2003.

Rowden, Clair. *Performing Salome, Revealing Stories.* New York: Routledge, 2016.

Rubin, Miri. *Corpus Christi: The Eucharist in Late Medieval Culture.* Cambridge: Cambridge University Press, 1991.

Russell, Jeffrey Burton. *Witchcraft in the Middle Ages.* Ithaca, NY: Cornell University Press, 1972.

Ryrie, Alec. *Being Protestant in Reformation Britain.* Oxford: Oxford University Press, 2015.

Schemmann, Ulrike. *Confessional Literature and Lay Education: The "Manuel dé pechez" as a Book of Good Conduct and Guide to Personal Religion.* Düsseldorf: Droste, 2000.

Schmitt, Jean-Claude. *Ghosts in the Middle Ages: The Living and the Dead in Medieval Society.* Translated by Teresa Lavender Fagan. Chicago: University of Chicago Press, 2007.

Schulenburg, Jane Tibbetts. *Forgetful of Their Sex: Female Sanctity and Society, ca. 500–1100.* Chicago: University of Chicago Press, 2001.

———. "Gender, Celibacy, and Proscriptions of Sacred Space: Symbol and Practice." In *Women's Space: Patronage, Place, and Gender in the Medieval Church.* Edited by Virginia Chieffo Raguin and Sarah Stanbury. Albany: State University of New York Press, 2005.

Bibliography

Shepard, Alexandra. *Meanings of Manhood in Early Modern England*. Oxford; New York: Oxford University Press, 2006.

Silen, Karen. "Elisabeth of Spalbeek: Dancing the Passion." In *Women's Work: Making Dance in Europe before 1800*. Edited by Lynn Matluck Brooks. Madison: University of Wisconsin Press, 2007.

Smith, Kathryn A. "'A Lanterne of Lyght to the People': English Narrative Alabaster Images of John the Baptist in Their Visual, Religious, and Social Contexts." *Studies in Iconography* 42 (2021): 53–94.

Smith, Lesley. *The Glossa Ordinaria: The Making of a Medieval Bible Commentary*. Leiden; Boston: Brill, 2009.

Spencer, H. L. "Middle English Sermons." In *The Sermon*. Edited by Beverly Mayne Kienzle. Turnhout: Brepols, 2000.

Spencer, H. Leith. *English Preaching in the Late Middle Ages*. Oxford; New York: Clarendon Press, 1993.

Stanley, Eric. "Dance, Dancers and Dancing in Anglo-Saxon England." *Dance Research: The Journal of the Society for Dance Research* 9, no. 2 (1991): 18–31.

Steenbrugge, Charlotte. *Drama and Sermon in Late Medieval England: Performance, Authority, Devotion*. Kalamazoo, MI: Medieval Institute Publications, 2017.

Steinmetz, David C. "Calvin and the Patristic Exegesis of Paul." In *The Bible in the Sixteenth Century*. Edited by David C. Steinmetz. London: Duke University Press, 1990.

Stevens, John. *Words and Music in the Middle Ages: Song, Narrative, Dance, and Drama, 1050–1350*. Cambridge: Cambridge University Press, 1986.

Stocker, Margarita. "Short Story, Maximal Imbroglio: Salome Ancient and Modern." In *From the Margins 2: Women of the New Testament and Their Afterlives*. Edited by Christine E. Joynes and Christopher Rowland. Sheffield: Phoenix Press, 2009.

Straple-Sovers, Rebecca. "Kinesic Analysis: A Theoretical Approach to Reading Bodily Movement in Literature." In *The Cursed Carolers in Context*. Edited by Lynneth Miller Renberg and Bradley Phillis. New York: Routledge, 2021.

Sutherland, Annie. *English Psalms in the Middle Ages, 1300–1450*. Oxford; New York: Oxford University Press, 2015.

Taylor, Larissa, ed. *Preachers and People in the Reformations and Early Modern Period*. Leiden: Brill, 2001.

Taylor, Robert A., Wendy Pfeffer, Randall A. Rosenfeld, and Lys Anne Shore Weiss. "The Bele Alis Sermon: Homiletic Song and Dance." *Florilegium* 24 (2007): 173–191.

Thayer, Anne T. "The Medieval Sermon: Text, Performance, Insight." In *Understanding Medieval Primary Sources: Using Historical Sources to Discover Medieval Europe*. Edited by Joel T. Rosenthal. New York: Routledge, 2012.

———. *Penitence, Preaching and the Coming of the Reformation*. New York: Taylor & Francis, 2017.

Bibliography

Thibodeaux, Jennifer D. *The Manly Priest: Clerical Celibacy, Masculinity, and Reform in England and Normandy, 1066-1300*. Philadelphia: University of Pennsylvania Press, 2015.

Thomas, Keith. *Religion and the Decline of Magic*. New York: Scribner, 1971.

Thompson, Stith. *Motif-Index of Folk-Literature: A Classification of Narrative Elements in Folktales, Ballads, Myths, Fables, Mediaeval Romances, Exempla, Fabliaux, Jest-Books, and Local Legends*. Bloomington: Indiana University Press, 1955.

Tlusty, B. Ann. *Alcohol in the Early Modern World: A Cultural History*. New York: Bloomsbury, 2021.

Tubach, Frederic C. *Index Exemplorum: A Handbook of Medieval Religious Tales*. Helsinki: Suomalainen Tiedeakatemia, 1981.

van Liere, Frans. *An Introduction to the Medieval Bible*. Cambridge: Cambridge University Press, 2014.

Van Oort, Jessica. "The Minstrel Dances in Good Company: Del Tumbeor Nostre Dame." *Dance Chronicle* 34, no. 2 (May 2011): 239–275.

Varholy, Cristine M. "'But She Woulde Not Consent': Women's Narratives of Sexual Assault and Compulsion in Early Modern London." In *Violence, Politics, and Gender in Early Modern England*, Edited by Joseph P. Ward. New York: Palgrave Macmillan, 2008.

Volk-Birke, Sabine. *Chaucer and Medieval Preaching: Rhetoric for Listeners in Sermons and Poetry*. Tübingen: Gunter Narr Verlag, 1991.

Wabuda, Susan. *Preaching during the English Reformation*. Cambridge: Cambridge University Press, 2008.

Waite, Gary K. *Eradicating the Devil's Minions: Anabaptists and Witches in Reformation Europe, 1525-1600*. Toronto: University of Toronto Press, 2007.

———. *Heresy, Magic and Witchcraft in Early Modern Europe*. Basingstoke: Palgrave, 2003.

Wall, John N. "Virtual Paul's Cross: The Experience of Public Preaching after the Reformation." In *Paul's Cross and the Culture of Persuasion in England, 1520-1640*. Edited by Torrance Kirby and P. G. Stanwood. Leiden: Brill, 2014.

Walsham, Alexandra. *The Reformation of the Landscape: Religion, Identity, and Memory in Early Modern Britain and Ireland*. Oxford; New York: Oxford University Press, 2012.

Warren, Nancy Bradley. *Chaucer and Religious Controversy in the Medieval and Early Modern Eras*. Notre Dame, IN: University of Notre Dame Press, 2019.

Wayno, Jeffrey M. "Rethinking the Fourth Lateran Council of 1215." *Speculum* 93, no. 3 (June 29, 2018): 611–637.

Wenzel, Siegfried. *Preaching in the Age of Chaucer: Selected Sermons in Translation*. Washington, DC: Catholic University of America Press, 2008.

Westlake, H. F. *The Parish Gilds of Mediæval England*. New York: Macmillan, 1919.

Whiting, Robert. *The Reformation of the English Parish Church*. Cambridge: Cambridge University Press, 2014.

Bibliography

Wiesner, Merry E. *Christianity and Sexuality in the Early Modern World: Regulating Desire, Reforming Practice*. London; New York: Routledge, 2005.

———. *Witchcraft in Early Modern Europe*. Boston: Houghton Mifflin, 2007.

Williamson, Paul, and Fergus Cannan. *Object of Devotion: Medieval English Alabaster Sculpture from the Victoria and Albert Museum*. Alexandria, VA; London: Art Services International, 2011.

Winerock, Emily F. "Churchyard Capers: The Controversial Use of Church Space for Dancing in Early Modern England." In *The Sacralization of Space and Behavior in the Early Modern World: Studies and Sources*. Edited by Jennifer Mara De Silva. Farnham: Ashgate, 2015.

———. "Reformation and Revelry: The Practices and Politics of Dancing in Early Modern England, c. 1550–1640." Ph.D. diss., University of Toronto, 2012.

Wood, Andy. *Faith, Hope and Charity: English Neighbourhoods, 1500–1640*. Cambridge: Cambridge University Press, 2020.

Wright, Craig M. *The Maze and the Warrior: Symbols in Architecture, Theology, and Music*. Cambridge, MA: Harvard University Press, 2001.

Wrightson, Keith. "The Politics of the Parish in Early Modern England." In *The Experience of Authority in Early Modern England*. Edited by P. Griffiths, A. Fox, and S. Hindle. London: Palgrave, 1996.

Yount, Pamela J. "*Handlyng Synne*: An Unconventional Conventional Poem." M.A. thesis, Vanderbilt University, 1982.

Ziolkowski, Jan M. *The Juggler of Notre Dame and the Medievalizing of Modernity*. Cambridge: Open Book, 2018.

INDEX

1534 Act of Supremacy   23, 25
Adams, Thomas   46–7, 85–6, 99–100,
    157 n.1, 171 n.44, 195
adiaphora   4, 8, 17, 26, 36, 41, 44, 49,
    54, 74, 80, 89, 103, 107, 189, 192
adultery   37, 57, 106
    Herod and Herodias'   112–13, 115,
        124, 126, 137, 144, 153, 154
    in scripture   144, 167
    in sermons and glosses   124, 126,
        128, 180
Albigensian Crusade   19, 43
alehouse   65, 172, 181
Aquinas, Thomas   110 n.14, 111,
    113–16, 118, 138–9
Arcangeli, Alessandro   13, 21 n.8, 56–7
Arundel prohibitions   24
Augustine   4, 90, 137
Authorized Version   30 n.41, 133–4, 168

Barker, Christopher   134–5, 183 n.82
Barr, Beth Allison   32, 73
Becon, Thomas   79, 142, 196
Bennett, Judith   3–4, 12, 175
Berkshire   16, 82, 187–8, 190
birthday   105–6, 108, 114, 125, 136,
    138
Book of Sports   2, 43, 48, 77
bowling   39, 48, 90
Bullinger, Heinrich   79, 83, 179 n.71
Bynum, Caroline Walker   4, 51, 58, 59,
    61

Calvin, John   42 n.78, 46, 80, 86 n.30,
    136–7, 169 n.34, 195
Cambridgeshire   82, 180
carolers   40, 77, 100, 118, 185
Catena Aurea   111, 113–14

Catholic
    Catholics   47, 101, 177
    church   46, 134, 179
    clergy   158
    idolatry   148
    papist   16 n.32, 47, 148, 179, 182,
        185
    pope   16, 23, 100, 148
    teaching and practice   23, 102, 141
        n.27, 159
Certain Sermons and Homilies   80,
    146–7, 148 n.49
Chaganti, Seeta   11, 52
chastity   35, 116, 127, 148, 164–5, 167,
    169 n.34, 170
Christ   1, 33, 48, 55, 59, 91, 99, 101,
    164, 192
    allegory concerning   112–15
    body of   143
    commands of   99, 167
    dancing after   3, 85, 100, 106
    salvation through   42, 150–1
Chrysostom, John   4, 71, 90, 116, 126,
    137–9, 164
churchwardens   37–8, 47, 81–2, 93, 119
    n.46, 187, 191
churchyard   29, 36, 55, 57, 63, 74, 139,
    178
    as sacred space   57, 60, 72, 79–80,
        189
    dancing in   3, 21, 48, 52, 54, 56,
        64–5, 69, 77, 81–2, 94, 182, 185
clerical celibacy   71–2, 174–5
commentaries   14, 110–11, 117, 131,
    133–4, 139, 153
Corpus Christi   24, 32, 58
Council of Avignon   21
Cranmer, Thomas   23, 83, 167, 197

249

Index

Crusades 6, 19, 36, 43
cursed dancers 14, 51–4, 56–8, 61–71, 74, 83, 92, 107, 124, 144, 185, 189
cursing 60, 63, 69, 74, 82, 86

dance, styles of
  carole 77, 92, 100
  courtly 10, 137, 152, 183
  Easter 1, 55, 118
  galliard 85–6
  lavolta 86
  liturgical 54–5
  morris 2, 38–9, 47, 77, 82–3, 87, 96, 146, 152, 172, 176, 180, 183
  wedding 2, 137, 138–40, 154, 181
dancing mania 97, 123–4
dancing plague 94
dauerwondern 59–60
David 167, 177, 183
  dance of 1, 34–5, 48, 106, 117, 162, 182
  example of 116, 132
  see also Salome
Day, John 142, 158–9, 169, 197
Decretum 44
Delilah 161–2
demons 3, 21, 97, 123
  demon possessed 118, 132
  demonic 101
  devils 60, 84, 86, 97, 118
Devil, the 42–3, 46, 95, 97–101, 136, 148, 154, 161, 167, 178–80, 194
  dance after 2–3, 84–6, 90–1
  pipes of 85, 158
  sermon tales about 66, 71, 75
  servants of 16
  women as the tools of 148–9
  work of 164
  worship of 97
dicing, dice 43, 47, 83, 85, 176
Dickason, Kathryn 5, 11, 54, 99, 106
Dinah 165–6, 171
Douglas, Audrey 13, 88, 91
drinking, drunkenness 57, 175
  in parish life 99, 181
  in sermons 35, 42, 46, 65, 77, 81, 83–4, 157, 163, 167
Duffy, Eamon 12–3, 61

Ecclesiastes 34–5, 141, 150
effeminacy 160, 174–84, 189
  unmanly 160, 177
Eire, Carlos 6, 43, 46, 48
Elizabeth I 23, 79
  Elizabethan settlement 23
Elliott, Dyan 5, 7, 61, 63 n.36
Ely 47, 82
Eucharist 58–60, 79
  transubstantiation 32, 59–60
exegesis 32–3, 106, 131, 133, 136, 140
  allegorical 1–2, 106–7, 111–18, 123–4, 130, 131–3, 135–6, 140, 151
Exempla 40, 51, 59–60, 68, 83, 124
  on dance 38, 41, 53–4, 56–7, 60, 62–4, 66–7, 75, 124
  on women 70–1, 73, 75
  teaching tool 32–3
Exodus 34 n.53, 60, 117, 124

false Christians 42–3, 47, 177
Festial 24, 28 n.28, 29, 32, 120, 125, 127
Fetherston, Christopher 136–7, 139
fornication 46, 70, 181, 187–8
Fourth Lateran Council 28, 32, 38, 41, 44, 65, 73, 89, 113, 189
  canons 6, 19, 24, 43, 45
  implementation of 20, 26, 45
  lay education 19–22, 26
  reform 6, 14–15, 19, 45–6, 49, 51, 71, 187
  suppressing heresy 19–20, 43, 45
Foxe, John 85, 216
French, Katherine 13, 36–8, 58, 61, 72–3, 91, 118

games 40, 56, 60, 64–5, 92, 176, 183
Geneva Bible 133–5
Gifford, George 102, 147, 158–9, 199
gloss 14, 113, 131, 140, 148, 153–4
  relationship to sermons 106–7, 110–11, 117, 129, 133–6
Glossa Ordinaria 109, 111–16, 125–6, 130
gluttony 31, 57, 65
golden calf 34 n.53, 60

Index

Golden Legend see Legenda Aurea
gossip   27, 44, 56, 65–7, 70, 74, 107, 161, 178
Gowing, Laura   10, 66
Gratian   44
Gregorian reforms   71
Grosseteste, Robert   24
guild   38, 88–9
  parish   24, 36, 88, 90
  tailors'   86–7, 89–90, 93, 119
  trade   88

Handlyng Synne   24, 51, 54 n.8, 59, 62–71, 74–5, 120, 126 *See also* Robert Mannyng
heaven   3, 21, 32, 86, 100, 150, 153, 157–8, 162, 168, 183, 194
  heavenly dances   21, 85, 121
hell   3, 31, 85–7, 99–100, 143, 150, 157–8, 168, 180, 183, 194
Henry VIII   22–3, 25
Herefordshire   39, 81, 143, 146
heresy   19–20, 43–5, 97, 99
heretics   6, 10, 43, 45, 49, 96
hermaphrodites   177
Herod   105, 107–9, 120, 128, 133, 142, 147, 162–3, 167, 190
  allegorical interpretations of   112, 114–15
  punishment of   121–2
  sins of   106, 124–7, 129, 135–6, 144–8, 153–4
Herodias   105, 107–10, 120, 133, 136–7, 141 n.27, 145, 149–51, 162, 167, 190
  allegorical interpretations of   114–15
  example of sin   135, 137, 142, 153–4
  punishment of   121–2
  sins of   124–8, 144
Hooper, John   23, 165–6
household, households   136–7, 163, 169–73, 179
  domesticity   119, 170–1, 190

Idley, Peter   53, 63, 67, 69–71, 74
idolatry   6, 43, 60, 68, 93, 141, 144
  idolater   183

idolatrous women   16, 100
idols   46–7, 80, 149
  in sermons   80, 98, 100, 148, 180
Innocent III   19
Instructions to His Son   53, 67

James I   77, 97–8
jangling   65–9, 72
Jephthah's daughter   34 n.53, 161
Jerome   103, 113, 116, 125, 137
Jewel, John   101, 200, 201
Jews   20, 43, 45, 47, 79, 99, 112–13, 115, 147, 192
Jezebel   16, 100, 148 n.50, 162–3
Job, book of   34, 149, 168–9, 171
  Job 21:11-12   30 n.41, 168–9, 171
John the Baptist   105–7, 109–10, 123, 129, 133, 174
  decollation of   118
  depiction of in art   118–20
  head of   122, 125–6, 135, 142, 145, 147, 153
  in glosses, sermons, or commentaries   16, 100, 114–15, 120–22, 125–7, 131, 135–6, 143–5, 148, 167
  nativity of   116, 118–9

Karras, Ruth Mazo   68, 75
Kempe, Margery   32–3
King James Bible *see Authorized Version*
kingship   141, 145
Kölbigk dancers   53 n.7, 82, 123–4 *see also* cursed dancers

Lambeth council   24
Langton, Stephen   1–2, 159
Latimer, Hugh   84, 220
Laudian   23, 33
Le Goff, Jacques   51, 58, 61
Legenda Aurea   51, 58, 61, 120–2, 124–7
Liber Exemplorum   40, 84, 97
liturgy   2, 23, 44, 46, 51, 54–5, 58, 77, 102
Lollardy   24, 45
London   29, 158, 173, 195
Lowin, John   131, 177

251

Index

lust 35, 56–7, 62, 70–1, 97, 100, 124, 128–9, 145, 163, 167
Luther, Martin 80, 195
Lyra, Nicholas of 111, 113–17

Maleficia 97–8
Malleus maleficarum 96–7
Mannyng, Robert 60, 62, 69
Manuel des péchés 53, 64, 66–7, 74, 120
Mark 6 30 n.41, 107–9, 111–13, 115–16, 133, 135
martyrdom 16, 62, 100, 118–19, 121–2, 142–3
masculinity 48, 68, 175, 177–8, 183, 185
  masculine 72, 149, 161, 171, 182
material piety 8, 58–61, 73
matter 4, 40, 51–2, 58, 61–2, 79
  dangerous 51
  holy 22, 58–9, 70, 74
  profane 59, 74
  sacred 51–2, 58–60, 80
Matthew 14 107–9, 111–16, 134–5
Mayer, John 136, 138–40, 202
Michal 48, 162
Miriam 117, 151–2, 161
Mirk, John 24, 29, 32, 120, 124, 127
monastic orders
  Augustinian 27 n.28, 29, 110
  Dominican 28–9, 123
  Franciscan 28–9
  Mendicant 28–9, 32, 62, 110
Moore, R.I. 25, 43, 45
Moses 42
Muslim 20
mystery plays 24, 55
mysticism 61, 74
  mystics 117

nobility 118, 150–2, 162, 183
  aristocracy 152
Northern Homily Cycle 24, 120, 126

oath 105–6, 114, 126, 128, 136, 141 n.27, 144, 146–8
  Herod's 108–9, 115–16, 120 n.51, 126–7, 133–4, 138 n.21, 147, 154
  swearing 146, 157
  vow 70–1, 147–8

Of Shrifte and Penance 62–3, 65, 67

pagan 46–7
pamphlet 14, 131, 155
parish festivities
  ales 2
  dances 2, 34, 92, 120, 131, 152
  dancing days 86–7, 91–5, 101–2
  hobby horse dances 152
  hocktide 55, 73
  maidens' lights 2, 38, 55, 90–1, 152
  processionals 2, 38, 55, 60, 73, 91, 92–3, 102, 119, 152
  Rogation 91–2
  St. John's day 93, 118–19, 124, 129, 131
  Whitsunday 38, 55, 91–4
  wives' dances 38, 92
pastoral care 19–20, 53, 56, 73
Paul's Cross sermons 29, 90, 161
Peckham, John 24
penance 11, 33, 44
periculoso 45
pipes 34, 47, 85, 91, 158, 185
Poore, Richard 24
Postilla literalis 111, 114
Protestant 23, 30, 47, 159, 192
  culture 9
  ideas about society/domesticity 95, 171, 190
  theology 27, 161
Psalms, book of 34, 54, 116, 151
Puritan 23, 102, 141 n.27, 159, 161

rape 164–6, 171, 173–4
  assault 172–4
Records of Early English Drama 14, 39
Reformations 3, 48, 80, 91, 131–3, 136, 140, 162
  early modern 22, 25, 41, 49, 192
  Edwardian 23
  English 2, 14, 22–5, 37, 77–9, 84, 88, 95, 170, 194
  European 2
  Henrician 23
  impact on laity 6–8, 33, 37, 43, 88, 95, 170
  Marian 23

252

Index

sixteenth century 6, 19, 79, 133

Sabbatarianism 77–9, 83–4, 143
Sabbath 57, 62, 65, 77–9, 82–3, 86–7,
    91, 96, 102, 180–1
    breaking the 15, 78, 80–1, 84, 90, 93
    dancing on the 81–4, 86–7, 90–1,
      94, 165, 188, 190–1
sacrament 19, 26–7, 59, 60, 185
sacred space 6–7, 14–15, 59, 65, 70,
    78–9, 93, 117, 139, 141
    boundaries of 45, 50, 57–8, 71, 77,
      92, 193
    protection of 50, 52–5, 62, 67–75,
      89, 95, 105, 113, 187, 189
    violation of 3, 21–2, 57, 63–4, 72,
      81, 83–4, 91, 161, 173
sacred time 15, 21, 50–5, 57–8, 77,
    78–81, 84, 90, 92–3, 95, 105, 189
Salisbury 86–8, 92, 94, 102, 119
Salisbury statues 45
Salome 15–16, 34, 105–10, 116–18,
    120, 127, 134–5, 142, 146–7, 158,
    161, 163
    allegorical interpretations of 106–7,
      111–17, 123–4, 131–3, 136, 140
    compared to David 149–5, 162, 192
    example of sin 100, 123–4, 126,
      129–32, 135–7, 140–2, 167, 189
    punishment of 121–2, 124, 142
    sins of 121, 124, 126–8, 132, 140,
      144–5, 148, 162, 190
sanctorale sermons 28, 30
Satan 15, 100, 105, 116, 136, 148, 154,
    194 *see also* the Devil
scripture 19, 22, 25–6, 39, 41, 80, 133,
    136, 163, 177
    false understanding of 113, 115
    in sermons 30–1, 33, 35–6, 43, 126,
      128, 141, 147, 162, 168, 171, 176,
      178
    scripture commentaries 135
    translations 33, 38, 174
    with reference to dance 33–6
sermon cycles 10 n.20, 27–8, 62,
    110–11, 118, 121, 128
seven deadly sins 26, 56, 62
sexual sin 53, 57, 64, 70, 132, 149, 193

by women 146, 172–3
    in glosses and commentaries 69,
      107, 116, 134–5, 138
    in parish life 182, 188
    in sermons 36, 126, 128, 144–5,
      148, 164, 167–8, 178–80
Simeon of Durham 71–2
slander 67, 83, 181
Solomon 35, 149, 165
Somerset 16, 39, 92, 139–40, 165,
    183–4, 190
South English Legendary 24
Speculum Sacerdotale 24, 120, 122,
    125, 127
St. Cuthbert 71–2
Sussex 86, 94, 143, 178
Synod of Oxford 24, 26
synodal decrees 24, 27, 56, 64–5

temporale sermons 28
Ten Commandments 26, 57, 62, 144
    first commandment 70
    third commandment 57, 62, 65
    fourth commandment 79
Thayer, Anne 25, 33
true religion 6–7, 16, 22, 25–6, 43,
    47–8, 166
Tymme, Thomas 135, 137–9
Tyndale Bible 133–4

vanity 147–9, 163–4, 171, 178
Virgin Mary 1, 32, 44, 48, 170
visitation records 3, 38–9, 47, 82, 190
Vitry, Jacques de 75, 91
Voragine, Jacobus de 51–2, 61
Vulgate 1 n.1, 108–9, 125

Wabuda, Susan 27, 33
wanton 49, 64, 135, 153, 177, 179
    dancing 35, 47, 64, 90, 135, 137,
      144–5, 153, 163, 167, 181
    songs 178
    wantonness 34 n. 53, 35, 135–6,
      162, 164–5
wench 120, 122, 127–8, 172
Whittingham, William 134–5
Wimbledon, Thomas 29–31
Winerock, Emily 13, 39

Index

witchcraft   78, 91, 95–103, 148, 160–1,
    189
   dances   15, 97, 99
   trials   43, 95, 99, 101–3
witches   96–103
witches' Sabbath   96
wives   71, 93–4, 140, 165, 191
Wood, Andy   159, 171
wrestling   39, 56, 64–5
Wycliffe's Bible translation   109, 133

Wycliffite sermons   120, 125, 128

York   139
Yorkshire West Riding   181
young men   151, 167, 178, 181
young women
   girls   41, 93
   maidens   32, 68–9, 138, 150–1, 163,
    166, 178
   virgins   167

GENDER IN THE MIDDLE AGES

I   *Gender and Medieval Drama,* Katie Normington, 2006

II   *Gender and Petty Crime in Late Medieval England: The Local Courts in Kent, 1460–1560*, Karen Jones, 2006

III   *The Pastoral Care of Women in Late Medieval England*, Beth Allison Barr, 2008

IV   *Gender, Nation and Conquest in the Works of William of Malmesbury*, Kirsten A. Fenton, 2008

V   *Monsters, Gender and Sexuality in Medieval English Literature*, Dana M. Oswald, 2010

VI   *Medieval Anchoritisms: Gender, Space and the Solitary Life*, Liz Herbert McAvoy, 2011

VII   *Middle-Aged Women in the Middle Ages*, edited by Sue Niebrzydowski, 2011

VIII   *Married Women and the Law in Premodern Northwest Europe*, edited by Cordelia Beattie and Matthew Frank Stevens, 2013

IX   *Religious Men and Masculine Identity in the Middle Ages*, edited by P. H. Cullum and Katherine J. Lewis, 2013

X   *Reconsidering Gender, Time and Memory in Medieval Culture*, edited by Elizabeth Cox, Liz Herbert McAvoy and Roberta Magnani, 2015

XI   *Medicine, Religion and Gender in Medieval Culture*, edited by Naoë Kukita Yoshikawa, 2015

XII   *The Unspeakable, Gender and Sexuality in Medieval Literature, 1000–1400*, Victoria Blud, 2017

XIII   *Popular Memory and Gender in Medieval England: Men, Women, and Testimony in the Church Courts, c.1200–1500*, Bronach C. Kane, 2019

XIV   *Authority, Gender and Space in the Anglo-Norman World, 900–1200*, Katherine Weikert, 2020

XV   *Female Desire in Chaucer's* Legend of Good Women *and Middle English Romance*, Lucy M. Allen-Goss, 2020

XVI   *Treason and Masculinity in Medieval England: Gender, Law and Political Culture*, E. Amanda McVitty, 2020

XVII   *Holy Harlots in Medieval English Religious Literature: Authority, Exemplarity and Femininity*, Juliette Vuille, 2021

XVIII   *Addressing Women in Early Medieval Religious Texts*, Kathryn Maude, 2021